The City and the Architecture of Change: The Work and Radical Visions of Cedric Price

Tanja Herdt

 PARK BOOKS

"Philosophy is perfectly right in saying that life must be understood backward. But then one forgets the other clause – that it must be lived forward."   Søren Kierkegaard

1   Ian Finch, "Fun Palace Architect",
The Guardian, **1964**

Preface

Since I began my research, I have had many conversations about Cedric Price. Whenever his name was mentioned in conferences and seminars, it immediately provoked a reaction: he polarised the people I was talking to, who responded either with enthusiastic commentaries or ironic smiles. Price's name unfailingly seemed to challenge the people I met to make their own stance clear. In the best-case scenario, this led to an interesting conversation about the nature of architecture or the role of the architect.

I have been told numerous stories and anecdotes about Price in those kinds of situations. Most of those were related to the "myth" surrounding him. People who knew him personally would cite his ever-sophisticated air, complete with a cigar and a stiff-collared shirt that he always purchased from the same British hotelier supplies outlet. His appearance had imprinted itself particularly clearly in the memories of people who felt it was in stark contrast to the experimental projects that he presented in lectures and publications, drawing on all his rhetorical eloquence and his excellent draughtsmanship skills. Opportunities to discuss the actual substance of Price's projects were much rarer. That may be because there is limited awareness of the diversity and scope of his oeuvre. On the other hand, the Fun Palace was almost always mentioned, along with the 1964 photomontage in which Price portrayed the building's support structure standing among the industrial landscape of London's East End. That project did not simply bring him overnight fame in the early 1960s; to this very day the design's forcefulness and forward-looking thrust exert a huge pull on architects of all generations.

Others remembered his sketch *The City as an Egg*, in which Price drew on an essay by his friend Reyner Banham and used the egg as an example to elucidate how the European city had evolved. The illustration's humour appealed to many of my conversation partners. More importantly, the sketch documents the 1950s' and 1960s' discourse on a new interpretation of modern architecture, which had a significant impact on the evolution of Price's own design stance. Banham's essay "The City as Scrambled Egg" alluded to Le Corbusier's ideas on the reconstruction of European cities after the Second World War. However, in the light of mass society's rapid development, Banham and Price held that urban architecture could no longer be determined by modernist architecture's formal aesthetic principles. In their view the results, such as car-friendly remodelling of city centres and standardised mass housing schemes, no longer tallied with the needs of city dwellers, but were instead simply manifestations of public-sector planning and its planning elites.

Humour is widely recognised as a typical British way of reflecting on one's position within society, including one's relationship to elites and authority. And indeed, there was clearly something deeper underpinning Price's witty approach to architecture: a level of serious reflection and a desire to encourage in his projects planning to become more open and to advance a usage-based culture at the heart of architecture. His choice of representational forms was part of

1

his strategy to encourage ideological debates on urban architecture's values and content in everyday city life once again.

His deep-rooted humanism is a hallmark of Price's work and renders the city as a built environment a central topic in his oeuvre. In his view, the various dimensions of its social and built space within the city represented the "ecology of the societal". Many architects' crystal-clear recollections of his *The City as an Egg* sketch reflect not least the enduring success of his 'democratic' approach in conveying architectural concepts. At the same time, it should be noted that his architecture projects are in many respects cast in an especially British vein. If we are to understand them, these projects must be considered in the context of the socio-political developments of Price's day and in the light of Anglo-Saxon traditions and schools of architecture.

Price's particular self-perception and understanding of architectural practice have often led to his work being categorised to this day as so-called *radical architecture*.[1] Yet, Price did think of himself neither as a theorist nor a visionary. He found it regrettable that he never managed to shake off his early self-description as an "anti-architect".[2] Price's work, including his project documentation, reveals that he saw himself rather as a pragmatist who, through his projects, aspired to make a constructive contribution to modernising his own discipline. Therein also lies the reason why he cast his projects in terms of experimental research and development work, focusing on expanding the boundaries of his profession's established practices and mindsets, often enough calling precisely these aspects into question. As a result, already early in his career Price had assumed an outsider's role in the British architecture world. His playful questioning of post-war architectural paradigms earned him the reputation of an eccentric. Yet he himself viewed his projects as a bid to ensure that his discipline would reflect the contemporary world and engage in a process of renewal which, as far as he was concerned, was the only viable alternative: "I'm only radical because the architectural profession has got lost."[3]

Rather than radically abandoning the concepts of Modernist architecture, his work returns to the ideas that originally inspired those concepts. Noting that cities were undergoing radical changes due to widespread deployment of science and technology, Price concluded that reappropriating the urban realm called for equally novel and innovative responses. Whereas his willingness to experiment led, for example, to considerable delays in project completion for the London Zoo Aviary, it is important to note that Price did not use technology as an end in itself. Instead, technology was a means to do justice to city dwellers' social need for self-expression. In this spirit he opposed in the late 1990s the English Heritage's efforts to have the Inter-Action Centre listed. Price took instead the view that the temporary building should only continue to exist for as long as it could offer an appropriate response to users' needs.[4]

This book aims to present the particularities of the design approach that Price developed. At the heart of this are the recognition of the city as a socio-technical system, observations on the influence of industrial design and everyday culture on architecture, and the re-evaluation of the role of science and technology in architectural design. By addressing these topics, Price developed a relational understanding of space, which took city dwellers and their options for action and social relationships as the points of departure. In depicting his interdisciplinary methodology, which encompasses cultural, social and natural sciences considerations, I aim to move beyond the interest in Price himself. I hope this approach will allow for the interesting conversations I have already enjoyed on the "Price myth" to be succeeded by many further discussions about his projects.

Acknowledgments

This book could not have been realised without the active support of many colleagues and friends. It is based on my dissertation, which was developed thanks to funding from ETH Zurich and the Swiss National Science Foundation. I would like here to express my thanks once again to everyone who assisted and supported me while I was writing that dissertation. The reworking and publication were funded through the Zürcher Hochschule der Künste (Zurich University of the Arts); I would like to express here how extraordinarily grateful I am to them. Thanks are also due to the Canadian Centre for Architecture, CCA, in Montréal, its staff and director, Mirko Zardini, as well as to Phillys Lambert, whose initiative has enabled the work of her friend Cedric Price to be rediscovered today. Finally, I am most grateful to my husband Andreas, who has supported me and my work on this book right from the very beginning.

1 Cedric Price, "PRICE", Series 2/4, Photomontage for the Sheffield University Festival, ca. 1966.

2 Cedric Price, "PRICE", Series 3/4, Photomontage for the Sheffield University Festival, ca. 1966.

Instruments
of Change

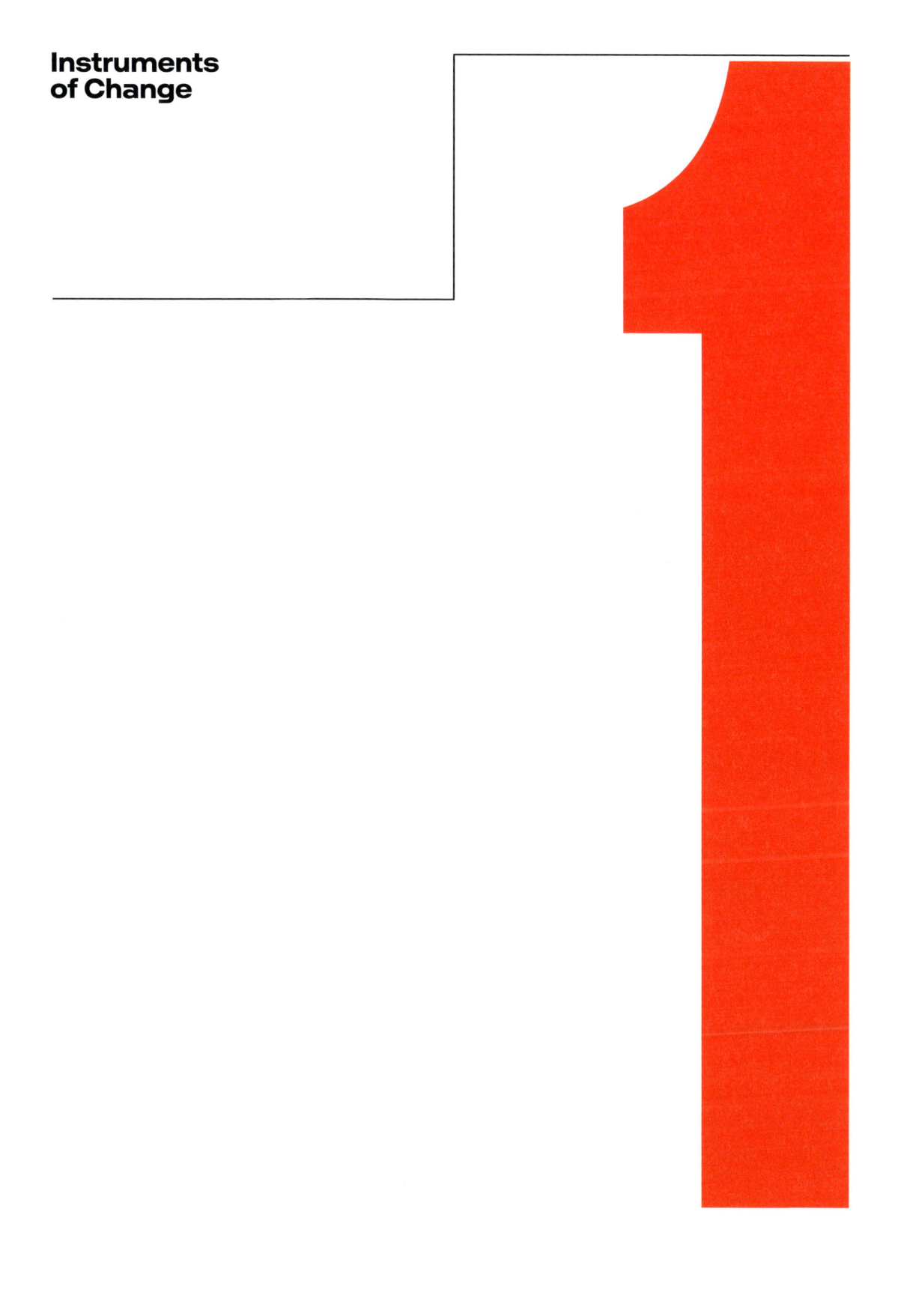

Architecture as Environment: The Role of Science and Technology

In 1956 Cedric Price moved into his first flat in London, which had two rooms. One was the bedroom, the other was the kitchen, bathroom, living room and work space rolled into one.[1] By way of furniture, Price constructed a table over the bath. That was where he worked, cooked and hosted guests. The flat's simple fittings corresponded to the general standard of rented accommodation in London during the 1950s. Although state programmes to combat the housing shortage were in full swing, very few London flats at the time had modern heating, plumbing or kitchens. This was in stark contrast to the range of consumer goods then available. Cars, refrigerators, televisions and transistor radios were becoming commonplace among British households[2] and signalled the new, media-based "mass society" emulating the American model.

When the British tourism trade fair was held in 1961, Price therefore compared the degree of comfort his accommodation offered with that of the latest mobile homes. The latter reflected cutting-edge developments in the consumer goods market and were equipped with fitted kitchens and moulded-plastic shower units. For Price, residential architecture lagged behind other contemporary innovations in two respects: its typical fittings and fixtures did not incorporate the most recent technology, and British urban architecture could no longer keep pace with the population's evolving lifestyles. These observations set the tone for the autonomous architectural approach that Price began to develop in the early 1960s, which would inform his work throughout his career.

His student years in London at the Architectural Association School of Architecture (AA) and the early years of his architectural career saw profound structural and societal change. The advent of the mass media and mass consumer markets in the 1950s had transformed British lifestyles, and at the same time increasing automation in industrial manufacturing and the burgeoning service sector continued to affect employment and labour structures. Employees had more free time and consequently more opportunities to pursue their interests.[3] New societal achievements in the form of media culture, consumerism and leisure conveyed a sense of freedom and self-determination that was entirely out of kilter with housing and living conditions for most of the British public. In the light of these developments, Price realised that architecture could only become more closely aligned with its users' needs by upgrading domestic amenities to offer the same ease of use and top-notch performance found in widely available consumer goods.[4]

The impact of the emerging information and service society did not merely affect urban lifestyles, but also brought about enormous changes in the existing building stock in response to the shifting needs of business and the general public. After the Second World War, reconstruction in London had been coloured by measures to make the capital car-friendly and turn the centre into a global financial hub. Many nineteenth-century working-class districts as well as industrial and port facilities were demolished due to deindustrialisation and government slum clearance programmes. Replacing this housing stock was a slow

1 process and tended to concentrate on large-scale mass housing projects, mostly constructed in other areas within the metropolitan agglomeration, far from the site of the cleared slums. As well as triggering an acute housing crisis, this also led to a loss of public space and community-focused sites where local inhabitants could express their cultural identity.

At the 8th CIAM congress, "The Heart Of The City" in 1951, the London-based Modern Architectural Research Group (MARS) had already focussed on these issues, reflecting on urban built identity. This debate would define architectural discourse and education at British universities until well into the 1970s. The theory of Modernist architecture being shaped by the expression of community[5] that was developed by MARS members Arthur Korn and Felix Samuely was a key influence on the young Cedric Price's work on urban planning, construction and structural integrity.

However, the discrepancy between technological change and urban architecture and lifestyles raised central questions for Price about modern architecture's limitations, which he explored in numerous articles and essays. Reacting against functionalist planning premises, he commented for example on the car-friendly redevelopment project for London's Piccadilly Circus by underscoring the site's significance as a locus of large-scale societal events. In Price's view Piccadilly Circus was more than just a traffic intersection, for, with its neon signs and information displays, it served an important function as a meeting point for people from all walks of life, on election day or New Year's Eve.[6]

In his articles Price always adopted an integrative view of the city, shaped by an awareness of culture, and considered the built environment in light of its multiple strata of utilisation, technical infrastructure and architectonic design. In his view, only the sum of all its spatial characteristics had rendered Piccadilly Circus culturally significant. Inverting this perspective, Price became convinced at a very early stage in his career that architecture must move beyond technological considerations to take account of social imperatives too in order to find a fitting response to the altered circumstances of city life.

Technology is the Answer But What was the Question?

After completing his studies at the AA in 1959, Cedric Price worked briefly in various architectural offices[7] before setting up his own practice in 1960. Price used his first projects, a conversion of a holiday home in Oldham (1956) and the new-build Gamekeeper's Cottage (1961), to draw initial conclusions about designs for housing that would fit with the zeitgeist.[8] As the owners promptly made extensive alterations to both projects, Price concluded that the spatial division he had proposed was too rigid to keep pace with the changing circumstances of the people living in these houses.[9] Growing out of these initial experiences with shifting utilisation of his projects, Price subsequently began to develop an adaptable home architecture, which he elaborated in his designs for the Potteries Thinkbelt project (1964) and his entry for the "Steel Housing Competition" (1966).

In both projects Price used existing system-build and industrial prefabrication concepts, which he combined to generate new variants for single-storey detached homes. The construction industry's system-build houses, 160,000 of which had been erected in Great Britain alone as emergency accommodation after the Second World War, served as a reference point in this endeavour, along with various examples of modern single-family domestic architecture that were already well-known at the time, including Philip Johnson's New Canaan House (1949) and Ludwig Mies van der Rohe's Farnsworth House (1950/51). Price was above all interested in industrial manufacturing techniques, viewing these, entirely in keeping with Konrad Wachsmann's manifesto *Wendepunkt im Bauen*, as integral to a genuinely contemporary construction process.[10]

He used these techniques in the "Steel Housing Competition" to create a flexible spatial organisation for housing. The residential construction system he designed comprised a hall made up of industrially manufactured steel frames. Prefabricated space cells were fitted into the hall's open space, thus generating the house's functional division. His design was highly adaptable thanks to scope to rearrange the space cells within the hall, along with the wide range of different options for fittings and fixtures that could be incorporated into the cells. Picking up on practices already prevalent in the automobile industry, Price planned to have the cells produced with a wide range of different fittings and fixtures included at the manufacturing stage. Combining the hall with a variety of space cells, six possible configurations for a house emerged, each corresponding to a different lifestyle, ranging from the classical family unit to a flat-share model.[11] Price had grasped the evolutionary scope of this space formation principle thanks to Basil Spence's 1951 Sea and Ships Pavilion at the Festival of Britain, and he also tapped into this design principle in various other projects, such as the Inter-Action Centre.[12]

In his entry for the "Steel Housing Competition", Price's interest in a truly contemporary technical articulation of domestic architecture comes together with his desire for social reform. Channelling the spirit of the 1960s, his competition entry calls into question social conventions of the family and shared living space, opening up prospects to reformulate such norms. For Price, electronics and device-based technology offered an opportunity to overcome rigid floor plans in residential architecture. He incorporated a plethora of technical devices for air conditioning, lighting control and sound insulation with a view to making houses adaptable to users' needs.[13] As he had previously noted in 1961 in the journal *Time & Tide*, radio and television also influenced the ways in which houses were used, and thus had ramifications for the culture of shared living. Since televisions had become widespread in British households, people no longer shared meals in the kitchen but ate in the living room instead.[14] This led Price to conclude that technological innovations in electronics and consumer goods would emancipate homes from traditional, predetermined room functions: "The house is no longer acceptable as a pre-set ordering mechanism for family life."[15]

Architecture critic Reyner Banham, summing up the message of his 1960 *Theory and Design in the First Machine Age*, also underscored the significance of technology in liberating users from architecture's formal design elements. In his view, industrialisation and its impact on society had generated various forms of functional style since the early twentieth century. An updated variant of functionalist Modernism in post-war Britain would create a link to developments unfolding in the second, electronics-driven machine age.[16] Banham took Philip Johnson's Glass House in New Canaan as an example to elucidate a central motif of his engagement with mass-market technical developments.[17] Electrically controlled under-floor heating in the Glass House had freed the living space from all architectonic design elements related to service infrastructure. Opening up unprecedented possibilities for the architecture of everyday life, the utilisation-neutral space of the Glass House could be freely shaped in line with users' wishes: "An environment suited to what you are going to do next […] move away from the fire or turn on the air-conditioning, it is the same basic human gesture you are making."[18] In an illustration for Banham's essay, *A Home Is Not a House*, French architect François Dallegret conveyed this idea in an eye-catching image depicting the naked architecture critic sitting cross-legged in an inflatable capsule – with only a few electronic devices set around him.[19] In what was dubbed the "environment-bubble", the house was reduced to a climate capsule: a blank canvas for any use its occupants might choose, thanks to the use of technology to control interior conditions. In Banham's view the functional and representative purposes of architecture's formal design elements, such as walls, apertures and façade, were replaced by a technically equipped environment that could directly fulfil its users' needs.[20]

Banham's ideas were particularly important to Price in developing his own design practice at the start of his career in the early 1960s. Banham and Price were lifelong friends and influenced each other's thinking on reinvigorating Functionalist architectural language. Price met Banham through the latter's activities in the Independent Group and at the Institute of Contemporary Arts (ICA). As a student research assistant at the ICA, Price had helped to set up the exhibition *This is Tomorrow*, which gave him deeper insights into work by the members of the group.[21] His contact with Banham, Richard Hamilton and John McHale in particular gave rise to long-lasting, productive exchanges on the development of mass culture and its implications for art and spatial production. In their exhibition piece *Fun House*, Richard Hamilton, John McHale and John Voelker had anticipated the idea of environment architecture in an artistic vein. Their installation depicted domestic space as a staged interior world, opening up to consumer society's experience-fixated culture through new media such as the radio, record player and television set: pop songs, stars, advertising were key features.[22]

Artistic engagement with American Pop culture[23] served as a springboard for Price's own work on environment architecture, characterised by technological innovations and mass culture. He believed that current technological innovations should be incorporated into this architecture as instruments of self-determination. Price illustrated this socio-critical dimension in his 1966 photomontages for Sheffield University Festival.[24] One depicts a miniskirt-clad woman pushing a church, balanced on an inflatable cushion, out of a village.[25]

A second woman is buying blueprints for a home from a dispensing machine, as casually as if she were picking a song on a jukebox.[26]

"Environment" Architecture

At virtually the same time as his designs for homes, Price began work on his first projects for larger public buildings, such as the London Zoo Aviary (1960–1965) and the Fun Palace (1961–1964).[27] Price saw himself as an "architect-engineer" in his approach to these projects. He described how they came into being as "carefully designed technological architecture", developed in the light of rational concerns that informed the entire process, from the initial design phase right through to construction and utilisation. This stance is more an articulation of his design attitude and working methods than a description of the projects' aesthetic cast. In keeping with the Oxford English Dictionary's definition, Price understood "technology" as "the science of industrial arts", positioning his design concept as being closely linked to engineering and the applied sciences, which optimised the functionality of a building through technical innovations and construction techniques.[28]

Architecture-engineer and inventor Richard Buckminster Fuller had already established a role model for realisation of functional environment architecture in his Dymaxion House project (1927–1930).[29] Price had engaged with this design for a prefabricated home during his youth.[30] However, he did not meet Fuller until 1958, through Reyner Banham and the Independent Group.[31] Two of the group's members, John McHale and Lawrence Alloway, had been observing Fuller's take on domestic architecture with great interest. Their engagement, as well as publication of Fuller's works in the context of the 1961 UIA Congress in London, made a much broader audience in early-1960s Britain aware of Fuller's design approach.[32]

Fuller advised Price during the development phase of his projects and supported the younger architect when he was setting up his practice.[33] In 1962 he granted Price a licence to build geodesic domes in Great Britain, which allowed Price to draw on the patent to implement his own commissions. Fuller also put Price in touch with the director of the American Museum in Bath, Ian McCallum, who was planning a new auditorium as an events venue and museum extension. The design for the Claverton Dome (1961–1963) comprised a geodesic dome with seating in the auditorium set around a central stage. The dome's self-supporting roof could be elevated with a hydraulic system, enabling up to 1,000 people to access the interior simultaneously.[34]

Due to the technical complexity of constructing the auditorium and the costs involved, the Claverton Dome was never built. However, his work on the project gave Price an opportunity to gain expertise in all the details of dome structures.[35] One particular source of inspiration was the Garden of Eden Project, an experimental house conceived by Fuller in 1952 as an exhibition piece for the Museum of Modern Art in New York.[36] Fuller sent Price the plans for the two-storey residential dome, which he had designed as an interior space controlled using technology.

had the lifting capacity to carry the building, but the fuel capacity to fly it all the way to the North Pole as well. Therefore I saw that it would be possible for us to deliver scientific buildings, which I prefer to call environment controls, to very remote places. If we did develop such tools, it would mean that men would be able to make a better theoretical choice of their distribution around the Earth instead of being pushed around by their environment.

Let us try to understand what is going on. There are two clearly different kinds of activities that are familiar to us: what we should call 'high scientific priority" activity of the kind that goes into the developing of rockets and very fast aircraft, the development of atomic fission and so forth; and then very everyday kinds of activity—designing objects such as houses, where there may not even be an architect, let alone an engineer. There is, however, a very important fundamental difference in the "high scientific priority" activity.

World War I marks the moment when Man went off the sensory spectrum. Until then, those who were the most powerful men around the Earth, who mastered the oceans with their ships of commerce and their navies, judged things very much in the terms of their physical senses. They made their decisions in the terms of things they could touch, smell, hear and, particularly, see. Such men were masters at taking inventory of world economics—knowing the distributions of

FIGURE 1a *(above, left). Wire-wheel principle: Prototype Dymaxion House of 1927. Like a bicycle wheel, the "rim" and "hub" are under compression and the "spokes" are under tension, making a strong structure weighing only 3 tons.* FIGURE 1b *(below). Geodesic dome principle: American Society of Metals 250 ft dome of 1959. The surface of the sphere is constructed of members which are not subject to any bending stress and which share any load throughout the network.* FIGURE 1c *(above, right). Tensegrity (tensional integrity) principle: University of Michigan experimental tetrahedron. Unlike brick-on-brick compressional systems in which tension is a secondary function, in tensegrity the compressional components are "islanded" or discontinuous and only the tensional network is continuous throughout the structure. The tensional members exploit the property that the tensional strength, unlike compressional strength, is independent of length/width ratio. Tensegrity structures can be one-third of the weight of geodesic structures.*

3   Richard Buckminster Fuller, Dymaxion House and Tensegrity structure, New Scientist, 1962.

Price drew in particular on his studies of the regulation mechanisms and circulatory systems for ventilation, water and lighting in integrating such technical circuits into his own projects, for example in the London Zoo Aviary and the Fun Palace. A further notion he picked up on for the Fun Palace was the concept of electronic controls for spatial levels that could be set by users via "push button control".[37]

While the dome structure's technical details drew on Fuller's methodologies, Price also pursued his own ideas in devising projects based on the dome patents. For example, rather than choosing metal for the Claverton Dome, he opted for plastic components, viewing this as a fitting contemporary interpretation of Fuller's constructive principles in the light of the most recent manufacturing technologies. In the early 1960s, plastic had come to dominate the consumer goods industry, although it was not yet widely used in the construction industry.[38]

In this respect Price followed a central design principle of his mentor, who saw the work of the architect as being much closer to that of an engineer and experimenter than had traditionally been the case. Fuller viewed his residential dome design as a research and development project that fostered progress on integrating the latest production and manufacturing technologies.[39] He saw his projects as an "experimental laboratory", a kind of scientific/technical test assembly in which he could produce prototype-style results. This stance was rooted in a socio-political motivation and a positivist view of architecture that Price also shared. From this perspective, industrialisation and the evolution of democratic mass society meant that architects had assumed social responsibility and must focus on improving people's living conditions. For Fuller the architect's remit was therefore to design products that drew on the potential of industrial manufacturing and gleaned inspiration from the most recent scientific findings. In the spirit of the design science revolution described by Fuller, the architect could thus make technical innovations available to as many people as possible.[40]

London Zoo Aviary

Price drew on Fuller's scientific/technical design strategy in both the London Zoo Aviary and the Fun Palace Project, which his studio worked on at roughly the same time. The London Zoo Aviary afforded Price an opportunity to experiment, which he hoped would foster further progress on integrating technical systems and developing prefabricated components. Fuller supported and accompanied Price during the five years that he worked on the project, right up to completion of the aviary in 1965. However the substantive thrust of Price's designs gradually began to move away from Fuller's ideas. Optimising the engineering technology was not the sole focus for Price, for the spatial staging of the "environment" was also crucial for him. This autonomous interpretation of Fuller's design principles subsequently caused a rift in Price's relationship with his mentor. Although they maintained close links, both chose to pursue different trajectories in their design approaches.

In November 1960, the Zoological Society of London had commissioned Princess Margaret's husband, photographer Antony Armstrong-Jones, to design an aviary for London Zoo, and he hired Cedric Price to work on the project as an architect. Price was keen to design the aviary as an unsupported shell structure,[41] a highly ambitious constructional undertaking, which was to be executed as a "tensegrity" structure. The load-bearing system, deploying minimal materials, had been developed by Buckminster Fuller and his student Kenneth Snelson, but was so complex that it had not previously been implemented within a built structure.[42] Price developed the design in conjunction with structural engineer Frank Newby, who also produced the plans for realisation of the complex load-bearing system.[43] In addition to his role in the Aviary's construction, Newby also became an important partner in translating Price's ideas into built form in other projects. Both were pupils of Felix J. Samuely and adopted an architectural approach informed by constructional concerns, with Functionalist perspective and a penchant for industrially prefabricated elements as its main hallmarks.[44] Working under the aegis of project engineer Samuely, Newby had designed the Festival of Britain's Skylon, which had become a symbol of Britain's fresh start in the post-war era.[45] Price had studied structural design with Samuely, and was particularly impressed by his work on lightweight shell structures and their dynamic load distribution; he described Samuely as "my hero as far as structure went".[46]

The load-bearing system Price und Newby developed for the aviary consisted of two tetrahedrons made from aluminium bars anchored in the ground, and connected by tension cables, thus defining the aviary's internal volume. A tensed metal mesh was wrapped around the edges of the tetrahedrons, delimiting the space and providing additional bracing to augment the structural integrity. The structural system distributed the loads dynamically; i.e. all the constructional components were simultaneously part of the load-bearing structure, determining both the building's appearance and its load-bearing performance. Under this enclosing structure, extending along a canal, a space entirely free of supporting elements came into being, seemingly a continuation of the surrounding area, thanks to its minimalistic construction.

Laborious tests on the materials' characteristics and load-bearing capacity were required to develop and construct this complex structural frame, with Fuller providing input from afar.[47] Selecting aluminium as the material for construction, Price explicitly focused the project on research and development studies. Although cast aluminium components were already in use in the aviation industry, manufacturing aluminium building components was not yet standard practice in the construction industry, which largely worked with steel.[48] Fuller therefore emphasised to Price how risky it would be to engage in such time-consuming development work in a public construction project.[49] Far from deterring Price, the challenge appeared to spur him on.

All the aviary's structural elements were developed from scratch and tested by Price and Newby. Particularly striking aspects here included the stainless steel forgings and the welds joining the aluminium elements, which required rigorous structural engineering testing to appraise their load-bearing capacity.[50] For these tests the project team cooperated with the Engineering Department at Southampton University, which ran X-ray and ultrasonic checks in

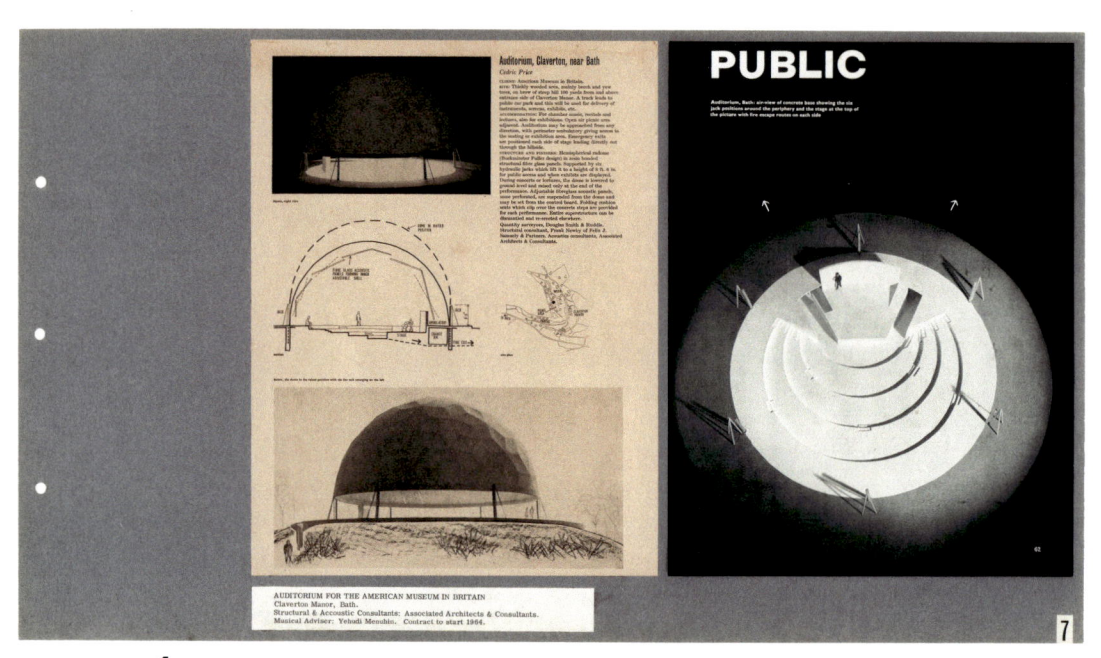

4 Cedric Price, Auditorium for the American Museum in Britain, Claverton near Bath, ca. 1963.

1

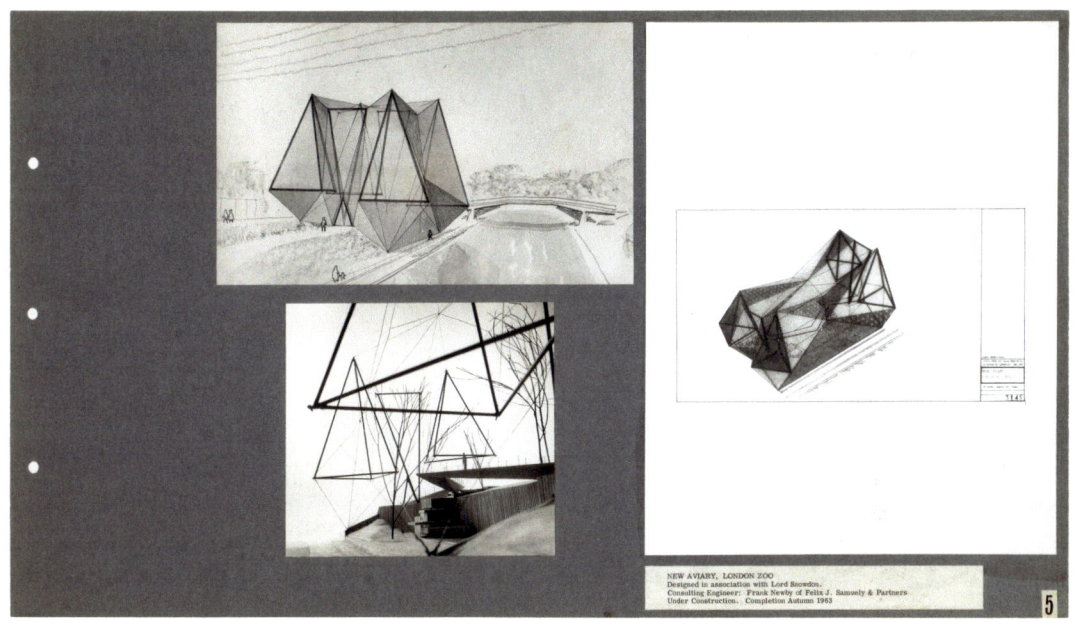

NEW AVIARY, LONDON ZOO
Designed in association with Lord Snowdon.
Consulting Engineer: Frank Newby of Felix J. Samuely & Partners
Under Construction. Completion Autumn 1963

5

5   Cedric Price, New Aviary:
London Zoo, Photograph of model, ca. **1963**.

6   Cedric Price, New Aviary:
London Zoo, Axonometric projection, ca. **1963**.

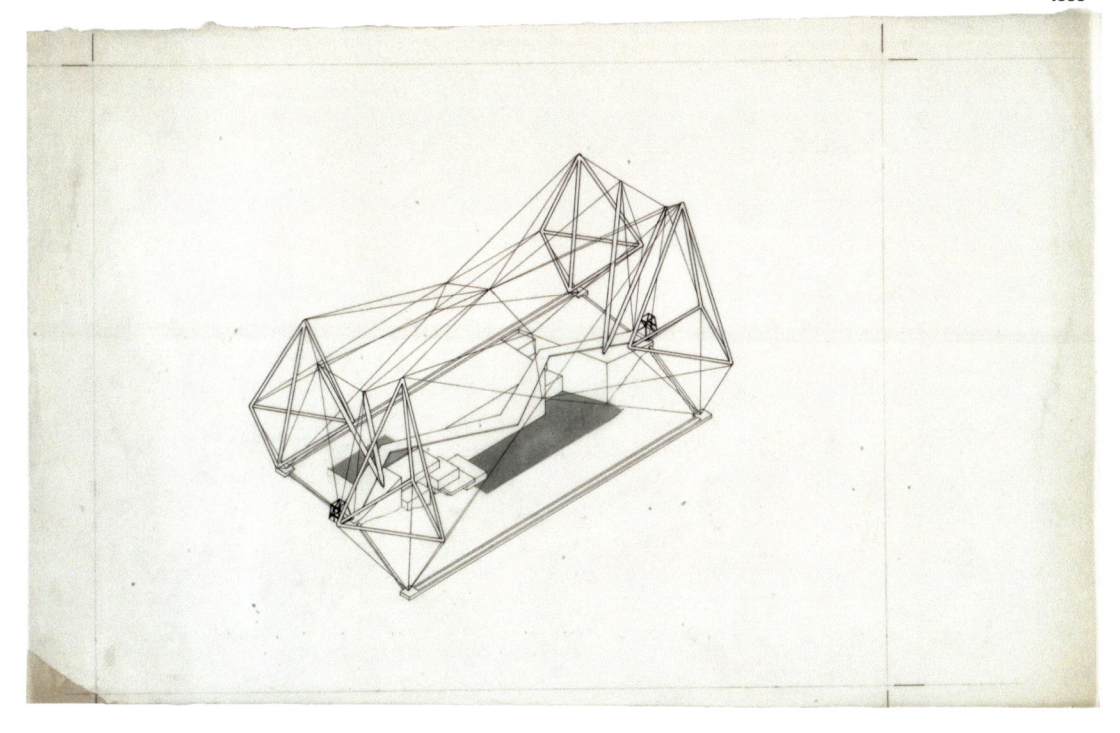

1

7 Cedric Price, New Aviary:
London Zoo, Exterior view, **2008**.

8 Cedric Price, New Aviary:
London Zoo, Roof structure, **2008**.

its stress test and wind canal set-up, as well as computer simulations to check the aviary's behaviour under load.[51] It would have been impossible to realise Price's design without these high-tech procedures. In this respect the aviary's construction also involved developing a prototype system with which Price aspired to set new structural standards for materials integration and construction techniques.

Price's development-oriented design strategy also extended beyond the construction methods for the outer shell. He also considered how the aviary's design would impact on utilisation of the space when configuring the interior. The area within the structure was planted with trees and bushes and landscaped to reflect the birds' natural habitats.[52] Drawing on the Garden of Eden Project as a source of inspiration, an artificial inner universe was created, striking a careful balance between various environmental parameters. As an ornithological research unit, the aviary also needed to consider how the birds would be affected by their surroundings. The system Price devised combined individual elements, such as planting design and the structures within the space and water supply, and had to include means of observing how these aspects interacted, as well as coordinating their functioning.[53] Another equally significant consideration for Price in designing this environment was the space's impact on visitors.[54]

Price divided the area inside the aviary into two sections with a rocky landscape area and an artificial water course. The upper level functioned as a pathway that steered the visitors' attention, with the lower level serving as an enclosure for the birds. For visitors walking through the structure this created a sense of viewing the birds in their natural environment. To heighten this impression, Price created places that afforded a particularly clear view of specific elements, such as nesting areas.[55] Controlling the individual design elements was therefore about more than maintaining the artificial habitat with its various functions: it was also crucial to the staging of the visitors' experience. As Reyner Banham wrote when the aviary was opened, the mise-en-scène of the interior space overcame the aesthetic impression of a cage.[56] He viewed the London Zoo Aviary as an example of a new generation of exhibition pavilions that enabled direct forms of spatial experience thanks to new structural and servicing technologies.[57] In contrast to Fuller, Price had not opted for a global resource-optimised system for the aviary but had instead put himself in the visitors' shoes and built an experiential space that melded naturally with its surroundings. Charles R. Faust, San Diego Zoo's garden designer, described the effect evoked by the project in a letter to Price: "Even a person with a limited sensitivity to his environment would find it difficult not to react to the dramatic experience …"[58]

Reactions were not however universally positive, for harsh criticism was also levelled at the aviary, partly because the laborious development work delayed completion for more than three years.[59] In addition, the construction of the load-bearing structure did not sit well with many engineers' preconceptions, for Price's choice of aluminium was difficult to reconcile with the general structural-engineering tenet of optimising structural integrity.[60] However Price countered this critique, arguing that he had pioneered a development addressing industrial standards for aluminium construction rather than targeted resource optimisation in the load-bearing structure: "No one (before had) made a tube that big."[61] Furthermore, Price moved far beyond the frame of technical engineering categories by expanding his perspective to include the space's psychological impact on visitors.

Buckminster Fuller also raised a number of sometimes harsh critiques of the building. He took issue with what he saw as Price's lack of coherence in design decisions relevant for the structure's functionality. To cite just one example, he objected to the mesh composed of squares used in the aviary's enclosing envelope, as a triangular mesh would have corresponded more closely to the structure's performance under load. In the light of aspirations to create a soaring engineering achievement, Fuller felt that choosing a "wire mesh fence" for a building under the patronage of the Royal Family was both aesthetically and politically inappropriate.[62]

Price had selected an existing product with a square mesh format to stretch across the pylon frame. Although this created a stable structural frame, the mesh's geometry was at odds with the load distribution in the structural system. In this case however he preferred to work with a readily available industrial product, although developing his own component would have reflected the imperatives of his brief more closely. In this respect, Price interpreted the design science revolution more radically than his mentor. Working to develop a specific structural detail was only crucial for Price if it generated greater utility for society or the individual. Given the highly specific geometry of the load-bearing structure, any triangular-mesh grid he might have developed would only have been viable for this particular project. In this respect Price accorded greater importance in his design to social utility than to the building's aesthetics and engineering optimisation.[63]

It proved largely impossible to bridge this fundamental difference between his practice and Fuller's emphasis on engineering concerns. There was more than a pinch of arrogance in Fuller's reaction when Price, after four years of cooperation, began to pursue his own path, which no longer corresponded to his mentor's design ideals: "I would not dare to say that to you, risking our friendship, if I did not feel it to be all true and clearer to my transatlantic perspective and a long time developmental experience than it could be to you."[64] In subsequent projects however the question of architecture's "utility value", i.e. its usefulness to society and individuals, became an increasingly important focus for Price. Although they remained friends until Fuller's death in 1983, it was however no longer possible for Price to envisage reinstating a professional cooperation with Fuller, despite Price's continuing admiration for his mentor.[65]

The Fun Palace's Machine Architecture

When he was only twenty-nine, Price was catapulted to international fame with his 1964 plans for a cultural centre in London's East End. The active involvement of theatre director Joan Littlewood (1914–2002) in the project, coupled with support from influential British intellectuals and politicians, meant that national and international media proclaimed the Fun Palace to be a pioneering social project that marked the dawn of a new era. Conveying as it did the sense of an imminent societal transformation rooted in mass media and market technological innovations,[66] the project was an unparalleled success in striking a chord with the mood of its day.

The cutaway view from Price's 1964 public presentation of the Fun Palace's interior reveals movable lecture theatres and stages suspended from the ceiling of an open steel structure.[67] It shows a gantry crane, set at an oblique angle above the roof of the hall's structural frame, used to move the various room elements, walkways, and platforms to form a range of different compositions.[68] The aim was to allow the Fun Palace's cultural programme to be adapted to users' wishes at stipulated intervals. In addition, the interior was equipped with heating, air-conditioning, lighting and sound infrastructure to generate different ambiences in the various sections of the structure. In this respect the project was a further iteration of an experiential space underpinned by technical support.

As Price worked on the London Zoo Aviary and the Fun Palace more or less in parallel between 1961 and 1964, there was considerable cross-fertilisation between the projects' design tactics and methodologies. Echoing the approach he adopted for the Aviary, the architect focused in the Fun Palace on producing an artificial environment in which conditions within the structure were controlled using its mechanical and electronic infrastructure. However, the two projects pursued entirely different intentions and aims. While the London Zoo Aviary design focused on shaping conditions within the structure's environment, the Fun Palace concentrated on incorporating users' changing social activities to create a new arena for cultural production and community.

Tapping into the most up-to-date technology, the structural frame envisaged for the Fun Palace was configured to promote access to cultural activities such as theatre and concerts, courses and discussions for a mass audience.

LEA RIVER SITE

9   Cedric Price, "Lea River Site",
Fun Palace: Perspective for Lea Valley, ca. 1964.

The design was therefore reminiscent of a machine. In keeping with this, the Fun Palace's architecture was composed of standardised, sometimes mobile, elements that could be regulated mechanically, electrically or electronically. The vision that had previously informed Price's housing designs is apparent again here: an open room structure and technology to allow adaptable organisation of space as a function of users' wishes. The Fun Palace mechanisms were configured to appeal to the desire for cultural expression and community.

It was an ambitious project. This was partly because it was the diametric opposite of hitherto standard approaches to architectural production: rather than expressing a cultural institution's programme in a fixed built form, the Fun Palace sought to trigger dynamic interactions between the architecture and visitors' activities. "Bottom-up" cultural production was the vision that resonated in the project drawings. Visitors were to play an active part in shaping the cultural programme offered in the Fun Palace rather than just consuming activities passively. This would create a place defined by entertainment and education, bridging the divide between high culture and its quotidian counterpart, and in the process also overcoming the British class system's social divisions.

The main Fun Palace Project was the first in a series of designs that Price developed for the Fun Palace Trust in the period up to 1974. The association, with more than forty active members from academia, the world of politics and the general public, was founded under Joan Littlewood's leadership to promote an experiment in cultural reinvigoration of society – by constructing the Fun Palace.[69] The project's supporters included public figures such as violinist Yehudi Menuhin (1916–1999), the British Labour politician Ian Mikardo (1908–1993) and the physicist and later Nobel Peace Prize winner Sir Józef Rotblat (1908–2005). They saw their involvement as a form of socio-political engagement and a contribution to renewing post-war society, which was to be shaped democratically and in keeping with the libertarian values they held dear.[70] In their vision of the Fun Palace, technology as part of everyday culture did more than open up access to comfort and consumerism, for it also afforded new possibilities for individual expression, education and self-organisation within society. Against the threatening backdrop of the Cold War and the massive structural transformations manifested in redevelopment of industrial centres, the project's gestation was shaped by the emerging culture of community in the early 1960s. The damage wreaked by the Second World War was still apparent in London, and the positive vibe of growing affluence was increasingly overshadowed by a sense of passivity and threat. Seeking to strengthen society "at grassroots level", nurturing values such as exchange and mutual understanding through a cultural, educational project was a crucial concern.

Value-based communities in the emerging industrial society also took centre stage in debates in architectural circles on urban design for the future, especially in the wake of the renewed interest in American historian Lewis Mumford's work and the reception of his book *The City in History*, published in 1961. Particular attention was focused in this context on how technology could be deployed as a tool for regeneration in conjunction with new approaches in art and architecture.[71] This subtext also coloured Price's work on the Fun Palace Project. Integration of technology and the development of a construction system based on an industrial manufacturing perspective were the design leitmotifs that suffused his plans for the new environment. The principal element that distinguished his first sketches for the Fun Palace from his previous work was however his response to Joan Littlewood's ideas concerning an interactive theatre space. As well as initiating the project, Littlewood was also the client and became a close friend of Price from 1961 on. After an initial phase in which Price began drawing up plans for the Fun Palace under his own steam, although he had not been commissioned to do so, Littlewood financed Price's development work.[72] She was fifty-six years old at the time, with a long-standing desire to create a "people's workshop – a leisure land of occupational, vocational, instructional and creative fun", which she considered as the consummation of her ideas on participatory theatre.[73] Her productions, modelled on the Agitprop movement and Bertolt Brecht's Epic Theatre, centred on improvisation and audience reflection on events unfolding on the stage.[74] In Littlewood's view, theatre should not merely be passively consumed but actively experienced, particularly in an era marked by the advent of consumerism and mass society. She therefore sought to open up the conventional theatrical setting in her work by dissolving the boundaries between representation and observation, between stage and reality.[75] Littlewood imagined the Fun Palace as an arena in which the stage, self-awareness and experience would be inextricably intermeshed: "[...] all my life I've been trying to get such a place. A place in fact, where millions who search for 'something to do' will find it here and compound it with that something that comes with self accomplishment."[76]

Chiming with Littlewood's vision, the Fun Palace was conceived as a cultural and event venue that would provide the spatial and technical tools for active participation in cultural life.[77] Price described Littlewood's motivation as a reflection of her wish to create a new form of artistic expression for the theatre that could be directly experienced in a situational frame: "[...] she wanted to see some situation [...] where the ability for random humour and beastliness could result in a productive exchange which was not measurable, but was just fun when it happened."[78] Building on this understanding of "fun", the project's programme and contents were supposed to grow organically from visitors' interests. Instead of working with specific definitions, Littlewood therefore articulated the Fun Palace programme in the form of a question. As the heading on the cover of the advertising brochure proclaimed, the Fun Palace was: "Everybody's: What is it?"[79]

From the outset, the Fun Palace's architecture was developed without any concrete stipulations for its spatial programme. Instead, the building's openness became the design principle. Price's plans drew on his study for the Donmar Warehouse Theatre's rehearsal stage, which Joan Littlewood had commissioned in 1961.[80] For this location he had conceived a stage construction that could be moved in all dimensions, allowing a broad spectrum of presentations to co-exist. The architecture simply provided the functional infrastructure with which visitors could pursue their different interests.[81]

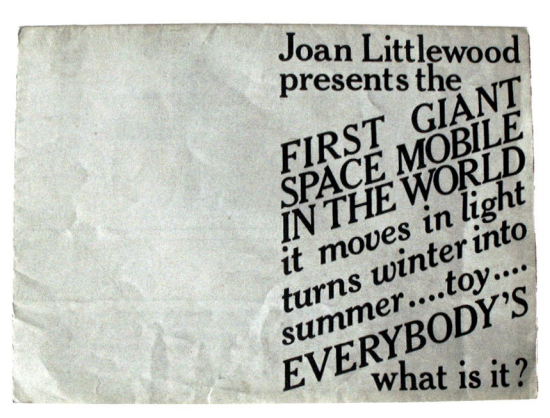

10 Joan Littlewood and Cedric Price, Fun Palace Leaflet: Cover, ca. 1964.

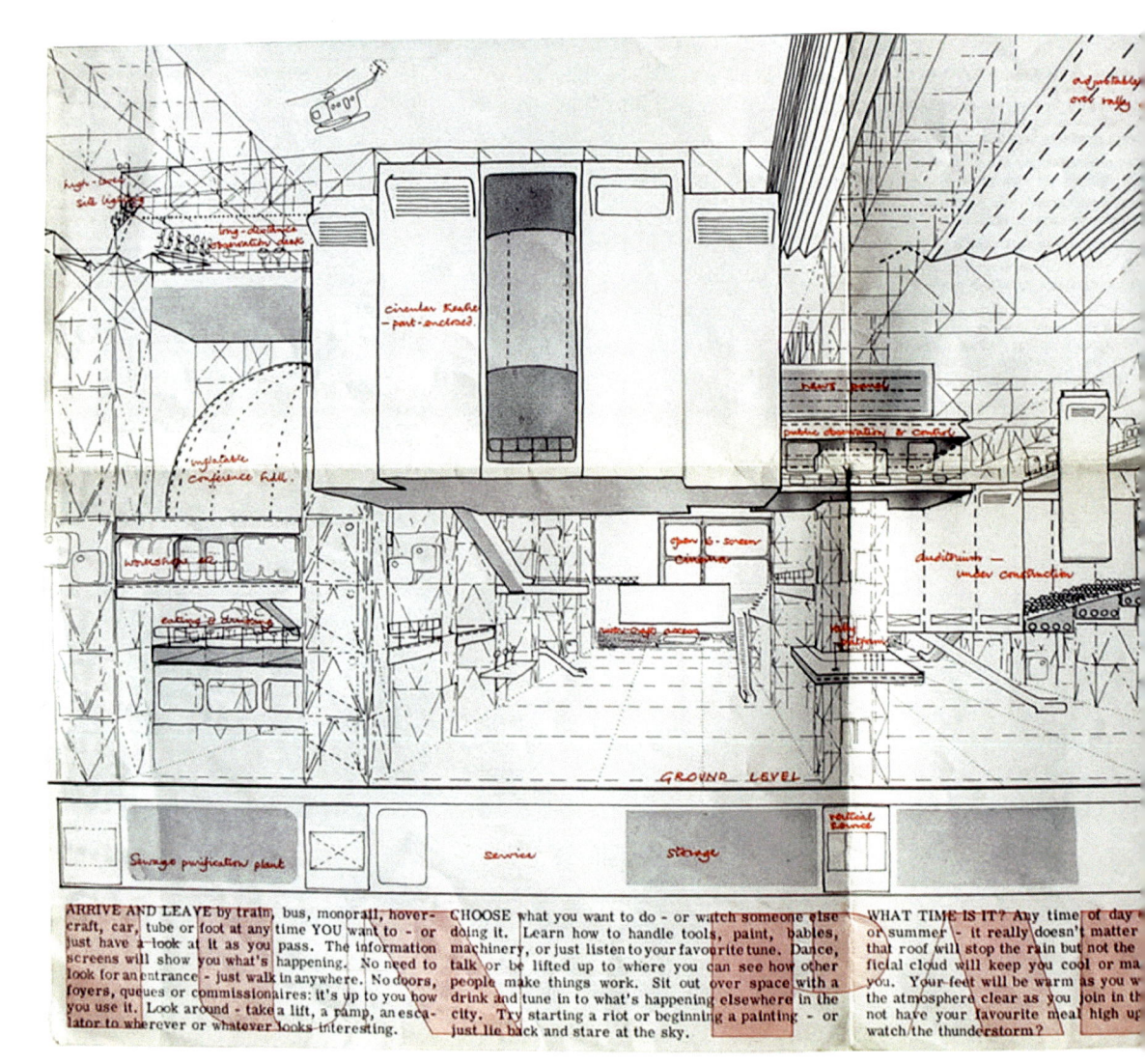

11 Joan Littlewood and Cedric Price, Fun Palace Leaflet: Interior pages, ca. 1964.

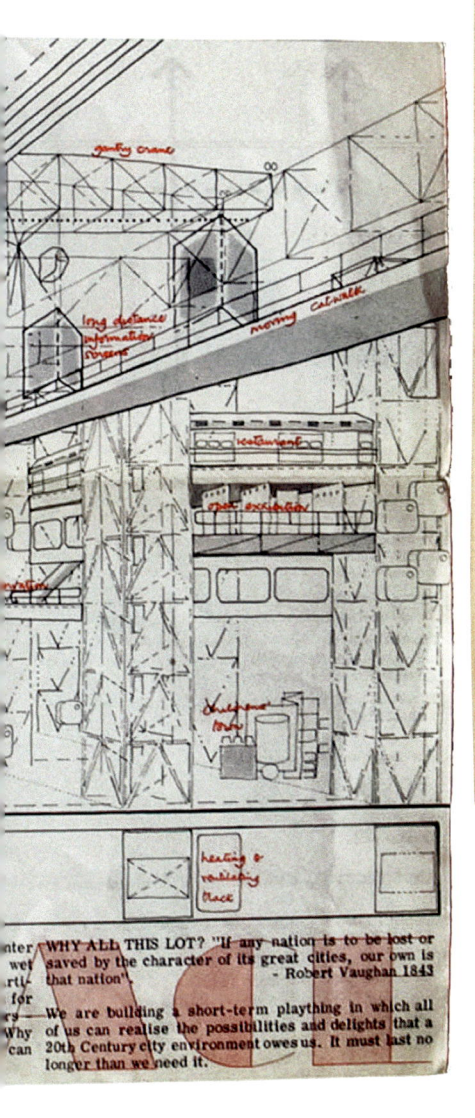

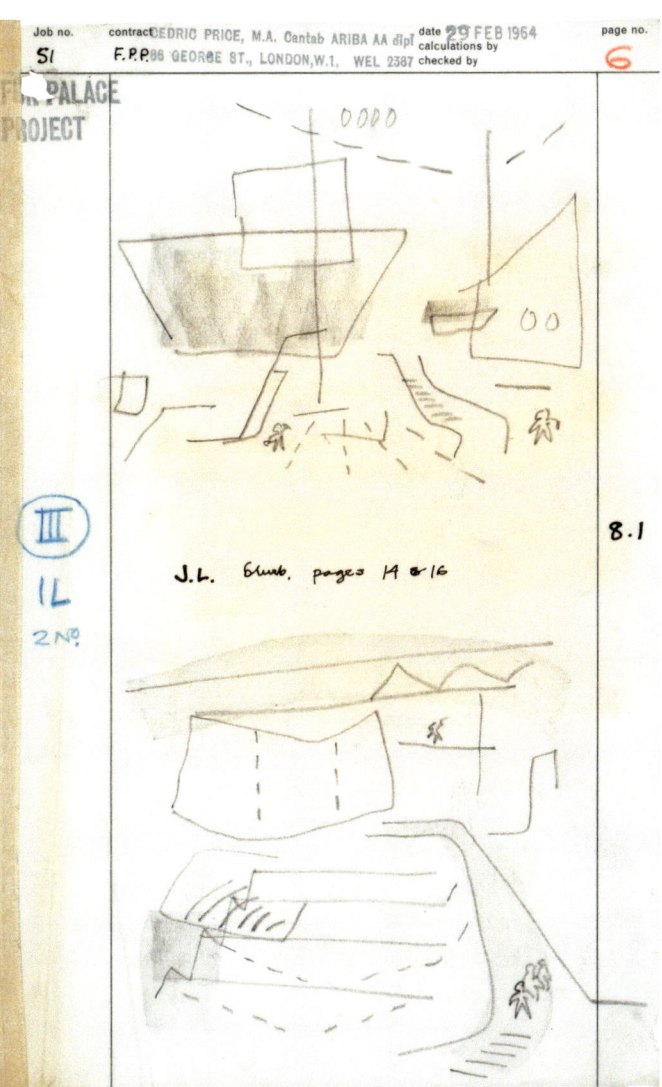

12 Cedric Price, Fun Palace Project, Interior sketches, **1964**.

Littlewood drew her ideas on constructing the open theatre space from the 1920s Soviet avant-garde reform programmes, which tallied with her belief in theatre as an instrument for politicising society.[82] This involved creating stagings close to life as a means of addressing quotidian conflicts. In putting these concepts into practice she used the pared-down means deployed by Erwin Piscator and Vsevolod Meyerhold. Their Functionalist set design, inspired by the aesthetic of industrial culture, influenced Price's plans for the Fun Palace, as the description of Piscator's stage aesthetic reveals: "There are few stages indeed which have the mechanical precision and efficiency of an ordinary modern factory [...] with mobile bridges, elevators, cranes, motors, great scene docks and moving platforms."[83]

12
13
14

With a view to enabling simultaneous activities and variable configuration of the spaces in the Fun Palace, Cedric Price, echoing his approach for the London Zoo Aviary, made a structural frame the central design element, this time in the form of a hall structure.[84] Working in conjunction with Newby, Price developed a steel structural system to contain all the building's architectonic components. The 260 × 114 m hall[85] was ten storeys high and spanned by an open truss structure.[86] It had a visitor capacity of 5,000. On the longitudinal sides of the hall, embedded in a double row of vertical stairwells, various floor levels accommodated servicing areas, galleries, restaurants and lifts. The hall was divided once more along the middle axis by stairwells leading to the suspended stages and platforms in the interior space.[87]

The visible truss structure Price and Newby envisioned referenced nineteenth-century architectural engineering and the typology of the exhibition hall, as exemplified in London's Crystal Palace (1851) or the Grand Palais in Paris (1900).[88] Within these structures a mass audience had enjoyed the first opportunity to find out about the societal and technical innovations of their era. This tradition of the large exhibition hall as a locus of cultural identity and large-scale societal events formed the point of departure for Price's creative reinterpretation in the Fun Palace. The design language Price tapped into in conceiving the Fun Palace did however have a direct precursor in the Sea and Ships Pavilion.[89] The exhibition hall typology linked two functional concepts of steel and glass architecture that Price used in the Fun Palace Project. Working with industrially manufactured materials on the one hand opened up the floor plan. On the other hand, the chosen type of construction freed the inner space from environmental conditions in its surroundings to an unprecedented degree. Both Price and Newby saw the USA's steel architecture as a logical continuation of this development, embodied for example in Fuller's dome projects, Konrad Wachsmann's work or Ludwig Mies van der Rohe's buildings for the IIT Campus. Price and Newby were familiar with these points of reference from their joint study trip to Chicago and the Californian coast.[90] In designing the Fun Palace's structural system, they explicitly aimed to continue the tradition of Functionalist Modernism outlined by Reyner Banham in *Revolution in Architecture*.[91] However, Price updated this tradition, whilst also approaching it from a somewhat different angle.

"Kit of Parts"

Price developed the Fun Palace hall as a modular system. He described the principle he used in construction as a "kit of parts".[92] The modular scheme was his design response to the desire to open up the building to respond to visitors' needs. Eleven horizontal structural components were envisaged for this construction kit, supplemented by wall panels to close off the rooms.[93] The hall was to offer a frame for cultural projects to come into being by combining a range of elements on various scales and with different features: "A galaxy of load bearing links, all straight & respectable."[94]

15
16

In adopting this approach Price referenced the Chicago School in the early days of high-rise construction and Louis Sullivan's "form follows function".[95] In keeping with the principle of fitness for purpose, any change in a building's function should also be reflected in a change in its form. The Fun Palace's shifting configurations were a strikingly clear manifestation of this principle. A different utilisation could be accommodated on every storey within the hall's structural frame, and each space within it could be reconfigured. Flexibility and multi-functionality determined the Fun Palace's spatial programme, and were also Price's aesthetic lodestones for the project. The façade evoked the machine architecture design principle vis-à-vis the outside world. Price described it as a stratification of various kinds of use: "An opportunity for sandwich banners."[96]

New relations between the individual components of the "kit of parts" could be established again and again without calling into question the hall's fundamental structure.[97] In this respect the Fun Palace was grounded in a structural design concept in which varied configurations offered scope for a range of organisational forms for the building.[98] The "kit of parts" idea can also be found in the early 1960s in work by architects such as Jean Prouvé, Buckminster Fuller and the Archigram Group.[99] In 1964 Warren Chalk, Peter Cook and Dennis Crompton began to explore a design approach with multiple affinities to the Fun Palace in their work on the Plug-in City (1964–66).[100] Prefabricated accommodation capsules in the Plug-in City could be suspended in a large open scaffolding structure that unfurled along individual infrastructure components of the city.[101]

Looking back, Reyner Banham used the term megastructure to describe this kind of large-scale structural framing architecture.[102] He identified its hallmark characteristics in the distinction drawn between the load-bearing structure and the finishing and services. The varying lifecycles of these elements opened up possibilities for the adjustment and renewal of the overall system. However, Banham viewed Price's Fun Palace and Archigram's Plug-in City as endpoints in this development.[103] For him, these projects had evolved out of Team 10's Structuralist designs, and from work by architects such as Yona Friedman and the Japanese Metabolists.[104] A member of the latter group, Fumihiko Maki, had already presented an initial definition of the megastructure in his 1964 book *Investigations In Collective Form*. For Maki the megastructure as a

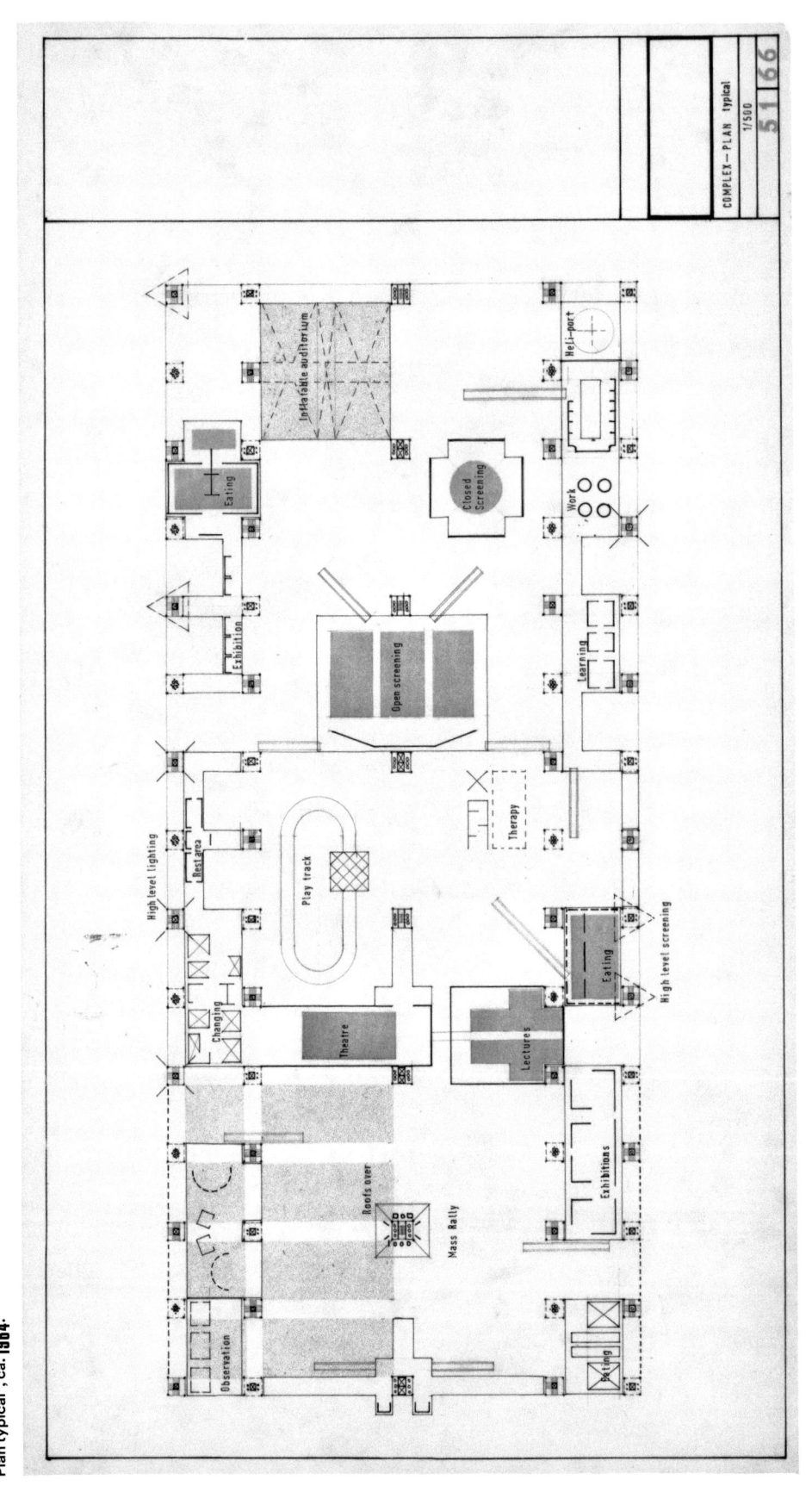

1

13 Cedric Price, "Complex: Plan typical", ca. 1964.

14 Cedric Price, "Complex: Typical short section", ca. 1964.

1

15 Cedric Price, "a galaxy of load bearing links", structural elements of the Fun Palace, ca. 1964.

16 Cedric Price, untitled, Sketch of Fun Palace with technical equipment and skin in pink and orange. ca. **1964**.

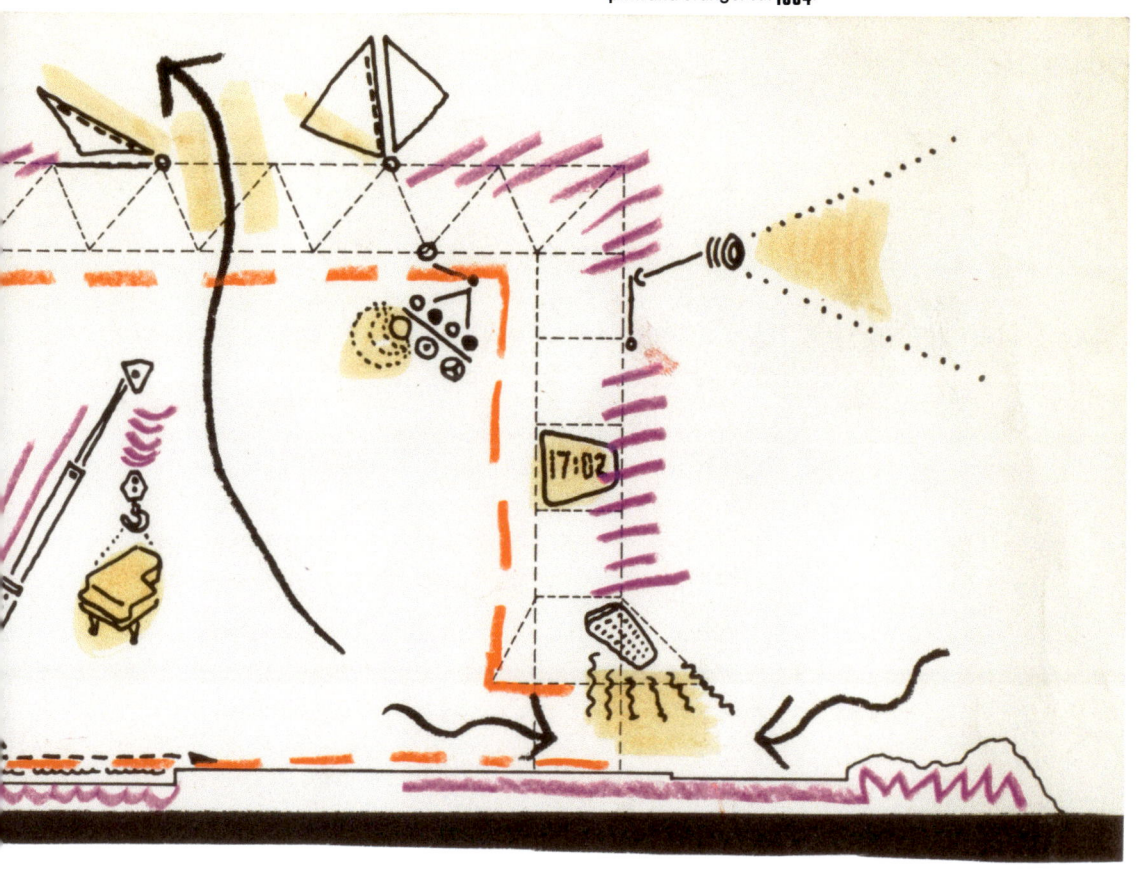

form of collective production of space had only become possible thanks to industrial manufacturing techniques. Its structure was based on a components system that linked the scale of each individual structure to the city's collective scale. The megastructure's form and configuration depended on a plethora of individual decisions made by the people living in it and therefore eluded the influence of the architect drawing up the plans.[105]

The Fun Palace was in equal measure an example of this phenomenon and an exception to it. In contrast to designs for what were dubbed "cluster buildings", the Fun Palace did not include modules to extend its structure outwards. Instead the project integrated variable ordering as a feature of its interior space. Price concentrated on the technical and constructional configuration of the building's structural integrity to ensure adaptability. Transforming the cultural programme and presenting multiple activities simultaneously were for him hallmarks of a new technologically-oriented era, and he took the view that transposing these considerations into built form involved much more than just the structural system's constructional aspects. In the detailed configuration of his plans, Price drew on both the most modern manufacturing techniques and the latest developments in building services engineering.

"A Home is not a House"

The architectural brief from the Fun Palace Trust stipulated that the hall construction should be adaptable, both thanks to its mechanical construction and an electronic regulation system for the space. The building's openness was to be manifested by creating a comfortable and welcoming atmosphere with the assistance of building services such as air heating, stage lighting and an electronically adjustable façade made of plastic membranes.[106] Price designed the structural frame for the Fun Palace as part of a three-dimensional infrastructure system that allowed building services to be incorporated anywhere within the space, with support from a supply and information network for electricity, water, information, etc.[107] Electronic regulation devices and the technical fittings would mean that the luminosity, acoustics and temperature in the individual sections of the hall could be adjusted independently.[108] The Fun Palace's load-bearing structure thus became an infrastructure tailor-made for users and their needs: " – in effect a 'plug-in' service grid."[109]

Price's inspiration in developing the requisite constructional details was drawn from manufacturing techniques used in the automobile industry, which produced a range of models based on a single technical chassis platform. For the Fun Palace he designed uniform floor platforms which could be connected with the technical infrastructure.[110] With these platforms as a foundation, a plethora of different spatial functions could be combined with simple or more complex room modules.[111] Contemporary examples of this approach in other fields abounded. In 1960s Britain, the car had become an affordable, mass-consumer product,[112] and popular models such as the Ford 17 M P3 offered similar technical amenities, such as a music system, and electronic roof-opening and ventilation systems.[113]

As an industrially produced machine, the Fun Palace was intended to enable differentiated regulation of the environmental factors throughout the ensemble.[114]

Drawing on Fuller's principle of universal architecture, Price's Fun Palace design was also informed by research and development considerations.[115] He began for example to develop an acoustic concept with engineer Sandy Brown to ensure variable electronic regulation of the amplification and sound protection required in the various spaces.[116] Like many of the technical systems in the Fun Palace, this form of electronic acoustic support was relatively new and largely untested in architecture previously. The methodology Price adopted in this context was always shaped by an experimental design strategy that aspired to promote industrialisation in construction by integrating technical innovations: "'Space' is meaningless. We have relationships – but no space" as Fuller had noted.[117] At the same time, in the Fun Palace design Price moved further away from the goals pursued by Fuller, who had always deployed the most up-to-date technological tools to control environmental conditions and energy flows within particular spaces.[118] In contrast, Price's use of technology was much more focused on the individual, and his or her wishes and activities.

Qualities such as informality, spontaneity and scope for creative expression were the vital parameters for Joan Littlewood and the Fun Palace's other initiators. The plans for a service architecture regulated by electronics systems, with which Price sought to transpose these qualities into the Fun Palace's design, fulfilled all the requirements for the building's temporality.

Ideas for the activities that would unfold in the space were derived from Littlewood's theatrical practice. The improvisation technique she had developed concentrated on experimenting with new role models and experiencing one's own personality. She interpreted these characteristics as offering an opportunity for new shared experiences in space, with no predetermined architectural constraints: "[…] the essence of the place will be its informality: nothing is to be for more than ten years […]; no legacy of noble contemporary architecture quickly dating; no municipal geranium beds or fixed teak benches."[119] She interpreted change and adaptability in this context as almost "natural" qualities of the building. In keeping with this spirit, she envisioned the Fun Palace's cultural activities forming part of a landscape of leisure in which people could stroll freely among a regularly updated range of pursuits and could encounter others in a setting akin to nineteenth-century pleasure gardens.[120] As indicated in the London Civic Trust's specifications, the building was envisaged as a component within a planned park ensemble that would extend along the banks of the river Lea in the east of London.[121]

In her script for the Fun Palace film, Littlewood ascribed landscape-like qualities to the programme, sketching these out in romanticising and metaphorical terms. The short commercial for the project used fog machines, devices for creating electrostatic clouds and an artificial sun to create a backdrop of nature that users could alter as they saw fit. All the control mechanisms to regulate the ambience within the space were to be put in users' hands, allowing them to exert a direct influence on the design of their surroundings, a "weather control at your disposal".[122] The electronic systems deployed in the Fun Palace were in this respect linked to the vision of creating an unmediated and hence more natural setting (i.e. one more suited to human nature).

Cedric Price's plans for the Fun Palace leave unresolved the question of whether it was to be an interior or an exterior space.[123] The Fun Palace's technical infrastructure, as well as producing a range of particular indoor-climatic states, aimed to embed the space in a natural "flow of space and time".[124] That also explains why Price did not produce plans showing an entrance zone. He designed the ground floor to be open on all sides, allowing the space to be entered at any time on this level with no spatial barrier. An information system underpinned by video cameras and monitors was envisaged to steer visitor flows and provide users with advance information about the schedule and locations of events in the complex. Access regulation was thus displaced from the architectonic shaping of space into the realm of information and building services. Embedded electronic information systems aimed to guarantee the building's radical openness and enable unrestricted access to the Fun Palace's cultural activities. As if seeking to fulfil a basic human need, the project initiators' goal was to open the Fun Palace's cultural space to everyone around the clock: "No need to look for an entrance, just walk in anywhere, no doors, foyers, queues or commissioners ..."[125]

Banham's 1965 essay "A Home Is Not a House" articulated the theoretical pendant to this societal vision of an environment-creating architecture regulated by technology. In this essay, he described pop music and the car as new forms of cultural expression, manifestations of a self-determined culture of pleasure. Banham believed that this was triggered by electronics and automated manufacturing techniques.[126] The transistor radio, for example, had transformed music, previously framed as high culture, into a mass cultural phenomenon. However, radio programming had remained largely unchanged until this point.[127] In the light of such considerations, Banham called for architecture to adjust its design principles to contemporary cultural transformations. Sigfried Giedion's 1948 *Mechanization Takes Command* had urged a new equilibrium between the individual and the collective sphere in modern architecture. In his book Giedion had interpreted the history of mechanisation as one of increasing subjugation of human beings to the dictates of machines.[128] Banham, like Price and the Fun Palace Trust, countered this notion with a vision of architecture that would open up scope for individual self-development by integrating electronic systems.

The Cybernetics Committee

Openness was a hallmark of the Fun Palace in multiple respects: the building had neither a rigidly defined spatial programme nor a fixed division of space. Alongside its adaptable spatial structure and technical equipment, the Fun Palace therefore required an organisation principle to regulate the sequencing and arrangement of activities within it. Price also identified a substantive link between automation in industrial manufacturing and the ways in which an individualised lifestyle culture was articulated. Given their small scale, the instruments deployed in the automobile industry's regulatory systems for measurements and adjustments[129] faded into the background in the face of the human scale of a building.

For Price, automated regulation systems provided an opportunity to handle spatial organisation of the Fun Palace's activities.[130] The building's technical infrastructure was therefore to include sensors and feedback mechanisms so that the mobile building structure could adapt almost invisibly to users' activities. In "A Home Is Not a House", Banham had described a space equipped with this type of technical amenities as using "softer hardware".[131]

In spring 1964, the Fun Palace Trust set up a dedicated committee, bringing together more than twenty-six scientists, academics and politicians, to develop the programme and organise how to regulate it.[132] It was headed by cyberneticist Gordon Pask, who, a year earlier, had devised a control system for Joan Littlewood's theatre productions that allowed audiences to influence the course of the plays.[133] The Fun Palace Trust's Cybernetics Committee set itself the goal of enabling virtually spontaneous utilisation of the Fun Palace, supported by the rational model of system regulation and instruments drawn from applied mathematics: "Random choice for a mobile society."[134] Cybernetics seemed a viable means of organising rapid fluctuations in the number of visitors and their distribution within the space. Cybernetic forecasting would allow each visitor an opportunity for individual self-determined use of the possibilities the space provided.[135]

17
18
19

Fundamental technical and mathematical concepts such as regulation, information and systems had been applied to the human social universe with the aid of cybernetics since the 1940s. Conversely, findings from this realm also began to restructure that social universe, for example in the organisation of work and communication.[136] Systems theory was tied into a plethora of entirely different objectives and contents, reflecting the political orientations underpinning its practical applications. In Communist states cybernetics was viewed as a scientific instrument for optimisation, used to secure social equality. In contrast, in the Fun Palace cybernetics was deployed to strike the right balance between visitors' individual interests and those of the community as a whole, in the process generating new possibilities of social interaction.

Work on the project's organisational principle unfolded parallel to development of the spatial design principles, as relations between the construction components had to be established to ensure the space's programmability. Price worked in close conjunction with Pask to achieve this, as well as with the other committee members, who elaborated ideas and decisions for the programmes and regulatory systems in regular meetings. On the one hand they aimed to make the regulatory mechanisms as simple as possible; on the other hand the committee agreed that the solution chosen to implement these mechanisms should not jeopardise the spontaneity of interactions in the building.

With these objectives in mind, the committee's scientists developed regulatory systems on three interacting levels. As their top priority they examined interactions between the building and its surroundings, the city. They defined regulation of the building's mechanical system as their second focal point. In addition, they believed systems could be developed to foster social interactions between

17 Cedric Price, "Star gazing", Punch card, ca. 1964.

18 Cedric Price, Fun Palace questionnaire, ca. 1964.

1

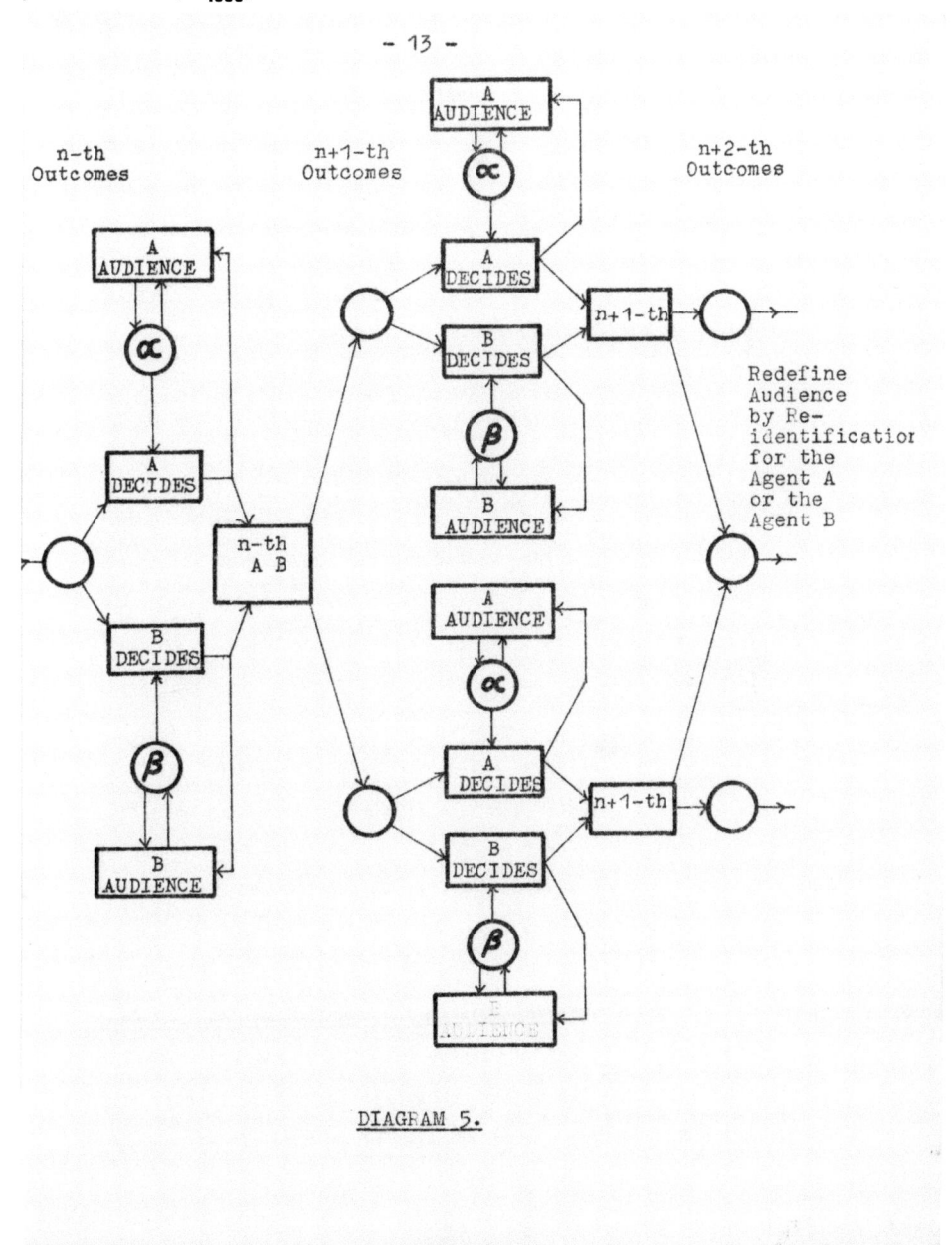

DIAGRAM 5.

	GENERAL ACOUSTIC CONTROL	LOCAL ACOUSTIC CONTROL	GENERAL HEATING	LOCAL HEATING	SPECIAL ILLUMINATION	LOCAL LIGHTING	ELECTRIC POWER	PRESSURE POWER	VACUUM POWER	WATER & WATER WASTE	CONDITIONED AIR & EXTRACT	NATURAL LIGHT	BLACKOUT
RALLIES closed	●	●	●		●								
RALLIES open air		●			●								
RECITALS	●	●			□						□		
CONCERTS	●	●		●	●						●		
THEATRE	●	●		●	●			●			●	●	
CINEMA closed	●			●							●	●	
CINEMA open		●			●						●	●	
LECTURES											●	●	
LESSONS	●			●		●	●				□	□	□
MEETINGS & SEMINARS	●		●			●					□	□	□
DANCE AREAS		●	●		●			□			□		
WORKSHOPS		●	●			●	●	●	●				
REHEARSALS	●		●		●			●				●	
EXHIBITIONS	●	●	●		●		□	□		□	□	●	
BARS [snacks]	●		●			●	●		●	●	●		
RESTAURANTS	●			●		●			●	●	●		
PLAYGROUNDS			●				●	●		●		□	
GYMNASTICS			●								●		

□ optional
● obligatory

SERVICING FOR MASS ACTIVITIES

51 59

20 Cedric Price, "Servicing for Mass Activities", Table, ca. 1964.

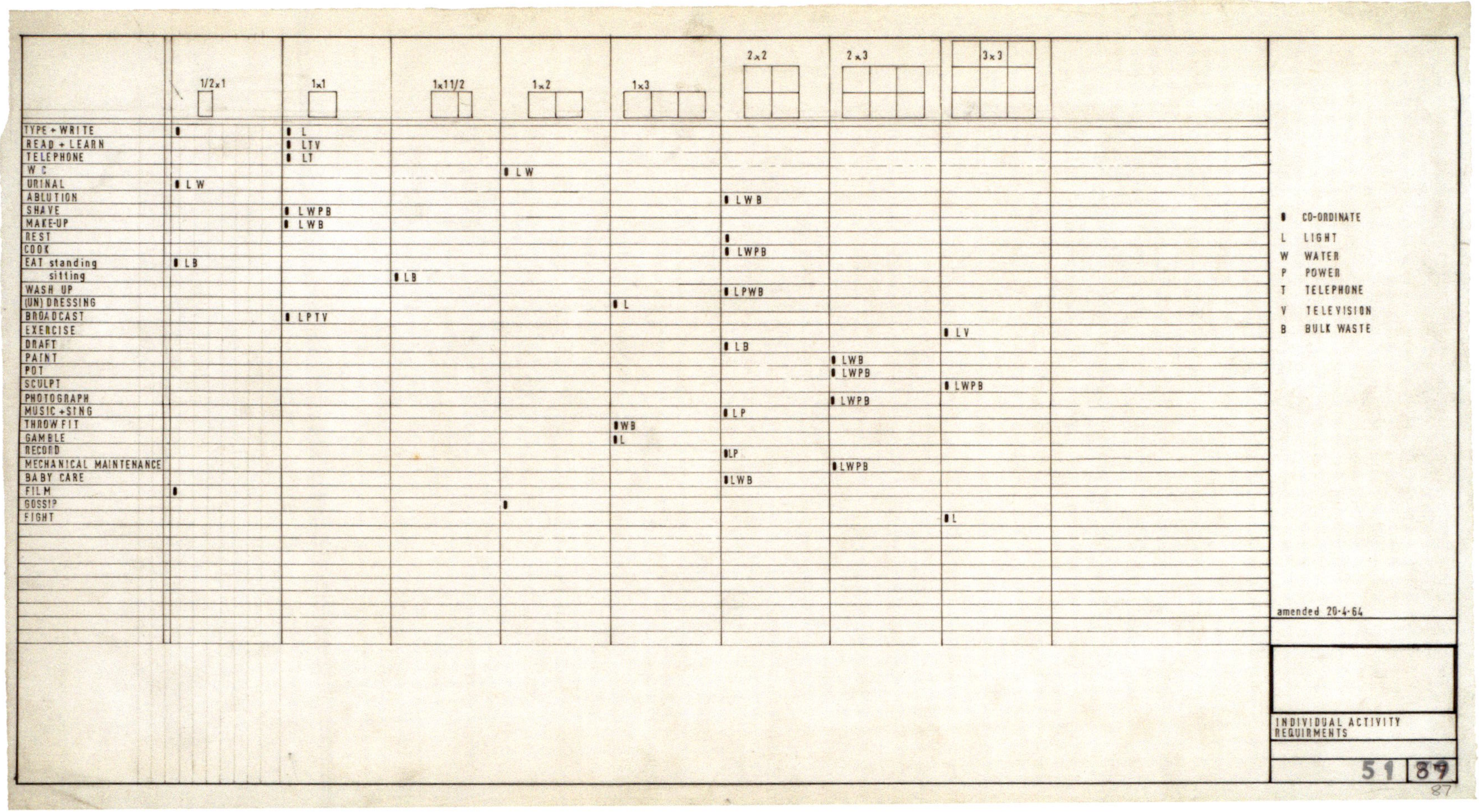

	1/2 x 1	1x1	1x1 1/2	1x2	1x3	2x2	2x3	3x3	
TYPE + WRITE	●	L							
READ + LEARN		LTV							
TELEPHONE		LT							
W C				● LW					
URINAL	● LW								
ABLUTION						● LWB			
SHAVE		● LWPB							
MAKE-UP		● LWB							
REST						●			
COOK						● LWPB			
EAT standing	● LB								
sitting			● LB						
WASH UP						● LPWB			
(UN) DRESSING					● L				
BROADCAST		● LPTV							
EXERCISE								● LV	
DRAFT				● LB					
PAINT							● LWB		
POT							● LWPB		
SCULPT								● LWPB	
PHOTOGRAPH							● LWPB		
MUSIC + SING						● LP			
THROW FIT					● WB				
GAMBLE					● L				
RECORD						● LP			
MECHANICAL MAINTENANCE							● LWPB		
BABY CARE						● LWB			
FILM	●								
GOSSIP				●					
FIGHT								● L	

● CO-ORDINATE
L LIGHT
W WATER
P POWER
T TELEPHONE
V TELEVISION
B BULK WASTE

amended 20-4-64

INDIVIDUAL ACTIVITY REQUIREMENTS

51 87

21 Cedric Price, "Individual Activity Requirements", Table, ca. 1964.

individual users.[137] The intended immediacy of activities at the Fun Palace could only be attained through the interplay of all these levels, on various different scales; as Reyner Banham later put it: "The environment was suited to what you are going to do next [...] An indeterminate participatory open-ended situation."[138]

Gordon Pask was in no doubt that cybernetics could become a kind of architectural meta-language. He enumerated three additional factors for Cedric Price that the plans for the Fun Palace should address. First of all, the architecture should take account of visitor flows moving around the building; secondly, it should incorporate an information system and the requisite infrastructure; and thirdly, it should define the system's connective qualities in the form of flexible access systems.[139]

The idea that certain "visiting patterns" could filter through into the configuration of the building was crucially important for Gordon Pask. He was aware that identifying such ordering patterns posed huge challenges for the building's architectural design.[140] In developing the Fun Palace's machine architecture, Price therefore also assumed the role of an organiser who developed a range of functional possibilities, which he recorded in diagrams and matrices. To cite just one example, he connected a series of possible programmes with various room sizes in these matrices, in order to obtain information about the mutual dependencies of these parameters for the design. These tabular presentations served as the underpinning for simple algorithms for programming the space.

To gain a clearer understanding of the interactions between the building and its surroundings, Cedric Price examined the ramifications of the building's internal organisation on visitor movements. He developed an extremely nuanced circulation system, with which he intended to reflect the complex cybernetic regulatory systems in the physical construction.[141] His design included a plethora of alternative pathways, implemented by incorporating electronic building components such as moving walkways and escalators running at varying speeds.[142] Price also introduced flexible connecting platforms and equipped every second access tower in the structural frame to become a "service tower", each of which could be connected to three other towers in the central axis.[143] Six pivotable escalators between the towers would accommodate additional vertical connection options.[144] The combinatorial scope afforded by the escalators alone meant that Price could create several thousand distinct options for connections within

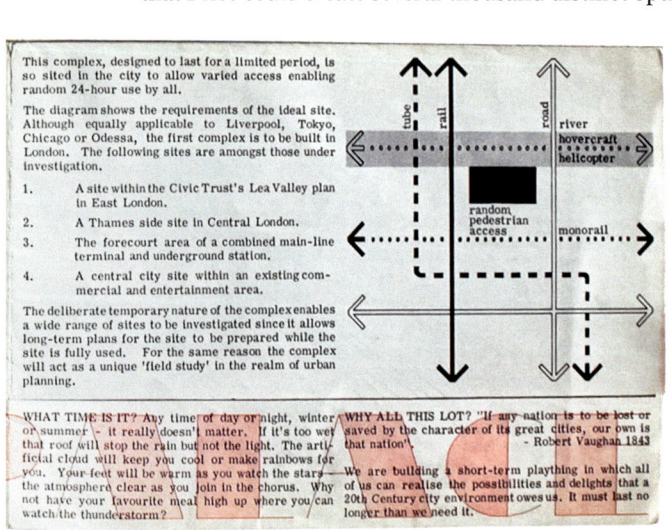

Joan Littlewood and Cedric Price, Fun Palace Leaflet: Interior pages, ca. 1964.

the building. These devices enabled him to create a complex, three-dimensional grid of intersections to afford visitors as much freedom of movement as possible.

Given the multitude of combinatorial possibilities that arose from the Fun Palace's machine architecture, Pask realised that devising a regulatory system for the building was directly linked to how manageable its complexity would be. The defining hallmarks of the Fun Palace, namely a wealth of simultaneous events and interactions, made absolute control of the space impossible. The sheer quantity of potential combinations arising simply from the three levels for system regulation generated a huge number of events, impossible to predict in detail, within the system's planned application patterns. Pask therefore attempted on the one hand to simplify the cybernetic system by drawing on statistical methods,[145] while on the other hand Price and Pask used social science surveys to delimit the extent of potential uses. Here they distinguished between predetermined use patterns, such as a concert with an audience of 3,000, and spontaneously generated configuration patterns that would come into being through the combination of individual activities. With a view to gauging the probability of various utilisation patterns, Price sent more than 160 questionnaires to friends and acquaintances.[146] However, the greatest influence on the Fun Palace's regulatory system was not utilisation patterns but visitor flows inside the building occasioned by a particular combination of activities.[147] Nevertheless, the committee viewed optimum spatial arrangement of the programmes as a purely combinatorial problem that could be optimised using an electronic computational process, coupled with control and feedback mechanisms fitted in the building.[148] The committee planned to use video recordings and real-time transmission to compare information on expected visitor numbers with the figures for users actually in the building.[149] The vertical connection routes in the building were to provide additional support for this approach by automatically recording visitor numbers via photoelectric sensors.[150] Capacities for individual events calculated using this method were to be displayed publicly on screens around the complex and in the adjacent streets.[151] Before even entering the Fun Palace visitors would be able to decide about the kind of visit they would make and how long they would stay.[152]

Consequently, even though the space inside the building was to be enormously flexible, Cedric Price nonetheless had to incorporate activities in its surroundings into his planning. The building's internal organisation was thus directly dependent on patterns of movement outside it. In this context the use of cybernetics in the Fun Palace dissolved the architectonic division between interior and exterior. Rather than being clearly demarcated as monumental architecture from events in its immediate context, the Fun Palace's machine architecture was conceived as part of the network of traffic and information flows surrounding it, whose influence extended far beyond the actual Fun Palace structure. In seeking to anticipate the building's internal organisation, it became crucial to consider it within a broader framing, as part of a network of urban infrastructures. The characteristics, movements and relationships of those infrastructures could be gathered using information technology so that, drawing on the action/reaction principle, the building would automatically adapt to the conditions in its environment.[153]

1 Cedric Price, sketch with ball pen on yellow paper, ca. 1964.

The Equilibrium of Urban Forces

Networks

When the Beatles first played live on British television, in October 1963, audience figures hit an unprecedented 15 million.[1] Events like this demonstrated the immense public impact that television was beginning to have in Great Britain. It was a medium that shaped public opinion, provided entertainment and offered opportunities for a new sense of community to emerge. That identity-creating dimension made it an apt conduit for conveying new urban lifestyles. Beatlemania made its mark on the physical city too. Hundreds of waiting fans blocked the streets outside the Palladium Theatre during the band's performance, tipping central London traffic into chaos.[2] The number of private vehicles on the city's streets had more than tripled since the 1950s.[3] As a result of this increased traffic, the technological changes brought about by mass culture also began to be manifested in public space. Streets and squares were redeveloped to suit drivers. The street as a place where people lingered had vanished and large-scale public events increasingly unfurled on television screens in British living rooms.

1

Just a few months later, in summer 1964, Joan Littlewood realised what a hugely relevant medium television could be for the Fun Palace Project. She produced an advertising film[4] aimed at convincing Londoners of the project's appeal. The film, intended for the BBC but never completed, presented the Fun Palace as modern metropolitan architecture, in which mobility and the mass media came together and brought about a step-change in exchanges between people. Functioning as a "valve",[5] the Fun Palace's open architecture was conceived to bring together various forms of cultural renewal and form a new culture of urban living. The concepts devised by the Cybernetics Committee presented the Fun Palace as embodying utterly new qualities, thanks to the ways that it linked in to the urban infrastructure, as strikingly illustrated in the film. Echoing the Situationists, who had explored an individual filter for spatial experience as they strolled on their *dérives* around cities such as Paris and Amsterdam, people casually walking past the Fun Palace would already be able to experience its impact.[6] There was also a media-based twist to the scheme in its function as a cultural hotspot, for various media channels were to be incorporated inside the building, allowing visitors to experience local and global events as they hit the headlines.

This performative conception of space drew inspiration from the work of artist Constant Nieuwenhuys, whose 1963 London lectures on the New Babylon project Price had attended with friends from the Archigram Group.[7] Nieuwenhuys' project envisaged a new form for society, with humans in the role of the so-called *homo ludens*,[8] living as footloose nomads. In this vision the city, rather than being defined as just a collection of buildings, was instead characterised by constant comings and goings, mainly serving urbanites' need to communicate and exchange ideas.[9] Drawing on this notion, the Archigram Group's *Living City* exhibition dubbed the connection between mobility, infrastructure and spontaneous urban experience "the time/movement/situation thing".[10]

Cedric Price picked up on this new way of looking at the city in the Fun Palace, aiming to make it a node of urban infrastructure that would offer a forum for situation-based experiences. Serving as a prototype for cultural architecture that chimed with the zeitgeist, the Fun Palace design pulled together a diverse spectrum of infrastructure types, envisioning that their signature connectivity would generate an entirely new form of experience.[11]

This conception of situationally adaptable space reveals an unexpected correlation between cybernetics and architecture. In applied mathematics, transport or information technology, intersections can be represented in the mathematical node and network model.[12] Thinking along similar lines, Price appraised the qualities expressed by his architectural design through the prism of the connections created by its infrastructure linkages and access points. Coming at the same issue from a different angle, the Cybernetics Committee used the mathematical concept of the network to address visitor flows and control of the building's spatial configuration. In these references to the notion of the network, cybernetics and architecture used a shared language that made it possible to consider the project's interaction option in terms of both spatial geometry and statistics.[13]

Taking the performative character of the network model as his point of departure, Price designed the Fun Palace as a node in the urban infrastructure network rather than as a stand-alone work of architecture. Through connections to as many different urban transport modes as possible, the project was integrated into the city's infrastructure system. Price also envisaged similar buildings set at other nodes to offer Londoners an aleatory experience of public space, shifting as a function of the specific situation.[14] In addition to the Mill Meads site, three further locations were foreseen for the Fun Palace: in Euston, on the Isle of Dogs and in Camberwell.[15] Littlewood, Price and Pask envisioned that the Fun Palace network would even reach beyond the city, creating a global system of interaction. To that end, Fun Palace Trust members had already started to nurture contacts in Liverpool, Glasgow and Chicago. A further node in this public network of culture was to be New York, under the aegis of Philip Johnson;[16] Tokyo and Odessa[17] would figure too, shifting the Fun Palace network outside the frame of Cold War ideological constraints. Against the backdrop of the nuclear threat, which had just come to a head (most recently in the 1962 Cuba crisis), the Fun Palace's network embodied a more global and international spirit, celebrating new communication and exchange technologies not merely as tools to augment individual freedom but as instruments of international understanding.

The cybernetic system Gordon Pask developed was grounded in the principle of self-similarity: different scale-levels in a system that build on repetition of structures. The architectural design reflected this functionally, with structural components, spaces and platforms that fitted together to form an overarching spatial system, subsumed into a network of cultural sites spanning the entire planet. Conceiving the Fun Palace's networks as part of a broader global network thus tapped into the incipient globalised worldview intrinsic to the information

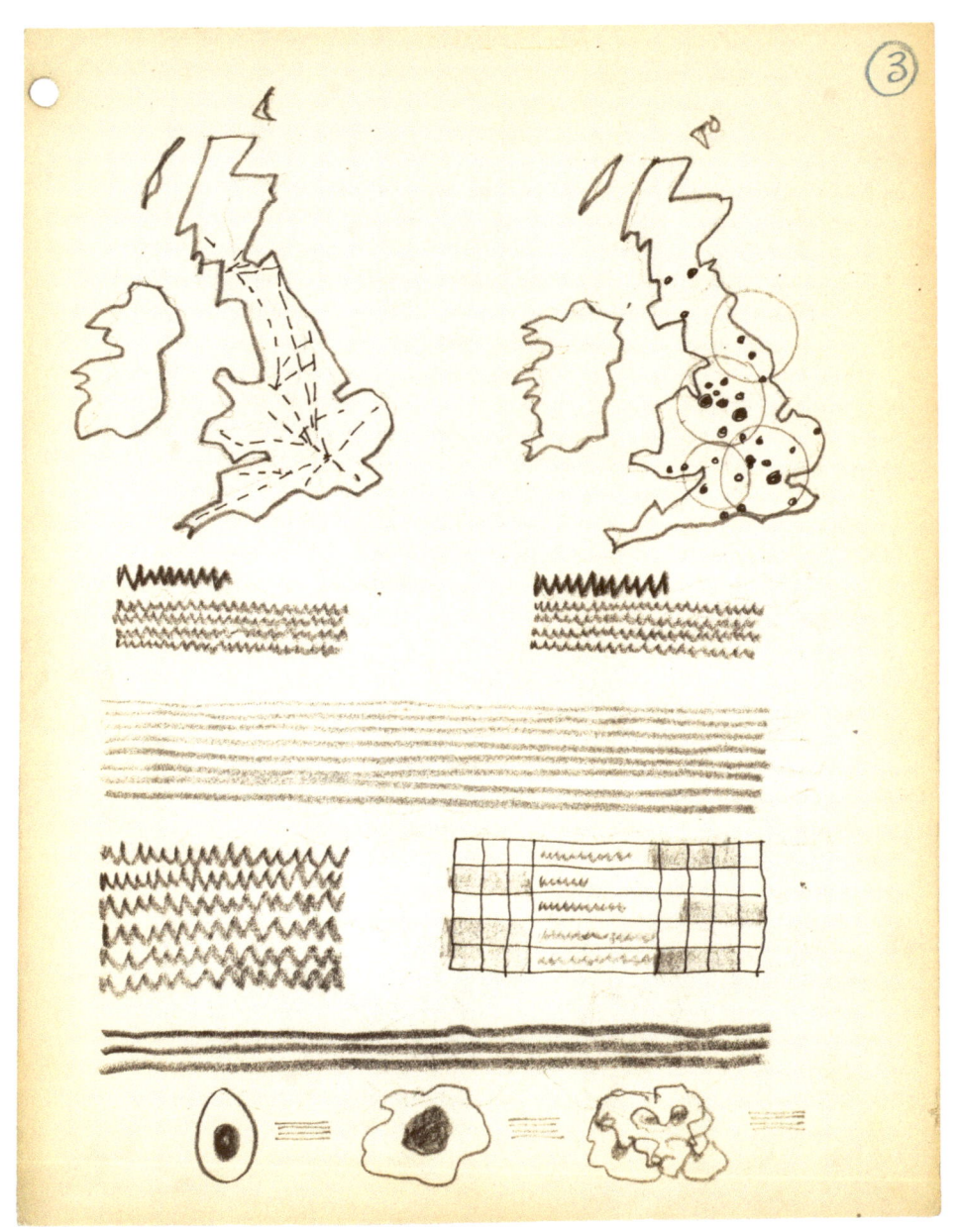

2   Cedric Price, *Fun Palace*, layout draft for: Fun Palace Leaflet, sheet 3, ca. 1964.

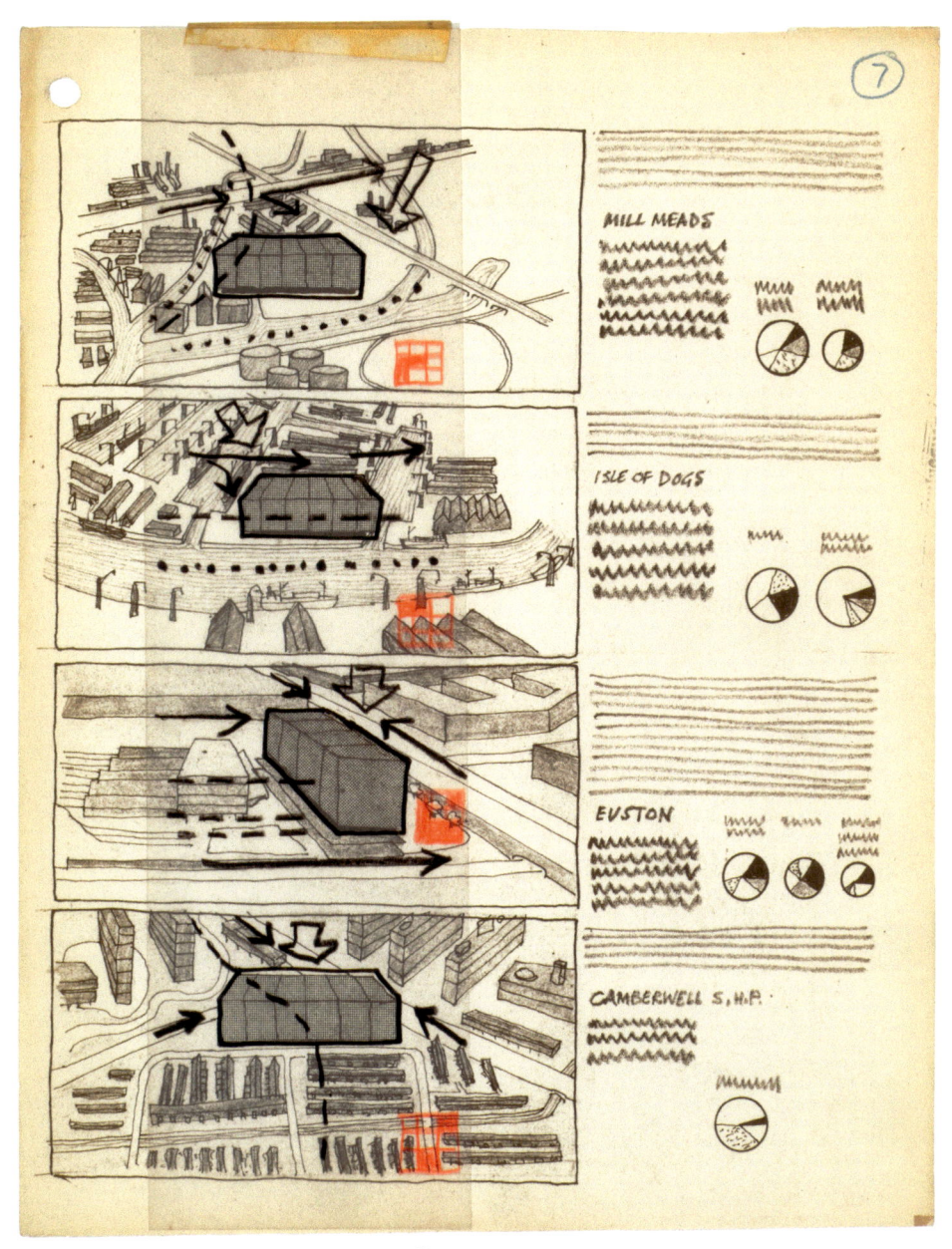

3   Cedric Price, *Fun Palace*, layout
draft for: Fun Palace Leaflet, sheet 7, ca. 1964.

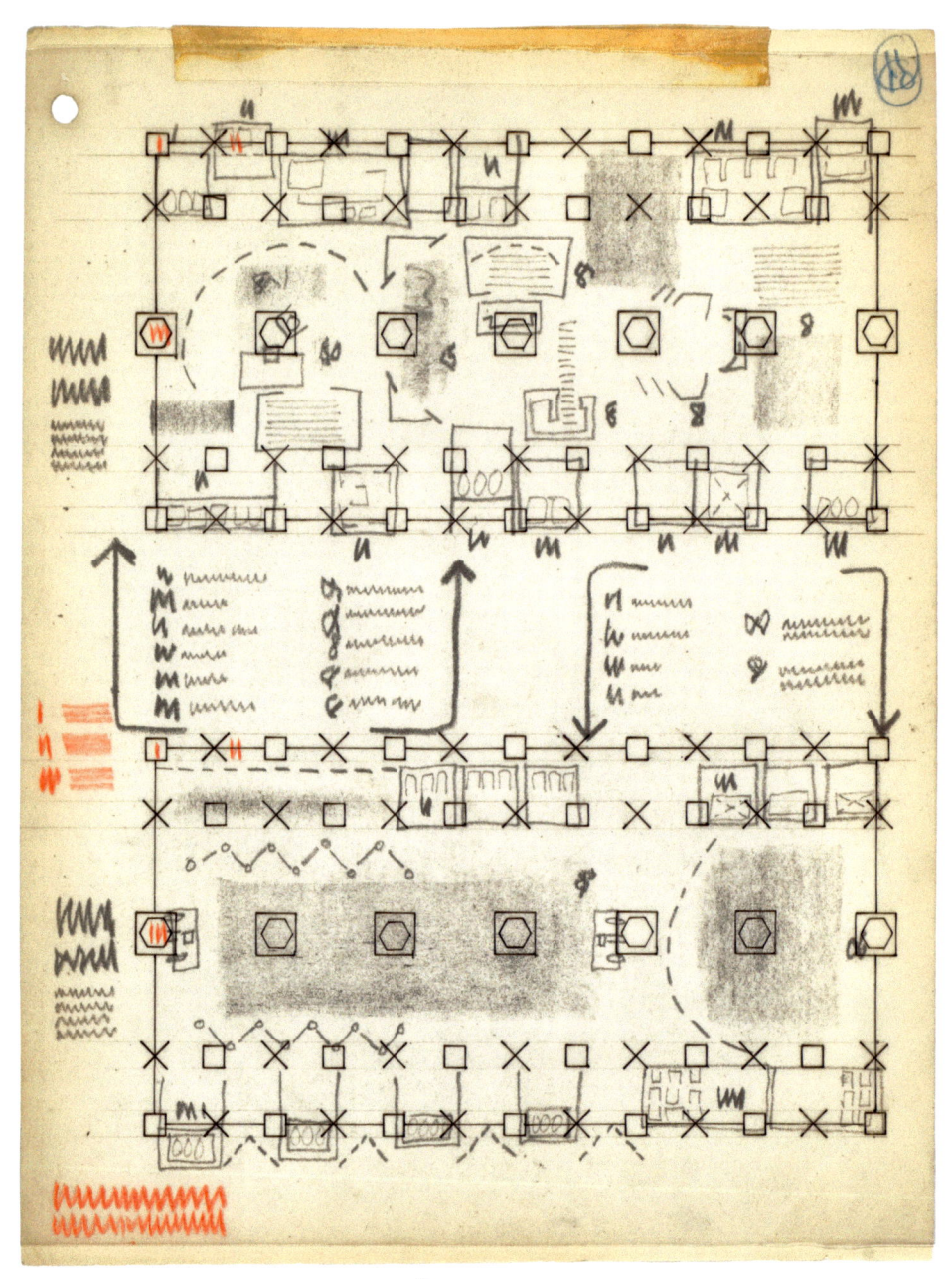

4 Cedric Price, *Fun Palace*, layout
draft for: Fun Palace Leaflet, sheet 18, ca. 1964.

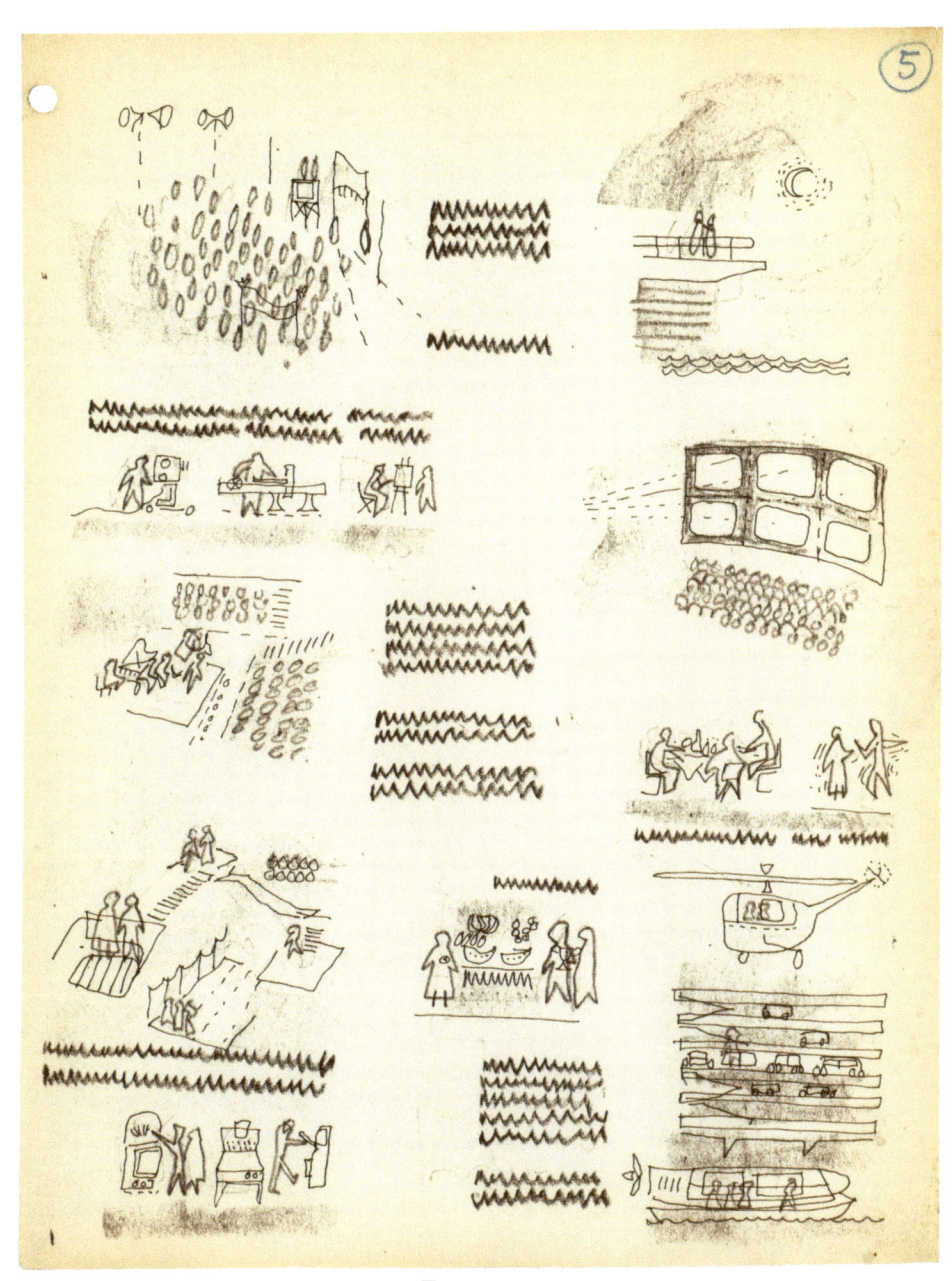

5 Cedric Price, *Fun Palace*, layout draft for: Fun Palace Leaflet, sheet 5, ca. 1964.

and service society, moving beyond physical spatial boundaries to create direct connections between the activities of individuals, institutions and states.

The scientific prerequisites for realising complex networks and systems were still in their early days in the early 1960s.[18] Network analysis had only just become a scientific research topic, deployed, for example, in NASA's major development programmes.[19] The scalability at the heart of the Fun Palace's network model made it significantly more challenging to implement cybernetic regulation systems here. The scientists in the Cybernetics Committee were well aware that the Fun Palace's network model went far beyond the control methods available at that time. They saw their work as a pioneering technical achievement, involving working at the cutting-edge of their respective disciplines rather than simply implementing readily realisable solutions. As a result, they saw the Fun Palace in terms of a research brief, exploring the applicability and societal utility of control systems.[20] However, the Cybernetics Committee's work was not couched as a thought experiment, for it was just at one remove from the latest scientific innovations.[21] As NASA's space programme clearly demonstrated, practical implementation of scientific principles was above all a question of time and money.

Microcosm of Society, Macrocosm of the World

This kind of experimentation with control and regulation systems formed the scientific framework for a much broader engagement with the social organisation of space in the Cybernetics Committee's work. Cybernetics interdisciplinary tack offered the committee ways to look at human psychology in the social and the political realm as part of a systemic whole rooted in the principle of action and reaction. The various technical options, including control and regulation technology, which they integrated into the Fun Palace were conceived to trigger new forms of encounter and entertainment as a way of facilitating direct experience of this cultural space.[22]

The committee's founding document specifically addressed how the Fun Palace's architecture and activity programme could create an environment that fostered and enhanced such social interaction and exchanges.[23] Within the overarching cybernetics research perspective, strategies from a wide range of very different disciplines came into play in devising the programmes and content that would flesh out the project: work on psychology of perception by Prof. Richard Langton Gregory, Sir Ross Chesterman's pedagogical concepts and cybernetician Stafford Beer's management theories, to cite just a few examples.[24]

Network-driven thinking proved particularly appealing to the Cybernetics Committee, framing the Fun Palace as a qualitative supplement to the city's existing systems, cultural and social activities. By creating such network links, the Fun Palace Projects aimed to foster exchanges, social participation and a new sense of community that would dovetail with daily life in the modern world. As the minutes of one of Cybernetics Committee meetings put it: "Fun in the Fun Palace context might be defined as 'participation'."[25]

The Fun Palace was to be equipped with cutting-edge information technology as a "city in the air",[26] bringing together all urban communication systems. This would enable it to produce a new kind of public sphere by reflecting diverse, complex simultaneous activities in the city. This strategy aimed to empower visitors to grasp the social identity of their surroundings, and boost their awareness of world affairs. The plans included broadcasting real-time recordings from various locations around London, reflecting everyday life.[27] Such direct information sought to conjure up a new media-based context for community life.[28] In this, the Fun Palace would be a multiplier and a gateway to the world, a "one-stop shop" simultaneously reproducing all aspects of British culture and daily life, as well as topical world affairs. This was all done with a view to promoting unfettered participation in public life and helping to create a more level playing field, as a response to the contradictions and social inequalities in access to culture, education and information that plagued London in the early 1960s.

Joan Littlewood's work on the Fun Palace film indicates how much living conditions in London shaped the direction that the project assumed. In the first part of the film she documented everyday life in London's East End,[29] turning the spotlight on the increasingly derelict working-class districts and London's waning industrial culture.[30] This is where the contrast between the rapidly vanishing culture of industrial labour and London's budding role as a service metropolis was at its most visible. Right next to the city centre, where office high-rises heralded over 56,000 new service-sector jobs, port and furniture industry workers faced a nose-dive in employment; as those jobs vanished, the culture of workers in those industries disappeared too.[31] In response to the decline of London's East End, the local authorities had authorised demolition of large swathes of nineteenth-century working-class housing. Whenever areas were cleared, London County Council's planning department[32] tried to rapidly

6 Cedric Price, Perspective drawing on paper, nocturnal view of the Fun Palace in Mill Meads, pencil, undated.

create as much new accomodation as possible by constructing new housing estates.[33] Fanned by a policy of economic incentives, more than 2,700 high-rise apartment blocks were built in the Greater London area up to the mid-1960s.[34] In the City of London, adjoining the East End, the huge amount of land that became available for building projects unleashed a speculative construction boom, and a flurry of office blocks shot up; this also meant that transport infrastructure expanded dramatically, for road construction was indirectly co-financed when contracts for construction schemes were awarded.[35] This huge building boom had a devastating effect on social amenities and shared open spaces. As Sir Colin Buchanan underscored in his report *Traffic in Towns,*[36] expanding mobility infrastructure had become a crucial town planning issue across Great Britain and posed a threat to many urban areas that had developed organically over the course of history. Modern planning's dominant tenets of production and efficiency meant scant attention was paid to the idea of the garden and the community, which had still figured in early twentieth-century workers' estates. As a result, public space was reallocated to other uses right across London. Against the backdrop of these developments, the Fun Palace was also motivated by the vision of creating a new public space where the city's culture could once again develop freely, unreglemented by planning constraints.

Architects and critics questioned the enormous pace of redevelopment in London. Reyner Banham contended that it revealed CIAM Functionalism's misdirected ambitions, turned on their head and transformed into something inhumane: "Yet it is clear that by the 1960s modern architects had argued themselves into a dilemma from which there was no logical escape. While the architectural profession would not relinquish its distinct 'Modern' claim to responsibility for 'the design of the whole human environment', it had now been forced to recognize that the homogeneously designed total architecture demanded by such as Walter Gropius would be as dead, as culturally thin, as any other perfect machine."[37] Contrasting with the conservative strand of British architectural traditions, Peter Cook from Archigram voiced the concerns of a younger generation of architects, calling for a renewal of Functionalist architecture "[…] with forms and spaces which seems to reject the precepts of 'Modern' yet in fact retains those precepts. We have chosen to bypass the decaying Bauhaus image which is an insult to functionalism".[38] It was a time of radical change; architects such as Price and Peter Cook were searching for new forms of expression for Functionalist modern architecture, and to put the relationship between the idea of community and emergent mass culture, with its individualising tendencies, on a new footing.

Price and Cook found role models for reinterpretations of Modernist Functionalist architecture close at hand. Denys Lasdun's design for Keeling House (1954–1957) had used cluster typology to produce a new "sense of belonging" in modern architecture.[39] Price had become acquainted with Lasdun's social interpretation of Functionalist architecture when working at Fry, Drew, Drake & Lasdun.[40] Whilst working on the Fun Palace Project, Price had also had an opportunity to visit the newly inaugurated Economist Building. In their design for this complex, Alison and Peter Smithson tackled public space in high-rise construction for the first time, seeking to express this idea through the urban planning trope they adopted for the building. Price found the Economist Building's design both classical and revolutionary, and was struck by the Smithsons' highly aesthetic and formal conception of architecture within an urban planning concept. Nonetheless, although he noted how the building responded to issues of accessibility and public space, he felt that it failed to take full account of how users would appropriate the space, as manifested for example in flows of passersby.[41]

In contrast to his role models,[42] redefining communal space was not a matter of architectonic form for Price. Instead he adopted an anthropological approach, and identified ongoing technological developments as the root cause of a transformation of society that extended deep into cultural production mechanisms. As new forms of mobility and communication evolved, Price observed a novel mode of lived culture coming into being, and in turn giving rise to a new urban form. Viewing the city's material expression as a product of everyday culture meant that "top-down" planning strategies to organise urban space were ill-equipped to respond to contemporary phenomena.[43]

The Game

In its role as a microcosm of society, the Fun Palace was therefore envisioned as a place where every user could influence the space and its utilisation. In order to offer a wide range of activities, the Cybernetics Committee set up the Form and Amenities Group to develop role plays, educational games and interactive installations.[44] These used screens, light, music and video projections (i.e new forms of consumer electronics and electronic control systems) to produce a specific kind of interactive experience. Growing out of an underlying conception of the Fun Palace as a locus of playful debate, IT and regulatory systems were devised to enable new forms of encounters and experience.

Games took on a central role in the design and regulation of the Fun Palace programme. On the one hand, games constituted a leisure pastime with no defined purpose. At the same time however, games also offered a new form of learning, grounded in purpose-driven rules and with scope to practice new skills. In the Fun Palace both these facets contributed to knowledge transfer and to upgrading social skills to handle the new technologies reshaping society. Explanations of technology (such as the X-ray microscope or rocket control systems) were planned to help users understand the invisible worlds of the micro and macrocosm, and consequently gain greater insights into international affairs and the defining political and social transformations of their era.[45] Price used information technology to provide scope for spontaneous, direct forms of experience, centered on visitors' corporeal experiences, personality and identity. Large-format installations were devised to give visitors access to new cultures or skills with the help of simulations.[46] Other game environments drew on technological tools to regulate the space, giving visitors new ways to interact with the building or other users.[47] Examples included admiring the wonders of the Orient on a flying carpet[48] or using gestures to alter the ambience in a particular space via an interactive light installation. The central intention underpinning all these ideas for games was to expand each player's individual frame of reference through performative experience in the space, affording opportunites to gain new knowledge or try out new roles. All the IT-based games provided a dynamic, open set-up, tailor-made to appeal to human curiosity, imagination and creativity. In the planning team's vision, the regulatory technology would fade into the background of the games, which would generate immediate, emotional experiences.

For the group's cyberneticians and mathematicians, especially Gordon Pask, games provided a chance for open-ended forms of regulation and participation to come into being, drawing on games theory.[49] This would make it possible to create a system capable of learning, with a view to generating a form of self-organisation. In this respect cybernetics formed an experimental bridge, linking a mathematical method for recording human behaviour to the actions of people playing, with no defined purpose to their games.[50]

Over and above the need to devise a programme for the building, games became important conceptually as a valuable socio-political model for the Fun Palace. Games' process-orientied rules and situational focus appealed to the Cybernetics Committee as a way of making rigid rules and ordering principles more flexible. From a social and psychological perspective, games could expand individual possibilities and spheres of experience. The committee was not just thinking of peaceful play, but of the entire spectrum of human emotions. There was to be room in the Fun Palace for spontaneous expressions of human nature: not just participation and dialogue, but also fury, struggle and gossip. One idea floated was for areas "where people can work off their agressions and high spirits [...] where they can work out creative ideas of their own".[51]

The Form and Amenities Group hoped that players would move beyond the constraints of rule-sets, and would generate new situations, experiences and creative processes when playing that had not been foreseen by the games' creators.[52] The term "fun" thus took on another layer of meaning, over and above its social significance, thanks to the idea of the game. The Fun Palace team associated various forms of playful engagement with the building with visitors' own creative accomplishments, which could produce open-ended, unexpected outcomes. Play was emphasised in the Fun Palace as a tool to attain the vision of a non-coercive community, rooted in human qualities like optimism, curiosity and conviviality, yet still offering room for example for anger or aggression as expressions of human emotionality.

This interpretation of play picked up on a more general trend in the social sciences, which addressed critiques of mechanistic views of society.[53] Drawing on the theatre as a model, sociologist Erving Goffman had for example interpreted interaction as a social role-based human behaviour, prescribed by comparisons between our internal self-image and appraisal by our immediate social context of particular roles.[54] The games developed for the Fun Palace, such as the "Identity Bar", where costumes let visitors slip into new identities, as well as the vision of the Fun Palace as a "theatrical space", made clear that the boundaries of socially determined role-based behaviour could also be called into question by this focus on play.[55]

For the project's initiators, the play principle as the foundation of social activities thus went hand-in-hand with a socio-political vision that proclaimed individual striving for self-realisation and happiness as a social achievement, produced by a culture of society that spanned the whole world.[56] The Fun Palace set out to create a space of dialogue, education and co-determination, using information processing principles to counter a goal-oriented, materialistic societal order under the sway of mechanical efficiency.[57]

"Labour, Action, Interaction"

This emphasis on play in the Fun Palace Project stood in stark contrast to the tight-knit, class-ridden structures of British society and its elites, who largely defined British politics, culture and society in the 1950s and 1960s. As protests during the 1956 Suez crisis had revealed, the younger generation particularly in Great Britain felt powerless in the face of the way that elite power dominated politics and society. For example, in the early 1960s the theatre was largely a leisure pursuit of the British upper class, and plays were subject to government censorship.[58] Access to higher education was equally restricted. In contrast, the vision of community-based culture guided by the philosophy of play offered scope for everyone to have an influence, and thus fostered a new, open culture of genuine participation in society. As Joan Littlewood emphasised in her project notes, fostering creative forces in the Fun Palace should also benefit people who previously had been unable to profit from societal transformation and upward mobility. Littlewood viewed play in a didactic sense, signifying access to education, and also saw it as a non-purposive form of labour: "Those who at present work in factories, mines and offices will be able to live as only a few people now can: choosing their own congenial work, doing as much or as little as they like. [...] We are going to create a university of the streets – not a 'gracious' park but a foretaste of the pleasures of the age of automation: a laboratory or a palace of fun [...]."[59]

The transformation of the world of work and the ensuing leisure-driven society that Littlewood addresses in this passage was the focus of considerable attention in political and academic circles, as well as in general public debate. In 1965 British social scientists forecast that working hours in Great Britain would fall to thirty-five hours a week by 2000, echoing the US economic model.[60] It was therefore assumed that everyone would have more free time for their own interests as a result of growing automation and the increasing efficiency of industrial manufacturing.[61] The transformation of the labour world was already high on the agenda in debates at the AA School of Architecture during Price's final year of studies there in 1958. As Kenneth Frampton recalls, over and above the rediscovery of Patrick Geddes' work, discussions on how societal change would affect architecture as a discipline focused on Hannah Arendt's book *The Human Condition*, also published in 1958.[62] Arendt reflected on the ramifications of mass culture for the notion of work in *The Human Condition*, pointing out that the transformation of work would lead to a shift in its meaning: what had once been seen as a life-sustaining activity – "labour" – would become a self-determined activity. She identified the origin of this form of work in the very attributes repeatedly underscored in the Fun Palace's conception: the human need for creative expression and social dialogue.[63] The Fun Palace Project was a conduit for Cedric Price, Joan Littlewood and the other members of the Cybernetics Committee to reflect on the future of work as a central issue in societal change. Their conception of the Fun Palace thus moved beyond its role as a cultural locus and meeting point, in which a new form of communality could be manifested; for the project's initiators, it was to act as a catalyst for a new form of society, no longer constructed around workers as passive consumers but informed instead by free human beings creating culture.[64]

In this respect, the work of both the Cybernetics Committee and Price himself drew on the 1950s and 1960s Social Democratic stance, viewing the emancipatory potential of technical progress as a logical consequence of automation in industrial manufacturing.[65] In 1963 the Labour Party, under the leadership of Harold B. Wilson, had just proclaimed industrial modernisation in the wake of the "white hot technological revolution", sparking debate on the leisure society in Great Britain.[66] The future Prime Minister linked implementation of technical and scientific innovations to social issues relating to the labour force, seeking to support workers through communication technologies and by expanding education: "We are restating our Socialism in terms of a scientific revolution."[67] Chiming with this spirit, the Fun Palace Project was viewed as a forum in which to realise these societal transformation processes, linking back as well to classical societal ideals, such as the call for prosperity, freedom and social justice. For Price, post-war society's technical opportunities were a chance to put into practice a diverse, varied culture of participation: "The Greek city state was small enough for this to happen, but Athenian 'freedom' was for a minority: it was based on the labour of a caste of slaves who had few rights. Our slaves are robots: in the age of automation all men can be free."[68]

In considering the role cybernetics could play in realisation of this socio-political vision The Cybernetics Committee picked up on ideas drawn from academic Socialism and Marxism, which were very much in vogue in the 1960s: science and technological progress as tools of emancipation that would help make an egalitarian society a reality. Seen through the prism of that mindset, the Fun Palace could become a place in which to renegotiate the contradictions between singular and community interests, between the interest of the individual and those of social classes, through technology-driven organisation of space. In this sense the the Fun Palace's technical toolkit was conceived as an apt means to foster "bottom-up" reform of society.

Control and Freedom

Questions of human behaviour and morality also loomed large for the Cybernetics Committee, given the Fun Palace's socio-political motivation. Advocating that the building should be open and self-organised meant addressing the rules and conditions for using it. The central question here was how to strike a balance between individual interests and those of the group as a whole.[69] As the architecture, in keeping with the Committee's vision, was no longer to form the framework determing how the space was used, a new framework of organisational conditions and rules became essential to provide guidance to visitors about the kind of behaviour considered appropriate in the building. The Committee's discussions therefore addressed questions of social control and fair allocation of space and activities. There was for example considerable discussion about managing conflicts of interest; should the wishes of the majority determine how rooms would be allocated? Preventing the use of violence in the building or barring certain people were also vital issues in this new context for the Committee, for such provisions would fundamentally restrict the pivotal principles of openness and participation.[70]

Psychological reflections on influencing behaviour assumed growing importance as the Committee pondered appropriate rules to govern the interplay between the public and private sphere in the Fun Palace. Joan Littlewood and some members of the Committee even thought about drawing up a code of conduct to introduce some degree of social control. They also considered devising a fictitious history of the Fun Palace, with a narrative that could serve as a basis for deriving traditions and community-based values.[71] The Committee thus hoped to be able to influence how visitors perceived themselves and behaved within the building, drawing on social identification to counterbalance the project's limited spatial organisation. Thought was also given to using technology-driven surveillance set-ups. If control by specially deployed "observers" proved insufficient, live transmissions on screens were planned, in order to foster mutual control of behaviour by visitors.[72]

Ultimately however the Cybernetics Committee's discussions on the bounds of freedom and on technical control instruments were inconclusive. It remained unclear how reinterpreting social actions would impact activities in the building. Yet questions related to controlling the space and defining the limits of individual freedom in the Fun Palace were extremely germane due to the Committee's political strategy and its aspirations to make the Fun Palace a locus of social and creative action to nurture societal renewal. They therefore categorically rejected interventions by the police or any other state authority inside the building. Some response was nonetheless called for to handle how the Fun Palace's technically constructed environment determined the social organisation of the space, and vice-versa. While the integrated technology would extend options for social interaction, the team behind the project nonetheless felt compelled to redefine the boundaries of social behaviour in the building.

Another moot point was how the cybernetic control system would enable participation without itself taking on authority in shaping the space. After all, the various configuration options had to be anticipated if the building's organisation was to respond to visitors' wishes.[73] The cybernetics concept thus stipulated a number of pre-selected possible consecutive utilisations, allowing visitors to pick from this selection. It was therefore not entirely apparent how much "bottom-up" control of the cybernetic system would be possible, just as it was not clear to what extent the technology would actually take on regulatory functions. The members of the Committee were well aware that this kind of technological regulation could be read in two opposing modes: as an act of emancipation or as the advent of a new surveillance culture. Minutes of the Committee's meetings reveal how optimism about the Fun Palace's technical possibilities mingled with doubts about the viability of their ideas. As British artist Roy Ascott noted: "All these issues raised questions of morality and legality."[74]

These dilemmas contributed to the criticism levelled at the Fun Palace right from the project's inception. Plans to build on a plot of land in London's Mill Meads were thwarted, because the neighbours were not convinced that the building, with its high-tech programming, would bring anything positive to their own lives. Worried that noise nuisance, alcohol abuse and gambling would infiltrate their immediate surroundings, they rejected the project at a neighbourhood meeting.[75] Local press coverage reveals that many Londoners, especially in the light of the threatening backdrop of the Cold War, felt that transferring decision-making powers to a mechanically controlled space was not democratisation, but heteronomy, and an assault on individual personal freedom. One journalist summarised public unease about the project in a nutshell, comparing Joan Littlewood's comments on Fun Palace activities with George Orwell's dystopian vision of the future in *1984*: "'An elaborate and general kind of control procedure can create moods and resolve conflict.' It sounds to me more like a sanatorium than a Fun Palace. And more like George Orwell than Joan Littlewood."[76]

This allusion to the technological surveillance evoked in *1984*, which reduced people to disempowered serfs in a surveillance society, reveals the huge misunderstanding that afflicted the project; a giant comprehension gap between Londoners' expectations and the Fun Palace's spatial and technological tools as integral elements in the concept developed by the project's initiators. The Fun Palace Trust had always counted on support from an enlightened citizenry that would recognise the project's beneficial social impact. They had nevertheless singularly failed to discuss and develop the Fun Palace's contents and goals with civil society and people living in the immediate vicinity. On the contrary: a group of experts took charge of planning, incorporating technologies that could also only be operated by specialists. The Fun Palace's underlying goal – opening up a whole spectrum of cultural and educational activites to a self-determined body of users – was in a very real sense imposed "from on high" on the people of London due to the way that the project was planned and organised. The tools that the Fun Palace Trust used, and its whole modus operandi, therefore fundamentally contradicted the project's stated intentions.

Neighbourhood resistance also disrupted plans to build a smaller version of the Fun Palace on wasteland in the London district of Camden. Price designed this version with the Fun Palace Trust in 1965, but the neighbours protested to the London planning authority.[77] Although this project was configured on a much smaller scale and did not use information technology, it again proved impossible to explain properly to local residents why an architecture with an open, shapeable design would be useful, or to convey the whole point of the project to them. Neighbourhood protests, coupled with criticism from the local press, led politicians and community representatives to cut off support to the Fun Palace, refusing to help with financing or in finding a site. Given that the project needed initial investment of over four million pounds, it became impossible to implement with such a dearth of public support and no cooperation from the public authorities.[78]

Joan Littlewood, Cedric Price and the Fun Palace Trust were thus faced with considerable setbacks: the pilot project in Camden Town had been put on ice in 1965, and the application for planning permission for the larger main project in Mill Meads was withdrawn. Nonetheless, they continued to pursue various projects to foster cultural activities in East London's neighbourhoods until 1975.[79] This work concentrated in particular on the area around the Theatre Royal in Stratford, which Joan Littlewood had used since 1953 for performances with her theatre company. Until well into the 1970s the lack of public space and cultural activities for the local populace was strikingly apparent in this area. Finally, in 1971 Cedric Price received a large-scale commission that allowed him to put his design strategy for an architecture grounded in social interaction into practice; the Inter-Action Centre, which included designs for a community and neighbourhood centre.[80]

The Fun Palace's influence resonated through all of Cedric Price's ensuing work. The project had brought him overnight fame when he was just twenty-nine years old. Thanks to Joan Littlewood's committed involvement, and support from influential British intellectuals and politicians, the Fun Palace was showcased in national and international media in Great Britain and the USA as a pioneering social project marking the advent of a new era. To a large extent this international public attention stemmed from the new architectural vernacular the Fun Palace proposed, which offered a convincing conduit to communicate ideas linked to an open, egalitarian society. Those attributes also made the project an important reference for the high-tech architectural style just emerging in the early 1970s in Great Britain, particularly in work by Norman Foster and Richard Rogers.[81] Inspired by this spirit, in 1971 Richard Rogers and Renzo Piano won the competition for the Centre Georges-Pompidou; as Rogers has stated, their design was crucially influenced by Price's work on the Fun Palace.[82]

Furthermore, in the Fun Palace Project Price had formulated all the important questions and stances that he would develop over the next fifteen years as he created his own autonomous design approach. Building on the notion of "grassroots" cultural production generated with the aid of technology, so central to his Fun Palace design, Price reappraised both the architect's role in town planning and the mechanisms involved in drawing up plans. His experiences reinforced Price's Constructivist understanding of space, which saw the urban fabric as a product of the social processes unfurling within the city. He subsequently expanded his design strategy by incorporating social-sciences concerns and a systemic twist into his architecture, again with the objective of fostering a new form of community.

Circlorama

In summer 1962 Price organised an exhibition in Glasgow that explored the region as the point of departure for a renaissance of society and for construction-driven renewal processes. The show referenced the reform strategies articulated by Scottish planning pioneer Patrick Geddes, who had formulated strategies for architectural and social renewal of industrial cities through the prism of the region in the late nineteenth century. Price's *Circlorama* installation offered visitors to the Glasgow Fair an overview of the city's future development projects from the roof of the Town Hall.[83] On three consecutive evenings he had the relevant areas of the city illuminated in various colours.[84] Accompanied by additional information about the plans, this aimed to spark off discussions and exchanges with visitors, which Price hoped would produce both fresh ideas and food for thought.

This unusual exhibition concept referenced a prominent urban planning project: Geddes' 1892 Edinburgh Outlook Tower. Just as Patrick Geddes had done, Price used projection in his exhibition to create an instrument for democratic participation in urban planning. Geddes set up the viewpoint with a camera obscura on the roof of the tower to give the people of Edinburgh an overview of their city's architectural and social development.[85] In his view, empirical studies offered scope to draw conclusions about universal features of the city's economic and social organisation. To Geddes, the panoramic view of Edinburgh revealed a superordinate model of society that could describe and disclose the underlying principles that give order to human civilisation and shared community life.[86] An exhibition in the tower also provided information about how the city was embedded in the broader geographic, economic and political context of the region and its importance for "good" governance.[87] In offering this information and the opportunity to view the city from the tower, Geddes sought to support efforts to achieve a shared political consensus, and thus to promote town planning focussed on citizens' wellbeing.

Geddes addressed these issues against the backdrop of urban industrialisation and the associated problems of overpopulation, hygiene, transport and food supply; he believed that integrating the city into the region would make it possible to strike a natural balance between political, social and economic forces, the foundation of urban culture.[88] Geddes' model was particularly innovative in its two-pronged interpretation of the city, as built environment and as a locus of interdependent economic and societal processes. He posited that the various strata of human cohabitation in a city, geographical area or economic zone, and indeed in politics and society as a whole, are equally significant in shaping urban form. That led him to conclude that a "good life" could only succeed in a city that managed to strike a balance between these elements.

Geddes' city-in-the-region concept offered Price a systematic perspective focused on balance, and also added a further conceptual layer to the Fun Palace's cybernetic strategies. The *Circlorama* project adopted not only Geddes' regional city concept, but also the educational thrust of its communicative method.[89] Price found himself grappling, like Geddes had seventy years earlier, with identifying an apt mode of urban living in the spirit of the "good life".[90] In contrast to Geddes, Price was confronted not with the problems of the burgeoning early twentieth-century industrial city, but with a different type of structural transformation: the advent of the information and service society, which coincided with the decline of industrial powerhouses like Glasgow and their culture of mining, heavy industry and factory work.[91] The starting point for his exhibition project was urban regeneration in the face of growing deindustrialisation. Symbolically opening up the Town Hall as a locus of political and administrative power, Price underscored his idea of reconstructing the urban community; this ceremonious staging at the Town Hall served "to invite the public in."[92]

City, Region and Technology: The Potteries.

Just over a year after the *Circlorama* installation in Glasgow, Cedric Price transposed the regional model of the city to his design for a university. Entirely at his own initiative, from 1964 to 1966 Price had been honing the details of a further variant of his design principles, which he developed parallel to his work on the Fun Palace Project. His Potteries Thinkbelt study incorporated a systematic conception based on nodes and networks as tools to regenerate an entire region. The study encompassed his plans to build a technical university in the North Staffordshire region known as the Potteries,[93] with the university premises distributed decentrally over the entire region. As Price's project report spelled out, he envisaged a network of university buildings, linked by the region's transport infrastructure. He saw this newly configured educational network as a planning instrument that would allow cities and districts to influence their future economic and social development.[94]

The region between Stoke-on-Trent, Price's hometown, and Newcastle-under-Lyme and Leicester emerged as a centre of the British ceramics industry in the mid-nineteenth century. Like most other industrial hubs in post-war England, the region suffered a downward spiral of constant economic decline in the early 1960s.[95] The impact of underinvestment in new infrastructure, factories and housing led Price to describe it as a "disaster area", "largely unchanged and uncared for since its industrial expansion through the 19th century."[96] His Potteries Thinkbelt responded to the region's ongoing decline and high unemployment with an education-driven project intended to trigger structural change and social renewal.[97]

Furthermore, Price understood his university design as an architectural response to the government's education policy goals.[98] The 1959 recommendations from the Central Advisory Council for Education (England) on opening up access to higher education to all social classes had unleashed a policy debate on social segregation in education and a shift in orientation was planned for the British education system. By dramatically expanding the educational sector, a vast segment of the British public was to receive access to higher education for the first time.[99]

Price's project picked up on the recommendations from the government-commissioned Robbins Report, which called for ongoing expansion of institutions of further education across the country to advance economic development.[100] However, Price was convinced that in order to attain this goal the prevailing attitude to planning university construction must be abandoned, for it was still tied up in traditional conceptions of the university as a self-contained, closed forum for academic education.[101] In his view the spatial segregation of educational institutions hampered badly needed exchanges between town and gown, cutting business centres off from potential catalysts for innovation. Price cited the expansion of what were known as "red brick universities"[102] to illustrate the flaws he identified in urban development policy. These educational establishments had been developed in the postwar period, and adhered to functionalist city planning principles.[103] However, this wave of university expansion had not noticeably improved economic development in English industrial cities such as Birmingham, Bristol or Sheffield.[104] In the Potteries Thinkbelt project Price therefore articulated his own ideas on how to implement universities for the masses. He endeavoured to demonstrate that successful networking between academia and

7   Cedric Price, "Master Diagram:
All elements and key", ca. 1964.

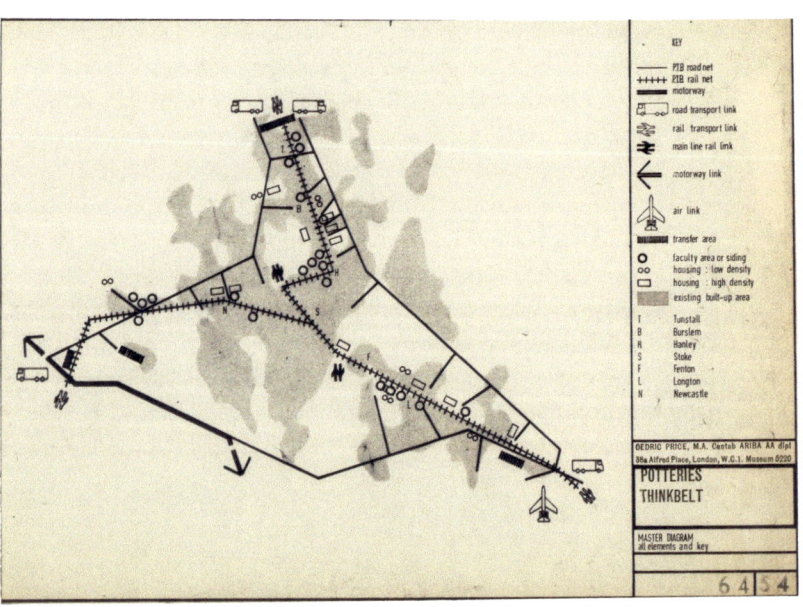

businesses would only work if architecture integrated both systems into the wider frame of the region. Adapting the national university system to an open education infrastructure would have far-reaching consequences for society, he believed, particulary given the scale of the undertaking and the looming changes in the world of work.

In his university study Price therefore engaged intensively with the housing situation, the employment challenges facing the Potteries area and the goal of a shared social identity. To encourage cooperation between existing industrial structures and the new university, Price envisaged research and development centres in former industrial sites, such as the steelworks at Shelton or the coalmine in Silverdale. He developed housing typologies positioned in various locations between existing settlements in the region. Price also designed three transfer areas with a high density of infrastructural amenities as central hubs, connecting both companies and university institutions to regional and national transport infrastructure.[105] His blueprint for the university encompassed an entire network of transport nodes to link residential, educational and industrial locations in the Potteries Thinkbelt. By plugging the university into the region's transport infrastructures, five existing universities, including Liverpool, Birmingham and Manchester, also fell within the Potteries Thinkbelt's immediate catchment area.

All the locations in his scheme were arranged along the railway routes to boost the university's integration into existing regional infrastructure. His design envisioned that rail tracks that once carried goods and raw materials between industrial sites would transport mobile teaching modules in dedicated university trains. Seminars could be held in these mobile classrooms, and students could also access information and teaching materials via television or video. Making these units mobile enabled decentralised access to information and knowledge in the region. The train compartments could be incorporated into the faculty building or stored, and subsequently redistributed.

Price's design viewed knowledge as a commodity that could be circulated via the same distribution and logistics mechanisms as other industrial commodities. As Price noted in the Potteries Thinkbelt, developments in communications and transport infrastructure in Great Britain had already created the preconditions for a decentralised organisational culture offering access to goods and knowledge everywhere.[106] He therefore likened the future form that knowledge mediation would assume to a supermarket stocking education alongside all the other daily staples.[107]

Chiming with these concepts, Price developed the university buildings as educational infrastructure, intended to ensure optimal distribution of knowledge in the region. His design for the transfer areas focused on bringing together every form of infrastructure that could encourage exchanges between the university and the region. For example, the range of training courses offered by the university aimed to reflect specific regional labour traditions, with the transfer areas providing the knowledge infrastructure to help students learn and research successfully. The broad spans of the steel structures in the Madley

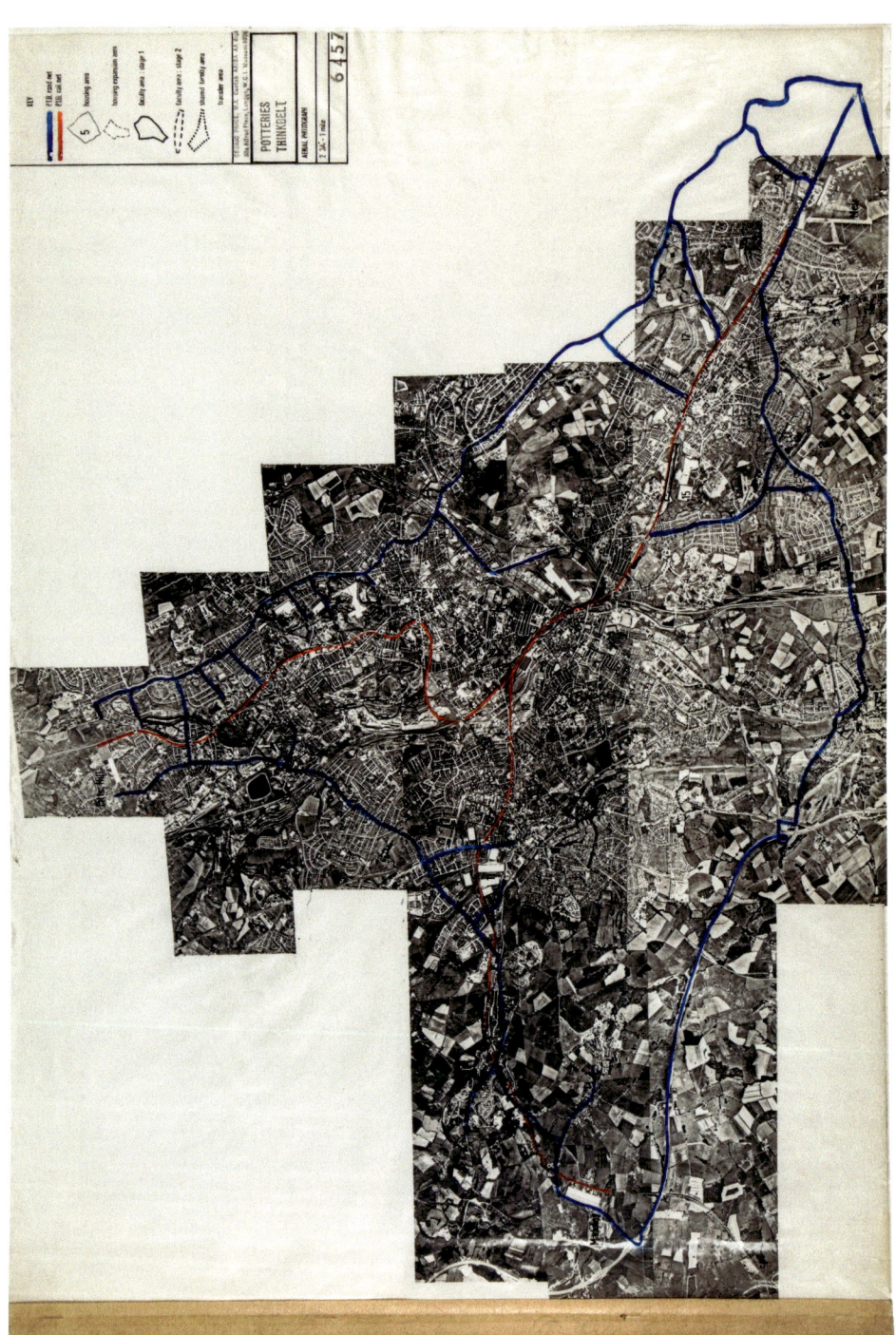

8 Cedric Price, "Aerial Photograph", aerial view with clear foil and red, blue and black felt pen, ca. 1964.

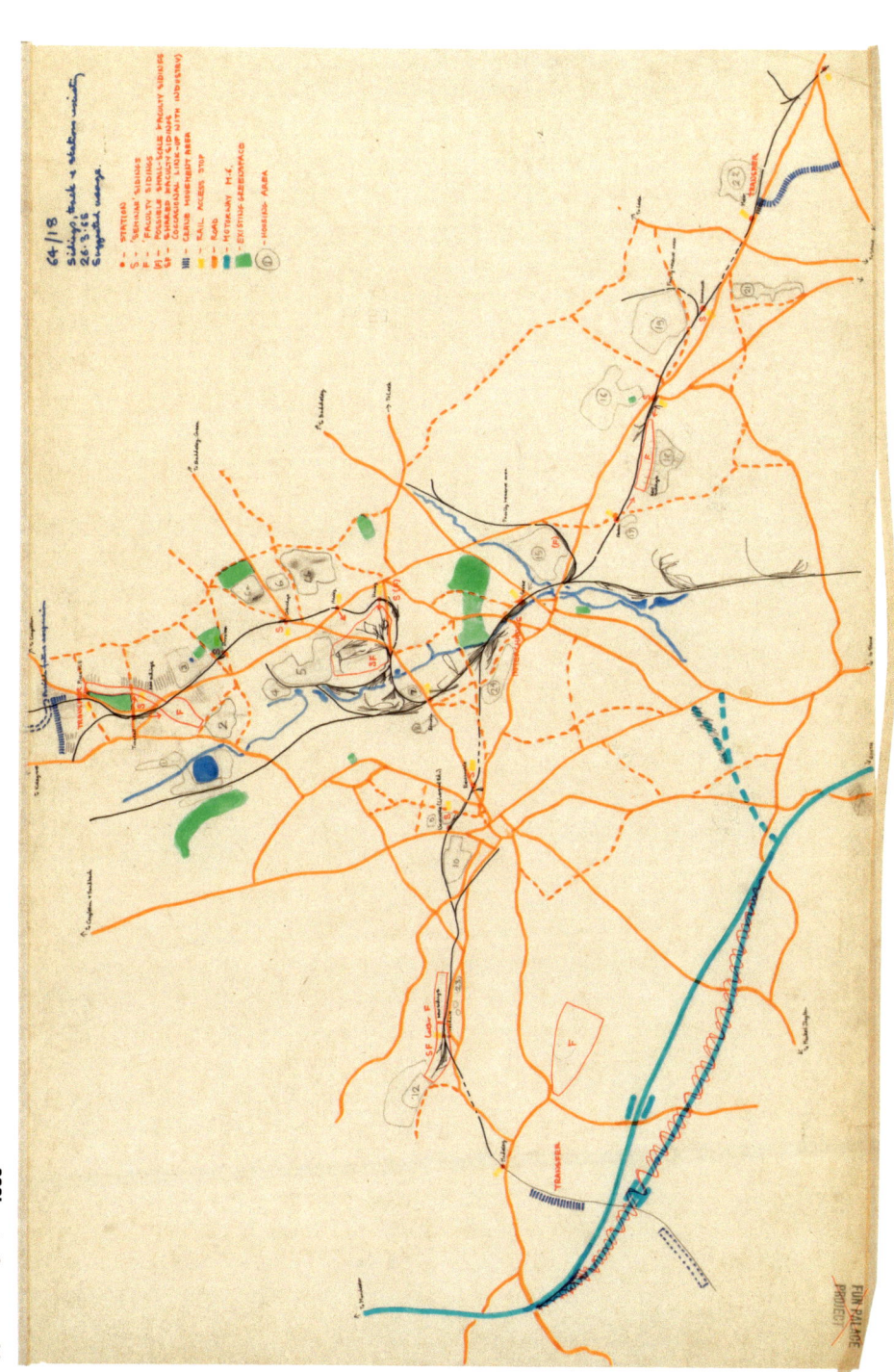

9 Cedric Price, "Sidings, tracks and stations existing suggested usage", ca. 1965.

Transfer Area provided a fitting structural frame for this, and did not presuppose any specific utilisations for the interiors.[108]

In this sense the university buildings for the Potteries Thinkbelt echoed the design means Price had integrated into the Fun Palace. Both projects deployed networking and mediation, and provided infrastructure that could adapt to the demands of changes in use. The Potteries Thinkbelt can be seen as the Fun Palace's twin; it also responded to the socio-political concept of an open, education-oriented social culture, transposing it to the regional scale. The networking principle Price deployed in both projects went entirely against the grain of modern town planning tenets, corresponding more closely to early approaches conceived by British planning pioneers, such as Geddes' idea of the "conurbation".[109] In addition, in the Potteries Thinkbelt project Price aimed to advance the evolution of the Functionalist architectural idiom, simultaneously drawing inspiration from his role models and seeking to demarcate his strategy from those adopted by his predecessors.

"Valley Section": The Ideal of Balance

Since the mid-1950s educational reform and the expanding university sector had provoked reflections in architectural circles about whether modernity's approach to urban planning design could meet these challenges.[110] Beginning in 1962, Denys Lasdun and Maxwell Fry worked on the buildings for the newly established East Anglia University in Norwich, drawing on "cluster buildings" principles.[111] The Smithsons' 1953 competition entry for the University of Sheffield had been conceived with a similar intent, also incorporating the cluster principle.[112] Their take on the university design, which was rooted in urban planning considerations, was elaborated in more detail in their "Cluster City" article through a study of Patrick Geddes' "valley section".[113] Geddes used schematic cross-sections through the valley of Edinburgh to depict historical typologies of settlement development as the product of harmonious exchanges between human beings and their environment. In what he called the "valley section", Geddes deployed taxonomic methodology and empirical observation (most likely drawing on his experience teaching zoology and botany) to divide the buildings in the area into four categories: farm, hamlet, village and town.[114] He viewed the built areas as a cultural product of conditions on the spot, poised in a natural equilibrium with their surroundings. The sequences of construction in the "valley section" therefore represented the aesthetic ideal of cultural balance, which he saw as becoming established in the region in keeping with the principles of the "good life".[115] He was convinced that comprehending a region's developmental processes would allow planners to influence the city and its living conditions.[116] The "valley section" represented an idealised depiction of the region as an expression of human labour. At the same time, Geddes also drew on it as a reference paradigm in elaborating his ideas on urban planning reform.

Eight years after the Smithsons' article sketched out a kind of manual to reform modern architecture in the spirit of the New Brutalism,

Price's revitalisation programme for the Potteries region was also guided by Geddes' idealised depictions of settlement typology. Price assumed that knowledge-driven work would in future replace industrial production as the economic foundation of society, meaning that a new form of urban design would also need to grow out of this altered regional economic basis: "[...] education and the need to exchange information can equate past needs of defence, energy and commerce as a generator of urban location and form: cities caused by learning."[117]

Price's three schematic sections through the region transposed Geddes' universal settlement types to his university project. Price's design for the envisaged interventions was framed by a comparison between the ideal state for the region and current conditions. This drew on his detailed analysis of the region, which mapped the geographic features and produced a classification of regional development through the prism of industrial history. For this analysis Price worked with aerial photos on which he marked all the abandoned industrial sites, indicating their spatial and landscape attributes.[118] In the first sectional representation, Price highlighted the spatial features of what he called subsidence areas, produced by clay mining or depositing of slag from ceramics production. He classified these areas as "uneven flooded or subsidence-prone ground". The second section focused on derelict land and areas close to factories, designated as "unpleasant immediate environment". Contrasting with this, the third section analysed the development potential of unutilised natural areas, close to rivers or to the steep slopes of, for example, former spoil tips. These were ranked as sites with a "good immediate environment".[119]

Price selected these unused sites as locations for four housing types; the specific configurations he opted for can be read as a continuation of Alison and Peter Smithson's typological studies.[120] The Smithsons, who were Team 10 members, had drawn on Geddes' ideas in developing their alternative design strategy for urban social renewal.[121] Price, fifteen years their junior, was aware of this work from his contacts with the Independent Group and his student days at the AA School of Architecture.[122] Translating contextual principles for organising space into the vernacular of modern domestic architecture, the Smithsons endeavoured to evolve a new architecture of community with stronger links to residents' lives.[123] Their contribution at the CIAM Congress "Habitat" was based on their study of traditional residential architecture in the schematic "valley section". Using four examples from the area around London, they derived formal design principles to appraise how the housing related to its environment, subsequently using this interpretative filter, which they dubbed the "scale of human association", to analyse modern residential typologies.[124] This method aimed to create natural growth and a situation-oriented positioning of new residential typologies, ranging from the simple single-family house to the apartment block.[125] However, the Smithsons' innovative strategy only encompassed individual buildings. Their reflections did not impinge at all on the guiding principle of modern urban planning, namely functional separation.[126]

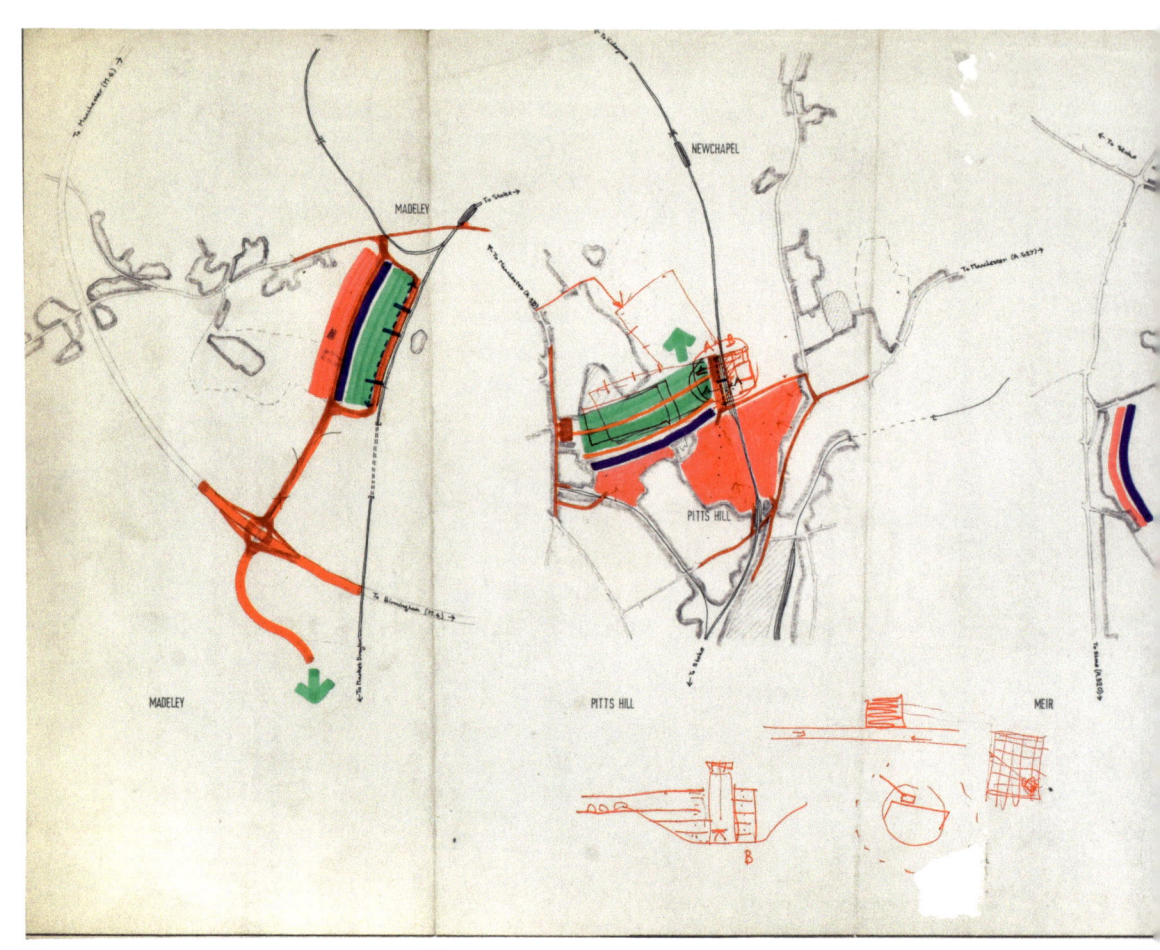

10   Cedric Price, "Transfer Areas:
Aerial Survey", ca. 1963.

11 Cedric Price, "Transfer Areas: Madley Axonometric View", ca. **1965**.

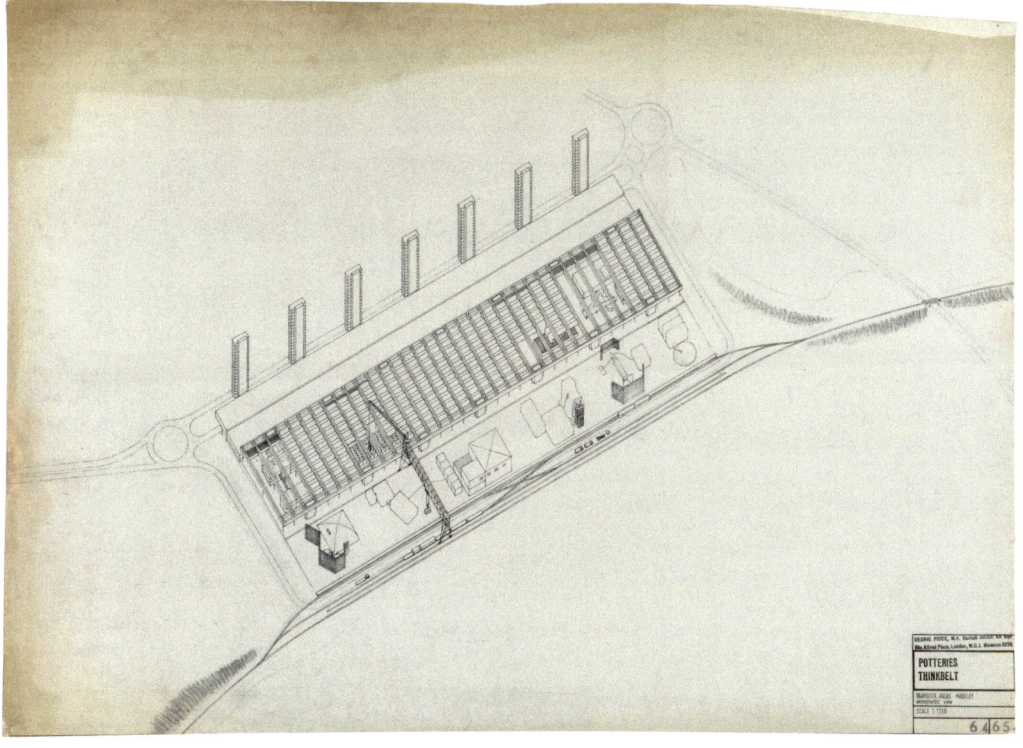

Price, like the Smithsons, regarded urban social renewal as closely linked to socially viable city growth, particularly against the backdrop of the baby boom. Implementation by state planning institutions of the university for the masses was however dictated by the selfsame Functionalist planning principles previously deployed in mass housing construction.[127] In this context Price cited the British government's construction of the so-called New Towns;[128] by the late 1950s, thirteen planned cities, each with a population of between 20,000 and 60,000, had sprung up under this scheme.[129] In 1964, when Price was working on his project for the Potteries Thinkbelt, the British Parliament had just voted in favour of a second phase of construction, which produced larger, noticeably car-friendly towns such as Milton Keynes, with up to 250,000 inhabitants.[130]

Price reacted to these trends in British mass housing construction by advocating a programme for the Potteries Thinkbelt that returned to the concepts that originally inspired the New Town movement. The garden city model was the key paradigm in the movement's response to expanding industrial cities, and linked urban growth to a renaissance of community-focused and civil society values. The garden city model had also inspired regional planning for London's growth after the Second World War, as elucidated in the Greater London Plan, a legally binding development blueprint for the city.[131] Observing implementation of this plan on the ground in the 1950s and 1960s, Price concluded that the pioneering planners' design approaches were thoroughly distorted by the way that the New Town programmes were implemented. In the Potteries Thinkbelt, Price therefore openly criticised official urban development principles, opting instead to emphasise the liberal traditions of the garden city movement, particularly its governing principles of self-organisation and autarchic living: "No more 'do-gooding' – everyone should be in a position, mentally, socially and economically not to require such 'hand downs'."[132]

In his proposals to integrate new housing for 40,000 people into the Potteries Thinkbelt, Price thus moved beyond the question of an appropriate form for urban growth to grapple with the qualities this growth should embody. Price opted to supplement the region's existing housing stock with his settlement typology designs, which aimed both to integrate students into the local population and to improve the general housing situation.[133] By equipping the settlements with their own infrastructure to supply their needs, for example for water and energy but also for schools and leisure amenities, he aimed to improve overall provision of services for adjacent neighbourhoods too. For Price, an overall strategy of regional growth and revitalisation entailed making the residential settlements autonomous while simultaneously connecting them to a new education infrastructure. In these apparently contradictory interventions he was pursuing the same objectives as earlier seminal thinkers like Geddes and Howard with their socially liberal ideas on urban expansion. The Potteries Thinkbelt aimed to make the region's inhabitants more independent and at the same time to foster the common good: "To increase the individual freedom of movement [...] amplifies the network to the benefit of the community as a whole."[134]

Price drew on the Smithsons' programmatic approaches in configuring the settlement typlologies. However, the real issue for him was not further developing the design for these typologies, as he aimed above all to underscore their function from a planning perspective. The typologies became his tools in settlement development as an integral part of his drive to re-establish the balance between economic and social forces in the region.[135] They were to function as what he called "catalysts" in this endeavour, or, in other words, to initiate a regenerative development process in the region, echoing similar scientific metaphors conceived by early-twentieth-century planning pioneers.

The smallest settlement unit Price devised was the "capsule housing" typology: a prefabricated housing capsule in deep-drawn plastic, in which one person could live self-sufficiently. It corresponded to Geddes' "farm" category. Price positioned them in the demanding landscape of the region's spoil tips and slag heaps, where they were to serve as "pioneers" for an incipient urbanisation process. The capsules' technical service infrastructure made it possible to set up housing in areas with few links to existing infrastructure.[136] Their layout echoed numerous space capsule designs from the 1950s and 1960s that experimented with new industrial manufacturing principles, including the visionary drawings by the Archigram Group, the Monsanto House of the Future (Hamilton and Goody, 1957) and designs for mobile capsules by Ionel Schein (1957) and Arthur Quarmby.[137] In the next step up, Price's correlation to Geddes' "hamlet" typology took the form of a decentralised settlement typology that he called "sprawl housing". In Price's plans this incorporated up to thirty open-plan single-family homes, grouped in a circle or line to form neighbourhoods. The houses were placed on platforms, between one and two metres above the ground depending on the terrain, and were connected by walkways, which meant they could also be built on undeveloped, uneven land.[138] The name Price picked for the typology alluded to its scope for flexible adaptation.[139] In contrast, in the natural areas and derelict industrial sites in the Potteries region, he deployed typologies that extended beyond Geddes' settlement classification.[140] Price's design for the settlement typology of the village was "battery housing": three-storey housing blocks oriented towards the interior of the block, with either one floor or the roof, depending on the situation, functioning as a shared open space.[141] The Smithsons had developed a similar typology in their 1952 Golden Lane Housing competition entry in London.[142] This typology could function in any settlement site in the region, just like Geddes' "hamlet". When no suitable outdoor space was available, the free storey or roof offered open, unconstrained spaces within the house, incorporating all the shared community spaces in the "village" within the housing block.[143]

For the urban scale of the small town, Price proposed a thirteen-storey housing block in the style of Le Corbusier's Unité d'Habitation. This housing type was to be constructed within various built enviroments, for example

12   Cedric Price, "Housing types
adaptation to site condition", ca. **1965**.

SITE CONDITION	CAPSULE	SPRAWL	BATTERY	CRATE
sloping, uneven, flooded or subsidence-prone ground	small unit size + linear layout allows use of steeply sloping sites with good views	small unit size, jacked supports and flexible service/access requirements allow siting in any ground condition	jacked supports allow siting on uneven, subsidence-prone, ground	no application
unpleasant immediate environment	no application	circular layout avoids contact with immediate surroundings	'promenade' allows construction of autonomous open-air environment	detachment from ground gives visual release from immediate surroundings
good immediate environment	small unit size allows use of sites hitherto impossible for housing	'Y' layout allows flexible siting with minimal disturbance to existing amenity	roof-deck parking variant	'frontier' condition at edge of built-up area

HOUSING TYPES : application to site conditions

6 4 70

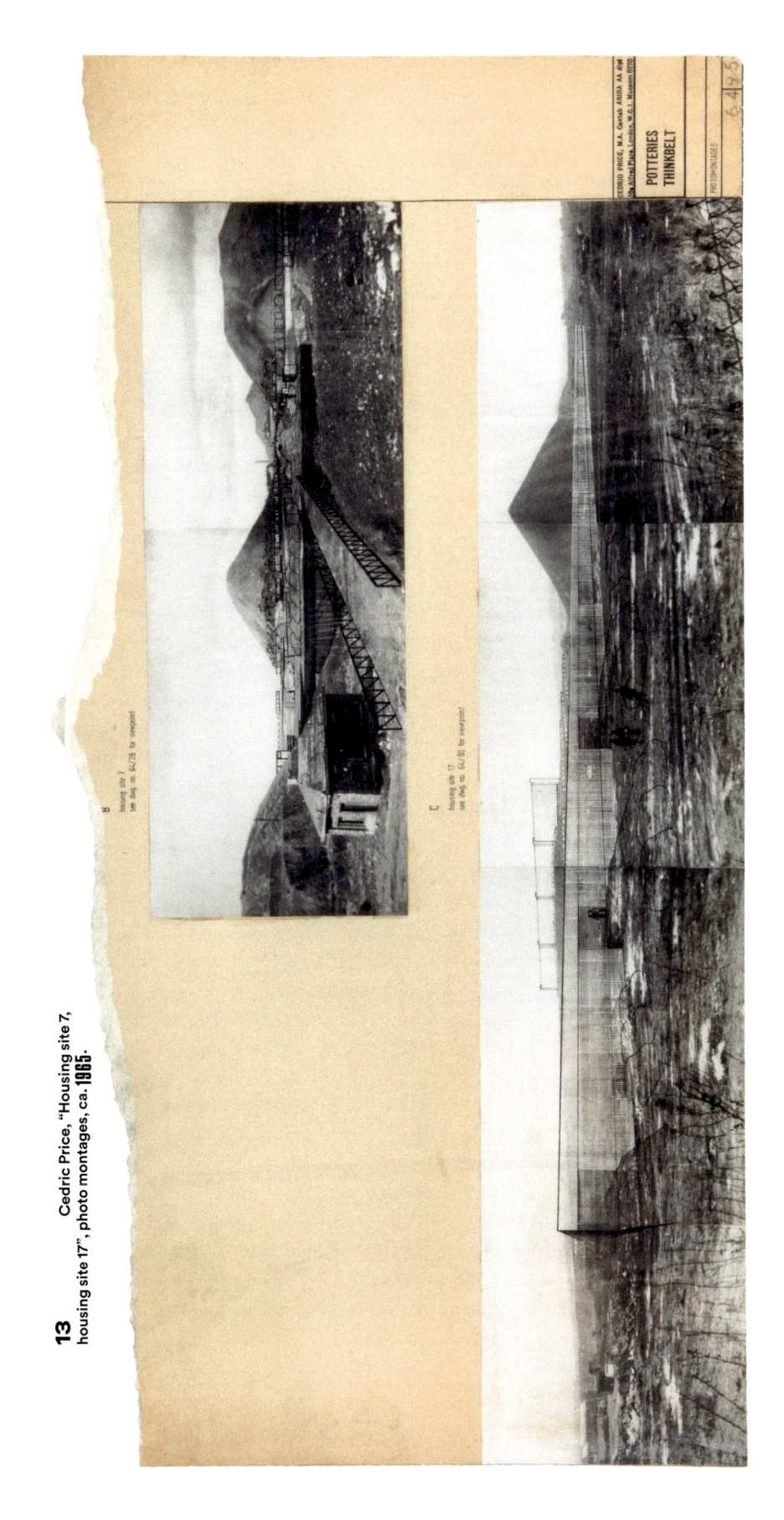

13 Cedric Price, "Housing site 7, housing site 17", photo montages, ca. 1965.

in industrial areas and residential areas, and would be visible from a distance across the open landscape.[144] The designation "crate housing" picked up on the metaphor of bottles in a rack that Le Corbusier used to describe his residential blocks' structural system.[145] Once again, Price took a typology with a form rooted in industrial manufacturing and updated it as part of his regional revitalisation concept. The stackable strucure and prefabricated capsules he developed for this housing type offered a range of variants for the individual units in each building.[146] Rather than starting from scratch and developing brand new typologies, Price's residential designs put a fresh spin on existing design strategies, and linked constructional principles from famous architectural role models with Geddes' "valley section" and its regional concepts. Price was simultaneously seeking to contribute to discourse on one of the key design issues of his day and to propose an independent response to articulation of community-based concerns in modern architecture.

Industrial manufacturing as a source of inspiration in architecture had been controversial for some time; Team 10 architects had already criticised their CIAM counterparts, including Walter Gropius and Le Corbusier, for adopting this tactic in the 1950s. In the Potteries Thinkbelt, Price posited that urban growth would only function in practice by tapping into industrial manufacturing and modular construction.[147] He saw industrial production as an instrument in a holistic planning approach that respected both the individual needs of people living in his buildings and community imperatives. Price therefore adopted aspects from both "valley section" models in formulating his contribution to the debate, combining elements of the modern settlement typology the Smithsons had developed almost ten years earlier with Patrick Geddes' regional model (structured in terms of historical developments).[148]

At the same time, Price moved away from the Smithsons' hierarchical city model in selecting his structuring principles for the Potteries Thinkbelt's regional plan.[149] Instead, his implementation of the "valley section" model incorporated various co-existing historical development phases, coupled with heterogenous typologies that could also stand side by side in any specific context. Like the Smithsons, Price saw his design decisions as a conduit for expressing an innovative approach to architectural design and planning. Rather than stipulating all the details in a masterplan, his built interventions in North Staffordshire aimed to trigger a primarily social developmental dynamic as the basis for gradual adaptation of the settlements.[150] Price elucidated this fundamental volte-face in his approach to urban planning design as his response to architects' tendency to overestimate the impact of their built interventions. For Price, the individual house was not the appropriate scale for urban renewal schemes, which also needed to consider connections between buildings and their complex utilisations.[151] Nevertheless, these links and usages, which change relatively slowly, are only gradually inscribed into regional architecture. Rejecting the tenet that architecture per se might offer some ad-hoc recipe for creating a new sense of urban community, Price highlighted architecture's role as a foundation that could allow this kind of culture to flourish.

Time-limited Architecture

The strategy that Price developed in the Potteries Thinkbelt built on Geddes' conception of dynamic regional development, and entailed making adjustments and adding space as time went by. This design vision for the region, rooted in ongoing development, is illustrated in his diagram indicating the planned lifecycle and utilisation timeframe for each building type, with forty years as the upper limit.[152] Price considered not just how long each building would survive, but also how often it would need to adapt to new uses. The time-based design premises for the four housing typologies ranged from short-term, mobile utilisation for the "capsule housing" to long-term, permanent use for the "crate housing".[153] The buildings' functional aspects, such as the load-bearing structure, supply infrastructure and interior configuration, were determined as a function of the planned lifecycle and changing uses envisaged for each typology.[154]

Price pursued his goal of making the region functionally adaptable by fine-tuning constructional and technical execution of the architecture he envisaged to produce variable forms of use. His floor-plan designs for typologies with a longer lifespan were deliberately much more open than in the short-duration mobile typologies, in which the internal space was much more clearly delineated. In this spirit, Price chose steel-reinforced concrete for the "crate housing" residential block; echoing Le Corbusier's Unité d'Habitation, it was made up of a cast-concrete skeleton and prefabricated room capsules. Openings in the walls allowed the prefabricated elements to be connected horizontally and vertically, affording scope for various apartment layouts. [155] He opted for a similar long-term development strategy for the "battery housing", keeping it open-ended by employing a space frame. The type of construction determined the form of the building envelope and the block's long-term urban planning role. Price's proposals for the flats' internal layout reflected the planned utilisation periods of seven to fifteen years, in clear contrast to the forty-year lifecyle he stipulated for the structural frame and the building envelope.[156] Consequently, while the building would continue to fulfil its urban planning function in the region over a longer timeframe, the interior space could be reconfigured to reflect changing lifestyles. A rather different tactic was used in the "sprawl housing" category, which offered scope in the medium term to alter both the internal layout and the settlement's configuration.[157] In these flats there was considerable freedom for inhabitants to alter the floor plans by shifting, removing or adding individual elements within the steel frame construction. Analagous methods allowed for the entire housing unit to be extended or scaled down. The cutting-edge, sandwich-structure composite method was used for the "capsule housing" prefabricated room elements. The short, planned lifecycle for this housing type – ten years for the cutting-edge sandwich-structure composite method – reflected the needs of the students living there; utilisation changed frequently as the flats were rented on a month-by-month basis. That made

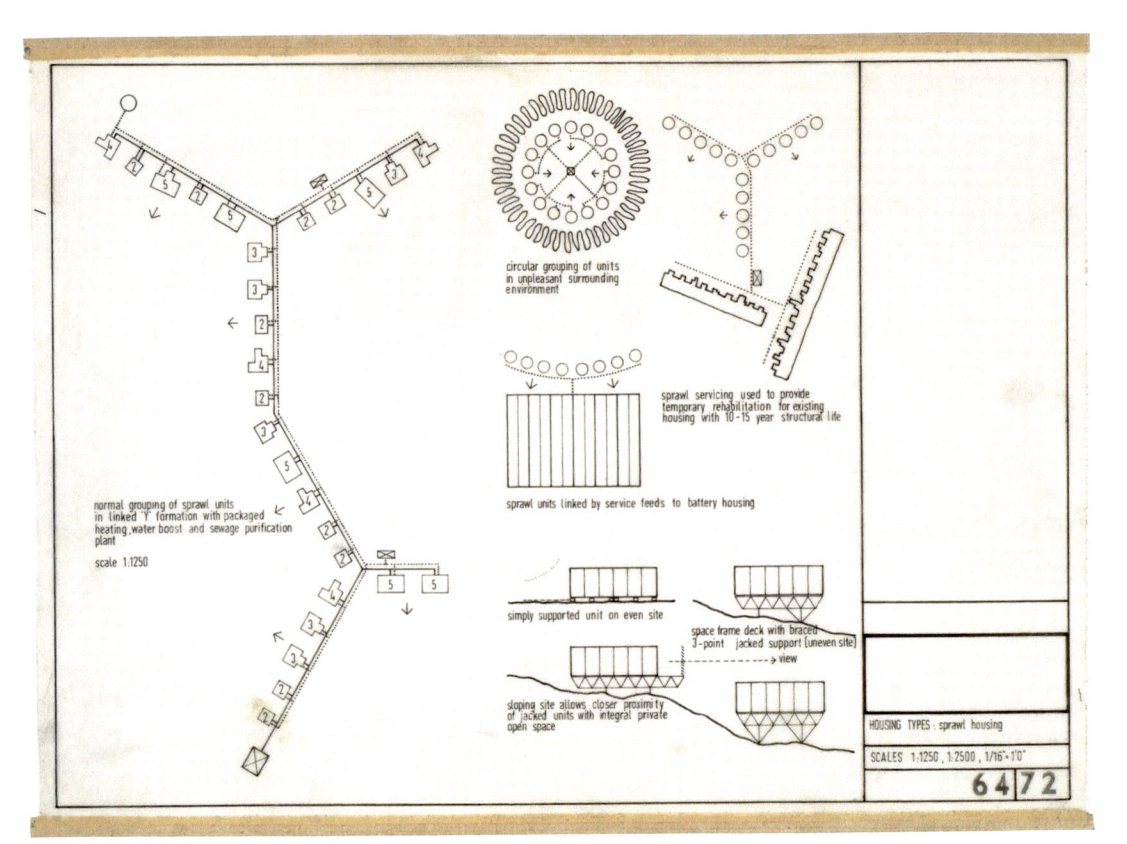

14 Cedric Price, "Housing types: battery housing", ca. 1964.

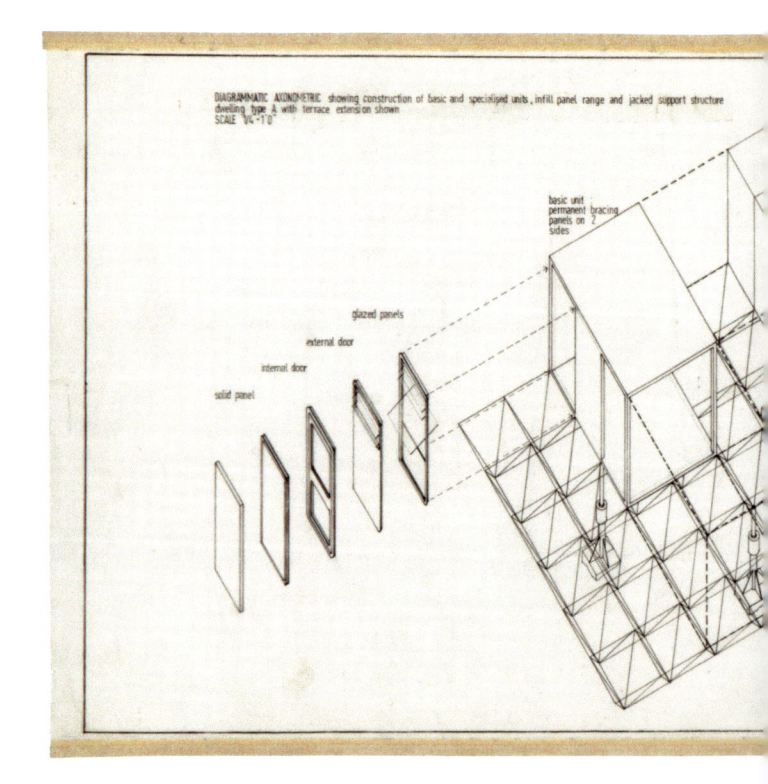

15　　　　Cedric Price, "Housing types: sprawl housing", ca. **1964**.

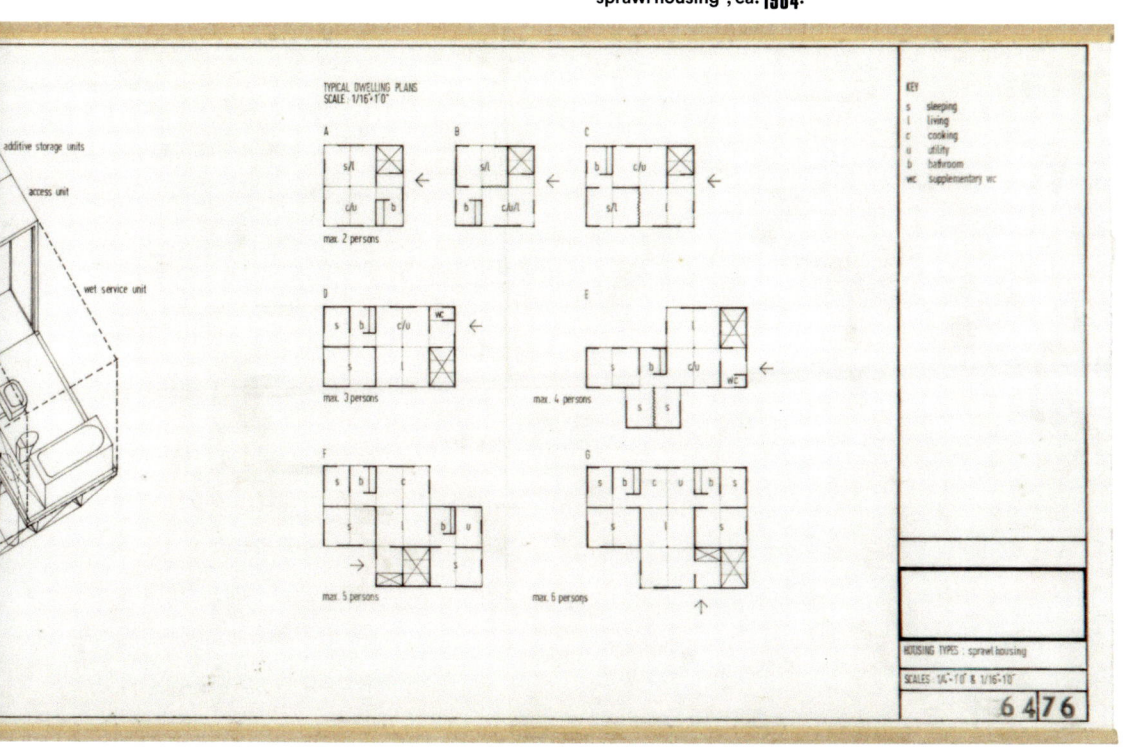

the "capsule housing" the most mobile, short-lived module in the Potteries Thinkbelt's university blueprint.[158]

Choosing to design adaptable architecture was about much more than simply responding to the liberal ideas of pioneering thinkers on urban design. It was also a clarion call for planning to become more open to bottom-up processes. The time-based diagrams depict an open university model, with knowledge offered as a service and mass product, in which users' specific needs mould the design of housing, faculty premises and development centres. As large-scale planning could not second-guess users' potential preferences, the buildings' innovative mobility and adaptability were the key to equipping the architecture to meet the challenges of societal transformation.

16

This kind of flexibility was first advocated in architectural criticism in 1961, responding to Louis Kahn's Richard Laboratories in Philadelphia.[159] The concept encapsulated the described endeavours to make architecture open or multifunctional without constraining users' freedom of choice by specific programming. The time factor Kahn introduced aimed to bring architecture closer to people and everyday life once again. Architectural design was growing away from older traditions that were all about picking the best possible way to execute a particular programme, and then shoehorning users into the concept: architecture now sought to offer adaptability in reaction to users' needs. In the Potteries Thinkbelt, Cedric Price tapped into the flexibility principle in addressing both levels of Geddes' concept of the region. On the one hand, Price's multifunctional programming for the buildings respected university users' freedom of decision, thus incorporating the dimension of social coexistence. In this sense the flexibility that lay at the core of the building typologies was Price's political response

16   Cedric Price, "Life span & Use cycle chart", diagram, ca. 1965.

to demands for open access to education. At the same time, flexible architecture aimed to have a positive impact on the region as an important component in its economic restructuring.

Lifespan-driven planning, conceived as an instrument of renewal, played a central part in Price's Functionalist architectural design. Adopting the design vernacular of consumer goods, he spoke of "planned obsolescence" to convey the idea of time-based development. Over and above its role in propping up consumerism, he believed this principle made it easier to adapt goods to technological progress and consumers' changing needs. To an ever greater extent than in the consumer goods market, it was of course vital to weigh up the pros and cons of short-term and long-term interventions in architecture. A precise grasp of the location in question was of the essence for Price in selecting a particular option, for short-term interventions alone could not do justice to the region's complex spatial, social and economic conditions: "If you have 100% planned obsolescence then there is no need for flexibility, if you have paper clothes then you don't have a little black dress that you can do everything with. One is the sort of alternative to the other because in architecture one is employing a discipline made up from the influences of both."[160]

A much longer timespan was therefore foreseen for much of the supply infrastructure, for example the "sprawl housing" energy supply, than for the individual buildings.[161] While the infrastructure was vital in Price's plans, not just for each individual settlement but for the whole community, with overarching significance for regional revitalisation, short-lifecycle buildings were intended to establish a new equilibirium between the built and social environment. By making his typologies adaptable, he aimed to make the region better equipped to react to social developments.[162]

Lifespan considerations were thus pivotal to Price's design strategy for infrastructure. In some cases long infrastructure lifecyles were not the answer, for they seemed starkly out of synch with social and economic development trends in English industrial cities. The scale of deindustrialisation in cities like Wigan or Leyland (close to Manchester), where urban structures had been defined primarily by heavy industry, made Price sceptical about large-scale revitalisation efforts in these areas. He instead proposed the radical route of demolition and even shorter lifespans for certain infrastructure, depending on its utility in specific contexts: "For example, services including secondary roads, must have an even shorter variable life than the housing. Thus eventually Wigan and Leyland could become a national park."[163]

In the three sections through the Potteries region, Price presented a textbook example of how adaptability over time would work. Every section expressed a clear statement about a time-dependent mix of long-term and more short-lived elements to keep social dynamism alive. Students' mobile lifestyles were factored in, but so were the settled lifestyles of extended families. His planning strategy did not however stipulate which programmes, amenities or social groups would take root in any particular neighbourhood over time. The project's infrastructure was conceived to allow all the elements

2

in each settlement to be reconfigured, and factored in exchanges and potential for further development as fundamental defining principles for the "city in the region". In this respect the Potteries Thinkbelt project followed in the footsteps of Patrick Geddes, as well as Alison and Peter Smithson. However Price's work on adaptable typologies in a regional planning scenario that spanned a forty-year time-frame extended far beyond their programmatic statements on time-oriented planning.[164] Emphasising technical progresss, his design stood resolutely at the heart of debates on the influence of science and technology on post-war urban development.

Time, Progress and Technology

Ideas developed by Lewis Mumford were also crucial to Price's elaboration of a time-based planning approach. As early as 1938, Mumford had pinpointed the capacity to evolve over time as a significant, specific attribute of urban culture and social co-existence. "Cities are a product of time. By the diversity of its time-structures, the city in part escapes the tyranny of a single present, and the monotony of a future that consists in repeating only a single beat in the past."[165] Building on the reception of Geddes' ideas in the wake of town planner Jaquelin Tyrwhitt's rediscovery of his work, intensive debate at the AA School of Architecture addressed alternative Functionalist planning, driven by culture and "natural" human development.[166] In this vein, Mumford applied Geddes' concepts to post-war society in his 1961 *Cities in History: Its Origins, Its Transformations, and Its Prospects*, underscoring the role played by technology as a driving force in renewing urban society and culture.[167]

Mumford singled out post-war technological innovations, particularly in communications and electronics, as the point of departure for the rapid pace of the developments sweeping through society. These instruments of technical progress fostered far-reaching exchanges of information, goods, ideas and skills. In 1915 Geddes had used the term "neotechnics" to express the impact of technical innovation on urban society, with technology establishing an important link between the evolving city and the natural environment cultivated by humans with the aid of technology. [168] In this context the city was seen as a product of human labour, its evolution driven by technical progress.[169]

The new channels for information transmission that arose with the advent of electronics marked the third phase in humanity's history of technical development for Mumford, and led to fresh developments in how society and space were structured.[170] Electronic communication technologies, receivers, transmitters, innovative information regulation and processing systems: they all added novel, invisible networks to the mix alongside visible urban infrastructure, and he believed they would generate a new mode of social co-existence. Mumford predicted that the spread of radio, electricity and automobiles would produce "organically" conceived communities in which these emerging technologies would unlock equal access to information, education and resources for everyone. Contrasting with industrial-era technologies grounded in mechanical principles and centralised energy supply, understanding the technologies of the electronic age called for a sound grasp of processes and practices.[171] Mumford therefore turned the spotlight on access to knowledge, viewed as a resource and economic fundamental, as the key for these new communities.[172]

Price's objectives in the Potteries Thinkbelt included create a synthesis of the multifarious ideas bubbling up in alternative Functionalist planning. To counteract government urban planning schemes, he tapped into the idea of "neotechnic communities" in proposing his alternative vision of planning. Price insisted that community-focused architecture must adapt the functions of the city's built fabric to respond to factors that architects had previously left out of the equation, namely dynamic urban development processes. Determining the specific, development-related conditions relevant to designs for individual structures meant appraising the entire urban system: "Too often architects assume a permanence of pattern, a permanence of habit investing in mortal lives of the occupants. [...] In a city where you can deal with a far less static thing than a little village, in a city you should encourage this ability to change."[173]

Viewing the city as a product of technological innovation, the next logical step for Price entailed making architecture open and adaptable, enabling it to respond to influences that would foster technical progress.[174] In this spirit, his design for the university facilities in the transfer areas envisages a linear sequence of open hall constructions to which smaller capsules could be added using a crane – analogous to the open-ended structures in the Fun Palace Project. The space within the capsules was more clearly delineated the further the buildings were from the crane. Price thus modulated the openness in his design configuration as a function of the transport infrastructure, which was in turn integrated into the regional university's overall network system.[175] That sheds light on the Potteries Thinkbelt as logistics-driven architecture, centred around efficient organisation of space. The city consequently became a locus of trade, communication and exchanges; for Price this meant that designing urban architecture was tantamount to providing an economic service, for it held the promise of improved quality of life for the local populace.

The new communication and information technologies played a particularly pivotal role within this strategy.[176] Over and above the region's physical infrastructure network, Price intended the regional university to introduce a new culture of individual learning thanks to a network of electronic communication technologies.[177] Unlimited access to information via a television and computer network, available everywhere around the clock, would allow individualised study reflecting students' specific interests and goals.[178] As in the Fun Palace, Price conceived the Potteries university within a larger national or even international network that would promote exchange of knowledge and place individual interests at centre stage. The multiple potential strata of relationship and communication in the Potteries Thinkbelt would allow studies to be devised with a focus on the individual and on lifelong learning. That gave the

Potteries Thinkbelt project a twofold role: it was to emphasise the interests of each individual and help to revitalise the region. As part of this process, communication technologies would unleash connective and emancipatory forces in the city, while constant exchanges would establish a natural balance in society.[179] On a plane that extended well beyond the tangible specifics of the university's functioning, the Potteries Thinkbelt design embodied a new societal model of the city in the electronic age. Technology was to enable the city to reinvigorate itself "under its own steam".

Information and communication media also figured in the British Parliament's efforts to offer a wider range of study options as part of the overarching reform of the educational system. The official strategy favoured the model of universities reaching out to students through television and radio. In 1965 an expert committee was set up with a remit to develop a media-supported, distance-learning university, and one of the members, Peter Laslett, asked Price to provide a commentary on his project. Laslett subsequently recommended that Price elaborate the economic and social functions of his project in greater detail, and play down the architectonic side, instead highlighting the organisational aspects of what was dubbed "soft servicing".[180] However Price opted instead to emphasise revitalisation of the region through urban planning rather than filling in more details of the Potteries Thinkbelt's educational dimension. He justified this by pointing out that he could only respond properly to these contemporary issues within the context of his own discipline, as an architect. Price, as well as submitting the project he had developed only to the government committee, also presented it in architectural circles, in lectures and articles.[181] Roughly four years after the the parliamentary committee discussed the Potteries Thinkbelt, the Open University was created in 1969: the world's first media-supported, distance-learning university.[182] However it completely ignored Price's idea that university infrastructure could be the seed crystal for revitalising former industrial regions.

"City as Scrambled Egg"

The city in the electronic age continued to play a pivotal role in Price's designs after he had concluded the Potteries Thinkbelt study. He saw the socio-political vision of a city that would run on the principles of interaction and communication as a viable way to adapt industrial-era Functionalist architecture to the imperatives of the information and service society. Mumford's ideas offered scope in his view to build on and develop Functionalist planning models, as did the thinking of reform-driven architects, such as Ebenezer Howard's "The Three Magnets" diagram.[183] The force-field metaphor underpinned both Ebenezer Howard and Patrick Geddes' reconception of the city as a space of social interaction. This metaphor also articulated the influence of technical innovation and science on the city's social and spatial organisation. This second plane of urban space viewed as a social and cultural arena became one of the conceptual backbones in Price's designs. He saw interaction as a principle that expressed labour and human culture, forming the fundament of a social culture that had been taking shape since industrialisation and was manifested in the form cities assumed.

17
18

       Price's famous *The City as An Egg* sketch expressed the fundamental principles of development throughout history.[184] It alluded to the essay by his friend Reyner Banham, "The City as Scrambled Egg", which included the egg metaphor as a polemic allusion to Le Corbusier, conveying Banham's critique of post-war modernist urban planning.[185] Banham contrasted the historicising image of a closed form as an expression of identity and community with a vision of the decentralised city, shaped by the dynamic everyday processes unfurling within it: "The true destination of the scrambled egg environment is to provide an infrastructure of usable facilities. The place where everybody has to go such as the centre of a New Town [...] is a dead letter in the kind of high mobile highly communicative society [...]."[186] From this perspective, the decentralised city of the electronic age had abandoned slavish obedience to a superordinate urban planning concept, and was directed solely by the logic of its production and distribution infrastructure. Both in the world of business and in everyday life, urban culture generated simultaneity and heterogeneity in various development areas, which influenced each other both in terms of their buildings and from a social and economic perspective.

       This reinterpretation of the field metaphor served as a foundation for Price's elaboration of his independent design stance. In his view, the quintessence of the architect's remit lay in targeted architectural interventions intended to influence the social and functional dynamics of individual developments.[187] He was convinced that this kind of built intervention, in conjunction with urban infrastructure systems, could steer the development of districts or neighbourhoods. Even in the 1990s, Price titled one of his projects "Magnet". In this study he proposed ten relatively small-scale interventions to make public space more accessible in several London districts.[188] Through the systemic impact of these schemes, Price aimed to bring about a transformation of the social setting and indirectly influence its spatial and social attributes.

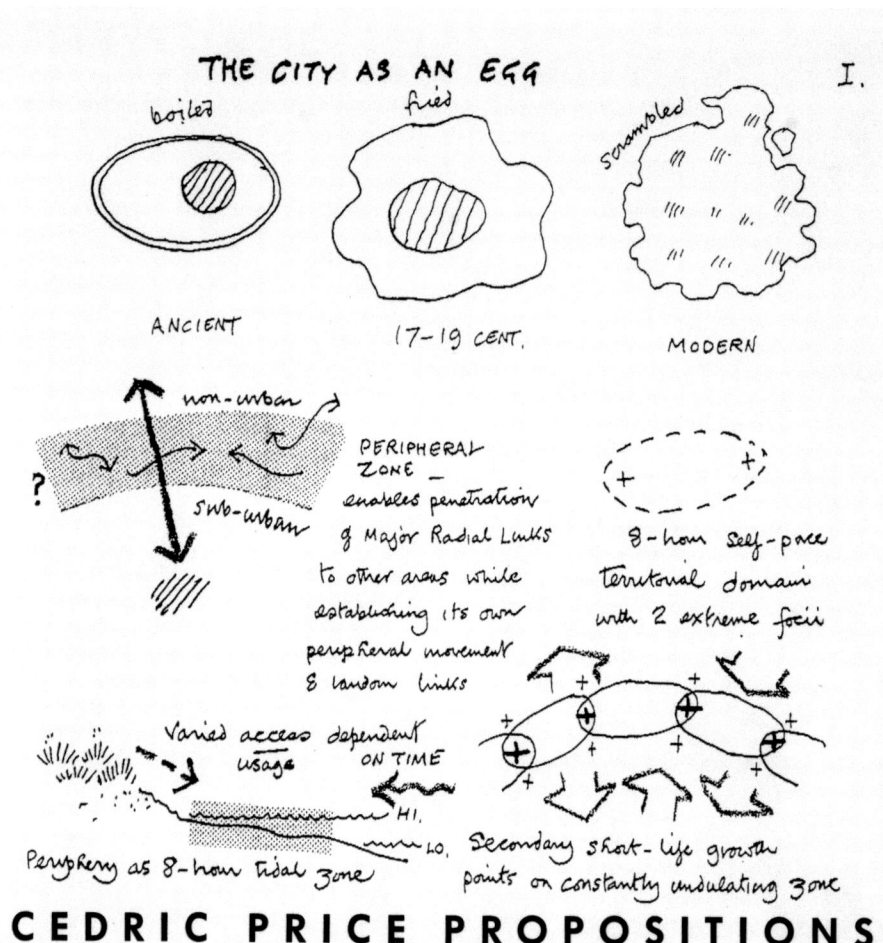

17 Cedric Price, *The City as an Egg*, Cedric Price Propositions I, undated.

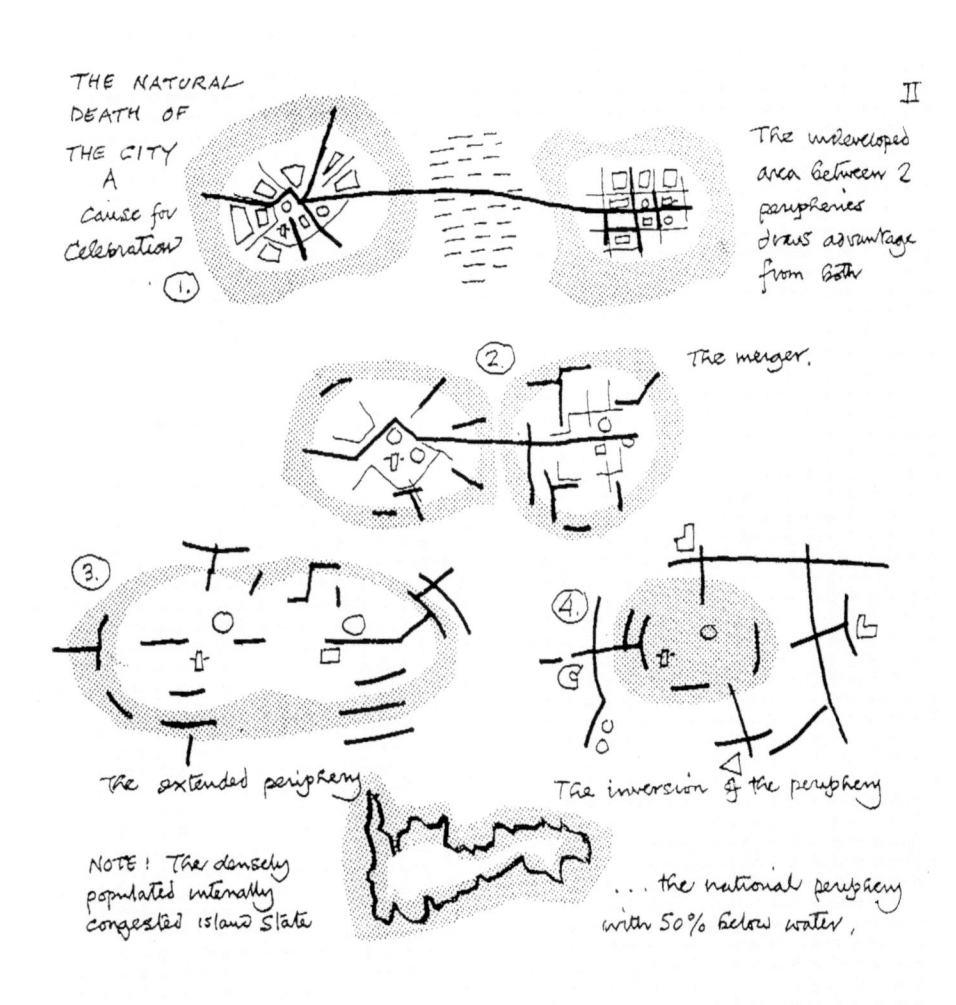

1   Author unknown, no title, Inter-
Action Centre, use diagram, undated.

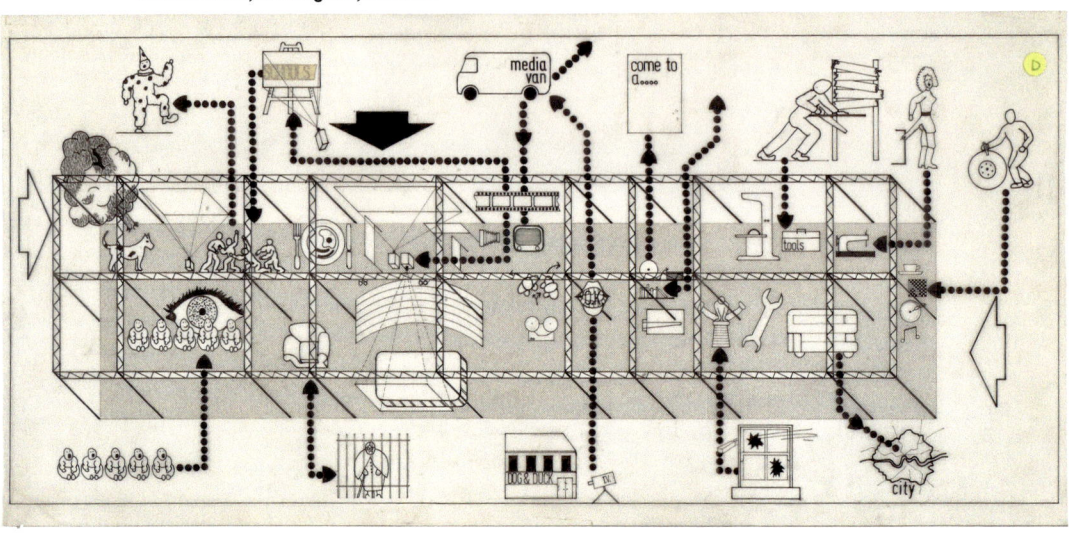

Ecologies

3

"The 'Invisible' Fun Palace"

In 1974, ten years after the first Fun Palace Project ended, the rock band The Who held a benefit concert outside Joan Littlewood's theatre in Stratford for the "invisible Fun Palace".[1] That was the band's way of supporting the Fun Palace Trust, which had continued to pursue its central vision of a new community-driven urban culture, organising cultural schemes and neighbourhood projects even after the main project initiative drew to a close in 1965.[2] The Trust's goal was still to set up cultural activities in London districts affected by slum-clearance programmes in order to foster neighbourhood social initiatives.

Joan Littlewood had leased unused plots of land near the theatre and started arranging activities there together with local inhabitants.[3] The theatre group's enduring close ties to the Fun Palace's objectives becomes apparent in the emphasis on urban transformation in its dramatic practice. This encompassed social renewal through learning-oriented projects and theatre work, as well as schemes to regenerate the built environment around the theatre.[4] It was a strategy that chimed with the Trust's emphasis on framing its activities as instruments for urban revitalisation, intended to improve the quality of life in the city and have a positive impact on neighbourhood development.

From 1965 to 1975, Price designed several smaller projects for local festivities and neighbourhood projects, such as the Camden Town Pilot Project (1965) and the Fun Palace Playground (1974) which, in contrast to the original project's industrial dimensions, were characterised by small-scale, straightforward interventions.[5] These projects unfolded within a fundamentally different frame. In Camden Town, for example, room-sized wooden cubes could be self-assembled by the neighbourhood centre's users, who also took charge of organising the activities there.[6] The Trust shifted its focus away from high-tech tools and large-format architecture in this design, investing instead in maintenance and organisational support for activities on the spot.[7]

In the Camden Town project Price deployed an additive principle based on the smallest spatial units.[8] Ease of assembly was one of the fundamental parameters shaping the construction system, which was made up of three variants on a prefabricated wooden cube.[9] Simple bracing infill units, forming the walls, floor and ceiling, could be slotted into the spatial framework defined by cubes, which could be stacked up to three storeys high.[10] It took just two people with a forklift truck to compose a huge spectrum of different combinations with the basic elements. Textile awnings stretched above the structure's interstices created room for activities that needed more space.[11] The simplicity of assembly and the option to create a mix of distinct functions enabled local inhabitants to "programme" this public space, heightening its significance for the neighbourhood: "A springboard to the needs and objectives of the community."[12]

1

2

Responding directly to the outcomes produced by state-sponsored mass housing construction, one of Price's central concerns in this project was to ensure his architecture could adapt to the neighbourhood's changing needs. The cellular construction he devised allowed the building to adapt almost "naturally" to the functional requirements of its surroundings.[13] In this respect Price's design was informed by Gordon Pask's cybernetic self-organisation model.[14] As a member of the Fun Palace Trust, Pask continued to participate in the initiative's activities and began to transpose his cybernetic perspective to the architecture/neighbourhood system. Pask's ideas of organisms' self-organisation and "learning capability" were particularly important as structural attributes that Price endeavoured to integrate into the project.

Price envisaged that fundamentally new impetuses for the building's programmes and activities would grow out of the project's adaptable potential.[15] In this vein, he studied a series of parameters that might impinge on the structure's growth and adaptation, and developed several configuration variants. The project could be extended along an internal access street in each growth phase.[16] Price clearly viewed his design simply as a springboard for future developments, describing it, in analogy with the biological processes Pask addressed, as a "catalyst" for new urban lifestyles.[17]

3
4
5

The constructional principle Price deployed in this project echoes early Structuralist designs, such as Kenzo Tange's Tokyo Bay Project and Candilis, Josic & Woods' award-winning 1963 competition design for the Freie Universität Berlin.[18] Arnulf Lüchinger later dubbed this principle "structure and coincidence" or "the two-components approach", with the built system flanked by a new organisational mode that determined the specific details of its configuration.[19] In developing the construction system Price drew on instruments devised by operations research, such as the "Critical Path Method", to get to grips with the complexity of the project's possible development trajectories, which he depicted in diagrams.[20] This enabled him to identify a range of potential developments and tap into these to optimise the course of the project, obviating the need to stipulate rigid constructional specifications in advance. Project management instruments would, he hoped, serve to integrate complexity, spontaneity and openness into his planning process. The cybernetic notion of communication, conceptualised as a means for planning to adapt to changing environmental conditions, was an important complement for Price to the mere "aesthetics of number" that Arnulf Lüchinger classified as the principle underpinning Structuralist architecture.[21]

"Situations"

After the Camden Town project was suspended in 1965, Price worked on study commissions and small-scale projects in which he engaged with the idea of self-organisation and ways of deploying knowledge and education as tools of urban revitalisation.[22] It was during this phase that he created a synthesis of many of his earlier approaches and ideas, blending them into an independent concept of design.

The period in which he was formulating this concept was shot through with incipient social disillusionment about the form that the leisure society took in

2 Cedric Price, Camden Town Pilot
Project, site plan, ca. 1965.

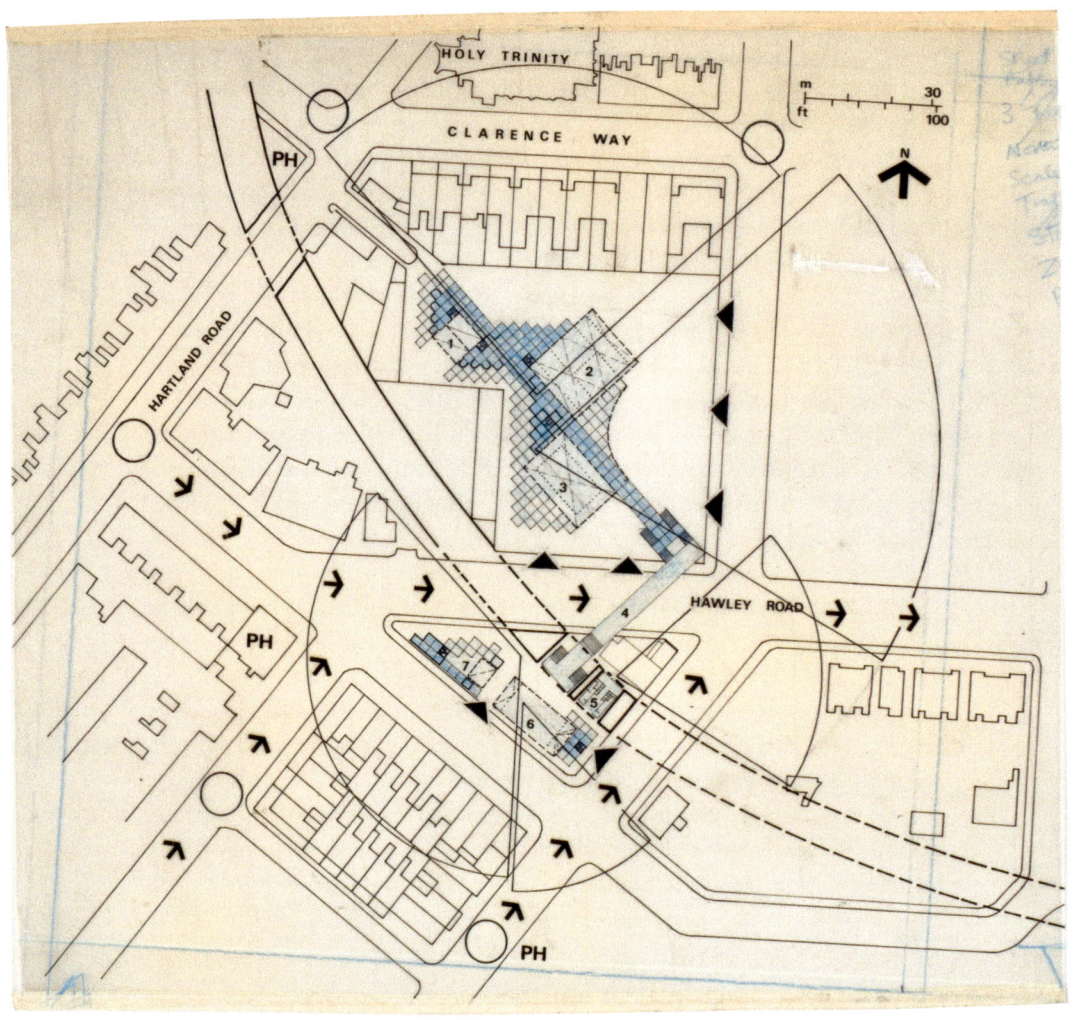

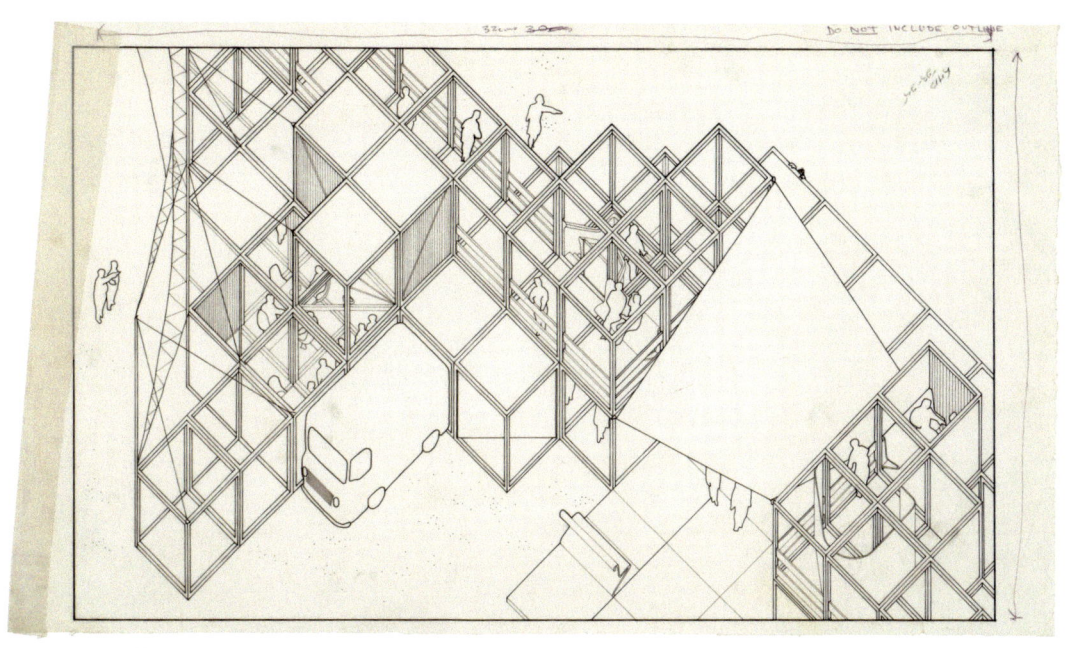

3   Cedric Price, Camden Town Pilot Project, axonometric projection, ca. **1965**.

4   Cedric Price, "Basis units + control systems: F.P. Pilot Project", ca. **1965**.

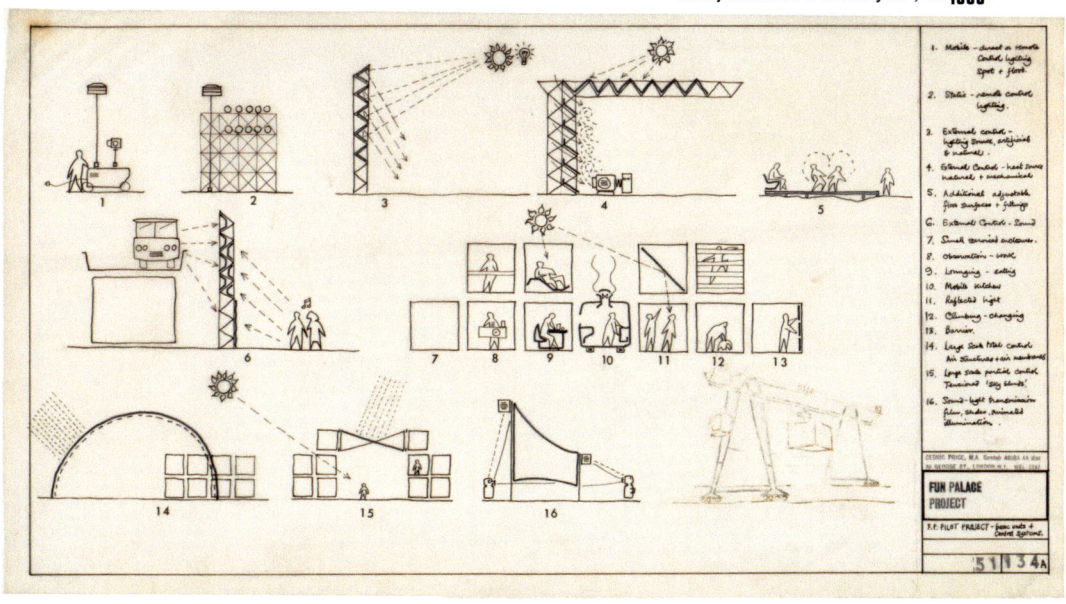

5   Cedric Price, Camden Town
Project, "Network Analysis", ca. **1965**.

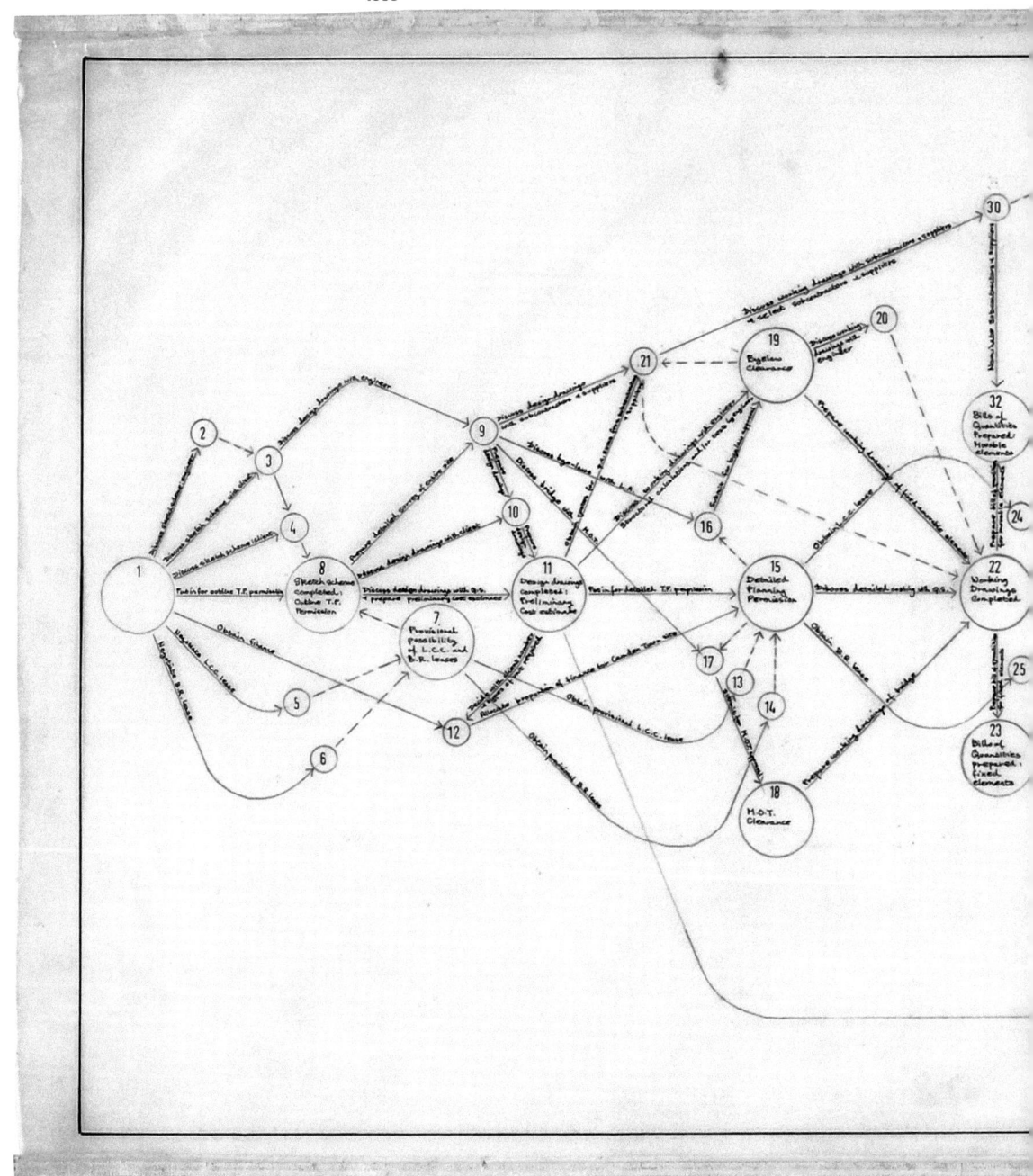

3

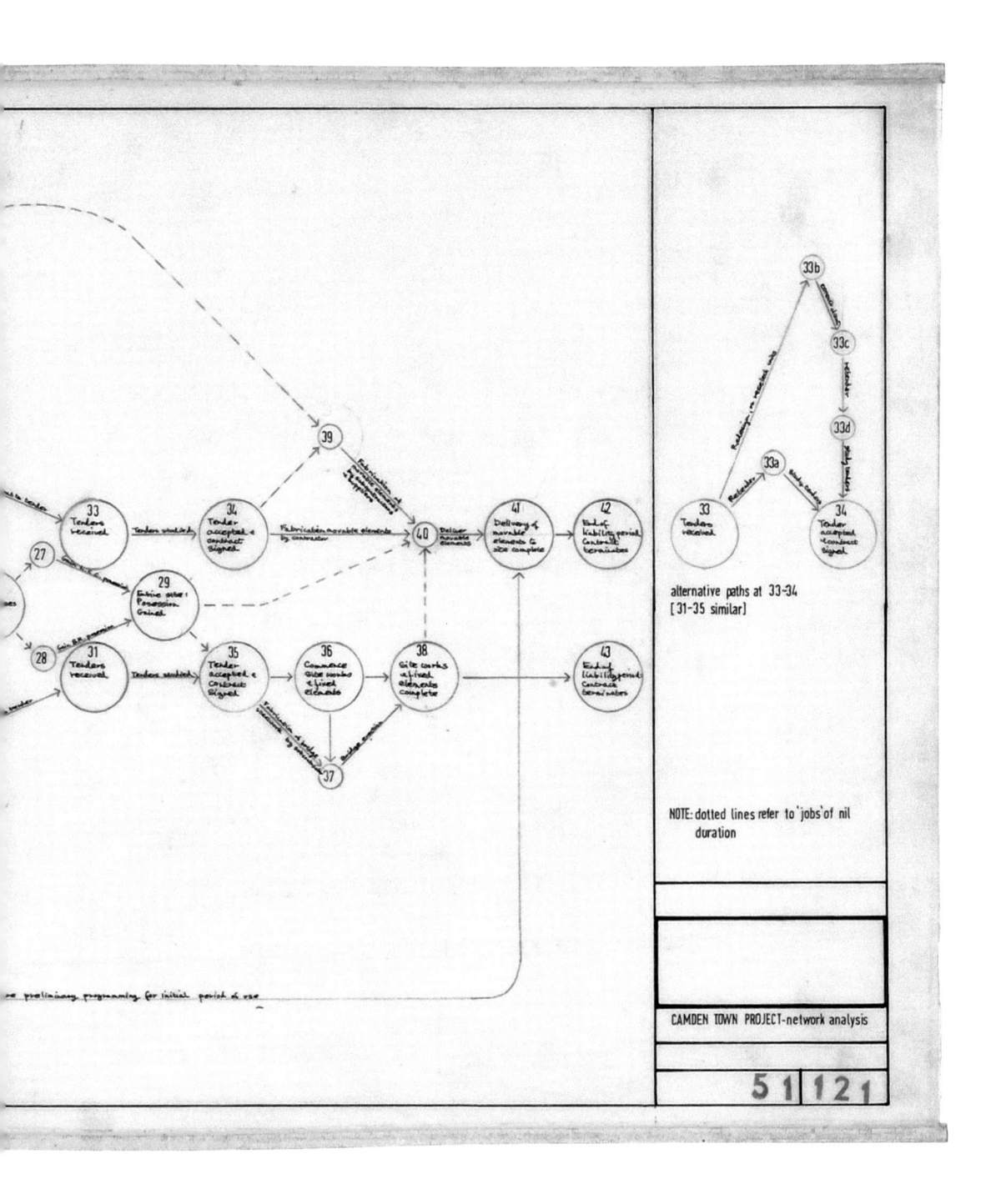

alternative paths at 33-34
[31-35 similar]

NOTE: dotted lines refer to 'jobs' of nil
duration

CAMDEN TOWN PROJECT-network analysis

5 1 1 2 1

97

practice, along with erosion of the belief that science and technology would help create a just world order. By the late 1960s hopes of progress had been dashed on many fronts: for example, the predicted drastic reduction in working hours for most employees had not come to pass.[23] The social imbalance in British society, rather than shrinking, was growing even more pronounced; unemployment and inflation were rising, and the country's economic situation had gone from bad to worse, culminating in devaluation of the pound in 1967.[24] In addition, Cedric Price and Reyner Banham had differences of opinion over a new aesthetic for architecture in the second machine age. Whereas Price took the view that a new architectural idiom should arise from the conditions of its use, for Banham the technological aesthetic of the Archigram Group's projects was a much better fit for the contemporary spirit of reinvigorated Modernism.[25]

Representatives of both camps came face to face at the IDEA (International Dialogue of Experimental Architecture) conference in summer 1966.[26] This meeting of young architectural talents had been organised with a view to forming an original avant-garde of experimental architecture. The group aimed to draw up contemporary design principles for mass-culture Functionalist architecture.[27] However, during the conference, Price realised that the political goals and aesthetic concepts addressed were so heterogeneous and complex that this attempt to establish a new avant-garde movement was destined to be just a flash in the pan.

His introductory speech asserted the role of temporality and adaptability as novel attributes of Functionalist architecture. In the title of his lecture, "Auto Destructive Architecture", he alluded to work by his friend Gustav Metzger,[28] who used destruction as an instrument in his Happenings to help consumers regain interpretative sovereignty over the world of things.[29]

In his lecture Price linked the notion of Happenings with process-driven architecture that seeks to derive social relevance by creating experiences of situationally adaptive space.[30] Echoing Banham's concept of architecture for a second machine age, Price also turned his attention to aesthetic representations of the social realm. Critiquing references to Futurist aesthetics in Archigram's work, he alluded indirectly to the latter's Plug-in City project, which deployed a visual language that Banham characterised as the contemporary form of Functionalist architecture.[31] Price, drawing a clear distinction between his work and Archigram's formal-aesthetic projects by emphasising his analytical, scientific method, underlined that understanding interactions, between city and society or between architects and users, is as germane to architectural design as building per se.[32] In this context Price pointed out the direct influence on architecture of scientific know-how gleaned from local technical infrastructure, such as cybernetics and information technology; this made it possible to represent the past or the aesthetic of the future, but also to depict current use, and hence the unplannable dimension.[33]

Amidst the flurry of heterogeneous design approaches presented in Folkestone, Price's call for situation-driven architecture shaped by tools from systems theory had little impact. Heavyweight ideological debates on power and the authority to devise definitions in architecture flared up during the conference, dividing advocates of architecture's social relevance and those developing a new aesthetic.[34] The discussions reflected architects' disillusionment with their discipline as an effective means of shaping society. Against the backdrop of an increasingly globalised world economy, architects were failing to attain the objectives they pursued, such as distributive justice and political co-decision. The 1966 and 1967 famines in Nigeria and India, former British colonies, suggested that self-determination alone does not lead to a just social order.[35] Furthermore, in 1965 the United States of America entered the Vietnam War; widespread coverage of the conflict demonstrated clearly that a social culture with a media underpinning does not necessarily contribute to understanding between peoples.

In this context, some conference participants objected to the project presented by Ron Herron, Walking City, finding it a cynical veneration of a Pop aesthetic with a morally obsolete architectural stance.[36] Similar misgivings led to Hans Hollein being described as a Nazi when he presented architecture in the form of an aircraft carrier in his collages.[37]

The experimental architecture scene had become politicised, in many different ways. The enormous spectrum of viewpoints and the diverse realms the architects addressed in their attempts to improve people's lives made the idea of forming a common movement and a new avant-garde – as Team 10 and the Independent Group had done in the 1950s – seem like an impossible dream.

"What About Learning?"

That same year, Price developed his first educational project in the form of the National School Plan (1965/66).[38] Marking the advent of a series of projects focused on education policy (reflected too in the Potteries Thinkbelt project), it sought to introduce a new culture of learning.[39] Price viewed his projects both as a necessary reaction to the changes sweeping society and as a response to debates on the direction his own discipline should pursue, offering a vision for the new course architecture would need to steer in future. One of the leitmotifs running through all the projects was Price's call for a new culture of self-organisation that would turn organisational processes on their heads. In the National School Plan, Price sketched out a long-term reform proposal to revamp architectural training at British universities. This was followed by two urban planning studies for educational networks in Aurora, Illinois, ("ATOM", 1967) and Detroit, Michigan, ("Detroit Thinkgrid", 1969), which dealt with ways to deploy educational schemes in neighbourhoods.

6

In 1970 Price could finally put his ideas for a new thrust in British architectural training into practice, building up the Polyark network (1970) as part of a study project. Like the other schemes mentioned above, it articulated the idea of pursuing urban revitalisation through educational infrastructure to open up new opportunities for development and self-help.

Concentrating his educational projects on the culture of self-organisation resonated with the mood across Europe in the late 1960s. The younger generation in particular were eager to overhaul society, as manifested in the 1968 student revolts in Paris and Berlin. Student protests in Great Britain however, unlike those in France and Germany, did not trigger an overarching debate on the country's closed social culture, but concentrated almost entirely on education and future prospects for various individual disciplines. While the protests were unfolding, Price accompanied a delegation of British student representatives to Paris, where they met architecture students at the École Nationale Supérieure des Beaux-Arts for discussions on the motivation and goals of their movement. When he returned to London, Price suggested using the Polyark study network as a highly pragmatic way to support the students' demands. Polyark, a social study network that Price ran for six years in cooperation with universities and colleges in London, aimed to link training more closely to practice and to create new options for independent study. The network acted as a go-between, linking university and the business world by fostering exchanges between students and entrepreneurs, as well as creating more options for self-organised study. It aimed to help reform British architectural education by expanding the frame of training and unlocking broader agency for architecture students.

7   In this project, funded by private donations, Price proposed tangible measures in reaction to calls for architecture to move in a new direction. Despite the student protests, the pedagogical concepts and structures in British architectural training had remained largely unchanged. Price was particularly critical of the excessive emphasis in teaching on formal, aesthetic design principles, neglecting the question of how people relate to their environment. That latter concern, a crucial facet of Price's vision of architecture, called for a much deeper engagement with other disciplines, such as engineering and social sciences, and for a greater emphasis on practical experience as part of the educational framework. Through lectures, exchange programmes, internships and mentoring schemes, Price attempted to counteract the rigidly organised structures of university degree courses It was especially important for him to underscore that Polyark first and foremost fostered students' independence and creativity.

    Drawing on the liberal paradigm of self-development and free decision-making, Price also viewed his role here as establishing a viable organisational structure rather than stipulating what students should learn. Within the Polyark structure, students would define the type of exchange within the project, based on their specific concerns. In the first year, for example, the programme's contents were determined through a partnership with North East London Polytechnic; two years later a cooperation with the AA and the journal *Architectural Design* reinterpreted Polyark's programme.[40] Under the aegis of the network, AA students for example organised a bus tour in February 1973. They travelled from university to university for two weeks in a converted double-decker bus with information materials on topical concerns like community action, and held workshops with other students on this nexus of issues.[41] The bus as a mobile educational facility was already well-established in London's alternative cultural scene, where it had become synonymous with self-organised, creative project

6 Cedric Price, "Atom", collage on photographic negative, undated.

7 Author unknown, "Polyark Lectures No. 1", poster, ca. **1970**.

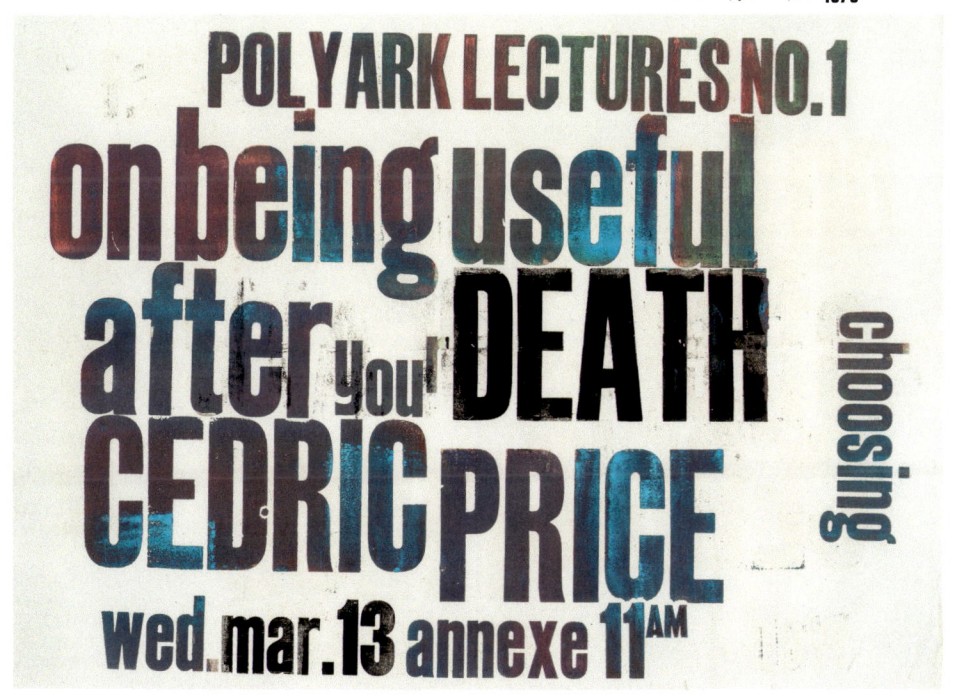

NEWsociety

20 March 1969 No 338 1s 6d weekly

Robert Holman	**WRONG POVERTY PROGRAMME**
John Berger	**MAGRITTE RECONSIDERED**
David Marquand	**EDUCATION BACKLASH**
Rayner Banham Paul Barker Peter Hall Cedric Price	**NON-PLAN: AN EXPERIMENT IN FREEDOM**

8   Reyner Banham, Paul Barker, Peter Hall and Cedric Price, Cover of: *New Society*, no. 338, 1969, with the article "Non-Plan: An Experiment in Freedom".

3

work. The Inter-Action Group's theatre company had been doing the rounds of working-class districts in London with the "Fun Art Bus" since 1971.[42] Even before this, the ANTFARM group's "Media Van" tour to American universities had celebrated the possibilities opened up by a mobile culture grounded in technology.[43] For Price, the Polyark network reflected the selfsame attributes of this innovative culture, in which exchange, mobility and cooperation would re-invent the knowledge society.[44] In this respect Polyark was a tangible manifestation of the architect's efforts to integrate his political convictions into university practice by establishing a new organisational principle.

"Non-Plan"

Price had also engaged with the notion of self-organisation previously, already addressing it during his studies. Giancarlo De Carlo and Colin Ward had introduced the concept of "bottom-up" planning into the Architectural Association's educational programme in the late 1950s.[45] While analysing self-organisation principles for the Fun Palace, Price drew on Colin Ward's Plotlands studies as an underpinning for the project's organisational rules.[46] The Plotlands were small pieces of land laid out in regular plots along the English coast with self-build homes largely constructed outside the conventional planning system. These settlements were not governed by an overarching planning scheme, but arose out of simple organisational principles, such as the orientation of the houses along the roads.[47] Thanks purely to initiatives by a number of individual landowners, well-functioning settlements emerged, and the Plotlands principle seemed to offer a genuine alternative to existing urban planning models.[48] Its associations with the idea of democratising planning appealed in particular to left-wing architects, who felt that the Plotlands picked up on and updated Socialist planning maxims from Britain's early industrial age.

8

Price was however soon disappointed to find that the new democratic planning models devised at universities did not filter through into practice as strategies to reform planning mechanisms. In 1969 he presented his ideas for a turnaround in planning methodology in "Non-Plan: An Experiment in Freedom", in conjunction with Reyner Banham, the journalist Paul Barker and geographer Peter Hall. They castigated the planning authorities' technocratic design aspirations as fundamentally out of step with contemporary trends in society. Until this point, planning had been moulded by a conception that gave greater weight to the "user" as a statistical average than to the individual needs of city dwellers. "Non-Plan" therefore proposed unleashing societal forces to feed into a diverse "bottom-up" planning strategy by devising appropriate regulatory provisions.

The "Non-Plan" manifesto was a direct response to the *Town and Country Planning Act*, adopted a few months earlier, which sought to reform British urban planning and make the ponderous state planning apparatus more flexible. The manifesto's authors felt however that this legislation did not go far enough.[49] They formulated a polemical counter-thesis: they proposed establishing three planning-free zones in the West Midlands agglomeration as an experiment to shed light on how everyday culture actually influenced settlement development. Free market forces alone were to guide development for twenty years in these areas, without the constraints of institutionalised planning rules and regulations. The authors were convinced that this experiment would offer insights into the question of urban form and functional viability by creating developments determined solely by city dwellers' needs.

They also envisaged that planning-free zones would offer greater scope for local inhabitants to take action. In the "Non-Plan" zones, tax law was to be liberalised, along with licensing provisions for pubs, restaurants and even radio stations, to create a liberal market-economy setting shaped by free entrepreneurship and thus more directly oriented to the local populace's needs. In this respect the authors also saw their manifesto as a deliberate counter-design to modern planning's idealised image of the body politic. They countered aspirations to equal treatment by focussing on the diversity of individual interests: "Non-Plan – or as it was originally and more accurately called Null-Plan (AD 5 1969) detailed the advantages of unevenness. [...] to be able to establish a new order of land, sea and air use which would be related more directly to the valid social and economic life span of such uses, *replace Utopia with Non-Plan*."[50] They tapped into market dynamism and free entrepreneurship as a substitute for leftist ideologies: "Marx is best known as the maker of plastic, battery driven dump trucks. Let's become that kind of Marxist."[51]

West Coast American cities, where the advent of mass culture had generated entirely new urban planning developments, served as role models for the manifesto.[52] Los Angeles represented a self-service culture defined by the mass market, cars and road infrastructure. "Non-Plan" feted the American city as an expression of an individualised lifestyle, drawing inspiration from Banham's radio lectures on Los Angeles,[53] Tom Wolfe's texts, and essays on architectural theory such as Charles Moore's "You have to Pay for the Public Life."[54] The socio-economic culture of freedom proposed in the "Non-Plan" would, its authors assumed, also give rise to a new urban form in Great Britain: "At least one would find out what people want; at the most one might discover the 'hidden' style of mid-twentieth-century Britain."[55]

With such references to the city's concealed style, the authors called for institutionalised planning instruments to be sidelined as a rational means to re-establish a "natural" urban order. Rather than being produced by specialised planning, this urban order would be an expression of the vital processes unfolding in the city, such as work and other activities. The lived culture of the urban populace lay at the heart of design strategies informed by this view of the city, which was profoundly influenced by concepts from social sciences. "Non-Plan" therefore moved beyond simply questioning established planning instruments to launch a debate on the architect's role and the remit that town planning should fulfil. Architects would have to work retrospectively in responding to the planning-free zones, deriving urban development rules from the outcomes produced by the experiment. In order to ensure academic review of the processes unfurling in those zones, changes in the built fabric were to be analysed after five, ten and twenty years.

Echoing Herbert Gans, the "Non-Plan" authors underscored their "desire to know instead of impose".[56] Planning was to be grounded in observation and analysis of the existing situation. "Non-Plan" therefore represented demands for greater attention to the dynamics of everyday life in urban planning, and for design interventions grounded in empirical data.[57]

Against the backdrop of the 1968 student protests, the "Non-Plan" authors identified cybernetics as the key technical innovation that had brought about enormous changes in lived urban culture, for it constituted the basis for industrial mass production and was a precursor of the mass media. In this period, three of the defining elements that filtered through into radical urban redevelopment involved the idea of "the mass": the mass market, mass media and mass housing construction. The manifesto also ascribed a key future role to cybernetics in implementing process-oriented, dynamic planning: "The cybernetic revolution makes our traditional planning technologically and intellectually obsolete, social change reinforces this conclusion."[58]

This cybernetic view of the city in "Non-Plan" represented a system-oriented conception of planning rooted in the principle of interaction and the dynamic process of striking a balance between differences. Cybernetics was thus viewed in a broader societal context in "Non-Plan" than in 1960s conceptions of this discipline. As the authors pointed out, new management methods rooted in operations research's mathematical approach had recently been developed, and were already being deployed in the social sciences and economics. That created an imperative for planning to address the organisational framework and decision-making issues, replacing conventional urban planning's rigid regulatory mechanisms with more flexible instruments.

Rather than taking structural policy as the point of departure, "Non-Plan" called for planning to be viewed from a system-oriented angle as a political process that must take account of the diversity, complexity and open-ended nature of urban functions. Viewed in these terms, planning should establish an equilibrium between built structures and the city's functions as part of an overall system.[59] In other words, "Non-Plan" did not demand zero planning but instead advocated a shift in design priorities, moving away from an exclusive focus on built structures to address the functions such structures fulfilled in the city.

Surprisingly, the publication of "Non-Plan" produced little response, despite its radical demands to utilise mass-culture technologies for people-oriented planning. As Peter Hall recalls, architects and social scientists dismissed the ideas of "Non-Plan" as being utterly divorced from reality.[60] One partial explanation for this cool reception is that the authors were engaging with a discourse about the ramifications of pop culture that was primarily being explored in the USA at this time. Furthermore, mass-market culture was not nearly such an established part of daily life in Great Britain as it was on the American West Coast.[61]

Learning from Las Vegas – published three years after "Non-Plan" – was the first detailed empirical documentation of how quotidian culture influenced urban form.[62] Like Cedric Price, Denise Scott-Brown's studies at the Architectural Association had influenced her analysis of everyday culture, but she conceived the link between the city's societal functions and its built form in terms of a new iconography of architecture. That stood in clear contrast to "Non-Plan", which proclaimed a new urbanism that would emphasise architecture's social function within the city's social system.[63]

This entirely different perception of the mass-culture city in the "Non-Plan" manifesto corresponded to the Functionalist concerns that continued to permeate Price's projects in the 1970s. Furthermore, Price was also fundamentally opposed to an iconographic reading of the city, as he made clear in a commentary on Kevin Lynch's *The Image of the City*.[64] Price did not merely find the quest for new formal modes of architectural expression irrelevant, but considered it to be a moral betrayal of the discipline's values: "The role of architecture as a provider of visually recognisable symbols of identity, place and activity becomes an increasingly attractive excuse for architects to revel in the immensity of their personal visual dexterity [...] Call it a fix or 'the image of a city', such overt self-consciousness is embarrassing only to a few – in general, it is both incomprehensible and irrelevant."[65]

Los Angeles: City of Ecologies

In the context of both the 1968 protests and the specifically British scenario, "Non-Plan" clearly also took a stance in relation to the left-wing protest movement and its calls for political co-decision.[66] Like PolyARK, "Non-Plan" rejected left-wing ideologisation of architecture. The action-oriented understanding of the social realm manifested in "Non-Plan" contradicted the Marxist conception of society that was popular in the 1970s. Rather than adopting the era's customary focus on social and economic inequalities and class struggle in societal analysis, Price developed an actor-centred understanding of society with his co-authors. He viewed both the city and its architecture as a product of everyday life and the culture of work, in other words as cultural artefacts in which power structures and the individual's actions and social relations were manifested.[67] This form of relational thinking determined Price's work in the early 1970s, even if the "ecology" label was not yet applied to his work at this point.

Banham's 1971 book on Los Angeles laid the conceptual groundwork for this mindset.[68] He dedicated *The Architecture of Four Ecologies* to Price, who had challenged him to stand up for Los Angeles as an alternative model of the modern city at a time when the modernist planning culture was suffering a massive loss of credibility.[69] Ever since the Independent Group's activities, Los Angeles had represented an idealised view of the city as a dynamic field in which everyone could live their own "California way of life" thanks to the possibilities afforded by the market, car-based mobility and communication technologies.[70] In his book Banham declared this new form of social order and its spatial articulation to be the model for an urban societal culture in which the dynamism of a new lifestyle unfolded as a "culture of 'fun'".[71] In Price's projects the term "fun" also played a decisive role in describing the reciprocal interactions between the individual and the city's social environment that his adaptable architecture aimed to achieve.[72] Banham, Cedric Price and Joan Littlewood thus deployed the same vocabulary to sketch out their concept of a cultural space in tune with the zeitgeist.[73] The local populace's activities and the site-specific circumstances were co-determinate and interdependent.

The Architecture of Four Ecologies was published at the end of a long phase of conceptual engagement with future urban developments, in which Los Angeles was referenced above all as a negative example of the consequences of modern settlement development. In 1971 neighbourhood conservation, vigorously advocated by grassroots movements, stood in stark contrast to Banham's ideal of a dynamic city in which modernisation was interpreted as an instrument to generate an emancipated lifestyle. Jane Jacobs' citizens' protest against highway expansion in New York's Greenwich Village was in full swing when Banham's book was published.[74]

Banham's optimistic, technology-oriented conception of the city was also linked to a new way of reading the urban context. He assumed the role of an empirical observer in his book, investigating urban space as an expression of a new kind of lived culture.[75] Los Angeles was described from a driver's perspective and the city was interpreted in terms of its various strata of utilisation.[76] Banham read the city as a palimpsest, with attributes determined by its geography, inhabitants, activities and artefacts. In echoing this view of the city, Price also pre-empted a decisive change in urban planning interpretation. The notion of urban design rooted in prototypes was replaced in his perception by an understanding of the city as ecology.

Banham's understanding of ecology was shaped by Patrick Geddes' statements on the city in the region. Banham added a further tier of cultural artefacts and everyday utensils to the strata envisaged in the nineteenth century for examining ecological systems, namely geography, community and economics.[77] Banham identified four distinct regions in Los Angeles – which he called "Surfurbia," "Autopia," "Plains of Id" and "Foothills" – as ecologies, reading their characterisation out of the social processes and functional connections on the spot. In addition, he cited the surfboard and the car as typical artefacts that shed light on the local population's lifestyles and attitude towards life.[78] The city was therefore not conceived in terms of interactions between strata observed in abstract terms, for example societal processes, environmental conditions and economic activities, in Banham's thinking, for his definition was guided much more by everyday activities and consequently by city dwellers per se. The concept of social ecology is therefore reinterpreted in Banham's descriptions of Los Angeles, transforming it into the broader notion of the ecology of the city, in which the entire lived culture of the city's inhabitants fed into a systematic mode of viewing urban space.[79] Viewed from this perspective, cultural phenomena are not explained solely by the history of the city and the built structure that has grown up within it, but are also determined by the processes and events that unfold in the cityscape, a phenomenon Banham explored with reference to new technical artefacts.[80] The architecture of ecology thus became part of what Banham dubbed the "history of the immediate future".[81] In keeping with this conceptional interpretation of the city, Cedric Price had characterised his design approach at the IDEA Conference as a "constructive use of the immediate future".[82]

Architecture of Ecology

Price's conception of architecture couched as a system took on new political relevance in the early 1970s. The 1973 oil crisis and the first United Nations Resolution on environmental policy in 1972 heralded a paradigm shift in planning, putting system-oriented thinking at the heart of design disciplines. This shift found symbolic expression in the images of Earth transmitted live on television from the Apollo 8 mission on 24th December 1968. This vista of the planet brought together the idea of emancipation through technology and a sense of confidence that humans could master their surroundings. However, the chance to view the blue planet from this perspective also heralded a mood-shift in the early 1970s, rooted in an awareness of Earth's fragile equilibrium as humans' habitat.

A system-focused view of the environment gained ground, drawing inspiration from the first conference on environmental protection, held in Stockholm, and the Club of Rome Report; systems theory consequently became a planning instrument and provided a new moral model for a just world order. The UN General Assembly Resolution 2398 convening the Stockholm conference noted that "the relationship between man and his environment is undergoing profound changes in the wake of modern scientific and technological developments".[83] The Resolution underscored that, although science and technology offered unprecedented opportunities, the consequences of rapid technical progress were the long-lasting and accelerated destruction of important attributes of the human environment.[84] Socio-political objectives such as diversity, participation and co-determination were to be secured as central values of a new order within society, with support from systems theory and the technical tools it offered. An overarching concept thus emerged in global politics, linking the quality of the built environment to the moral and political issue of a new culture of society.

In the context of this socio-political turning-point, the 1968 explosion at Ronan Point in London took on real symbolic relevance for architecture as a discipline. The results produced by the second phase of New Town construction had led to a dramatic upsurge in public criticism of urban reconstruction since the 1950s. This widespread discontent was directly linked to the construction methods used for serialised production of mass housing, such as the Large Panel System that London County Council (LCC) deployed for high-rise residential blocks. In May 1968, when a gas explosion led an entire corner of a high-rise block of flats at Ronan Point to collapse, causing three deaths, public anger fed into a broad-based rejection of Functionalist planning. Modernist construction styles were categorised in public discourse as synonymous with dehumanised centralised government planning policies and, more generally, with the negative consequences of societal modernisation processes.[85] One commentary in Architectural Design described the loss of public confidence in urban planning using one New Town, Cumbernauld, as an example: " [...] people in chatshows now dare to openly criticise the packed-ice pedestrian plazas of Cumbernauld; high rise living is held to be conducive to madness, and today the phrase 'modern architecture' has a lot to answer for [...]." The emerging paradigm shift had a direct impact on attempts amongst students to steer a different course in architecture: "Ronan Point fell down and ecology was invented."[86]

Younger architects in particular hoped that looking at the environment in terms of systems theory would ensure that relationships between humans and their environment became established across the board.[87] However, differences of opinion arose when it came to elaborating the details of the new paradigm of ecology in practice, with disagreement for example about the extent to which new technologies could make a productive contribution to this process. In addition, the challenge of fleshing out the abstract model of ecology with tangible design content also had to be addressed: "Facing architects, designers and planners is the almost impossible task of making that artificial environment integrated with nature within man. And for that we have no book, no rules, and architectural forms or details are of little if any help."[88]

In his education-based projects Price had already pre-empted the re-orientation of his discipline in the light of the crisis in modern architecture and the ensuing new challenges. Building on his reflections on systems theory and the idea of the environment, he developed this incipient stance into a fully fledged independent approach: an architecture of ecology. This also entailed interdisciplinary work with other authors. In the wake of Reyner Banham's extension of the ecology concept to include cultural artefacts, Gordon Pask's work on architecture and cybernetics also incorporated ideas on mass culture and society into a view of architectural production based on systems theory. Asserting that "the construction of a building is a system", Pask interpreted construction as entailing development of a social system too: structuring and interpreting not just material resources but also humans' relations to their environment and hence the social organisation of space.[89] From this perspective the architect acted within a system of social relationships and had to take up the challenge of striking a balance between this system and conditions in the natural environment by means of the buildings he constructed.

Fun Palace Playground

In his 1974 Fun Palace Playground design Cedric Price applied this new perspective to an architectural project for the first time. In this 1974 scheme, devised in the context of his involvement with the Fun Palace Trust's activities, he drew up the blueprint for the annual Easter Fair that Joan Littlewood organised with her theatre company in Stratford East to provide financial support to the local community projects.

Numerous other grassroots initiatives with similar goals, such as the Inter-Action Group, had also sprung up in London around this time. That gave rise to a heterogeneous "alternative" scene in early 1970s London, experimenting with models of community-based self-organisation in neighbourhood projects such as city farms and theatre initiatives. In this ambience, the Easter Fair blended political statement and personal commitment with a pop-style event and a street party.

9
10
11

Although a full-blown architectural design was not planned for the Fun Palace Playground, Price did produce plans for stage architecture for the festival site in front of the theatre.[90] He sketched the site as a three-dimensional space to be filled with activities, dividing it up into three horizontal zones. He defined the open festival square, with its layout of entry points, seats and stage, as the first zone. In the second zone, which began roughly three metres above the ground, he indicated all the technical and architectural elements that could be used to influence the site's spatial characteristics: the loudspeakers and stage floor, the film projector and lighting equipment. Price had the third zone start at a height of about six metres and defined it as encompassing the entire festival site. Although the cinema screen was the only design element that extended to this height, this third level was very important to Price's design, as it encompassed all the environmental factors, such as the acoustics, as well as lighting and shade at the festival site, in terms of their impact on the adjacent neighbourhood. As Price noted in his design sketches, the zones selected for the site design correlated with the influence of the fun fair on the neighbouring houses, which he wished to encompass within his plans by viewing the site as a three-dimensional field of activities and interactions. He thus mapped the system-oriented sphere of influence for the elements he designed, considering not just their positioning on the site but the much broader radius of their impact. Price viewed the site's design as an intervention in an existing system of relationships within the urban district. He noted on the edge of one of his sketches: "the reason for zoning is to encourage mutual benefit of all elements both inside & outside the 'site'."[91] The division of the spaces into superimposed functional zones (of the kind typically used in urban planning) meant that the various attributes of utilisation, and thus the open, multi-layered relations between humans and their surroundings, were set at the heart of this architectonic design.

This highlighting of multifunctionality and simultaneity as new qualities of functional zoning is underscored in a second comment in the margins of a drawing, which Price illustrated with a pyramid: "No clever monument of which only one use can be found at any one time."[92] Alluding to the Independent Group, which had referenced the 1913/1914 Werkbund discussion by selecting the pyramid as a symbol of the Functionalist city's planning hierarchy,[93] Price defined his design as a new monument of a Postmodernist urban planning order in which eliminating hierarchies would lead to an open, diverse architecture of ecology. In this respect, he also picked up on a debate that had been unfolding in the USA since the mid-1960s; it addressed the monument in fledgling pop culture, with Charles Moore for example identifying the new monuments of experience-driven society in collective loci such as Disneyland or the Los Angeles Freeway.[94] Positioning his approach within the context of this debate, Price emphasised the programmatic dimension of his design. He viewed the festival site, where constructed elements were kept to a minimum, as a collective place and a monument, that had an important status in the city's public consciousness due to its utilisation, even though it was so open-ended and deployed such a wide range of aesthetic idioms. In contrast to Charles Moore, Price found it important to highlight that the form of the space was not a backdrop for experiences, but emerged solely as a result of users' activities. Making his architecture adaptable to various situations took precedence for Price over a mise-en-scène of the space.[95] Consequently, a monument did not need to generate an admonitory or memorial air by deploying formal design references to history or a cultural tradition.[96] Instead, the monument simply celebrated visitors' activities, becoming in Price's eyes a monument to social agency, the present or, to use sociological terminology, performance.[97]

12 In this spirit the Fun Palace Playground also symbolised the creation of a personal space of experience that only assumed its form as a result of the event.[98]

McAppy: Architecture as Intervention in a Social System

The focus on the social organisation of space in Price's designs becomes particularly clear in the McAppy project, which Price developed from 1973 to 1976 for his friend, British building contractor Alistair McAlpine.[99] Rather than being primarily concerned with an architectural design, the project concentrated on examining the conditions under which such designs come into being. Traditionally, organisation of work on the building site fell within the remit of the architect. Post-war industrialisation of the construction business meant that issues relating to the construction process and quality assurance were however delegated to other professions. In 1972, the first national construction workers' strike revealed grave shortcomings in working conditions in the British building industry, leading to considerable economic and political pressure for changes in the sector.[100] Alistair McAlpine therefore commissioned Cedric Price to investigate his company's working conditions and make proposals to improve productivity and the quality of work.

Price's close relations with the trade unions, his membership of the Labour Party and his close friendship with influential British trade union official Norman Willis made him an ideal adviser for the firm, able to mediate between employee concerns and the company's interests. In this context, Price conceptualised work as a process of exchange influenced by factors such as employee satisfaction and safety in the workplace. On this basis, he viewed the building site as a system of spatial and social relationships, and endeavoured, with the aid of empirical social research, to glean insights into the reciprocal influences between the organisation of work in practical and spatial terms and the tools deployed to handle this.

3

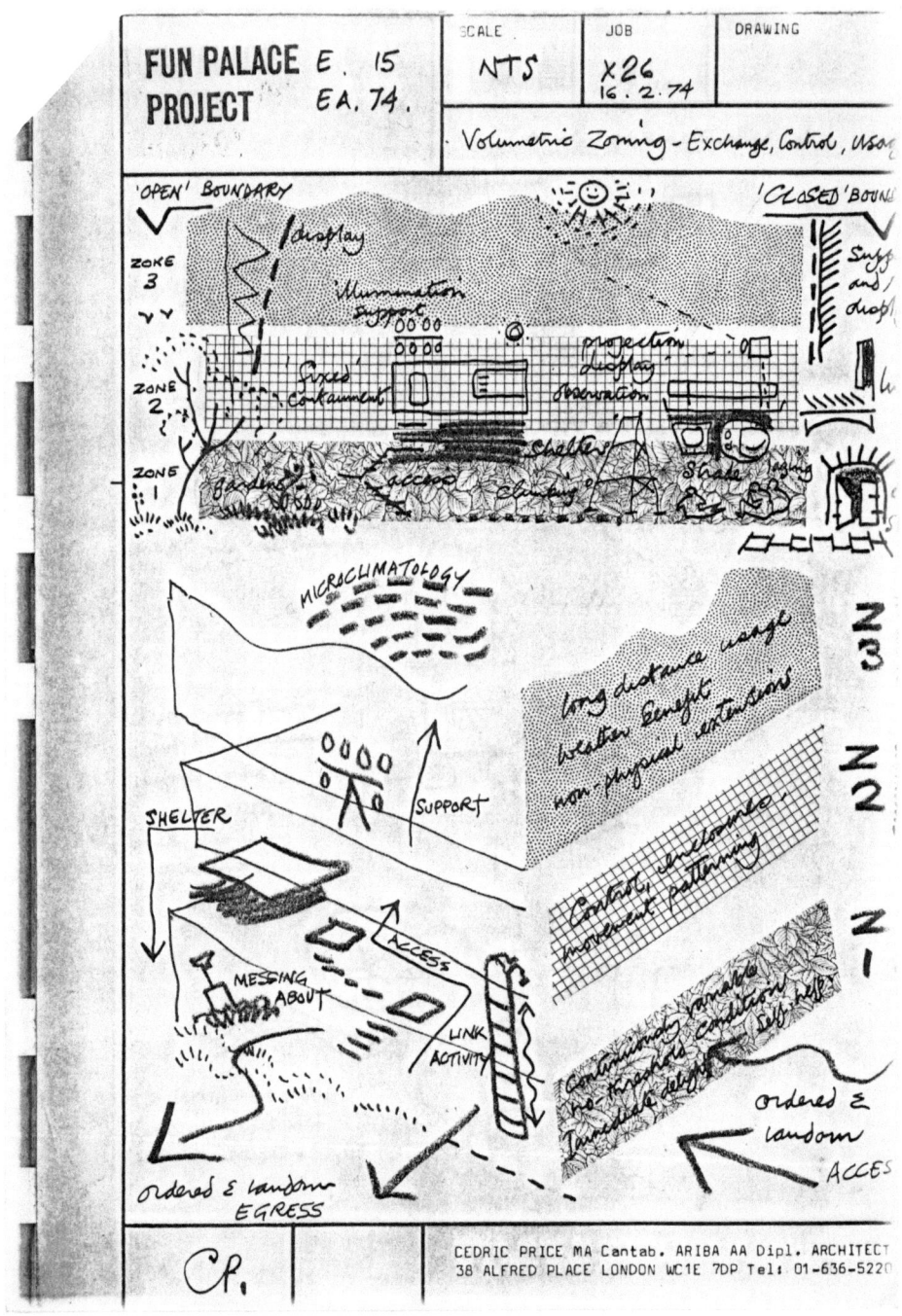

9 Cedric Price, "X26: Fun Palace
Project", Easter Fair, sketch, 1974.

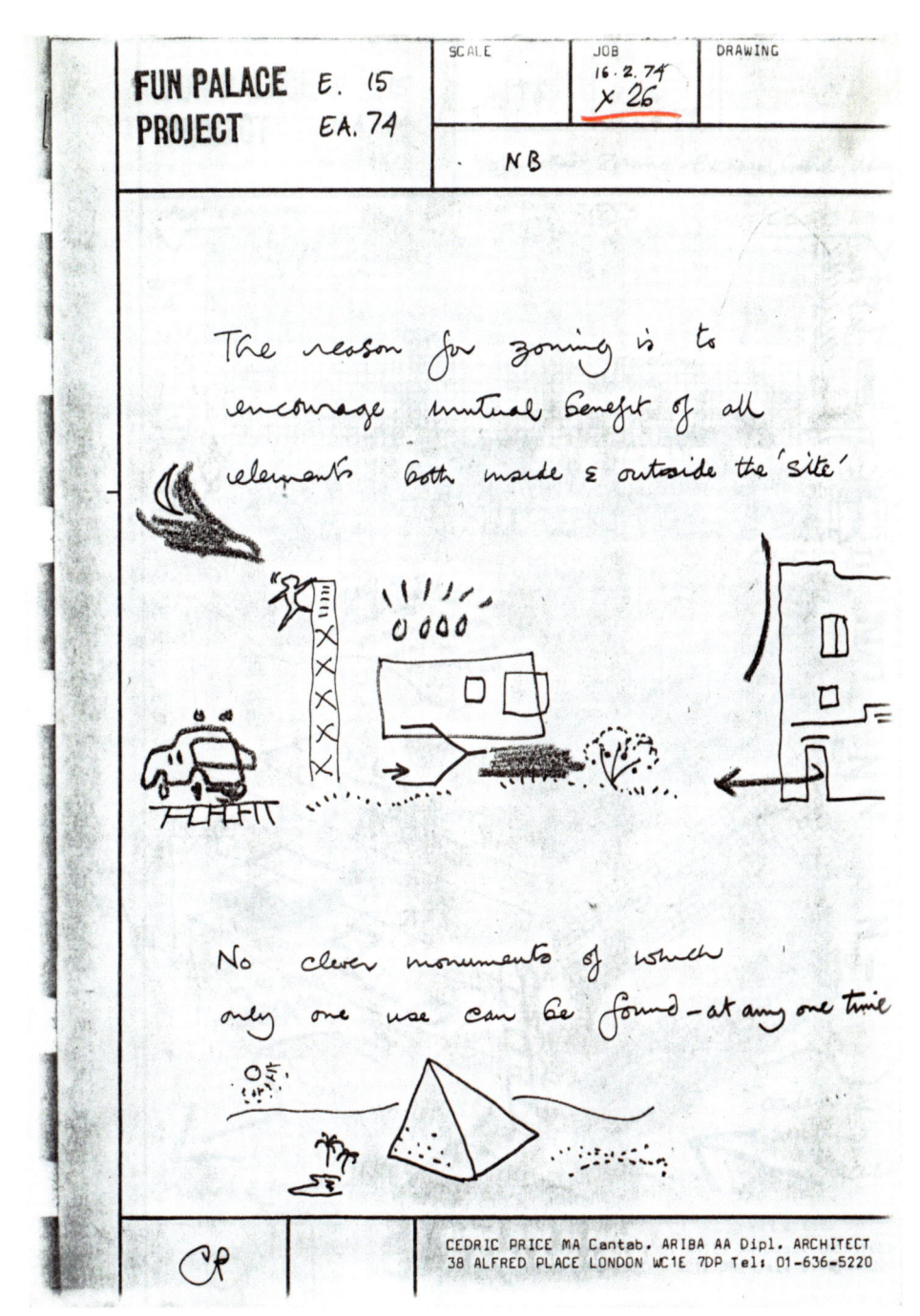

The reason for zoning is to encourage mutual benefit of all elements both inside & outside the 'site'

No clever monuments of which only one use can be found — at any one time

10   Cedric Price, "Volumetric Zoning: Fun Palace Project", Easter Fair, sketch, 1974.

11 Cedric Price, "Possibilities G: Fun Palace Project", South Bank, collage, ca. 1983.

In March 1973, Price began to devise a strategy for the requisite restructuring measures in conjunction with company management.[101] As he subsequently emphasised in his project report, he saw the firm assuming a pioneering national role thanks to this study, as the proposed improvements sent a more general message to the construction industry and the unions. Industrialisation meant the building industry increasingly required skilled workers, which meant that working conditions and the way that work was organised also had to adapt to changed market demands. Price therefore saw the project as a chance to develop recommendations for national quality standards while simultaneously improving the quality of the company's work.[102] To that end he distinguished between three levels of influence on which the firm could act: improving organisation in the workplace, re-arranging the workflow and providing support to the workforce. He was convinced that each of these categories offered an opportunity to restructure the firm "from the bottom up".

Price was convinced that restructuring the work flow would boost each worker's output and consequently professionalise the firm's work. "Shop-floor" influence was for example to be used to reduce conflicts between management and the workforce, cut sick leave and boost staff motivation and identification with the firm.[103] In conjunction with McAlpine, Price therefore developed a system-oriented company representation, encompassing mutual dependency and a conception of work as a process influenced by parameters that extended beyond economic issues to include psychological and physiological aspects, such as health and job satisfaction. The yardstick for the firm's productivity was therefore to be not just unit labour costs but rather how well workplace relations functioned. In the confidential minutes of one meeting Price noted: "A[listair] accepts people will no longer work to make him rich, but will support him if his presence makes them rich."[104]

In Cedric Price's view the backdrop to the ideas he developed entailed a sense of trust in a form of corporate development that would optimise profits solely through incentives and motivation. McAlpine shared this liberal attitude with Price, although each represented a very different form of liberalism. Price's attitude was coloured by his family's political background[105] and took its cue from nineteenth-century Socialist liberalism.[106] McAlpine in contrast adopted a "neo-liberal" stance, popularised in the 1950s by Milton Friedman or Friedrich von Hayek's economic theories.[107] Both attitudes could seemingly coexist happily in the McAppy project.

Price's examination covered only the London district for which Alistair McAlpine was personally responsible. As the firm was keen to see rapid improvements in the labour situation, a number of simple measures could be implemented after just a few months.[108] After an initial phase of field research on the company's building sites, analyses of workplace behaviour and amenities were conducted, and the first proposals for solutions were drawn up. Possible scenarios for restructuring were to be developed on this basis.[109] Price suggested constructional, organisational and technological measures related to equipment and amenities, which were subsequently tested for a year in real-world working

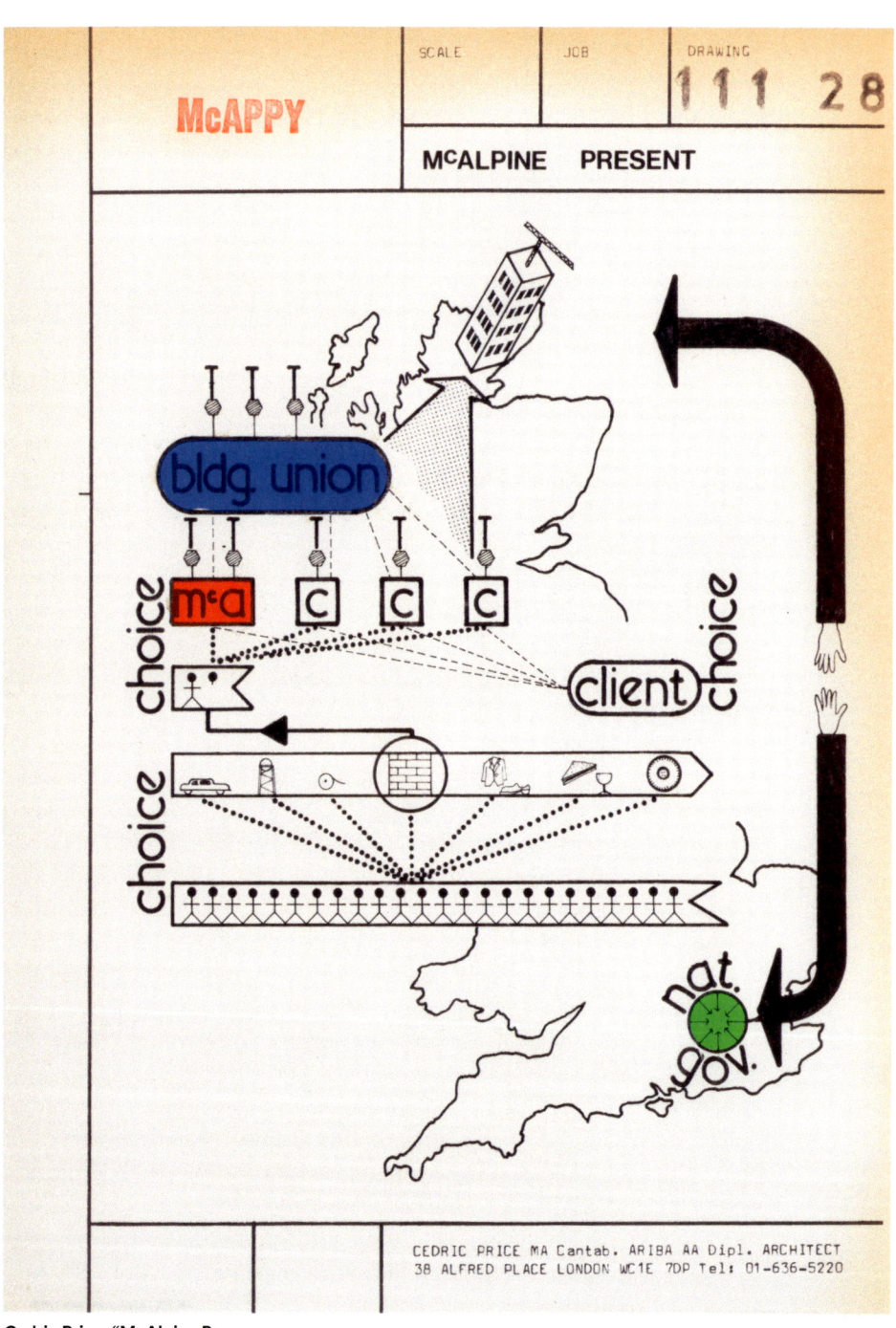

12 Cedric Price, "McAlpine Present", organisational diagram, 1974.

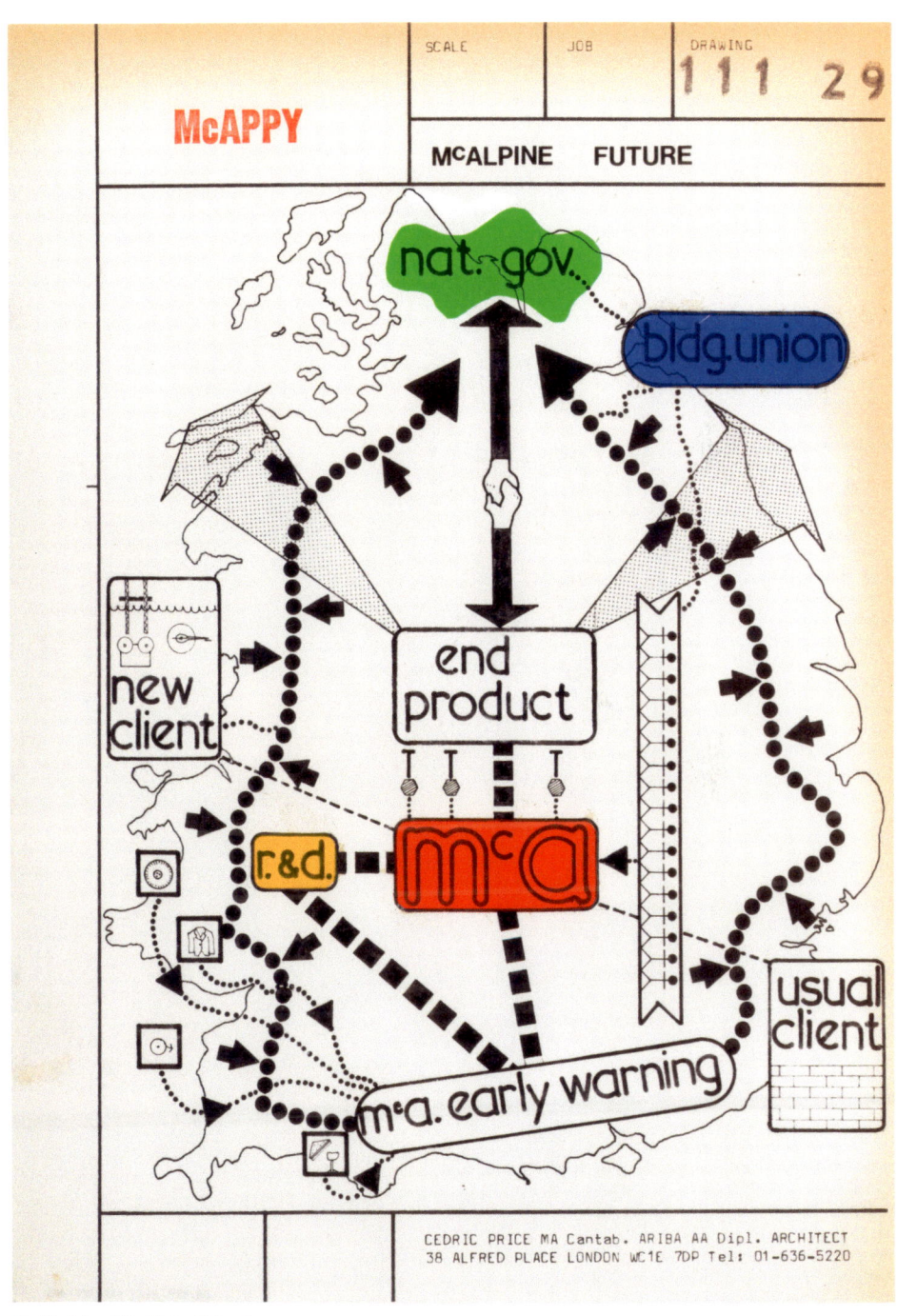

13   Cedric Price, "McAlpine Future",
organisational diagram, **1974**.

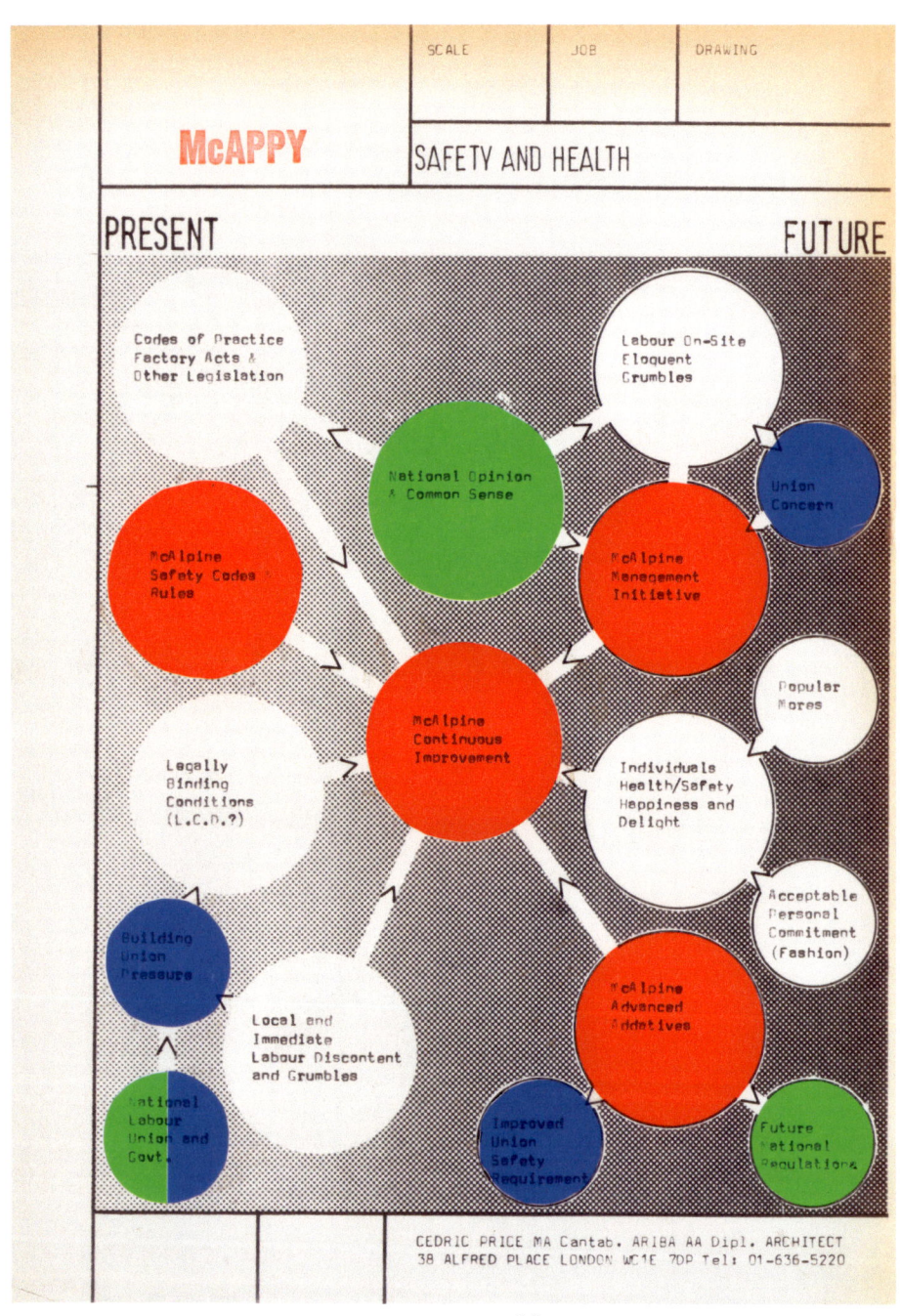

14   Cedric Price, "Safety and Health", organisational diagram, 1974.

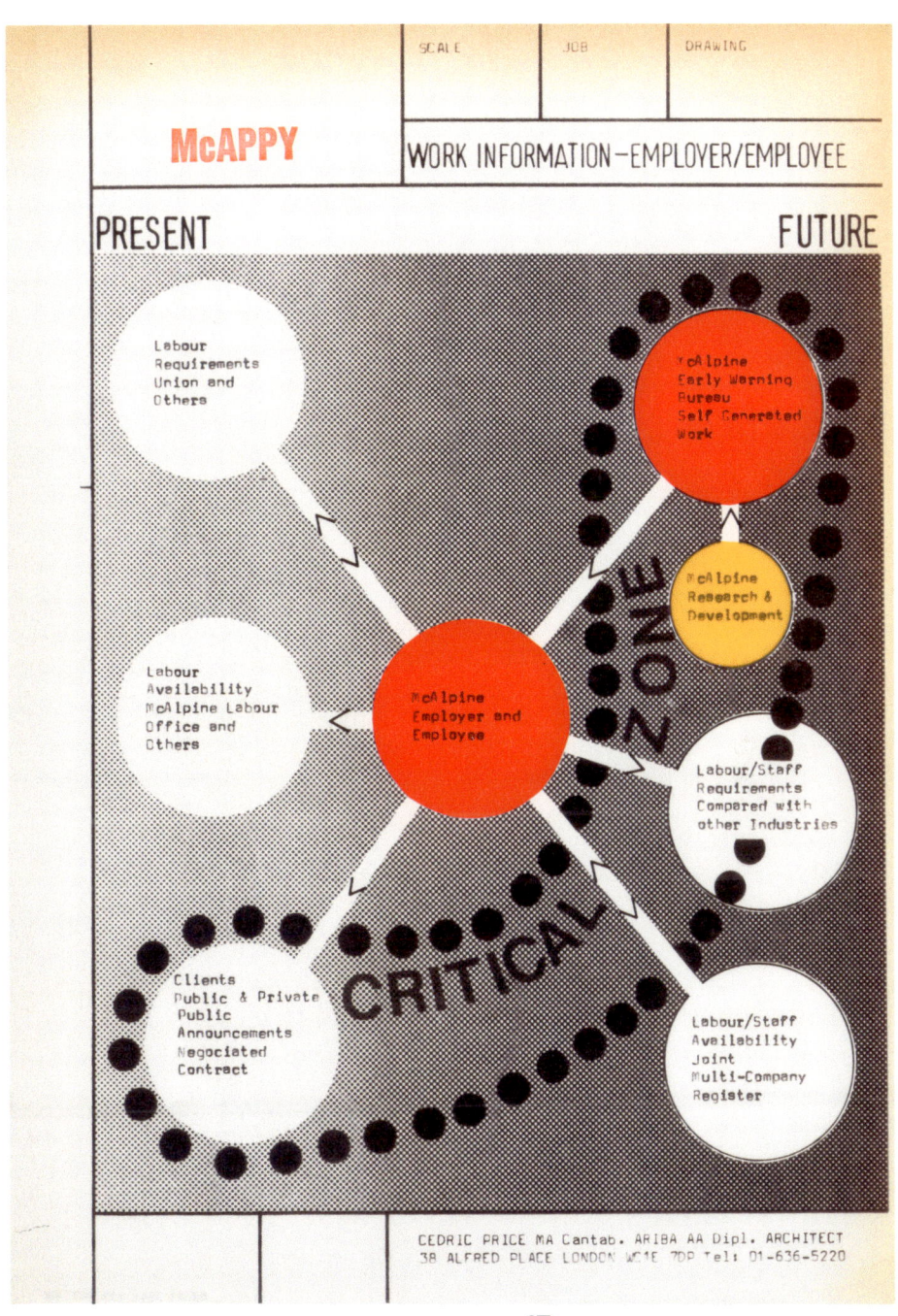

15 Cedric Price, "Work Information", organisational diagram, 1974.

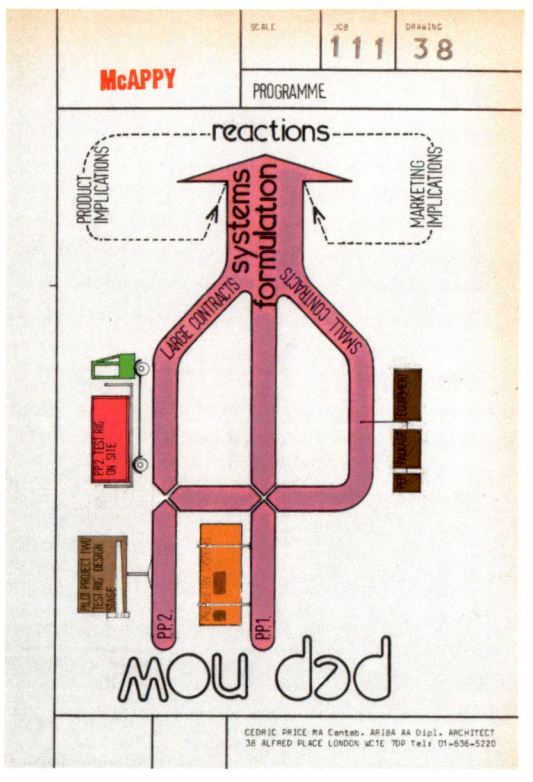

16 Cedric Price, "Programme Pep Now", organisational diagram, **1974**.

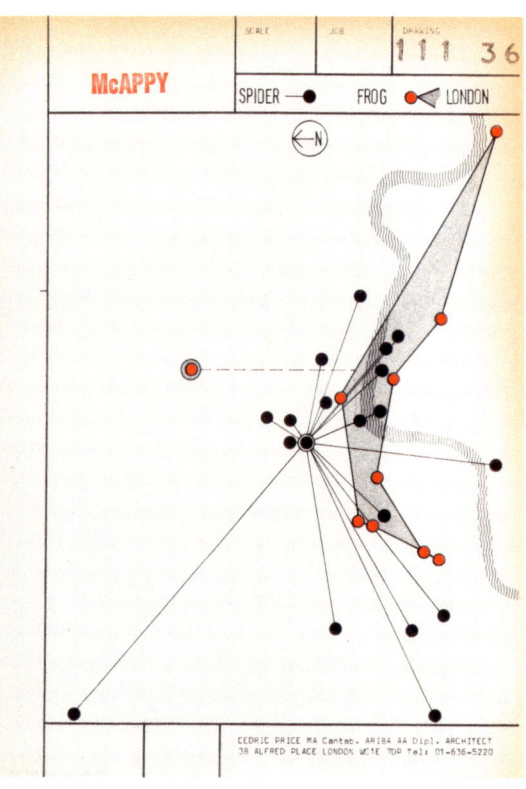

17 Cedric Price, "Spider/Frog", organisational diagram, **1974**.

conditions on a building site. In this pilot study Price sought to implement detailed constructional and organisational proposals and test their viability in practice.[110] He recorded progress in reports and organisational diagrams, subsequently incorporating the successful interventions into a manual and a list of measures. The manual constituted the actual product generated by this project. Alongside directly construction-related issues, it also tackled the introduction of new processes and organisational workflows – for example, continuous monitoring to secure quality assurance and improved safety in the workplace – and brought about fundamental changes in the firm's corporate culture.

During the first phase of field research, Price used instruments from the social sciences, such as participatory observations and surveys, to glean insights into the organisational connections and work practices of everyone involved in the construction work.[111] The observations and analysis involved not just Cedric Price but also his brother, David Price, and their colleagues Paul Hyett, Paul Burrows and Don Gray, who visited four building sites regularly over several months.[112] The documentary records made on the spot rapidly revealed a number of obvious problems. Most of the company's building sites for example did not have a room for workers to take breaks. Instead there were only simple lean-to constructions with completely inadequate light and heating. Rubbish lying around, exposed cables and poorly stored construction materials impeded work. The workforce did not have hard hats or other appropriate work clothes. The fences and warning signs used to keep passersby away from the site were also not fit for the purpose. In addition, there was often no first-aid room to give immediate assistance if accidents occurred. The analysis of shortcomings also examined in-house communication and human resources management. It was noted that the organisation of work on the building sites demanded a high degree of mobility: in addition more than thirty workers had to communicate with one foreman, which led to errors in executing the work. A glance at the wage structure also made clear that a McAlpine foreman earned less than a competing firm on the same building site offered. The flaws that emerged in the first investigation of the firm concerned various levels of work organisation but, as Cedric Price noted, contributed overall to making the company inefficient and unattractive. He summed up: "McAppy losing touch at the front."[113]

The improvements Price suggested tackled the building site's functional amenities and organisation as well as corporate structures, in-house communication and contractual agreements.[114] To ensure high-quality work, Cedric Price proposed a further training programme and a company pension scheme to help retain well-trained staff.[115] He developed two programmes to address functional facets of construction site organisation, which targeted work routines and spatial processes on the building site. His Portable Enclosures Programme (PEP) was aimed at enhancing spatial organisation on building sites through appropriate site infrastructure, the introduction of stackable building containers and workflow coordination.[116] Price focused on developing the spatial system as it offered scope for dynamic adaptation of the building site set-up in response to company imperatives and workers' needs.[117] The proposed system

CONTRACT   : ANGEL COURT, OFFICE DEVELOPMENT

LOCATION   : THROGMORTON STREET, LONDON EC1

DURATION   : 4½ YEARS : DECEMBER 1973 - MAY 1978

IN FEBRUARY 1974 McAPPY INVOLVEMENT AT ANGEL COURT COMMENCED.
THIS WAS AFTER INITIAL McA SITE OCCUPATION.

HOWEVER, BECAUSE OF DELAYS IN WORK COMMENCEMENT, IT WAS POSSIBLE
TO INFLUENCE SITE PLANNING AND THE FOLLOWING PAGES DESCRIBE THE RESULTS.

THIS EXTRACT FROM THE 'ANGEL COURT STORY', DESCRIBES A PART OF THE
McAPPY APPROACH TO SITE ORGANISATION AND EQUIPMENT.

THE FULL McAPPY PROGRAMME OF RESEARCH AND RECOMMENDATION IS DESCRIBED
IN McAPPY VOLUMES ONE AND TWO (JAN. '74 & JUNE '75).

IN

OUT

COPTHALL AVENUE

CHECKER

SITE ACCESS FOR VEHICLES

RECEIVED 2 8 FEB 1974

SIR ROBERT McALPINE & SONS LIMITED,
ANGEL COURT DEVELOPMENT

McAPPY

Cedric Price MA Cantab. RIBA AA Dipl. Architect
38 Alfred Place London WC1E 7DP Tel:01-636 5220

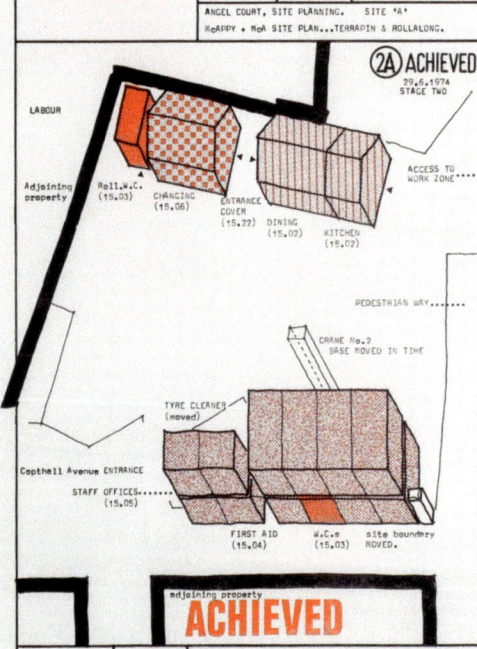

SCALE	JOB	DRAWING
....	111	192

ANGEL COURT, SITE PLANNING. SITE 'A'.
McAPPY + McA SITE PLAN...TERRAPIN & ROLLALONG.

McAPPY

(2A) ACHIEVED
29.6.1974
STAGE TWO

LABOUR

Adjoining property

Roll.W.C.
(15.03)

CHANGING
(15.06)

ENTRANCE
COVER
(15.22)

DINING
(15.02)

KITCHEN
(15.02)

ACCESS TO
WORK ZONE****

PEDESTRIAN WAY........

CRANE No.2
BASE MOVED IN TIME

TYRE CLEANER
(moved)

Copthall Avenue ENTRANCE

STAFF OFFICES........
(15.05)

FIRST AID   W.C.s   site boundary
(15.04)   (15.03)   MOVED.

adjoining property

ACHIEVED

REF:
CP DRG:079
29.3.1974

N

CEDRIC PRICE MA Cantab. ARIBA AA Dipl. ARCHITECT
38 ALFRED PLACE LONDON WC1E 7DP Tel: 01-636-5220

McAPPY

SCALE	JOB	DRAWING
......	111	195

ANGEL COURT. SITE PLANNING. SITE 'A'.
McAPPY + McA SITE PLAN, TERRAPIN & ROLLALONG.

(3A) ACHIEVED
12.10.1974

DRYING/
CHANGING.
(15.06)

Roll WC
(15.03)

KITCHEN
(15.02)

DINING
(15.02)

STORE (15.07)

WALKWAY

STORAGE ZONE.

SITE WALKWAY

CRANE No.2.

OFFICES
(15.05)

PED.
WAY

BN. SHOP.
(15.09/10)
STORAGE
OVER.

Copthall Avenue ENTRANCE.

STAFF OFFICES
(15.05)

FIRST AID   WC's   site boundary
(15.04)   (15.03)

PEDESTRIAN WAY

adjoining property

ACHIEVED

REF:
CP DWGS:
057 & 079

N

CEDRIC PRICE MA Cantab. ARIBA AA Dipl. ARCHITECT
38 ALFRED PLACE LONDON WC1E 7DP Tel: 01-636-5220

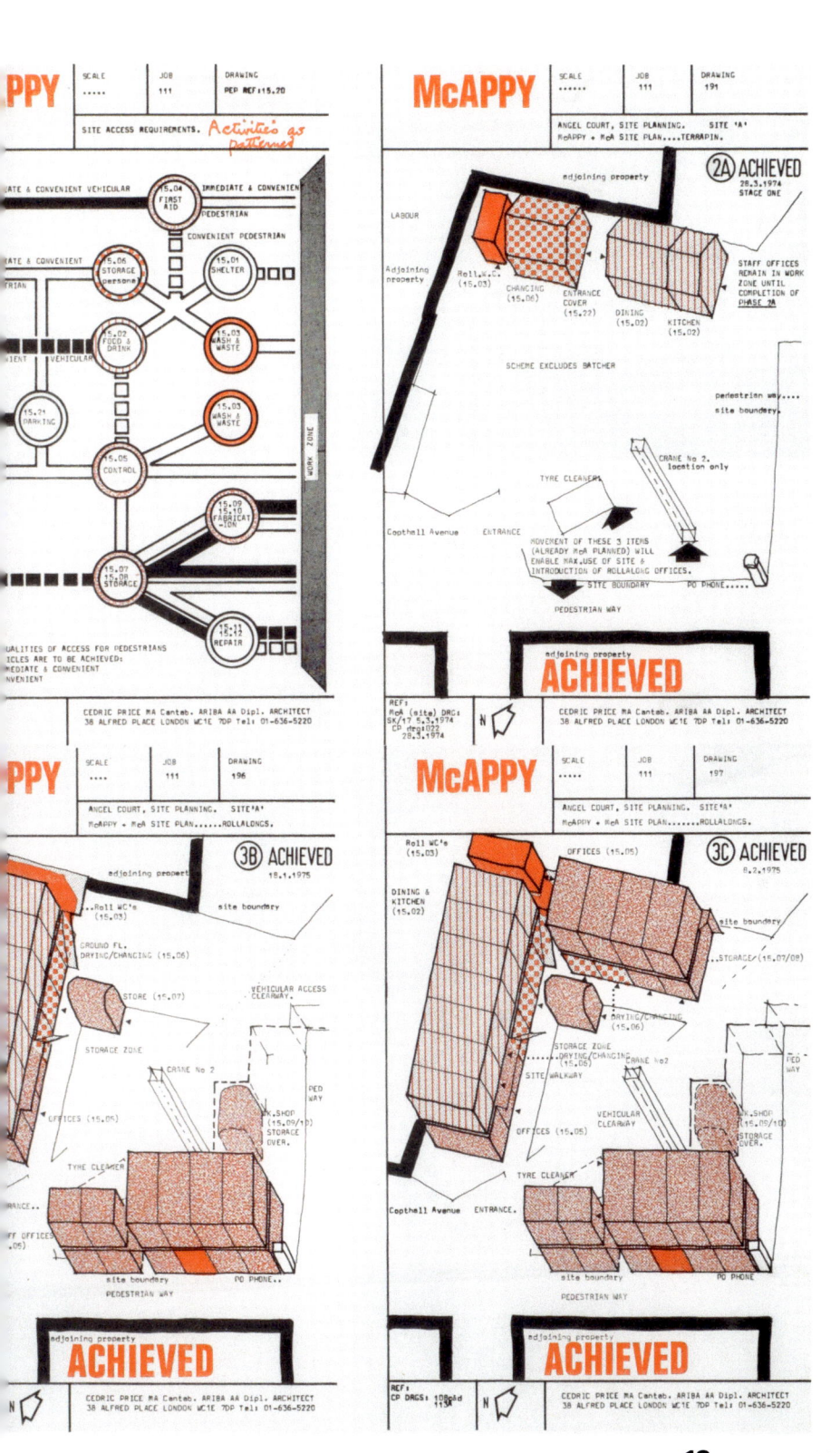

18 Cedric Price, McAppy, "The Angel Court Story: An Extract", ca. 1978, project presentation, part 1, ca. 1978.

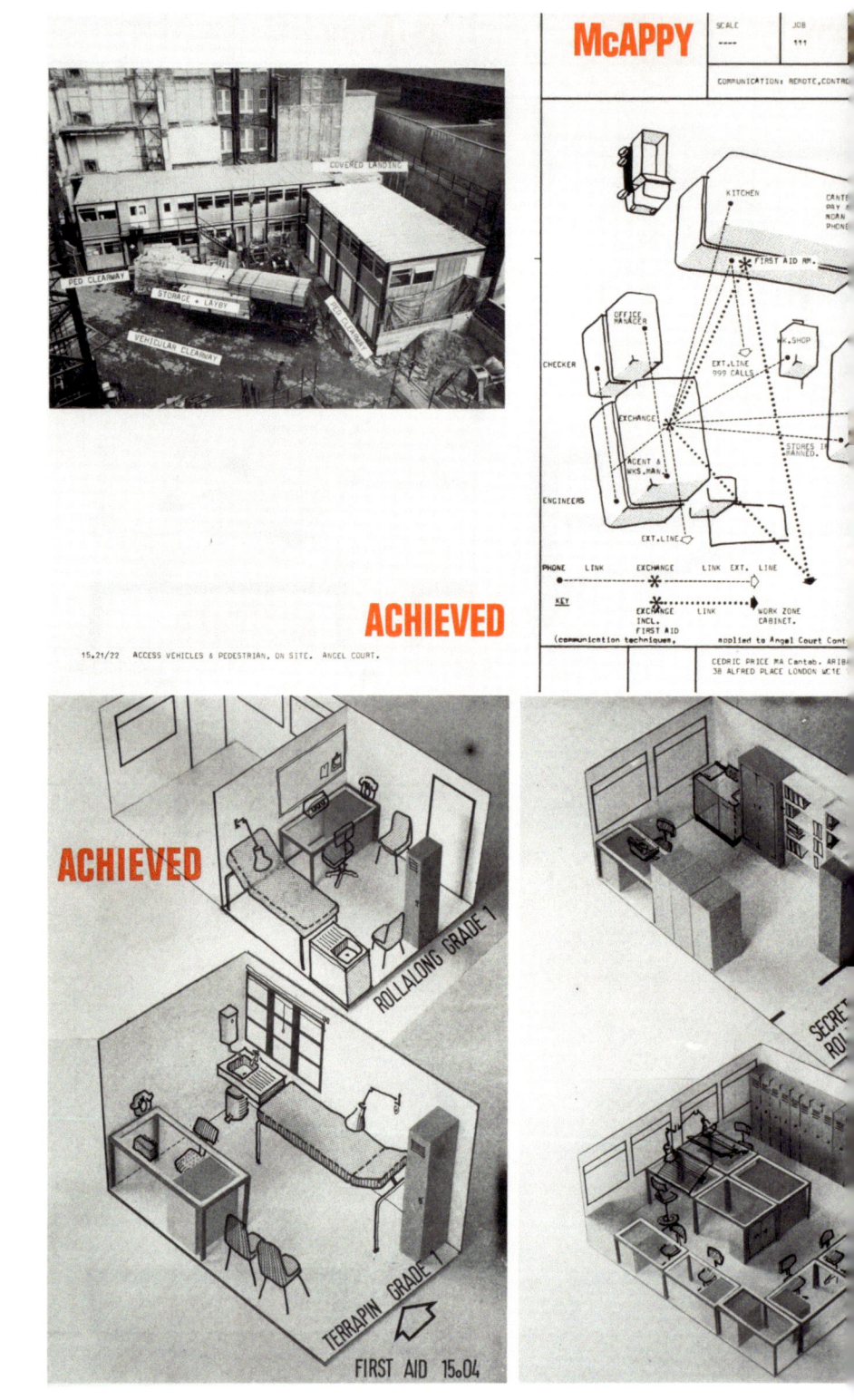

McAPPY

SCALE	JOB
----	111

COMMUNICATION: REMOTE, CONTROL

ACHIEVED

15.21/22 ACCESS VEHICLES & PEDESTRIAN, ON SITE. ANGEL COURT.

ACHIEVED

ROLLALONG GRADE 1

TERRAPIN GRADE 1

FIRST AID 15.04

SECRET ROI

CEDRIC PRICE MA Cantab. ARIBA
38 ALFRED PLACE LONDON WC1E

19 Cedric Price, McAppy, "The Angel Court Story: An Extract", project presentation, part 2, ca. **1978**.

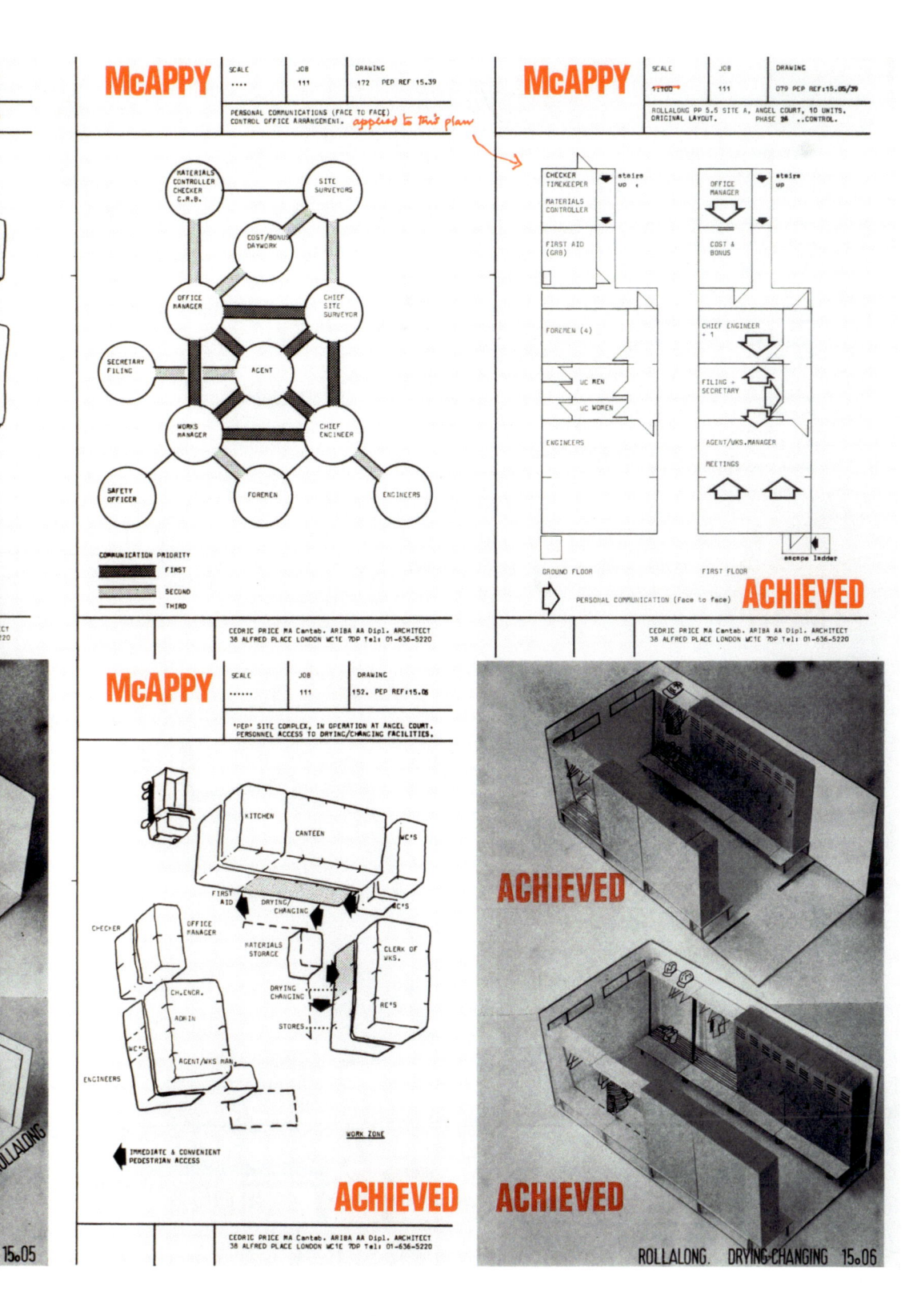

of prefabricated modules from the firm Rollalong could be stacked three storeys high using a steel frame developed by Frank Newby.[118] The second programme addressed the physiological and psychological aspects of working conditions, and encompassed measures on safety in the workplace and improved workflows. It was dubbed PAL, an acronym based on the terms "Protective Clothing", "Alimentation" and "Learning". Within the framework of this programme Price suggested for example introducing company work gear, with clothing specifically designed for this purpose.[119] He hoped to improve workers' morale and motivation by providing appropriate catering systems, changing rooms and showers in the workplace, which he planned to integrate into the mobile container system. Cedric Price thus came up with a very simple approach, tailor-made to respond to the most basic human needs, and broke down this design strategy into equally simple functional measures: "[…] good food, encouragement and dignity […] changing – lockers – showers."[120]

The systemic analysis Price presented to company management in his January 1974 project report viewed the building site as a functional system whose shortcomings could be identified and remedied through small-scale interventions that targeted amenities and workflows. Using the terms "social life" and "structural life", Price divided his proposals for reorganisation of the work into two categories.[121] The intervention level he classed as addressing "social life" primarily included the PAL programme's temporary measures. In contrast, the "structural life" category encompassed measures relating to all the social processes and structures that were so hard to change, for example long-established company work routines and communication processes, as well as the ways in which the space on the building site was organised.[122]

18
19 From February 1974 on, Price concentrated on implementing the PEP and PAL programmes on a functioning building site at London's Angel Court.[123] In his view, the pilot project was a way to alter work processes on the site through built and organisational interventions. The PEP programme aimed to create an appropriate framework for these changes by providing premises for a canteen, first aid unit, offices and changing rooms whose number, configuration and amenities could vary as a function of particular building phases.[124] This "bottom-up" spatial organisation was to be supplemented by the PAL programme, in which the logic underlying the design for the content of the new spaces would spring from utilisation, in other words, "from within". In his studies for the fittings, Price therefore developed a standard layout that could be adapted to needs on the spot after running utilisation tests. Price documented the resulting configuration variants in models and photomontages that could be referenced as a potential assortment of options.[125]

His proposals were rooted in sample-based studies directed at comprehending the current scenario at Angel Court. For example, together with his team he analysed the working relationships between Indian foreman Vad Sabharwal and his co-workers.[126] These surveys provided the foundation for structural diagrams in which Price portrayed workers' communicative behaviour as a system of spatial and organisational relationships.[127] Presenting his ideas in the form of abstract structural diagrams, Price subsequently attempted

3

to draw conclusions about functional dependencies within working relationships on the building site, and subsequently to determine the spatial and organisational interventions needed to improve the relevant processes.[128] During the project Price thus investigated for example the configuration of the offices, where best to locate the first-aid room and considered setting up telephone and "radio phone" stations.[129]

20

Price's functional analysis of labour relations on the building site reflected systems technology categories: "control, communication and system."[130] He had taken on board Gordon Pask's systemic approach to the built environment, which accorded a regulatory function to architecture within the social system of work. Price therefore viewed his interventions as fostering a functional dialogue that would allow him to influence use of the offices and building site facilities, as well as work behaviour on the building site. In the light of his nuanced observation of all the functional relations on the building site, each insight called for an independent solution. The broad spectrum of measures he used specifically targeted each flaw he identified, which meant his interventions took on a plethora of forms. The one essential common denominator was that all the measures were not imposed but proposed.

21
22

Price thus assumed for example that the risk of accidents on the building site could only be reduced by considering several issues together, each involving only minor changes to the existing organisational approach. Right at the start of his investigation Price had identified for example several causes for the high incidence of accidents on the building sites, such as lack of work clothing, poor spatial organisation and inadequate catering.[131] In response, he

20 Cedric Price, McAppy, "Angel Court", documentation of building site equipment, ca. 1975.

initiated broader reflections on user behaviour, relating to how the space was organised and used on a daily basis, and touching on issues like work gear, the canteen infrastructure and the meals on offer.[132] Price referred to this mode of combining a range of proposed spatial interventions with improvements in functional sequencing as "access/use location-strategy".[133]

"Diversity and Choice"

In this context Price set great store by ensuring that his planned interventions did not stipulate any particular form of use, but instead opened up new utilisation possibilities. In this light his interventions aimed to present proposals that every worker could accept (or not) as he or she saw fit.[134] Viable solutions in the McAppy project therefore often emerged from detailed observation of user behaviour. Visits to the building sites had for example revealed that accidents such as falls or fires were often caused as workers hung wet clothing over beams and girders to dry due to the lack of drying facilities. Price therefore installed changing rooms and equipped canteens and offices with extra coat hooks.[135] In addition, Price tried to discover during the project why the hard hats in the work gear he had introduced were not worn systematically. Over and above various organisational problems, he found out that many of the unskilled workers, who were migrants from the Indian region of Punjab, were Sikhs.[136] As Sikh customs insist that men must wear a turban in public, it was impossible for these workers to wear a hard hat. Price therefore gave his then co-worker Will Alsop the task of researching suitable materials to produce a hard hat that could be worn together with a turban. In this sense Price tried, using design means, to adjust the labour system on the building site to the workforce's particular needs and cultural practices.

One of the crucial consequences of this attitude was that the effectiveness of the McAppy project interventions could only be appraised once the construction workers had had an opportunity to accept, change or reject these measures. The impact of the interventions Price proposed therefore only became apparent in their practical implementation, necessitating a "monitoring" phase during the project.[137] In the "Non-Plan" manifesto Price had already indicated the importance of monitoring, but the idea of reviewing and adjusting design interventions in his work had not been put into practice until the McAppy project. Implementation of the PAL programme on the building site at Angel Court now allowed him to examine the degree of acceptance and viability of his interventions in practice. Some of his proposals, such as introducing work gloves and clothing with a uniform design, turned out to be impracticable and had to be reconsidered.[138]

Observing cause-and-effect relationships in the McAppy project gave Price a broader understanding of the areas that fell within the architect's remit: this involved much more than simply completing a design, for it also entailed adjusting the project subsequently in response to users' changing needs.

He conceptualised the architect's role as an intervention in the social system of ecology or as a design intervention that impinged on social communications: it was not just about designing a built structure.[139] However, that meant that the effect triggered by architecture could only come into play in a context of self-determined utilisation, for Price saw communication as a voluntary process. This informed selection as a parameter that runs through his projects, as he integrated multiple meanings into his work along with a wide range of different use options. In addition to the pivotal notion of "fun and delight", Price thus singled out the idea of "choice" as the second central concept in his design strategy. Implementing freedom of choice in architecture involved a two-pronged approach for Price. First of all, it entailed designing artefacts, by which he meant everyday utilitarian objects such as work gear, office equipment or the building's layout.[140] The second part of this strategy called for an extended dialogue between the designer, the building and the user to identify possibilities to adapt use: "[...] re-think, re-flect & re-choice as a continuous process [...]."[141]

To keep the ball rolling in this dialogue after the McAppy project's test planning phase, Price introduced a new operative unit for the firm, which included defining various job profiles. It included site control staff linking individual building sites and management in order to foster communication and ensure Price's measures for logistical and safety issues were put into practice.[142] This group was to include a site planner to coordinate the set-up of the building site and the time-schedule for the various construction phases. A site scout was to oversee implementation of these plans and related organisational aspects on the spot. Framing the other interventions, a roving medic was to tackle issues relating to safety in the workplace and preventative health care in the firm.[143] The aim was to trigger a self-regulating process to improve working conditions at McAlpine through a feedback system. To that end, Price included sixteen "low profile actions" in his manual, derived from the Angel Court test project; the site control staff could transpose these to specific scenarios on other building sites. The manual provided guidance on putting these measures into practice, with additional information on possible combinations of interventions, methods to use when introducing them and the time factor during implementation.[144] Yet in the concluding project report Price emphasised that the planning solutions identified in the test phase stemmed from a specific process of adapting to a particular site's imperatives and spatial configuration, making it impossible to transpose the proposed solutions directly to other locations. Any design solution was in his view tied into a communicative process intended to strike a balance between the forces at play. This perspective was entirely in keeping with the systems science notion of the building site as a social system. It meant that the individual measures were not the whole story: the only way to ensure that differing interests and requirements could be regulated independently on the spot was by integrating a communicative process as well.

Echoing the earlier Camden Town project, Price viewed his interventions in the McAppy project as catalysts for a process of change that would be directly rooted in workers' daily lives. The human environment that

3

21 Cedric Price Architects, "Locker/ Drying Facilities", photograph, from: "McAppy Angel Court Story", **1975**.

22 Cedric Price Architects, "Terrapin: Drying/Changing", photography, from: "Mc Appy Angel Court Story", **1975**.

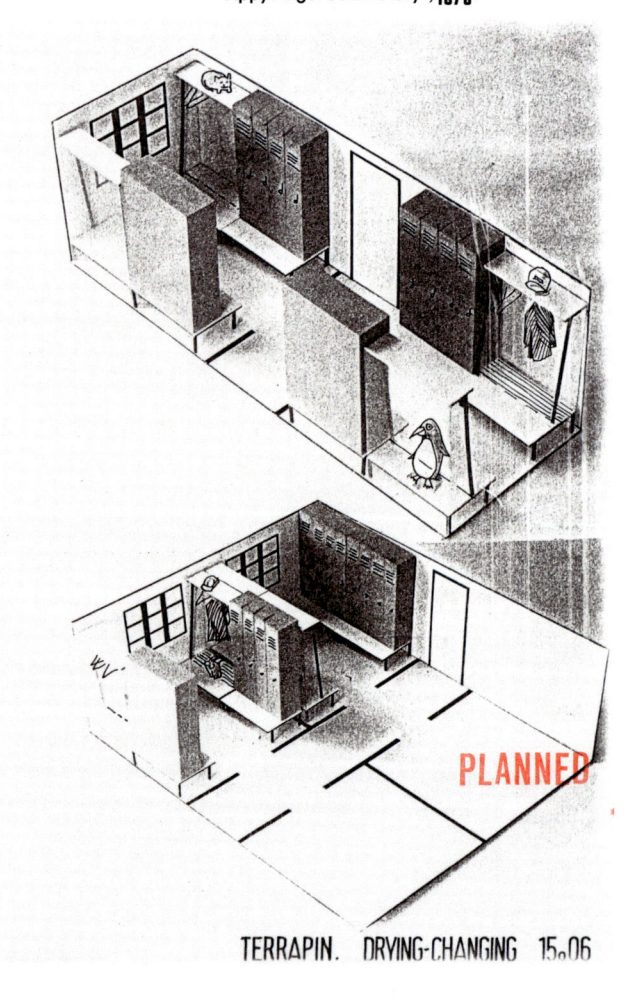

TERRAPIN. DRYING-CHANGING 15.06

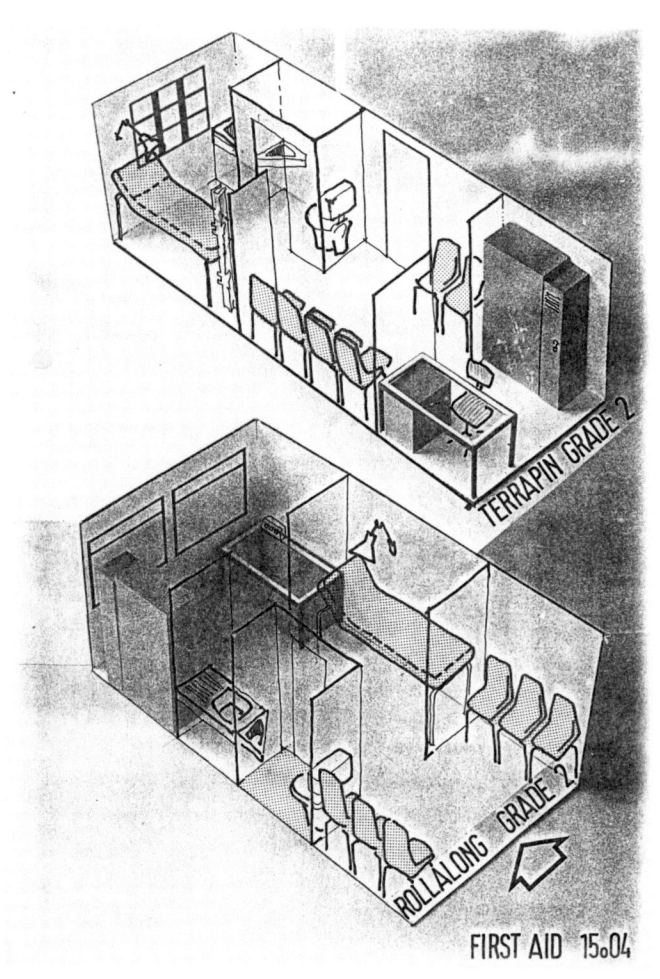

TERRAPIN GRADE 2

ROLLALONG GRADE 2

FIRST AID 15.04

23 Cedric Price Architects, "Portable Enclosures Programme: Example 'First Aid'", photography, from: "McAppy Angel Court Story", **1975**.

24 Cedric Price Architects, "First Aid", photography, from: "McAppy Angel Court Story", **1975**.

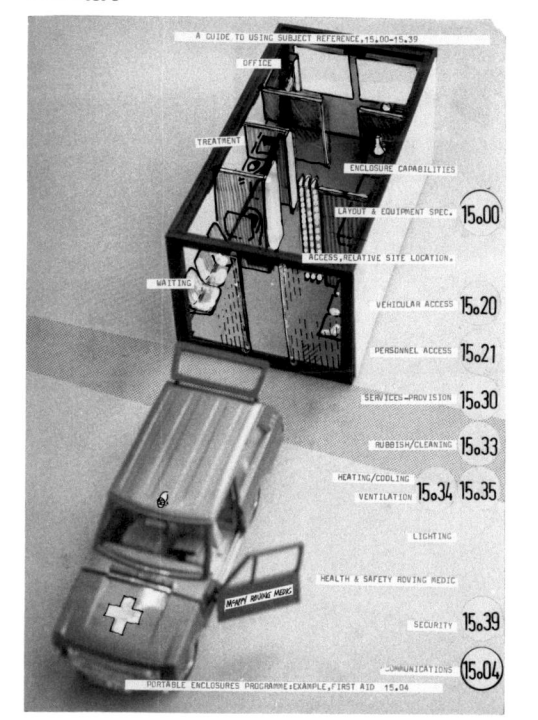

he deployed to expand users' scope for action embraced everyday objects and technical equipment as well as architecture.

In pursuing this transformatory goal, Price's proposals often responded to complex problems with extremely straightforward means.[145] In his view, each intervention had the potential to restructure the firm "from the bottom up". Initiated at grassroots level, the interventions were conceived to have a positive impact on more complex, broader processes in the overall workflow. In the McAppy project Price in this respect set the worker at the heart of all the building site's interactions and processes. The worker became both the central object of study, allowing Price to assess the ramifications of interventions implemented by the firm, and, at the same time, the crucial protagonist, for each worker's actions influence how the building site is organised – and consequently the firm's overall operational structure.[146] Price's strategy here was underpinned by a conviction that micro-level interventions would affect the macro-level of company structure, meaning that small interventions could also impinge on the firm's entire work ethos.[147]

Price's highly particular approach to the project mirrored the sea-change in the conception of work since the Second World War, which also entailed slotting this notion into an evolving socio-cultural frame. Since the advent of industrialisation, work had been appraised solely through the prism of economic categories like productivity and output. Ongoing automation of work processes triggered a growing awareness of human behaviour as a factor influencing efficiency in mechanised work. In 1951 British scientists came up with the term "socio-technological system" to describe the complex interdependencies of man and machine in industrialised labour processes.[148] In addition, in the mid-1960s operations research spawned the concept of micropolitics as a new organisational model for work.[149] British sociologist Tom Burns summarised the importance of informal labour relations in ensuring that employees develop strategic "self-motivation" over and above corporate goals, thus indirectly shaping the organisational system that governs their work.[150] Casting work in a new light as a system of labour relations meant that the quality of social interaction became a further important criterion, alongside productivity, for assessing workers' performance.[151] All these considerations led to a gradual shift in thinking right across society, as psychological and social factors in human behaviour were increasingly recognised as factors influencing the culture of work.[152]

In interpreting his own design work, Price also used affect-related qualities to describe the utilisation-driven attributes of his projects, turning the spotlight on relations between humans and their environment. As leitmotifs in his design approach, "fun" and "delight" represented endeavours to offer users a broader palette of options for active responses, generating a liberating sense of joy and participation.

This aspiration was already the crucial hallmark of Price's work in the Fun Palace Project. However it was only fifteen years later that Price found an opening to articulate his design practice, formulating his signature strategy for architectural design on the basis of the McAppy project. In his system-driven interpretation of architecture as an intervention in processes shaping the human habitat, a book or a clothes hook could constitute an appropriate intervention means in a particular situation. Price in this sense drew on a "material-semiotic method" in which people, ideas and objects enter into a new form of dialogue, thus altering the spectrum of action available to users. It was not the specific configuration details of the McAppy project that made it so unique and so successful: its impact lay in the modus operandi Price developed in striving to make the social attributes of utilisation a central design feature in his work.

Interestingly, Price's approach to design ignored the type of "postmodern" approaches emerging during the same period, such as the ideas formulated by Aldo Rossi in 1966.[153] Instead, by referencing topical sociopolitical issues in his projects, even in the 1970s Price continued to update earlier concepts from Functionalist Modernism. Think for example of the Potteries Thinkbelt project and his reflections in that project on recent British education legislation as a reaction to the ongoing structural transformation of the British economy, and indeed Price's response to new legislation on workplace safety in the McAppy project. In envisioning a design framework for neighbourhood revitalization in the Fun Palace Project and the Inter-Action Centre, Price turned the spotlight on the role of local citizens' initiatives and socially oriented activities, with a particular focus on the neighbourhood. The role of the architect for Price lay in devising design-driven interventions to establish a balance within society by creating access to important resources and extending scope for city dwellers to act. In the same spirit Gordon Pask compared the architect to the Victorian engineers who played such a vital role in defining the modern city's functional infrastructure in the nineteenth century. In this new phase of twentieth-century modernisation, the architect-engineer stepped into the role of developing urban social infrastructure through his buildings, dreaming up architecture that actively shaped possibilities for social exchange, and access to knowledge, education and cultural activities.

1 Cedric Price, "The cube as a hood", sketch, ca. 1977.

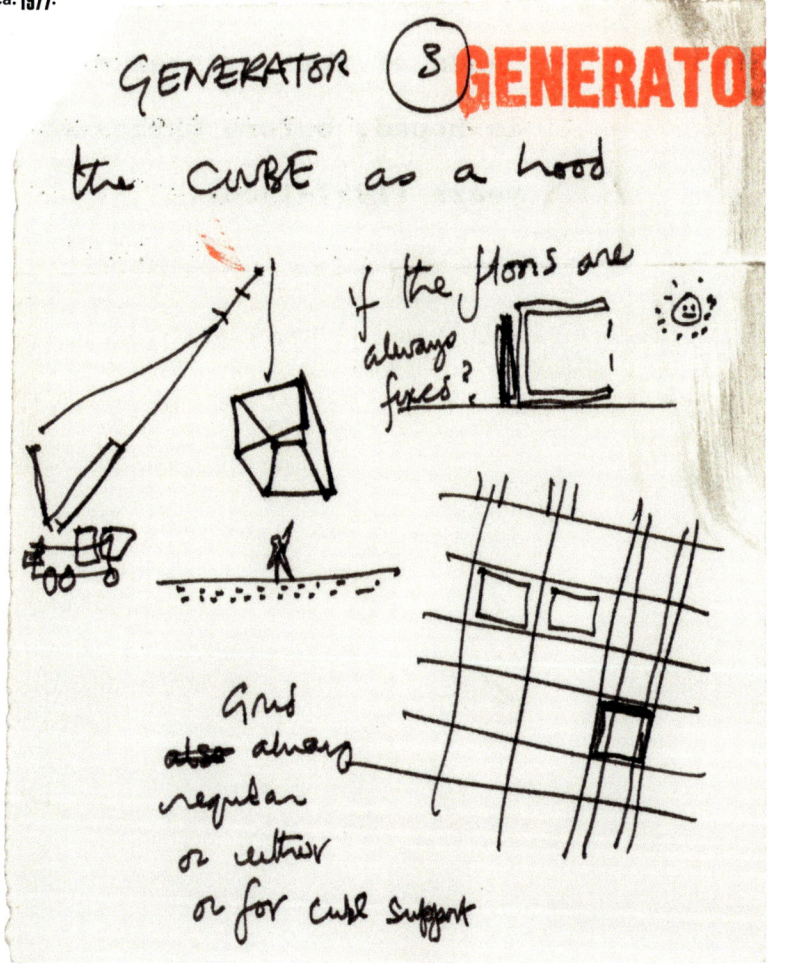

The Architecture
of the Others

4

4

In December 1977, American paper manufacturer, multimillionaire and patron of the arts Howard Gilman commissioned Cedric Price to build a "complex to be known as GENERATOR".[1] Shortly after concluding work on the McAppy project, Price thus had an opportunity to put his ideas on "architecture of ecology" into practice, creating a scheme that could serve as a role model. The invitation to tender for the Generator drafted by Gilman described it as a centre to promote the performing arts, to be constructed on Gilman Paper Company's White Oak Plantations in Florida. Gilman envisioned that it would offer dance ensembles and theatre groups an opportunity to work on new projects and choreographies, free of financial and spatial constraints.[2] In addition, he was keen to ensure the artists had everything they needed on the spot, both in terms of space and technology, with cutting-edge presentation and performance facilities.[3]

As soon as Price began to address the project, he broadened the planned programme, conceiving the Generator as an open forum to foster contacts and encounters, rather than purely a centre to host high culture. His proposal picked up on ideas he had evolved in the recently concluded McAppy project, incorporating further education schemes for the plantation workers alongside promotion of culture.[4] In Price's vision, courses and training programmes would lie at the heart of a new culture of work for the firm, so that "lifelong learning" would spark a democratic shift towards more open cultural production.[5]

1

With his philanthropist views, Gilman was receptive to Price's ideas and gave him free rein to forge ahead with further elaboration of the details for the project.[6] For Price this commission thus represented an opportunity to hone the design strategy he had pursued in his projects since the Fun Palace, and to create a truly contemporary cultural space. The first step involved drawing up a "work package" that Gilman could use to help identify the components needed to give a new orientation to the project in his firm.[7] As in the McAppy project, Price emphasised detailed analysis of the Gilman Paper Company's work culture to gain empirical data about the initial conditions for the project. In the light of Price's reinterpretation of the brief, the project now encompassed further education programmes and self-determined creative work, with the contents based on input from company employees. This new thrust for the project revisited a central leitmotif in Price's designs: the social organisation of space and ways to breathe new life into community culture. In describing the issues he wished to address in the Generator project, Price therefore underlined the goal of creating greater openness in the architecture and public space to foster a new culture of appropriation: "[…] an architectural complex with no previous title and no predefined use, only a desired end-effect."[8]

2
3
4

"The Menu"

The prototype Price developed for the Generator took his exploration of the underlying principles for his "architecture of enabling" to a new level thanks to the design freedom granted by his client coupled with the architect's own uncompromisingly consistent approach. The site Price selected was a roughly

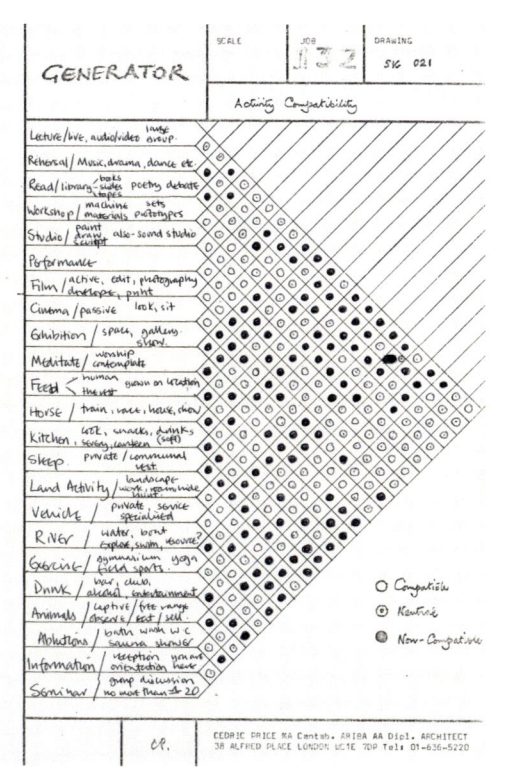

2 Cedric Price, "Activity compatibility, sk021 CP", diagram, 1977.

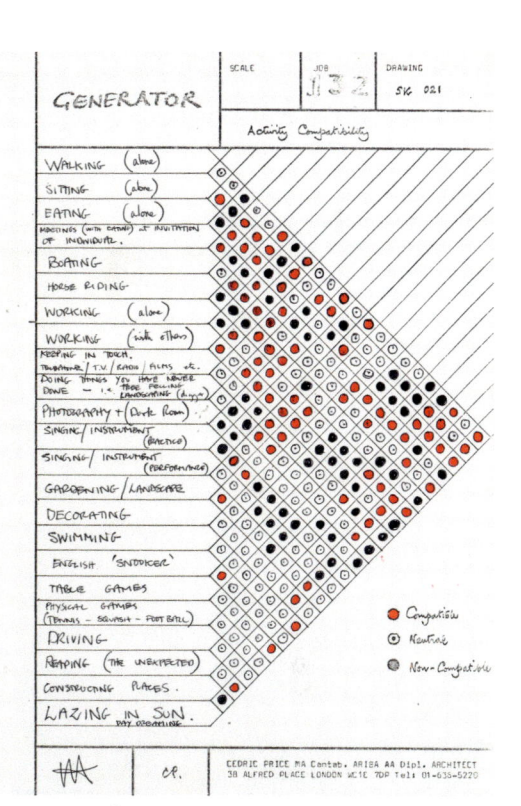

3 Cedric Price, "Activity compatibility, sk021 M", diagram, 1977.

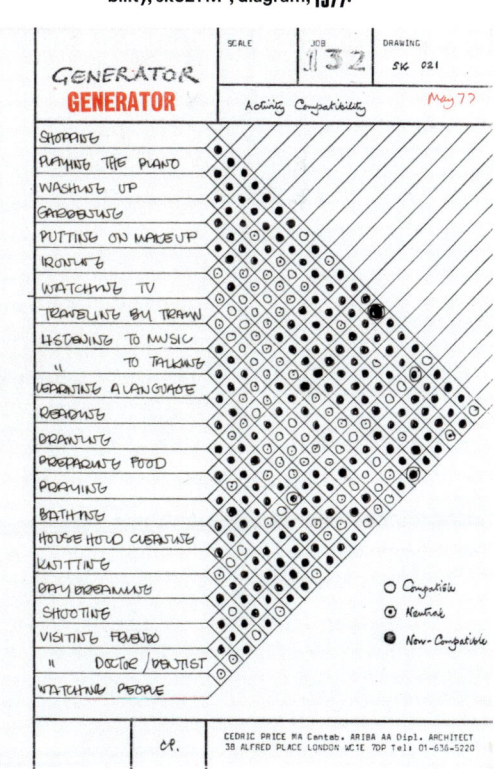

4 Cedric Price, "Activity compatibility, sk021 CP May 77", diagram, 1977.

120 × 80 metre clearing on the plantation, immediately adjacent to St. Marys River.[9] Tapping into its proximity to nature and the self-contained setting, in the midst of the forest's vast expanses, Price designed a "responsive environment" that could incorporate a whole host of spatial attributes and activities.[10]

Building on the principles of his Camden Town project, Price developed a modular construction system for the Generator with variable configuration of the components, which could also be stacked to form two storeys. Game theory and computers underpinned a range of innovative options for users to configure the space. The basic construction modules comprised a simple room-height wooden cube, finishing components for the interior and technical infrastructure, which Price distributed across the entire clearing as a 12 × 12 foot (3.65 × 3.65 m) foundation grid.[11] The cubes produced the structural frame for the living quarters, with scope to arrange up to 150 such units on the grid.[12] The single rooms housed private accommodation areas; combined in groups of two or three, they could be used as seminar or common rooms.[13] In addition Price also developed construction components for the Generator's outdoor areas: wood panels, stairs and ramps that could be connected to form pathways and open spaces, as well as frame structures, set at 45 degrees to the foundation grid, to hold awnings, privacy screening and electrical cabling.[14]

By selecting and recombining these components, a huge number of design variants could be created, each representing distinctive programmes and spatial qualities. Offering a broad spectrum of potential ways of configuring the space, the Generator could accommodate many different mixes of individual and group activities, including scope to remodel both interior and exterior spaces, which could flow seamlessly into each other, reflecting the local climatic conditions.[15] Users could also adapt the outdoor space in the clearing fairly spontaneously to suit the needs of each specific situation by simply moving the awnings and panels.

With his design for this combinatorial structural system, Price placed a clear emphasis on the process of creating the space within the ensemble, which could be shaped by all the users collectively during their time at the Generator. Over and above the constructional system, a further fundamental facet of Price's plans entailed designing an organisational structure and the associated processes, as a means to plan and implement re-arrangement of the ensemble.[16]

However, the Generator's design was not driven by a purely combinatorial principle, but was actually the outcome of a precise composition devised by Price to create an open, constantly changeable spatial ambience in the clearing. To that end Price adapted the grid so that it reflected the conditions on the site very precisely, taking account for example of the edge of the woods, the existing road and the shaded areas in the clearing.[17] The Generator's construction site was thus not a regular rectangle and the road that cut diagonally across the construction site divided it into two unequal triangular fields. The fixed shade-producing elements introduced a further sub-division, leaving just a few potential spots to site the larger rooms, such as the dance and performance hall. As the Generator's combinatorial principles thus produced only a limited

4

5 Cedric Price Architects, "Menu 15",
schematic plan, undated.

4

6 Cedric Price Architects, photograph of model mounted on cardboard, undated.

7 Author unknown, Generator model, "132 P129", Polaroid photograph, 1978.

8 Author unknown, Generator model, "132 P131", Polaroid photograph, 1978.

selection of configuration options, Price took particular care to adapt the ensemble to the conditions on the spot.[18]

Price's design deployed a rational optimisation method for this adaptation, describing the hallmarks of various configuration possibilities to gain a better understanding of their spatial attributes. This process allowed him to derive organisational principles from any initial composition, selected at random, and to specify the design for particular functions and atmosphere, for example by demarcating public and private space, producing sight lines and envisaging lighting scenarios. This produced what Price called the Menu, from which users could select predefined groups of rooms and programmes to use during their stay. This "'menu' of items [...] for space, control, containment and delight" comprised both a selection of possible spatial combinations and a set of instructions on the chronological sequence for these arrangements.[19]

As Price repeatedly emphasised in his comments on the project, by developing the Menu he planned to give visitors to the Generator the broadest possible range of different programmes to take account of many different individual tastes.[20] The menu metaphor set the tone for a new way of looking at production and use of architecture. Echoing the notion of a range of dishes offered in a restaurant, the Menu comprised a selection of spatial propositions, each with a pre-composed, pre-formulated size, atmosphere and function, although in principle the Generator's modular system would have allowed users to pick and choose much more freely from the constructional components. This menu analogy articulated Price's intention to give all the building's stakeholders a new, more active role in shaping the Generator. Users took on the role of guests, with a selection of various proposals and sequences at their fingertips; the way in which these were "utilised" was underpinned by culturally determined dispositions. Nonetheless, it was the architect who elaborated the Menu and designed the organisational structures for the "restaurant's" operation, determined by the undertaking's substantive programme, modus operandi and structures.[21] Specially trained staff took charge of day-to-day running of the Generator, supporting the guests as they made their selections and arranging the ensemble in keeping with guests' wishes. Through his choice of metaphor, Price paved the way for an understanding of his architecture as a cultural product, whose elements could be varied and consumed as if selecting from a multi-course menu. In this sense Price's design generated a built structure in which the degree of variability and openness were very precisely defined in advance, despite the scope to reconfigure the resultant outcome at any time in the spirit of an open process.

9
10

During the first eighteen months of his work on the project, Price focused on devising the Menu. During this process he designed an optimised configuration pattern that was to be incorporated into the Generator when the ensemble opened. To that end he drafted a number of configuration variants, working on printed representations of the grid and with a simple model, subsequently fine-tuning the outcomes produced by these variants to reach an optimised solution.[22] Tapping into the insights gleaned, Price subsequently teased out specific aspects of the design on a larger scale and carried out a second optimisation step.

9   Cedric Price, "Menu & Table
Settings & The Meal", sketch, undated.

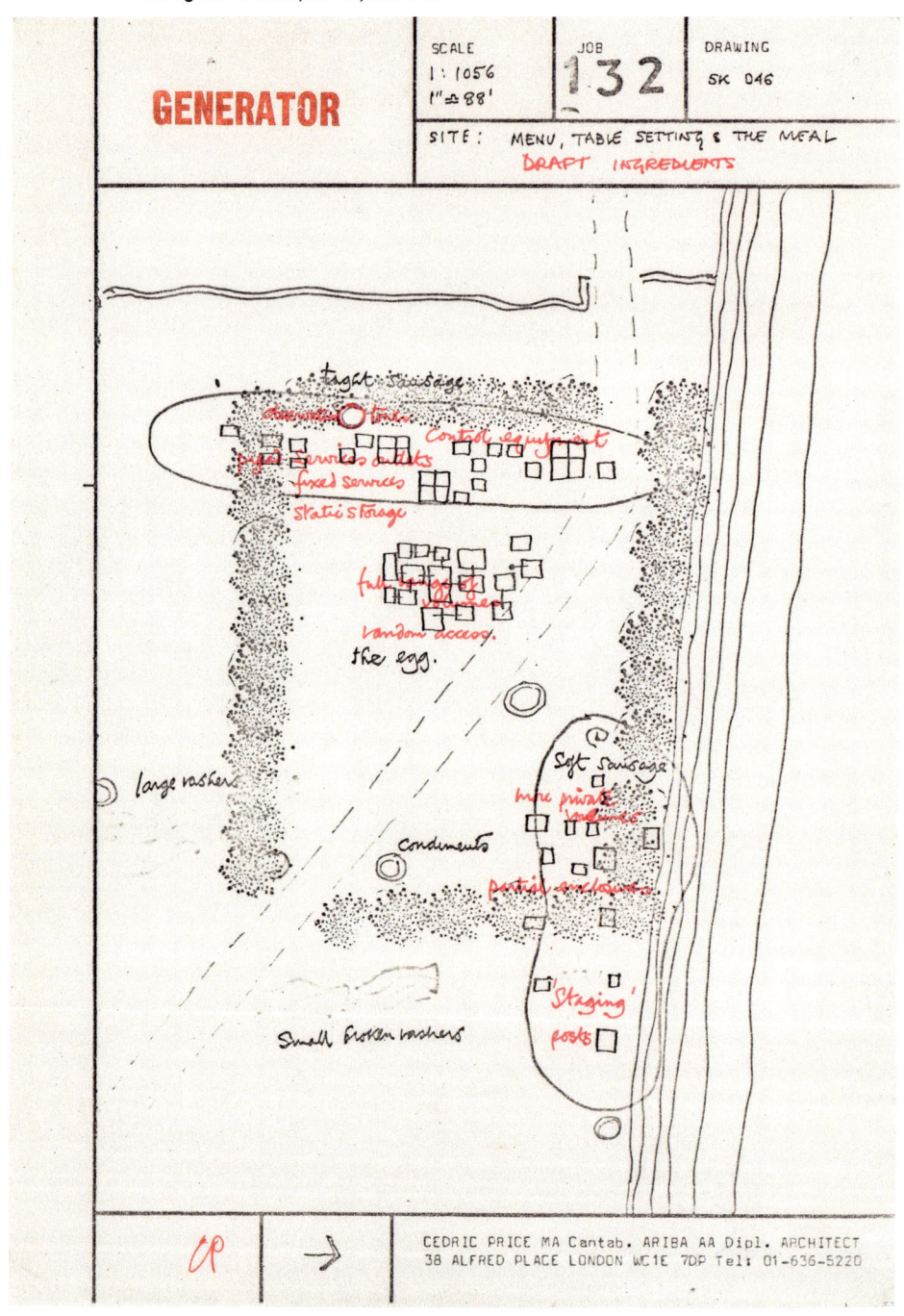

10 Cedric Price, "Menu 22",
4th October 1978, sketch, **1978**.

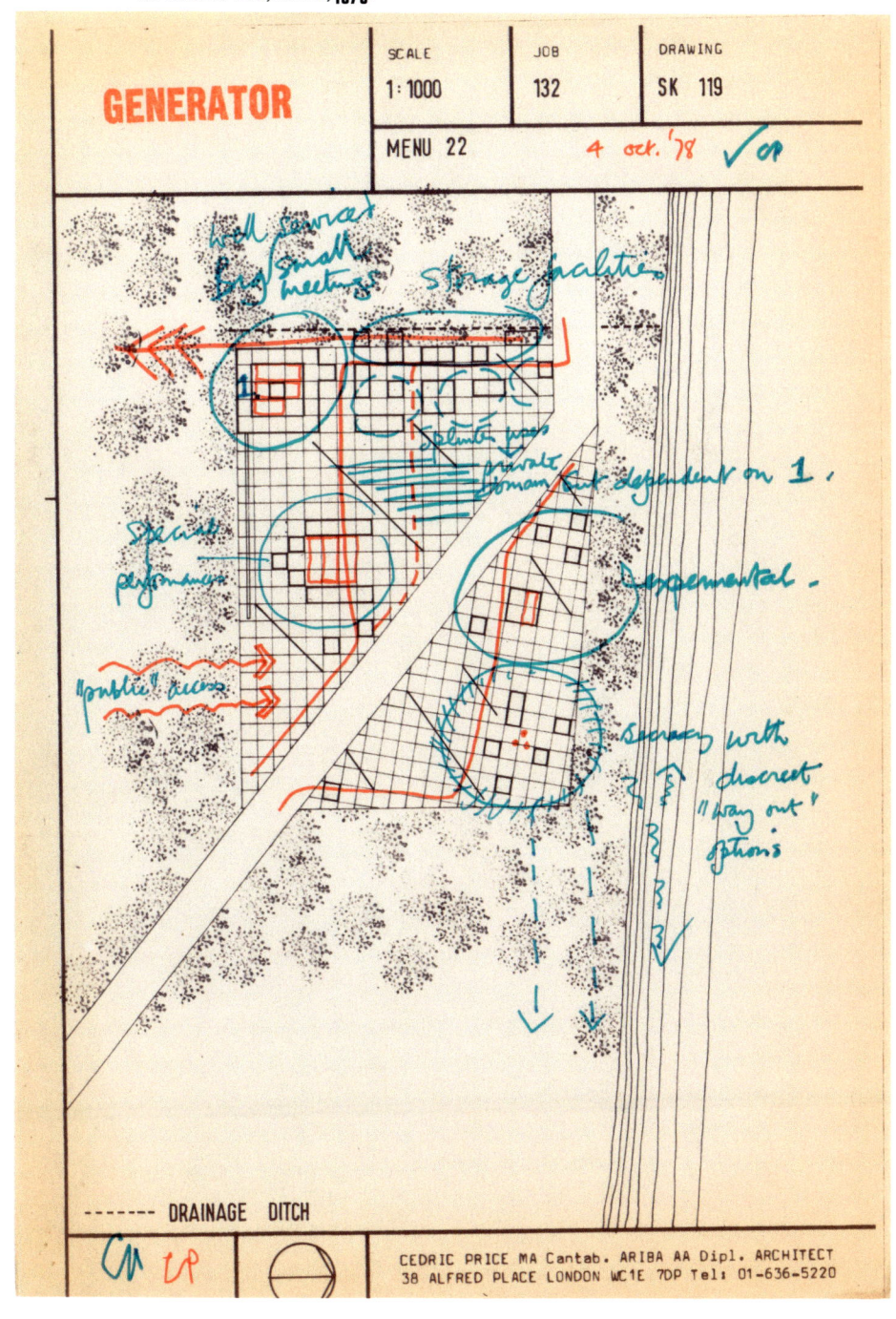

11 Cedric Price Architects, "Modular Activity Spaces", plan, undated.

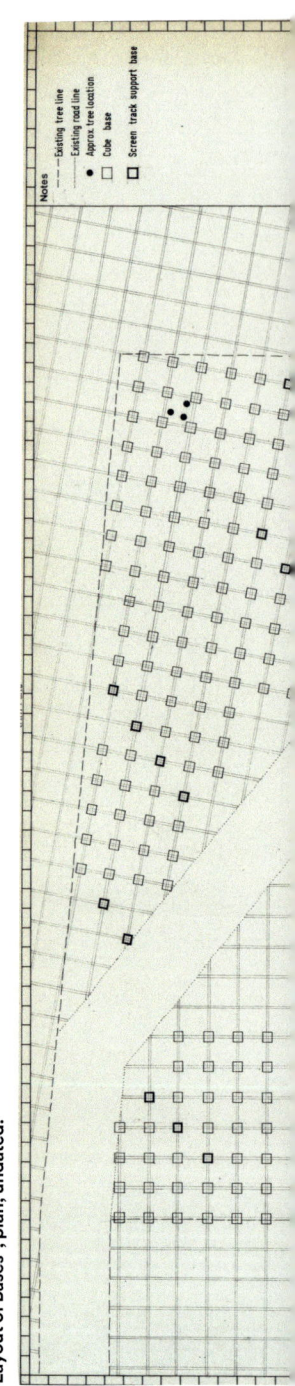

12 Cedric Price Architects, "Initial
Layout of Bases", plan, undated.

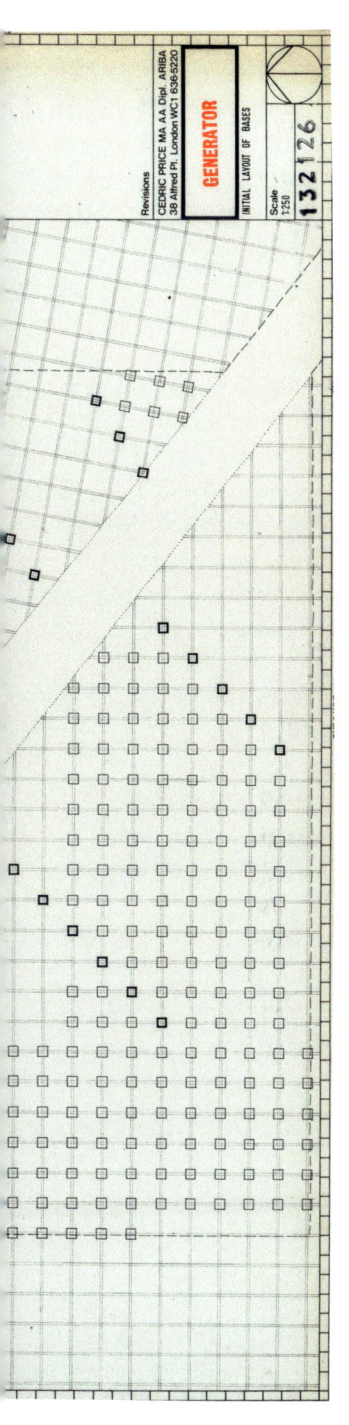

13 Cedric Price Architects, "Grid Layout + Menu 23 + External Spaces II", plan, 1979.

The blueprint for the Generator therefore grew out of a two-step "generative" design process. In the first step Price drew up several variants ("candidates") in order to derive general design criteria; he deployed these in the second phase to generate further design variants that were adapted to the needs of various user groups in the light of the particular programmes, room dimensions and environmental conditions required, ultimately arriving at a selection of optimised solutions.

Menu 15 was one of the first that Price ran through this rational optimisation process.[23] In it he drew a distinction between three cube categories, which were differentiated in terms of their grouping, aspect and utilisation, and could be combined on the basis of specific rules to form private or public spaces.[24] Price arranged large public spaces such as the theatre in a fixed cluster with generous roof spans, around which smaller rooms could be incorporated.[25] The second category he envisaged encompassed semi-public spaces for seminar and group work. A maximum of four cubes were joined together in this set-up, with easily recombinable finishings.[26] A third group contained free-standing cubes, earmarked for use as private bedrooms, sanitary facilities or for special functions, for example a sound studio.[27] Each of these three programmatic remits for the constructional system called for a different configuration in each cube to define its degree of openness or closure, with a particular spatial atmosphere ascribed to each potential iteration. For example Price used the epithet "Toughness" to denote the closed character of the large spatial cluster vis-à-vis changing external influences. Referencing the degree of enclosure or "Envelopness", he described complex configurations of cubes that extended over more than one grid unit with outdoor areas that could also be closed off. Price characterised the attributes of private cubes with the term "Control-richness", as users could opt spontaneously to create greater privacy in the outdoor space by folding out moveable wall components. He subsequently ascribed particular activities such as "sitting, eating, drinking, watching" to the cubes as a function of their space-defining attributes, for example the degree to which they were enclosed.[28] Allocation of particular fittings and fixtures meant the cubes took on specific functions in the ensemble's composition, as the type of finish embodied in these components determined the relationship between public and private space, and the proportion of open and closed elements in the ensemble as a whole. In further design steps Price tested various aspects of the configuration, for example the position and construction of large spaces for dance performances or how to arrange service infrastructure for the kitchen and storage areas, which were also to be housed in specially equipped cubes.[29] From design variant to design variant, the range of potential configuration variations dwindled, and ultimately Price formulated a temporary endpoint in his "generative" design process in "Menu 24". Subsequently Price concentrated on working out the design for individual elements and execution details for the building components.[30] His study for the Generator ended with "Menu 25", which marked an interim conclusion to his design process.[31]

Optimising the configuration possibilities meant that a very specific spatial atmosphere was conjured up in the Generator design, for during the design process Price had conducted a very precise study of the ways in which various ambiences could be created. The grid's asymmetrical orientation for example meant that no continuous visual axes could be formed in the grid's interstices, and thus there was no point in the clearing that offered a vista through the entire length of the ensemble. Entirely different experiences of space are generated within the various areas as a result of Price's choices in configuring the cubes, wall finishings and sun awnings, which mediated between the secluded private spaces and the open-access dance and workshop areas in a whole host of different ways. This multiple legibility of space was therefore not the fruit of an arbitrary adaptation process, but rather a design means consciously deployed by Price to generate an energy-laden, activity-related spatial atmosphere. Price referred to this facet of his design in terms of "the notion of a (friendly) energy able to pass a barrier [...]".[32] In his view this was precisely the kind of atmosphere to be found in urban districts such as Manhattan or in parts of central London, both of which he compared with the Generator design in collages. The decisive factor for atmospheric perception of space was in Price's opinion the relationship between built and public space, as reflected in the proportions of the urban grid in New York or London. In analysing these cities, he highlighted the residential block as a central design hallmark, pinpointing too how Central Park formed a kind of cavity in counterpoint to the dense built fabric of the cityscape.[33] Price's aspiration to create an energy-charged relationship between internal and external space is also conveyed in a key slogan he used to explain the project: "Never look empty, never feel full."[34]

14   In his studies of proportion, perspective drawings and models, Price repeatedly fine-tuned his focus on this atmosphere of change.[35] In his view the impact of the Generator ensemble essentially depended on visitors' visible interactions within the clearing and thus on perception of a certain density of activity, akin to that in urban piazzas or other public spaces in cities. In his studies on proportions, Cedric Price thus set up a direct link between human beings, their activities and the dimensions of particular spaces. Imitating this relationship accurately was one of the essential objectives in his cube studies.[36] The proportions of the grid, with its particular ratio of public and private space,

14   Author unknown, airbrush perspective, undated.

offered Price a means to establish a functional differentiation of space capable of accommodating a broad range of different lifestyles, along with the associated socio-economic, cultural, functional and constructional aspects.

Price planned a trial in a 1:1 scale model to assess the impact of the atmosphere created in the ensemble, clearly revealing how serious he was about ensuring his project design would serve as a foundation for a lifestyle defined by diversity and individual self-determination.[37] Even before this he had already conducted studies at the plantation in Florida with rudimentary wood and cardboard models to appraise the open spaces and sight lines between the cubes.[38]

15–
20

His comparative studies of Manhattan and London suggest that Price understood the Generator in terms of an inverted city block, seeking to transpose this urban atmosphere to the Generator's culture of living and working. The clearing thus forms the atmospheric framework of his "architecture of ecology": the dimensions of the constructional elements were in tune with the site to give visitors a sense of openness and freedom for creative development, yet at the same time could also create an impression of permanent activity and mutability within the space. In this respect, Price grounded his design in a conception of urbanity that he associated with attributes such as multi-functionality and simultaneity as expressions of an emancipated and individualised lifestyle. In his view, the ingredients needed to generate this included incorporation of technology into architecture, access to education and further training, and open public spaces, all of which figured in his conceptual programme. His description of the Generator as the quintessence of his "architecture of ecology" should also be read in this spirit: "It is a [...] realization of ACTION SPACE – a gradual transition between essentially outdoor and essentially indoor activities [...] There has become a deep involvement between site and structure."[39]

"Multi-Use Fixings"

In his preparatory work for the Generator, Price assumed that visitors would develop further versions of his Menu for their time in the building.[40] However Price's design for the Menu did not incorporate compositional rules applicable to all subsequent adaptation processes. Instead, the functional imperatives of the building components, the specific characteristics of their use and the associated constructive details determined the Generator's configuration rules and the options to vary the ensemble's ambience.[41] In addition, Price developed instructions for the building in the form of eight drawings depicting the individual steps of erecting the ensemble. The twenty-five Menus he devised were also a useful source for further elaboration of details relating to constructional and functional implementation based on the various component combinations.[42]

Parallel to his studies on menu variants, Price developed the detailing for the cubes and their fitting and fixtures right down to a scale of 1:5 to adapt all the conditions of their utilisation, for example the materiality, acoustics and lighting, to the ensemble's requirements.[43] He opted for a highly pared-down design approach in this respect to enable easy manipulation of the cubes by non-professionals: "With minimum of difficulty & maximum of delight."[44] He therefore envisaged that the simple wall elements, which could be open or filled-in, opened up or folded out in the different variants, would be fitted into the cube framework. Using studies with models, Price developed nine square structural elements for this purpose, each of which could be fitted with different infills to create views inwards or outwards.[45] The variable wall elements, which could be opened or closed to varying degrees, provided opportunities to create direct relationships with the surroundings. Visual relationships between the cubes were a central design criterion for these wall components, conceived to make the individual cubes part of the complex as a whole.[46]

21
22

Contrasting with these visual references to the outside world, the cubes' internal spatial attributes could be remodelled almost entirely independently of the external environmental conditions thanks to infrastructure such as air conditioning, a sound system, cable television, computers and telephones.[47] Together with the various wall components, these technical fittings and fixtures allowed each user options to engage with his or her surroundings in a whole host of different ways. That meant that the diverse spatial atmospheres Price aimed to generate would arise from actions undertaken by each user, based on selecting from various utility attributes of the cubes; the sum of these choices would combine to conjure up a particular scenario in the ensemble as a whole.

With a view to practical implementation of this diversity, Price developed ten variants of a simple hook-and-eye system with which each user could produce different degrees of opening in the cubes. This "multi-use fixing" could for example fix cubes in place and avoid slippage, or hold folding shutters open. The hook also could be used when lifting the roof element with the crane or to fix a ladder in place for access to the cube's roof.[48]

23
24

The key means for Price in stipulating the Generator's architectonic design was the detailing, which determined individual utilisation of the space. As in the McAppy project, Price viewed the robust and simple cast of his design as the key to self-determined re-shaping of the project by users. The Generator's composition grew out of the sum of individual decisions by users utilising the cubes across the entire ensemble. The cube defined the size of each space, regulated access and openings and made it possible to adapt the dimensions and nature of the spaces individually depending on the intended use of each cube. By setting users' actions at centre-stage, the cubes' design meant that the architecture of the Generator functioned primarily in terms of its order-creating function in the grid. As in his preceding projects, Price deployed an action-oriented design strategy for the Generator, in which the cubes' architectonic configuration determined the entire ensemble's utility properties: "The box as a generator – magnification & reduction."[49]

However, Cedric Price did not view his open blueprint as embodying a participative form of planning. Instead, his design strategy very deliberately accorded users only limited influence. On the whole Price was dismissive of user participation in the actual design process, believing this would give rise to

4

132
P48

132
P47

132
P45

132
P50

132
P52

132
P62

15–20 Author unknown,
1:1 Test, Polaroid photograph, undated.

Cedric Price MA Cantab. RIBA AA Dipl. Architect
38 Alfred Place London WC1E 7DP Tel: 01-636 5220

GENERATOR

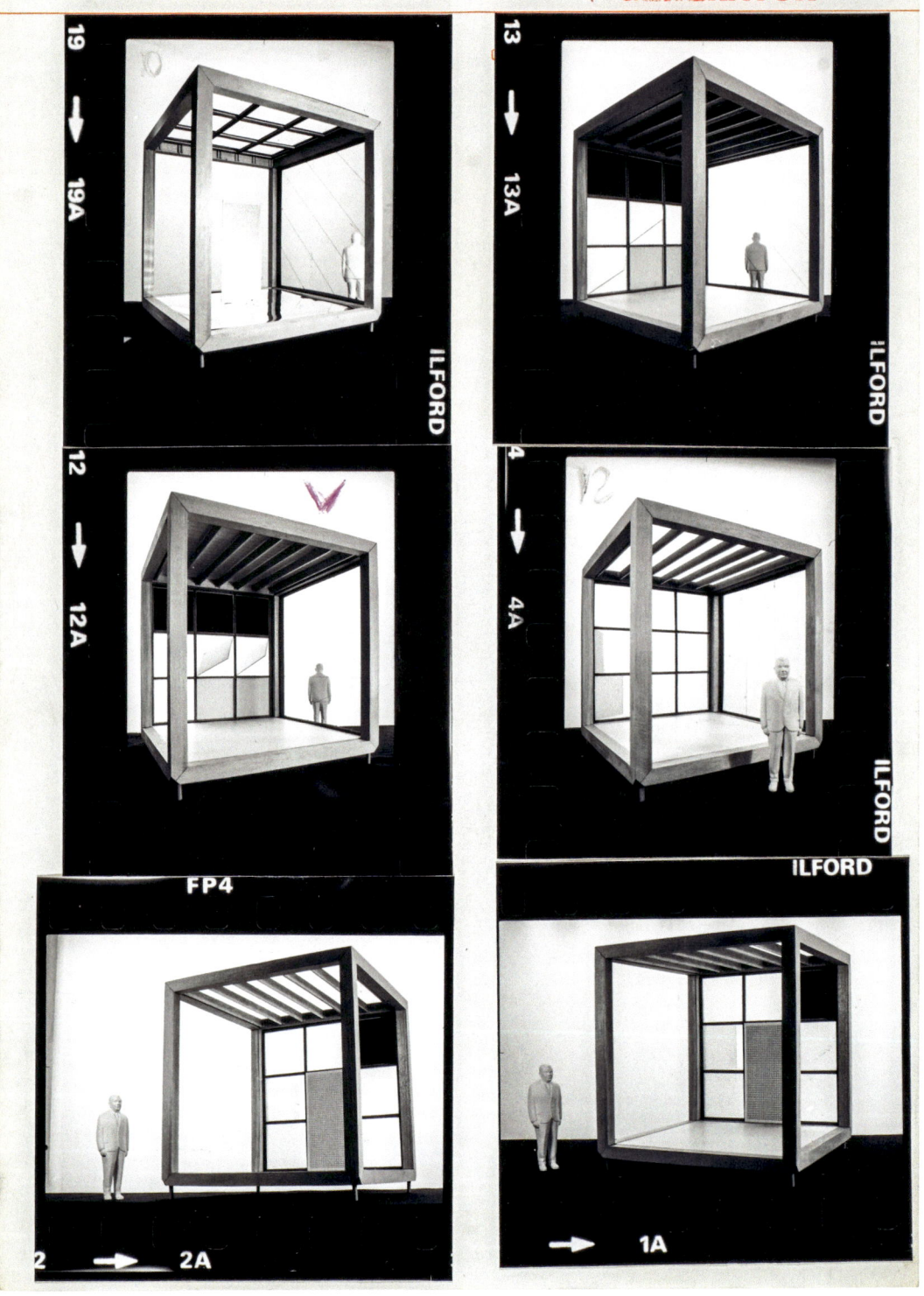

21   Cedric Price Architects, Generator cube, photocopy, ca. 1979.

22 Cedric Price Architects, Generator cube model, photograph, ca. 1979.

4

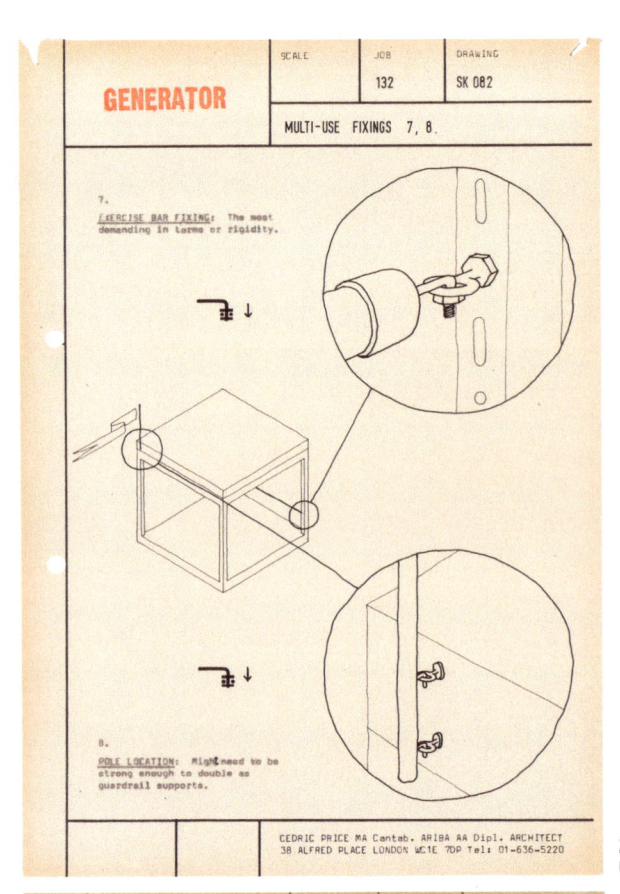

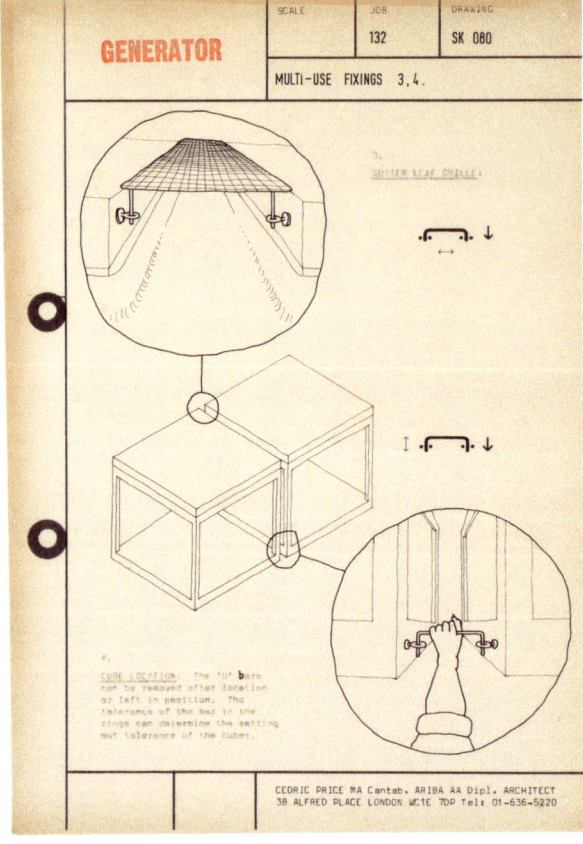

mediocre architecture. Design for Price was a job for an expert who translated needs and programmes into built form, precisely because every single user will tend to push for inclusion of as many of his or her own design preferences as possible: "I don't want to hear what forty-five people who have been asked to ring up the radio station think about this or that! [...] [I]t's almost as if everything is justified because the audience can participate. And therefore you get bad theatre, bad films, bad radio, bad television [...]."[50] That is why architecture in Price's view must adopt an unambiguous design stance and incorporate limiting stipulations, as absolute openness would simply make architecture arbitrary. As an alternative to such upstream participation, Price envisioned that users would have scope to make their own individual interpretations of the existing architecture and to configure the design through their activities and actions. He was convinced that knowledge and information about these utilisation possibilities, along with options for open access and use had much greater societal value than giving people a chance to participate in the design process per se. To elucidate his specific vision of an "architecture of enabling", Price drew on the example of church stairs, with steps infilled on the side to form a ramp. The design for these stairs would have to disclose both the new and original function if the added role of a ramp was to be legible. If this ambivalent mode of expression succeeded, the church stairs would be available, as a component of public space, to a new, wider group of people, who would be able to use the feature with bicycles, wheelchairs or skateboards.[51] In configuring the Generator's constructional details, Price attempted to open up space to multifunctional use, so that a much broader spectrum of users could access and use the centre. In this respect the Generator's design was rooted in the idea of inclusive architecture, fostering appropriation and self-organisation through its open utilisation attributes and combinatorial possibilities. However, precisely because the Generator's architecture was so open, its functional and spatial organisation depended to a large degree on user groups engaging with a decision-making process before pursuing their own activities within the ensemble.

The Polariser: The Social Organisation of Space

Price supplemented the Generator's architecture with an organisational principle intended to coordinate adaptation of the ensemble to visitor groups' needs.[52] In the form of the "Polariser" and the "Factor", Price had developed two job profiles to oversee operation of the ensemble.[53] The Polariser's role involved working with the visitor groups, compiling the programme and activities for their stay, and translating these into a spatial configuration proposal.[54] The so-called Factor was in charge of constructional transposition of the proposals on the grid.[55] Assisted by the plantation workers he was responsible for remodelling the Generator and taking care of maintenance. Price suggested Wallace Prince, White Oak's plantation manager, for this post, which would play a decisive role in implementation of the project and contacts with company staff. Price accorded

even greater importance however to the Polariser's role in the Generator's operation.[56] The Polariser was to take on the role of a manager and curator and, as a
"world scout", would be familiar with the international art and culture business,
tapping into this for the Generator.[57] Thanks to his solid grasp of the Generator's
design possibilities, the Polariser would in addition devise its spatial organisation in conjunction with users.[58] Barbara Jacobson, a former curator at MoMA
in New York, was Price's proposal for this post, envisaging that she would use
her art scene contacts to organise the Generator's first year and fill the ensemble
with programmes, companies and artists.[59]

25

The name Price chose for this curatorial position referenced the
polarisation filter and its function, which in this context signified identifying the
visitor groups' interests and orienting these towards a shared goal. He referred
to the Polariser's task as being "to give unity of direction",[60]an allusion to the
role of steering the visitor groups towards shared social organisation of space,
which could subsequently be realised in the Generator. That meant that the
Polariser's remit also encompassed moderating and organising the planning
process.[61] A playful communicative process was envisaged to adapt the site to
the needs of each group to provide optimum support to their creative work.[62]
Price viewed this dialogue between users and the Polariser as the central event
preceding reconfiguration of the Generator at the start of each stay. All these
lavish organisational measures aimed to create a working environment that
would be as conducive as possible to each group's needs, helping to unleash
creativity: "[…] a Generator – being a built complex that will enable those who
use it to think, create, invent and exchange with others in conditions hitherto
non existent."[63] Price thus made the ensemble's adaptability the very foundation
of his "architecture of enabling".

In Price's vision, the Polariser would need to do more than identify
appropriate programmes and users; the role would also involve drawing on
methods from psychology and organisational development to influence group
dynamics. The Polariser's job description was thus extended to pinpoint the
role of moderator, who would pick up on individual group members' wishes and
ideas and relate these to the group's planned activities.[64]

In turning to psychology Price once again deployed a functional design strategy previously used by the Modernist avant-garde. Scientific
insights from Gestalt psychology had influenced Neues Bauen architects as a
means of incorporating human perception and behaviour into their designs
for the urban context.[65] This approach worked on the assumption of a link between humans' inner perceptions and the external conditions of the built environment. Price highlighted the dynamism of this cause-and-effect relationship,
designing the Generator's logo in the style of the experiments with drawings
of cubes found in studies on dynamic spatial perception in the early twentieth
century.[66] In the 1920s, architectural theory on the dynamic spatial concept
posited that space could be organised and shaped in terms of movement and
human behaviour.[67] The grid layout and Price's studies on proportions formed
the basis to establish a relationship between the functional division of space

4

and users' impressions.[68] Building on this spatial concept, Price leveraged the group's social psychology and the individual's dynamic spatial perception, seeking to harness these mechanisms to organise the ensemble's adaptation processes and transformation.[69] This explanatory psychological approach provided the underpinning for Price's focus on developing a computer programme to assist visitor groups with decisions on organising space in and around the Generator. Price's stance gained confirmation from progress in mathematical systems analysis, which equipped social psychology with an important new tool to describe dynamic processes.[70]

Software and Hardware

The Polariser's job was much broader than simply involving visitors in functional configuration of the ensemble;[71] his organisational role would also be supported by a computer system that used game-theory principles to simulate the Menu's various configuration possibilities. Through this computer-based approach, Price hoped to establish a direct connection between social decision-making processes and the layout of space in the Generator. In late 1978, Price invited the architect John Frazer to accompany the Generator project as a "system consultant" in order to put this idea into practice.[72] At the time Frazer was working on Computer Aided Design (CAD) in the Faculty of Art at Ulster University in Ireland.[73] Within the framework of a two-year research grant, he planned to develop an "intelligent modelling system" to simulate the Generator's configuration patterns.[74] In 1979, he started writing a computer programme to make this possible.[75]

Menu design and the detailing of the cubes were already largely concluded by this point, and consequently the software was on the whole developed independently of the project work.[76] Price saw the software programming as a research and development task that would help improve the Generator's organisational processes. The programme was intended to speed up configuration, allowing users to grasp the Generator's spatial development possibilities before the ensemble was actually configured. In his project presentations Price emphasised that the computer was a tool to help visitor groups make decisions; in contrast to the Fun Palace Project, it would not provide information to technology that would take direct control of regulating the spatial components.[77]

The computer's sole role in the Generator project was to simulate configuration variants, from which visitor groups, in conjunction with the Polariser, could select the best possible design proposition.[78] In this respect the computer supported the production of design variants in the decision-making process Price devised for the Generator. Analogously to the method used, an architecture competition, visitors, together with the Polariser, would devise a programme in this multi-phase process, along with an initial design proposal for the ensemble, which a programmer would subsequently input into the computer.

25   Cedric Price Architects,
"Network", planning diagram, undated.

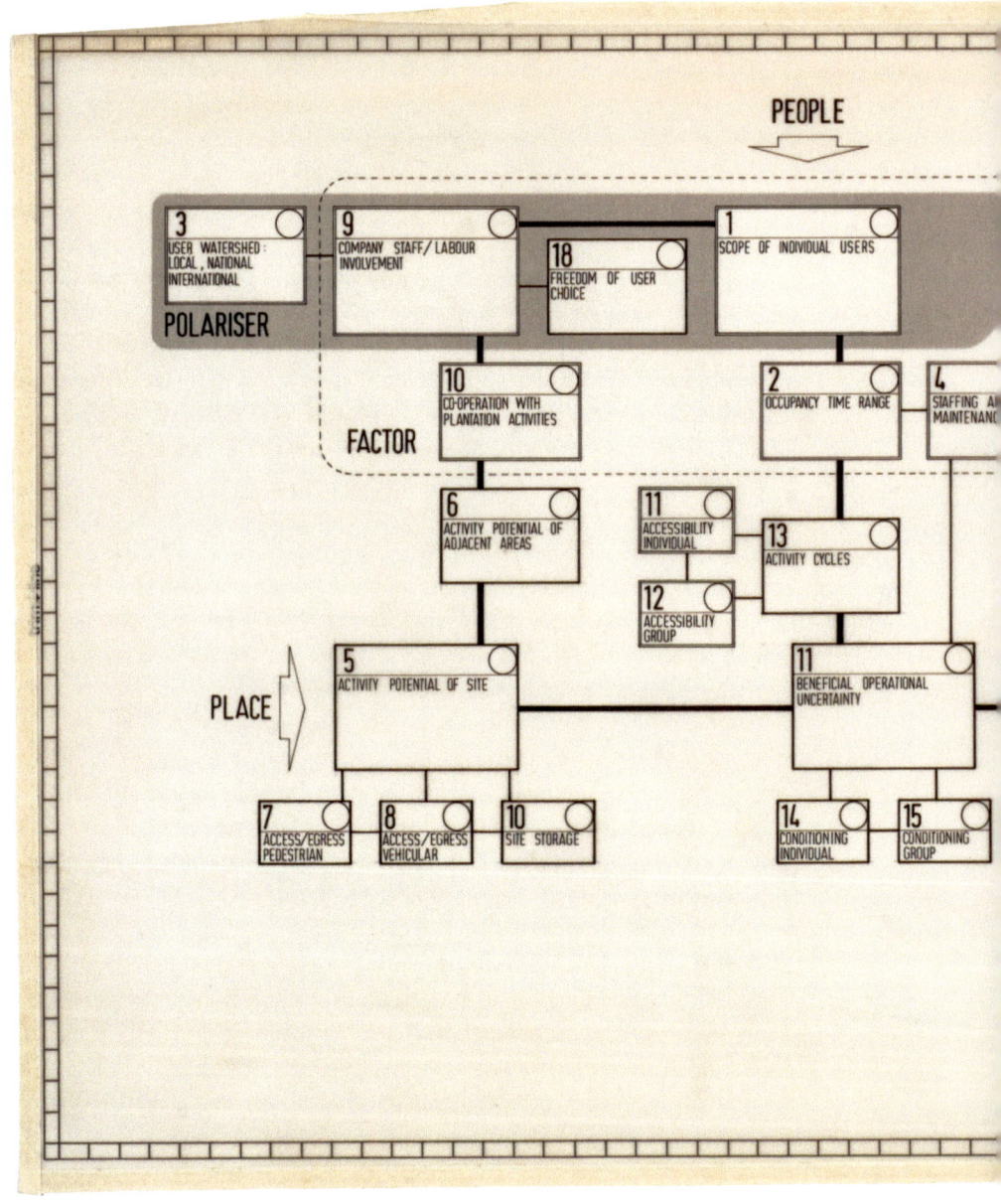

4

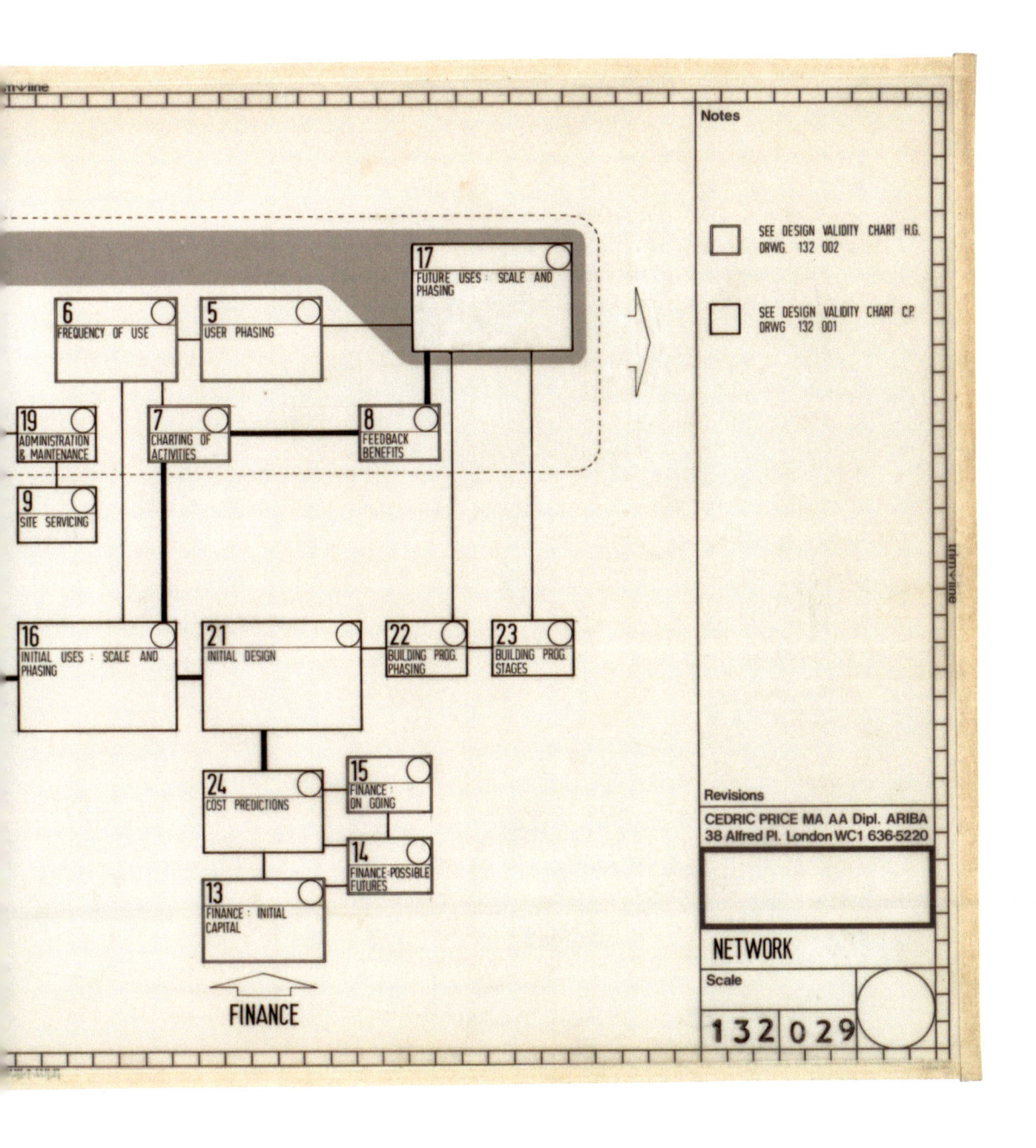

Notes

SEE DESIGN VALIDITY CHART H.G.
DRWG. 132 002

SEE DESIGN VALIDITY CHART C.P.
DRWG. 132 001

17 FUTURE USES : SCALE AND PHASING

6 FREQUENCY OF USE

5 USER PHASING

19 ADMINISTRATION & MAINTENANCE

7 CHARTING OF ACTIVITIES

8 FEEDBACK BENEFITS

9 SITE SERVICING

16 INITIAL USES : SCALE AND PHASING

21 INITIAL DESIGN

22 BUILDING PROG. PHASING

23 BUILDING PROG. STAGES

24 COST PREDICTIONS

15 FINANCE : ON GOING

14 FINANCE-POSSIBLE FUTURES

13 FINANCE : INITIAL CAPITAL

FINANCE

Revisions

CEDRIC PRICE MA AA Dipl. ARIBA
38 Alfred Pl. London WC1 636-5220

NETWORK

Scale

132 029

Incorporating new utilisation preferences, the computer would simulate and create a graphic depiction of the Generator's evolution.

John Frazer's software concept was grounded in the principle of the cellular automaton, a mathematical method also used for example in combinatorial game theory to simulate the development of spatio-dynamic ordering patterns within a closed field. It works as follows: The system to be examined is divided into uniform space cells, and various developmental stages of a spatial configuration are simulated in numerous consecutive iterations of simple mathematical functions. The increasing availability of computing power in microprocessors, made such simulations hugely popular in the 1970s, for example in "The Game of Life", which simulated complex growth processes based on two simple rules about the number of cells adjacent to any particular cell.[79] The Generator's grid-structured field and the three different cubes meant its architectonic design could easily be simulated using a cellular automaton. The computer programme John Frazer wrote to simulate the Generator's combinatorial processes concentrated on depicting the diversity and dynamism of adaptation processes on the site. Although this kind of process could be modelled without electronic data processing, computers dramatically improved the quality of the simulations, meaning that a much larger range of potential development variants could be tracked over a considerably longer time period. As this facilitated analysis of how individual decisions would affect the system as a whole, it became much more straightforward to develop suitable configuration variants.

Through the computer simulation Price attempted to open up a systemic way of looking at the Generator's development possibilities. The programme provided a rational instrument for users to coordinate their behaviour and compare its impact with the overarching interests of the group. Providing this additional information was a way to encourage "bottom-up" planning that would take rational individual behaviours as its point of departure in optimising adaptation of the overall system. Ever since his contacts with the Independent Group, Price had used physical metaphors like the field or the magnet to describe the socio-cultural determinants of space. Now he used the cellular automaton model to simulate the Generator's dynamic development as a field of experience and action.[80]

In order to achieve this goal, Price drew on 1960s and 1970s developments in social research and computer technology.[81] Game theory methods had become prevalent in social research to model behavioural studies, and made it possible to draw broadly applicable conclusions on the basis of individuals' behaviour. This methodology aimed to appraise a priori whether a particular action would serve the common good or be detrimental, irrespective of particular individual motivations. Price also worked with computers in attempting to resolve what is known as the "paradox of individual action", in other words, the way in which the sum of individual actions often produces results far removed from those intended by the individuals involved. The computer simulation Price used here aimed, with the help of game theory, to find a spatial solution that would contribute to the greatest possible good for the community.[82]

During this period the question of the functional relationship between individual actions and collective decisions was beginning to radically alter the way in which architecture viewed urban design. In 1971 for example Thomas C. Schelling, a Professor of Economics and Conflict Theory in the USA, also used a game theory model to explain how the individual inhabitants' choices of neighbours lead to residential segregation and hence to slum formation in cities. His model was based on the principle of situational logic, which explained social segregation through the prism of individuals' behaviour towards their neighbours (conflict or cooperation).[83] Shelling developed his model against the backdrop of grave incidents of racial discrimination in American cities.[84] In the 1960s and 1970s, government housing schemes, constructed in the 1950s in cities such as St. Louis, Philadelphia, Detroit or Chicago with the intention of offering equally cheap housing to the entire population, were particularly prone to failure due to the combined influence of market forces, the construction methods used and the preferences of those who lived in these schemes. In some cases this led to empty and decaying housing stock, for example in Pruitt-Igoe in St. Louis; its failure is still a topic of controversial debate even today. The enormous media impact of Pruitt-Igoe's demolition, which was broadcast live on television, meant that the scheme came in American public discourse to symbolise a failed government housing construction policy.[85] Architectural theorist Charles Jencks declared the day when Pruitt-Igoe was demolished in 1977 as marking the death of modern architecture, which had set itself up in opposition to popular culture as a result of institutionalised planning and had failed in the face of reality due to its flawed assumptions about how society functions.[86] Jencks' comments marked a historical turning point in architecture, heralding the advent of the postmodern era, with modern residential construction lambasted for having failed to fulfil its remit.

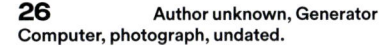

26   **Author unknown, Generator
Computer, photograph, undated.**

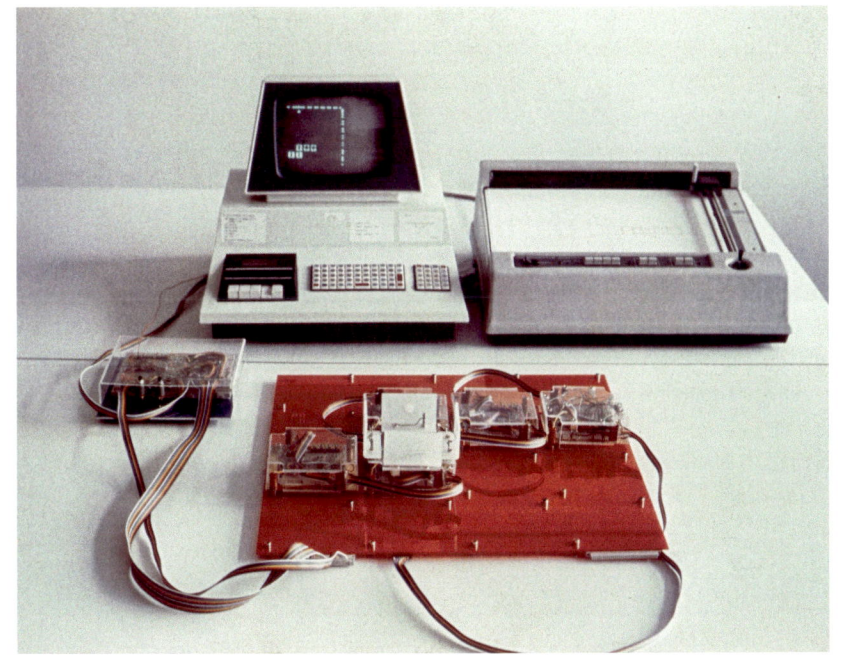

Programming instead of Programmes

In the "Non-Plan" manifesto Price had already made denigratory comments about modern planning methods that had lost touch with reality. In the light of the Watts Riots in Los Angeles, his co-author Reyner Banham pronounced that these methods had failed to attain their self-proclaimed goal of overcoming social inequalities using the tools of rational construction.[87] Nonetheless Price, like Banham, did not believe that Functionalist architecture per se had failed across the board. In the Generator he attempted instead to sketch out his ideas for a style of Functionalism in tune with the times, more strongly oriented to users' actual needs. Price sought to overcome the obvious discrepancy between reality and planning by using scientific methods drawn from psychology and sociology as well as new technical tools from systems science and information technology. In the Generator computer simulation, the rational model of the communal spaces stood in opposition to the individual's motivation and thus established a new relationship between the means and the ends: the additional insights gleaned were intended to support self-organisation of visitors to the ensemble. Just as his role model Patrick Geddes had done previously when constructing the Outlook Tower, Cedric Price introduced a new planning instrument aimed at collecting information and easing decision-making. Dating back to the Victorian age, this strategy was anchored in the notion of the responsible, enlightened citizen, provided with technical means for information-gathering and communication in order to make the best possible decision in the interests of the community as a whole.[88]

The Generator's programming also steered a new course, reflecting the underlying assumption of a situation-oriented logic in social decision-making processes. Rather than focussing primarily on democratic participation John Frazer concentrated in this context on the principle of the programme's self-organisation. With his software he sought to simulate quasi-evolutionary development of the project, generating future configurations from ordering patterns already stored. His proposed evolutionary design process even suggested writing computer programmes capable of learning, in order to make independent improvements to the configuration proposals on the basis of decisions already taken.[89]

After the launch in 1977 of the first Personal Computer, the Commodore PET 2001, Frazer also planned to equip each cube with its own microprocessor in order to display the cube's configuration on the Generator's grid in real time.[90] To test out this idea, he had a miniaturised model of individual cubes built, depicting their configuration on a screen and storing this information on a hard disc. The computer thus functioned as a design database that could be used for comparisons with further adaptations. In the long term, data storage in the system, coupled with the software's evolutionary design principle made it possible to refer back to user preferences, which could be entered into the simulation process as a further source of information.

Frazer's evolutionary design principle added an interactive optimisation process to the notion of self-organisation that Price had developed in the Menus.[91] Frazer envisioned that the computerised graphic depiction of variants would generate an interactive relationship between users and the software to enhance decision-making.[92] Both John Frazer and Cedric Price viewed the new communicative relationship between users and computers as an opportunity to generate a quasi-natural development of the ensemble's spatial set-up. Microprocessors and sensors were to be incorporated into the project, making this new form of interaction between the built system and users an immanent component of the Generator complex, as Price described on an optimistic note: "In this case the real world becomes the model of itself, understandable to the computer as a logical electronic model."[93]

Frazer was convinced that in a third developmental stage of the Generator software, the programme's scope for interactions could even make the Generator independent. The idea was that the software would draw on the case studies to devise a set of rules incorporating the requisite information about visitors' configuration preferences.[94] This concept worked on the assumption that the project had a natural evolutionary capacity, so that stable, recurring ordering patterns would emerge over time. By studying the various computer-generated configuration situations, all the specific rules could be deduced much more rapidly and effectively than with a manual recording system or by studying the real-life processes on the site. In this context the rules arose out of practical observation and not from the aesthetic principles that informed the design. In this instance however visitors' needs were subordinated to a principle of change that was viewed as being entirely natural. Frazer therefore compared his software principle with the process of morphogenesis, in other words the emergence of external characteristics of an organism, etc., in developmental biology.

The simulation method also aimed to allow the software to make unexpected proposals that burst out of the bounds of the immediate context and visitors' frames of reference. As John Frazer explained in a letter to Price, the software was to counter what he dubbed the "boredom concept" of optimisation by producing change and transformation, and thus responding to human needs and behaviour patterns like curiosity and activity.[95] Price viewed Frazer's proposal as a counter-design set in opposition to a technologically "optimised" environment, as the computer was also to respond to human attributes like boredom and creativity. The computer system therefore also symbolised the possibility of deriving fixed structures from the changing demands of users, without abandoning the characteristics Price enshrined in the Generator: an open community-based culture defined by openness, complexity, and diversity. In a 1980 article on the Generator, Price described the computer programme as an organic component of the project that imbued the ensemble with a vibrant, semi-natural order.[96]

In this vision of a quasi-natural development, Price's ideas of an "architecture of enabling" coincided with John Frazer's strategy of evolutionary software development. Both were driven by a desire to enhance human influence on space through a systematic understanding of the environment. In the process, they focused above all on taking account of users' emotions and behavioural patterns in situationally oriented design of the space. However, exerting influence in this way entailed designing a closed system that stipulated all the functional relationships between the constructional elements in advance. The Generator's design did allow visitors to impact the space in the short and medium term, yet the palette of options for such changes was restricted, as a selection could only be made from a limited number of pre-defined combinations. In this respect the Generator ensemble had all the attributes of the machine architecture that Price had previously elaborated in the Fun Palace. Moving beyond the approach he adopted in the Fun Palace, Price's introduction of the Polariser in the Generator project opened up a whole host of new possibilities for interacting with and appropriating development of the organisation processes and software, enabling visitors to perceive the ensemble as part of their self-defined environment. This sense of the ensemble as the visitors' quasi-natural environment could in Price's view be realised through self-organisation and simulation, generating interactions between the ensemble and visitors on various levels; at the same time, however, Price's design for the structural elements meant that he had already created all the conditions to create design links between the ensemble's closed system and the surrounding landscape. Visitors were to be encouraged to compose surroundings with multiple fine-tuned design facets, shaped by both by human interventions and external environmental conditions. In this particular understanding of an architectural system attuned to human perception, both Price and, somewhat later, John Frazer were influenced by Gordon Pask, in particular his work on scope for interactions in man-machine processes, as formulated in projects such as the Musicolour machine (1953) or the automated learning environment *EUCRATES* (1956).[97]

Furthermore, John Frazer's strategy of self-organisation and his aspirations to ensure evolutionary development of his computer programme suggested that Price's goal of striking a balance between individual and community interests would be achieved more or less naturally. John Frazer was convinced that the technical optimisation principle would allow the Generator to automatically make positive changes, as the programme imitated the natural principles of human behaviour and rational decision-making skills. This ordering, reason-based principle would gradually grow out of collective decisions and user behaviour with the assistance of technology. In this respect, the Generator computer simulation project is particularly revealing of the positivist attitude underpinning the entire Generator scheme.

The Generator's simulation programme was however never realised. In late 1979, Howard Gilman ordered a "temporary halt"[98] to the project and this was followed by repeated postponement of the requisite design work, which ultimately led to all work on the Generator project being abandoned. In addition, Frazer's reflections remained purely theoretical, particularly as the technical limitations of the data-processing and storage capacity available at the time hampered sufficient testing of his vision of self-organisation.

The Generator's Architecture of Enabling

The computer simulation Frazer developed was an important part of Price's architecture of social organisation, as it was conceived to enable users to perceive their environment and the impact of their own actions from an external perspective. The goal was to enable users to appraise their decisions objectively in terms of the overall system. This was paired with endeavours to incorporate spontaneity and chance thanks to the ensemble's adaptability, reflecting individuals' inner needs and creative expressivity. The design objectives thus entailed generating a systemic equilibrium that mediated between spontaneous construction of situations and simulations of future developmental possibilities.

As Price repeatedly underlined in his project notes, the Generator sought to produce a creative dimension that he dubbed "the unknown" or "the unexpected", although it was to be generated with support from rational construction and forecasting elements. In this respect the Generator's design entailed attempting to construct controlled uncontrolled events. The role of the architect in the planning process was akin to that of a director – with the key distinction that the Generator did not stipulate any staging instructions for a predetermined narrative. The architect's remit was to shape the framework for self-generating events; in this sense in the Generator Price constructed the functional conditions to frame an environment artificially shaped by humans.

In the Generator, though, the architect's role as the designer of structures and systems stood in fundamental contradiction to Price's efforts to integrate the wide range of differing individual and community needs into the complex on an equal footing. This becomes especially apparent in Price's intention to develop the Generator as a prototype that would encompass overarching design stipulations irrespective of specific situations and users. In pursuing this goal, Price was following in the footsteps of modern architecture's positivist design strategy, which in the early twentieth century had accelerated rationalisation of construction by developing prototypes in order to improve living conditions in industrial cities.[99] Picking up on and developing these ideas, Price's design was motivated by the notion that through science and technology this type of model could be designed for the creative lifestyle of the knowledge society.

Given the rapid development of automation deploying cybernetics and computerised tools, Price was convinced that this approach could be put into practice. Rational computation operations would therefore do more than create a new way of looking at the spatial circumstances of shared space: technology-supported dialogue could also stimulate emotions and ideas, thus appealing to the creative and emotional level of human interaction. Throughout the 1970s and 1980s, Price continued to adhere to the ideal of an egalitarian world community that would be rooted in scope for personal development in the knowledge society and would succeed thanks to the tools offered by technological progress, in integrating everyone, from the factory worker to the professional dancer, into a pluralistic societal structure.[100]

When it came to the Generator's design this aspiration suffered from an irreconcilable contradiction that Price attempted to overcome using systems theory. On the one hand Price deployed seriality and adaptability as design principles to overcome the contradictions between the individual and the community, while on the other hand transformation and adaptability were also intended to overcome the need for a concrete, situation-oriented design.[101] The root cause of the project's failure is also apparent in the fact that Price did in practice engage in direct cooperation with the firm's employees although the his implementation concept for the Generator relied on their willingness to play their part.[102] In contrast to his preceding projects, such as McAppy and the Inter-Action Centre, Price could not anchor the *Generator* project in either a specific social context or draw on a committed, motivated user group. As a result, the project lacked the vital connection with reality that Price had identified as the essential precondition for his situation-based and action-oriented designs.

As MoMA curator Pierre Apraxine commented, the project failed because it did not succeed in motivating the plantation workers and thus did not do justice to the idea of participation that for Price formed the key prerequisite for successful realisation of the project: "Cedric Price's proposal involved the active participation of the plantation workforce, which of course was the beauty of it. But the obvious maintenance requirements associated with such structure were considered a stumbling block and were opposed from within the Gilman Organization, despite Howard's efforts."[103] Letters from London requesting important information remained unanswered for weeks on end and the planned surveying of the clearing as well as preparations to construct the grid proceeded very slowly, despite repeated instructions to move ahead with these measures. "No consensus could be reached within management on the feasibility of the plan, and it had to be abandoned. Nevertheless, Howard went forward with his ideas [...] the brief was amply realized, although not on Price's terms [...]."[104] Cedric Price was thus unable to fulfil an elementary aspect of his "architecture of ecology" in the Generator project and it is still not clear whether he was aware of the immanent contradiction generated in his projects by his simultaneous aspirations to maintain design sovereignty whilst offering freedom to develop. His vision of co-decision was posited on personal initiative and empathy with the project, which in this case was merely anticipated by the client and the architect. Given the lack of any direct relationship to the context and the people involved, Price's aspiration to foster participation in the Generator was therefore doomed to remain purely abstract.

THE SYMBOL — any size — only one shape.

GENERATOR

CEDRIC PRICE MA Cantab. ARIBA AA Dipl. ARCHITECT
38 ALFRED PLACE LONDON WC1E 7DP Tel: 01-636 5220

27   Cedric Price Architects, "The Symbol – any size – only one shape", Polaroid photographs on paper, undated.

MAGNET 220

1 Author unknown, "Magnet 220", collage, ca. 1997.

Epilogue: The City and the Architecture of Change

The Generator was to be Price's last effort to design a complete, self-contained system. In his understanding of architectural practice, architecture could instead have an impact only if embedded within an already existing social and spatial context. Attributes of diversity and openness could not emerge within projects like the Generator, which started from a blank slate. Rather, he began to hold the urbanity of cities such as London or New York as synonymous with appropriate spatial articulation of society and its various cultures. In this respect he viewed the city as a place where the complex relationships between environment, geography and society were expressed in their entirety. In his subsequent work Price therefore saw the architect's task not in creating an ecology but in allowing the users the faculties of choice and discretion in an already existing urban system.

This definitive shift of orientation in his design methodology became apparent in the Magnets study, which he worked on in 1996 and 1997.[1] Here, Price aimed to promote public space through small-scale interventions. In ten neighbourhoods within the Greater London Metropolitan Area, which had become isolated due to newly built highways and railways, Price intended to spur novel connections, meeting points and places for people to sojourn.[2] To this task he developed infrastructures, such as bridges and platforms, each of which he assigned a sphere of influence; like magnets these structures should attract the surroundings' social dynamism and thus generate new activities. With this minimalistic approach for interventions in an existing social system, he let the dynamism of the urban context generate the programme and allowed for all kinds of appropriations of these places.

1
2
3
4

This principle also shaped many other projects of his, such as the Ducklands project, which Price devised for Hamburg in 1991, or his entry to the IFCCA ideas competition for Manhattan's West Side (1999).[3] As if to underscore this temporary endpoint in the evolution of his architectural strategy, he described his design principles in the exhibition catalogue for the Magnets project thus: "To establish a valid equation between contemporary social aspirations and architecture, it is essential to add to the latter doubt, delight and change as design criteria."[4]

Price thus succinctly summed up his ideas on how to continue and evolve the maxims of modern planning. Architecture should no longer be viewed in a therapeutic sense, i.e. as a means to overcome societal shortcomings; instead he demanded: "Like medicine it must move from the curative to the preventive."[5] Concurrent to his liberal values of free entrepreneurship and its conception of the user as a responsible and enlightened citizen, Price aspired to achieve an architecture that would foster self-organisation and adaptability over time. In his view modern architecture had turned against people and subordinated individual needs to maxims of efficiency. Price sought to counteract this development by incorporating emancipatory values such as diversity and individuality into his projects.

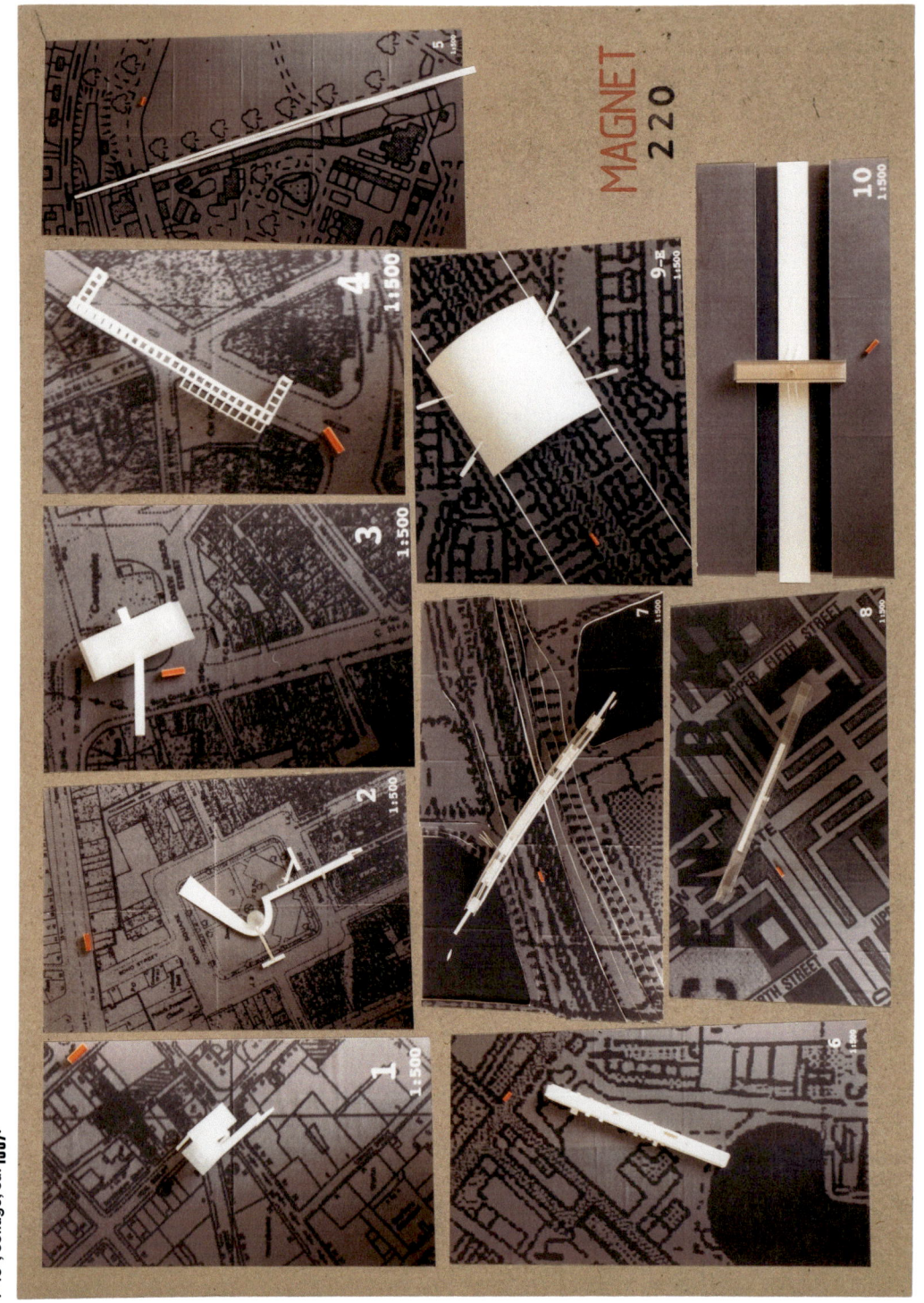

2 Author unknown, "Magnet 220: 1–10", collage, ca. **1997**.

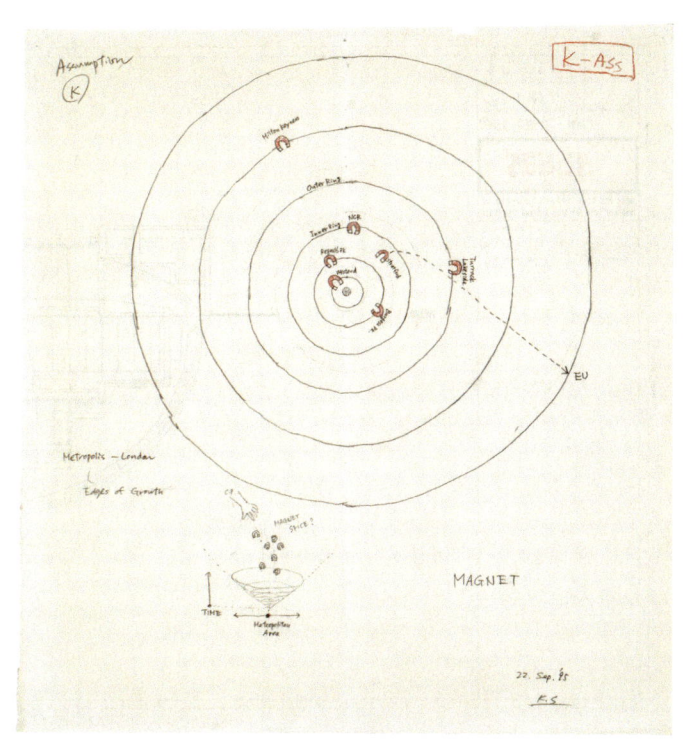

3 Author unknown, "Magnet K., 22", sketch, **1995**.

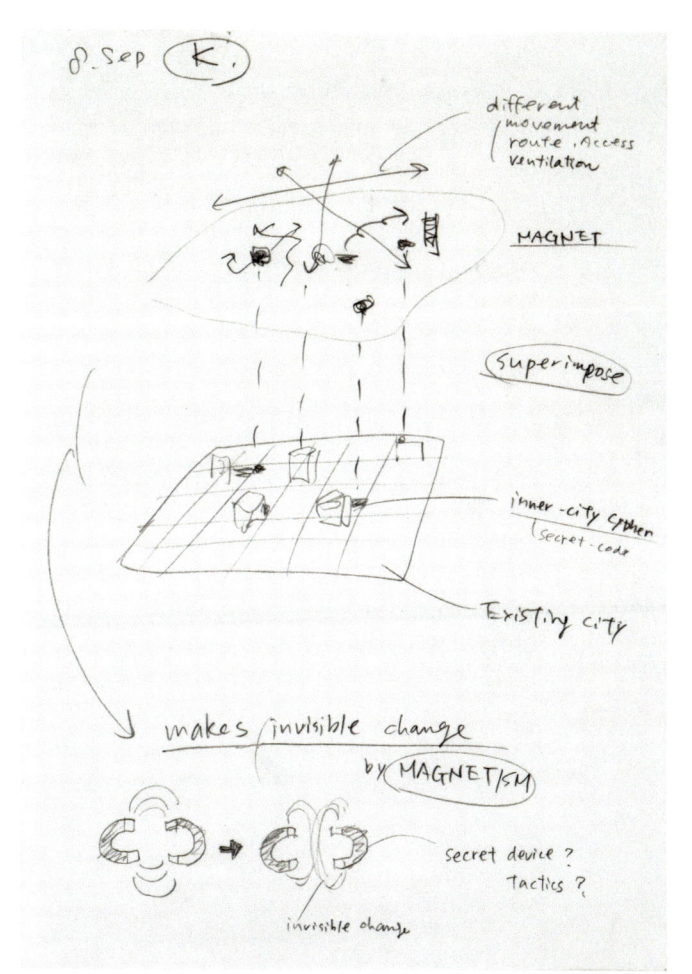

4 Author unknown, "Magnet K. Ass.", sketch, **1995**.

He believed that architecture could move on from questions of health and hygiene in the cities, which had been topical to Modernist architecture at the dawn of mass society. Contemporary architecture should instead turn its attention to new challenges that he saw arise from the emerging information and service society, such as the availability of knowledge and education or the access to places of public exchange and culture, which he viewed as fundamental requirements of human existence on a par with the importance that the Modernist avant-garde had accorded to housing.

The McAppy project and Price's work on the Inter-Action Centre can be seen as initial articulations of this stance, the practical means of which were both developed and tried out as if in a test bed. Whereas Price had developed the methodology for an open design practice in McAppy, in the Inter-Action Centre he successfully combined this approach with the technically oriented ideas of the Fun Palace. As a creative framework, the Inter-Action Centre was intended to bring together the activities of the local neighbourhood initiative, the Inter-Action Group, literally under one roof. However, in order to allow the initiative's diverse agenda and activities to continue changing and developing, a high degree of flexibility was required. Accordingly, Price conceived variable spaces for the cultural centre, which could be reconfigured and readapted again and again. For realising this "architecture of options" Price deployed the latest industrial prefabrication techniques as well as mobile spaces like Portakabins, but also a log cabin and a bus, all of which could be fitted into the roof grid in a range of variable configurations. Here, too, Price focused less on designing the building components than on devising a system and the corresponding structure that could contain potential combinations of these parts.

Putting his ideas into practice however proved not entirely unproblematic. Numerous difficulties arose first and foremost from the undefined process for participation in planning. A succession of contact persons and the complex decision-making process within the group were additional new challenges for the architect, which proved just as demanding as the lack of appropriate financing strategies or statutory provisions for implementing a temporary communal project at the time.

However, Price failed to appreciate the significance of negotiation processes for an open and adaptable architecture. Yet precisely such procedures would come to play an increasingly important role when realising this "bottom-up" type of architecture. It became apparent that suitable means of communication were amiss to convey to a non-expert audience the potential of the countless possibilities that were characteristic of Price's design. As a consequence, he had to develop his own visual language to convey to the Inter-Action Group just how flexible their communal centre would be and how responsive to capricious changes of their needs and desires. He had furthermore to take into account that, in general, the decision-making processes were less associated with well-defined individual interests but determined rather by a group of people representing highly heterogeneous ideas. Even though Price did address these challenges, he never fully articulated them, presumably because he did

5
6
7

not see himself in the role of a facilitator involving users and clients during the design stage already. Instead, and entirely in the spirit of the architect's classical role, he was not prepared to relinquish design sovereignty. His approach to designing architecture as infrastructure engaged solely in the optionality of spatial changes that the architect anticipated in advance.

While this aspiration of his had already informed the Fun Palace Project, it took more than fifteen years before Price began transforming it into an autonomous design approach. Taking the McAppy project as a starting point his ideas can be seen taking shape in his competition entry for Parc de la Villette in Paris (1983) and his study for London's South Bank (1983), in which he foreshadowed the London Eye by proposing the construction of a giant Ferris wheel. In his systemic interpretation of architecture as an intervention in the human living space, a book, a coat hook or a Ferris wheel could all be equally functional. In this sense Price developed a "material-semiotic method", in which people and things were to enter into a new form of dialogue. What makes his works so unique and so successful is therefore not the tangible shape he gave to his projects but rather the methods and strategy he developed in them.

Influenced by the technological transformations of his day, Price believed that architecture's main achievement lay in designing processes of emergence and change and that attributes such as accessibility and participation in social life should become newly ingrained in the city fabric. As his projects needed to be reshaped by users repeatedly over time, architecture depended on constant communication, exchange and negotiation. He thought that these processes would give rise to a new form of communality. He did not however engage himself in arbitrating the processes of appropriation and transformation. Instead, architecture remained in his design conception an object of technical rather than social interactions. To boost the individual's options for expression and, consequently, to reinforce his or her contribution to the community Price used information technology and building services. However, he did not see it as part of the architect's remit to shape the process of social interaction. This was to be achieved by civil society itself. Amongst other activities, Price was an advocate for these processes through his involvement in associations and organisations, as well as in his numerous pieces for journals such as *New Society* and *Architectural Design*. In his articles and columns he participated actively in the intensive debate on the societal role of the architect and his areas of responsibility, a discussion he also continued as a teacher and critic.

With the rise of a postmodern architectural practice and its formal expression at the beginning of the 1980s, however, the functional openness to which Price always referred was increasingly met with incomprehension. In deploying systems theory and industrial prefabrication, Price drew on means previously used to convey modernity's "grand narratives" of equality and compromise, even if he actually used these means to highlight the diversity of ideas and lifestyles encompassed within the notion of "living a good life".[6] To many of his colleagues his avant-garde attitude towards the mechanisms of modern

5 Author unknown, "Your Play Space Needs You", Talacre Action Group NWS and Inter-Action, poster, ca. **1971**.

6 Author unknown, West Kentish Town Neighbourhood Festival, Inter-Action Community Calender, **1977**.

ORIGINAL - OFFICE

7 Cedric Price Architects, photo-montage of the Inter-Action Centre, Camden Town, London, ca. 1976.

architecture felt more and more separated from the quest of finding formal expressions that underscored place and identity in architectural design.

8

Yet in today's context, Price's focus on openness and social interaction seems highly topical once again. In particular in light of the increasingly complex demands on cities' sustainable development in the information society, a number of questions arise, to which Price's ideas seem to be taking on new currency, for instance when negotiating the problems in regard to governance and freedom and the opportunities to participate in architectural production. The unbroken popularity of the Fun Palace Project can be explained by the fact that the project has become a utopian place of yearning, which is used to establish a bridge from the present day, with its complex problems of building, back to the era of modernism – in other words, to a time when architecture was an instrument of the welfare state and the architectural profession was attributed central importance in society. The building's equipment suggested furthermore that, with the aid of the latest technology, the qualities of Functionalist Modernism could be conferred to the era of the information and service society. In this respect, the socio-political vision of the Fun Palace Project comes very close to our present-day expectations of the capabilities of digital technologies, such as the internet and mobile communication, which we associate with values like freedom of expression and personal development. Moreover, in his subsequent projects Price made it equally clear that this socio-political vision is also linked to new social realities, such as the re-evaluation of public and private spheres and their respective limits.

Without being able to provide conclusive answers, Cedric Price devoted his work to these very questions. He challenged himself and the entire profession to find and refine contemporary fundamentals of a human-centric architecture, taking into account a critical attitude toward the use of new technologies. His lasting achievement can thus be seen in the foundation of a school of thought that deals with the human image in a technologized society and which decisively influenced architects of his subsequent generation, including Rem Koolhaas, Bernard Tschumi and Richard Rogers. This freedom of thought is worth rediscovering today.

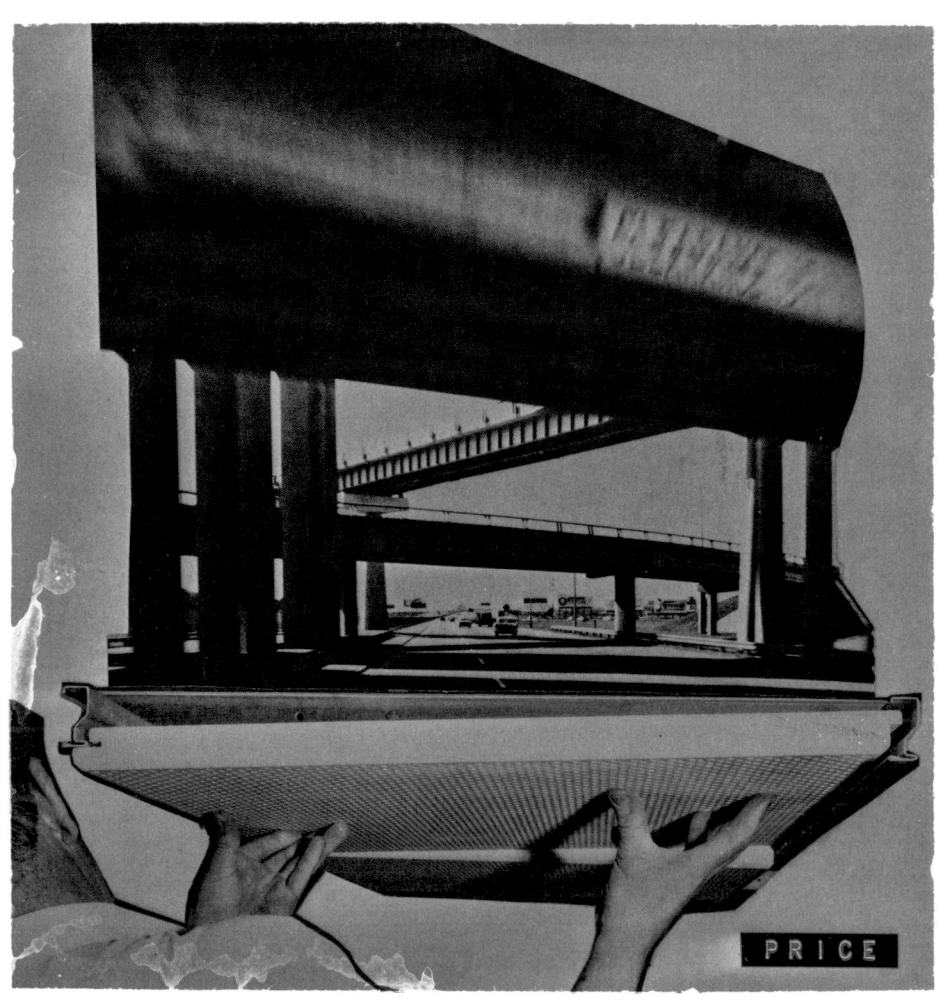

8 Cedric Price, "PRICE", series 4/4, collage for the Sheffield University Festival, ca. 1966.

Footnotes

Preface

1   The term is used to refer to groups such as Archigram, Archizoom and Superstudio, which had been commenting since the mid-1960s on the misguided evolution of progress-oriented Modernist architecture. See also, e.g. Simon Sadler, *Archigram: Architecture without architecture* (MIT Press, 2005).

2   Kenneth Powell, "Cedric Price", Obituary, *The Independent* (14th August 2003).

3   Ibid.

4   J. Stanley Mathews, "An Architecture for the New Britain: The Social Vision of Cedric Price's Fun Palace and Potteries", doctoral thesis submitted to Columbia University, New York, 2003.

1

1   Hans Ulrich Obrist, *Cedric Price*, The Conversation Series, 21 (Cologne: Verlag Walter König, 2009).

2   In 1960 most Londoners owned a radio or television, but did not have a bathroom or toilet in their home. "Statistics on Radio and Television 1950–1960", in *Historical Statistics*, UNESCO (1960), http://unesdoc.unesco.org/images/0003/000337/033739eo.pdf (consulted on 1st March 2010); Peter Geoffrey Hall, *Cities of Tomorrow. An Intellectual History of Urban Planning in the Twentieth Century*, 6th edition (London: Blackwell Publishers, 2001).

3   Sean Glynn and Alan Booth, *Modern Britain. An Economic and Social History*, (New York: Routledge, 1996).

4   Cedric Price, "Home, Sweet Home", *Time & Tide* (20th January 1961). Cedric Price Archive, Canadian Centre for Architecture, Montréal, document folder: DR:1995:0235:007:003.

5   Both articulated their specific interpretation of modern city architecture in 1941 in their reconstruction plan "A master plan for London". Dennis Sharp. "Gropius und Korn: Zwei Erfolgreiche Architekten im Exil", in *Kunst im Exil in Großbritannien 1933–1945* (Berlin: Fröhlich & Kaufmann, 1986).

6   Cedric Price, "What's the Use of Piccadilly?", *Time & Tide* (2nd March 1961).

7   Royston Landau. "Newby + Price", AA files in *Enigneers and Architects Series*, 27 (1994).

8   Cedric Price, "Conversion at Oldham, Lancashire", *Architectural Review*, No. 714 (June 1956); Cedric Price. "Beneficial Change", in *The Square Book* (London: Wiley Academy, 1984; reprint, 2003).

9   The couple who had commissioned him to design the Gamekeeper's Cottage had separated, which led to far-reaching changes in how the house was used.

10   Konrad Wachsmann, *Wendepunkt im Bauen*, (Wiesbaden: Krausskopf Verlag, 1959). An English translation of the manifesto, *The Turning Point of Building*, was published in 1961.

Cedric Price travelled together with a friend, engineer Frank Newby, to meet Konrad Wachsmann. Landau, "Newby + Price".

11   "From communal living to large self serviced 'cells' for each other." Cedric Price, "Steel Housing", concept text on reproduction film (not dated), Cedric Price Archive, Canadian Centre for Architecture, Montréal, document folder: DR:1995:0280:3/3:box 16, project #81.

12   The design had already made a lasting impression on Price during his first visit to London, as also becomes clear in his own later designs, particularly the Inter-Action Centre.

13   Cedric Price, "Steel Housing", in *The Square Book* (London: Wiley Academy, 1984; reprint, 2003).

14   Price, "Home, Sweet Home".

15   Cedric Price, "Towards a 24-Hour Economic Living Toy", *Interior Design* (September 1967), in *The Square Book*. The quotation is in capital letters in the original, giving it additional emphasis.

16   Reyner Banham, *Theory and Design in the First Machine Age*, (London: Architectural Press, 1960).

17   Johnson's pavilion was contemporaneous with Ludwig Mies van der Rohe's Farnsworth House (1946–1951).

18   Reyner Banham, "Towards a Pop Architecture", *Architectural Review* (July 1962): 43, reprinted in Reyner Banham, *Design by Choice* (London: Academy Editions, 1981).

19   Reyner Banham, "A Home Is Not a House", *Art in America* (April 1965): 73.

20   Banham, "Towards a Pop Architecture".

21   *This is Tomorrow* was held after the Independent Group had ended their joint activities in spring 1955. Its members were however still active in the ICA. Anne Massey, *The Independent Group. Modernism and Massculture in Britain 1945–1959*, (Manchester: Manchester University Press, 1995). Price was responsible for setting up the installation by Group 7, and met a lot of those involved in this context. He also frequently attended the architecture salons run by Banham and his wife, where architects of various generations would meet and discuss their ideas. Their circles included, along with many others, John and Magda McHale, Sir Colin Alexander St. John "Sandy" Wilson, James Stirling, Alan Colquhoun, Bob Maxwell, Cedric Price, who was fifteen years younger, and also Peter Cook. Mary Banham, Authorised interview with the author (London, 14th February 2007).

22   *Fun House* was curated by Richard Hamilton and John McHale in conjunction with John Voelker. Hans Ulrich Obrist. "On Early Influences. Interview with Richard Hamilton", The Tate Gallery, http://www.tate.org.uk/magazine/issue4/popdaddy.htm (consulted on 12th July 2010).

23   Richard Hamilton in particular, with whom Cedric Price had worked in the 1960s on installation projects, emphasised a connection between popular culture and the natural sciences and technology in his work. The impact of the technological development of machines, the influence of mobility and miniaturisation on everyday life and changes in the world of science were topics he had already addressed in the exhibitions *On Growth and Form*, 1951, and *Man, Machine and Motion*, 1955. Price worked with Richard Hamilton, and also with the artists Joe Tilson and Harold and Bernard Cohen on smaller installation projects in 1968. For example, an inflatable plastic column set up on St. James Square aimed to make passersby aware of their surroundings and of the square's beauty. Cedric Price. Letter to Walter Bird (1st June 1968). Cedric Price Archive, Canadian Centre for Architecture, Montréal, document folder: DR:1995:0014:080.

24   Cedric Price planned a piece for the festival in Sheffield in conjunction with a friend, the artist Feliks Topolski; it was to take the form of a folly, i.e. a decorative edifice or set-design-style architecture, originally deployed as an element in garden design in landscape parks and not fulfilling any practical purpose. It is however unclear whether the project was actually realised in this form. Cedric Price, "Sheffield University Festival 1966" (not dated), Cedric Price Archive, Canadian Centre for Architecture, Montréal, document folder: DR:1995:0221:017–018.

25 Cedric Price. Photo montage, negative (ca. 1966), Cedric Price Archive, Canadian Centre for Architecture, Montréal, document folder: DR:2008:003:0002, folder 8 (OSI Box).

26 Ibid.

27 Both projects ran in parallel from 1961 to 1965, with cross-fertilisation in their approaches and developments. The opening of the London Zoo Aviary was scheduled for 1963. However, there were delays in construction work, which was not completed until summer 1964. Cracks in structural connecting elements led to time-consuming checks and replacement of components, meaning that the building could not be officially opened until January 1965. On the opening, see: *Daily Express*, "Tony Shows the Cage", 15th January 1965. Cedric Price Archive, Canadian Centre for Architecture, Montréal, document folder: DR:1995:0185:275:003:3/4, 7/31.

28 Both quote and definition of "technology" in: Cedric Price, *Technology Is the Answer but What Was the Question?*, The Pidgeon Audiovisual Collection, (London: World Microfilms | Microworld House, 1979).

29 In *Theory and Design in the First Machine Age*, Banham had proclaimed Fuller's work to be a role model for architecture of the second machine age. Banham, *Theory and Design in the First Machine Age*.

30 Cedric Price, "Buckminster Fuller, 1895–1983" Obituary, *Architecural Design*, No. 4 (1983).

31 Banham, Authorised interview with the author.

32 John McHale, who later also worked for Buckminster Fuller, published an essay on Fuller in *Architectural Design* in 1961 on the occasion of the UIA's London Congress, "Architecture and Technology". On this point, see Peter Smithson's commentary on the differing areas of interest and approaches within the Independent Group in: Beatriz Colomina, "Friends of the Future. A Conversation with Peter Smithson", *The Independent Group 94* (October 2000): 3.

33 Fuller also invited Cedric Price to Carbondale for a lecture and recommended him in 1964 as a participant in Constantinos Doxiadis' Delos Symposium. Richard Buckminster Fuller. Letter to Cedric Price (6th May 1964). Cedric Price Archive, Canadian Centre for Architecture, Montréal, document folder: DR:1995:0188:525:3/5; Price, *The Square Book*.

34 In 1959 Ian McCallum had already seen Fuller's experimental residential dome in the garden at MoMA, and had contacted him as a result. Price's design for the auditorium was rejected by the American Museum's trustees in 1963. Ian McCallum, "Memorandum on the Plastic Radome Proposal by Cedric Price for the American Museum in Britain" (19th February 1964), Cedric Price Archive, Canadian Centre for Architecture, Montréal, document folder: DR:1995:0183:002.

35 Through John McHale, Buckminster Fuller had made detailed exposés and constructional descriptions of various earlier project designs available to Prince, enabling him to derive the constructional principles for the commission from these. Richard Buckminster Fuller, "To Ellen Marsh". Memorandum for the collection and archive of the Museum of Modern Art, New York (1st December 1961), Cedric Price Archive, Canadian Centre for Architecture, Montréal, document folder: DR:1995:0183:002.

36 The residential dome was initially meant to be shown together with a building by Frederick Kiesler in the exhibition *Two Houses: New Ways to Build at MoMA*. "Guide to the R. Buckminster Fuller Papers. M1090", Online-Archive California, http://www.oac.cdlib.org/view?docId=tf109n9832;query=M.-21-1%20;dsc.position=15001;style=oac4;view=dsc#hitNum1 (consulted on 2nd July 2010); "Chronology of the Department of Architecture and Design", Museum of Modern Art, New York (1964), https://www.moma.org/momaorg/shared/pdfs/docs/press_archives/3398/releases/MOMA_1964_Reopening_0024_1964-05.pdf?2010 (consulted on 2nd July 2010). The project was not realised and, just like Frederick Kiesler's Endless House Project, was only displayed as a model in Arthur Dexler's 1960 *Visionary Architecture* exhibition. Buckminster Fuller indicates however that a similar version of a dome construction was realised in Woods Hole. Fuller, "To Ellen Marsh".

37 Fuller, "To Ellen Marsh".

38 Price, "Buckminster Fuller, 1895–1983".

39 Fuller, "To Ellen Marsh".

40 Richard Buckminster Fuller. "The Comprehensive Designer" (1949), in *Your Private Sky*, Joachim Krause and Claude Lichtenstein, ed. (Baden: Lars Müller Verlag, 1999); Richard Buckminster Fuller. "Universal Architecture" (1932), in *Programs and Manifestoes on 20th-Century Architecture*, Ulrich Conrads, ed. (Cambridge, MA: MIT Press, 1970).

41 J. Stanley Mathews, "An Architecture for the New Britain. The Social Vision of Cedric Price's Fun Palace and Potteries Thinkbelt" (Doctoral thesis Columbia University, New York, 2003).

42 The Russian Constructivists had already considered approaches involving a similar construction method. Maria Gough, "In the Laboratory of Constructivism. Karl loganson's Cold Structures", *October* 84 (1998): 90.

43 "Report of the Zoological Society London" (20th April 1961), Cedric Price Archive, Canadian Centre for Architecture, Montréal, document folder: DR:2006:0023:1/31.

44 In this attitude both pick up on influences that stemmed from Buckminster Fuller. Landau, "Newby + Price".

45 "The Skylon South Bank Exhibition. Festival of Britain 1951". Truck postcard (not dated), Cedric Price Archive, Canadian Centre for Architecture, Montréal, document folder: DR:2004:box12.

46 Landau, "Newby + Price".

47 Reyner Banham, "Zoo À La Mode", *New Statesman* (12th March 1965).

48 As building materials, both aluminium and steel presupposed industrial production of components. Engineer John Mathy, who worked with Samuely, had experience in manufacturing moulded aluminium components from the aviation industry. His know-how proved helpful in producing the cast aluminium components. Landau, "Newby + Price".

49 "You will all have to use your highest strategic disciplines to pilot your way through the hazardous matter of doing experimental structural development in public." Richard Buckminster Fuller. Letter to Frank Newby (5th January 1964), Copy. Cedric Price Archive, Canadian Centre for Architecture, Montréal, document folder: DR:1995:0185:275:003:3/4.

50 The London Zoo Aviary was the first building in which aluminium welding was used. The technique had just been developed at the Westminster Engineering Cooperation in North Acton and was presented to the public at a press conference in February 1963. Westminster Engineering Cooperation. Press release (2nd May 1963), Cedric Price Archive, Canadian Centre for Architecture, Montréal, document folder: DR:2006:0023:015.

51 In the early 1960s computers were not yet in widespread use as data-processing tools and there were only very limited opportunities, for example in state institutes or universities, to actually use such devices. Landau, "Newby + Price". On the practical tests, see also: Institution of Civil Engineering. Letter to Cedric Price (18th July 1963; Kensington). Cedric Price Archive, Canadian Centre for Architecture, Montréal, document folder: DR:2006:0023:015.

52 Cedric Price suggested planting trees from an adjacent plot. Cedric Price. Letter to Shepheard, Bridgewater, Epstein Landscape Architects (25th January 1962). Cedric Price Archive, Canadian Centre for Architecture, Montréal, document folder: DR:2006:0023:015.

53 Cedric Price. Letter to James Bresford & Sons about the detailing of the pump system (1961). Cedric Price Archive, Canadian Centre for Architecture, Montréal, document folder: DR:2006:0023:015:3/31; Landau, "Newby + Price".

54 "[…] a place of public interest and enjoyment […]" Cedric Price, "The R. S. Reynolds Memorial Award Application" (1965), Cedric Price Archive, Canadian Centre for Architecture, Montréal, document folder: DR:1995:0185:275:003.

55 Cedric Price. Letter to General Dalton, London Zoological Society (1962). Cedric Price Archive, Canadian Centre for Architecture, Montréal, document folder: DR:2006:0023: 015:3/31.

56 Banham, "Zoo À La Mode".

57 A few years earlier the lightweight aluminium construction of the Skylon by the architects Powell & Moya, a project Frank Newby had also worked on, had been viewed as similarly exemplary. Isabelle Moffat, "A Horror of Abstract Thought. Postwar Britain and Hamilton's 1951 'Growth and Form' Exhibition", *The Independent Group* 94 (October 2000): 89.

58 Garden Designer Charles R. Faust. Letter to Cedric Price (31st August 1961). Cedric Price Archive, Canadian Centre for Architecture, Montréal, document folder: DR:2006:0023: 015:1/31.

59 Steven Mullin from Cedric Price's team reported that the mesh broke repeatedly. Droppings from the zoo's mascot, "Goldy the eagle", caused the mesh to corrode. On another occasion the mesh's welded joints broke due to an unexpectedly harsh frost. See also: *Daily Mail*, "Snowdon's Aviary Held up by Cable Trouble", 29th March 1963. Cedric Price Archive, Canadian Centre for Architecture, Montréal, document folder: DR:1995:0185: 275:002:4/31.

60 The cast aluminium components on the ends of the tetrahedron bars made the structure appear minimalistic, although its constructional approach and energy use meant it was not the optimum solution from the perspective of resource utilisation.

61 Landau, "Newby + Price".

62 Fuller, Letter to Frank Newby (5th January 1964).

63 Price continued his work on integration of industrial construction techniques into architecture in conjunction with Frank Newby. From 1966, they worked on a Ministry of Technology commission to research air-supported, load-bearing structures with the goal of documenting existing manufacturing techniques for these structures. Price subsequently set up the Lightweight Enclosures Unit (LEU) as a network promoting dissemination of important publications in this field. In 1974 the British Standards Institution gave Newby and Price the task of incorporating their know-how on air-supported load-bearing structures into a construction industry standard.

64 Fuller, Letter to Frank Newby (5th January 1964).

65 Price, "Buckminster Fuller, 1895–1983".

66 Gordon Pask, "Fun Palace Project. Cybernetics Committee. Introductory Document" (ca. 1964), Cedric Price Archive, Canadian Centre for Architecture, Montréal, document folder: DR:1995:0188:525:2/5.

67 Joan Littlewood and Cedric Price, "Joan Littlewood Presents the First Giant Space Mobile …". Copy (not dated), Cedric Price Archive, Canadian Centre for Architecture, Montréal, document folder: DR:1995:0188:526:1/5.

68 In this respect Cedric Price adopted a Structuralist approach in his designs, focusing on establishing different relationships between individual elements in the building. Joan Littlewood, "Fun Palace Film. Suggested Model Sequence" (not dated), Cedric Price Archive, Canadian Centre for Architecture, Montréal, document folder: DR:1995:0188:525:3/5.

69 Pask, "Fun Palace Project. Cybernetics Committee. Introductory Document". On the figures involved in the Fun Palace Project and relationships between them: Mathews, "An Architecture for the New Britain".

70 Pask, "Fun Palace Project. Cybernetics Committee. Introductory Document".

71 Casey N. Blake. "Introduction to Arts and Technics" (1952), in Lewis Mumford, *Art and Technics*, 2nd edition (New York: Columbia University Press, 2000).

72 Steven Mullin, Authorised interview with the author (London, 24th June 2006).

73 Joan Littlewood, *Joan's Book. Joan Littlewood's Peculiar History as She Tells It*, (London: Methuen; 2003).

74 Joan Littlewood, "Project". Script for the article *1984: Leisure and the arts; A Laboratory of fun* by Joan Littlewood and Cedric Price (30th January 1964), Cedric Price Archive, Canadian Centre for Architecture, Montréal, document folder: DR:1995:0188:525:1/5.

75 Joan Littlewood had initial experience with implementing the ideals of the Theatre Workshop in Centre 42, a project by leftist artists, including Arnold Wesker, Doris Lessing and Clive Barker, who opposed the commercialisation of art and organised festivals from 1961–1963. The project was suspended in 1963 as it was not financially viable. In the 1963 Donmar project Joan Littlewood once again attempted, in conjunction with Cedric Price, to set up an experimental theatre space. Robert Leach, *Theatre Workshop. Joan Littlewood and the Making of Modern British Theatre*, (Exeter: University of Exeter Press, 2006).

76 Melville Mark Associates. "Joan Littlewood's Fun Palace. A Peoples' Workshop" (Melville Mark, International Public Relations. Geneva, 11th May 1965), Cedric Price Archive, Canadian Centre for Architecture, Montréal, document folder: DR:1995: 0188:525:5/5.

77 The Fun Palace Project Report encapsulates the aims of the scheme in the following three goals: "–to provide facilities for conventional and unconventional entertainment; learning and investigation; expression of creative, constructive and imaginative ideas. –to provide any amenities, facilities and equipment as might reasonably be required by users. [...] –to give access to information and scientific knowledge not normally available to the majority of people." "Confidential Fun Palace Project Report" (March 1965), Cedric Price Archive, Canadian Centre for Architecture, Montréal, document folder: DR:1995:0188:525:2/5–5/5.

78 Cedric Price, "Chat. Extracts from the Tape", *Architectural Design* 41 (April 1971): 231.

79 Littlewood and Price, "Joan Littlewood Presents the First Giant Space Mobile …".

80 Mathews, "An Architecture for the New Britain".

81 For this project and for his initial studies for the Fun Palace, Price drew on Littlewood's input in the form of references to the 1930s Modernist avant-garde, Erwin Piscator and Vsevolod Meyerhold as well as to current developments in theatre building that deployed the latest construction and stage technology to establish all-round performance forms in the theatre. On the theatre of this period: Edward Braun, *Meyerhold. A Revolution in Theatre*, (University of Iowa Press, 1995).

82 Littlewood's role model here was Vsevolod Meyerhold, who used improvisation and opening-up of the space as techniques to contrast the natural being of humans with the mechanistic order of industrialised society. Throughout her career as a theatre director Joan Littlewood remained committed to this dramaturgical stance. Echoing Stanislavsky's theories on the theatre, Joan Littlewood called the theatre group she set up in 1935 in Manchester the "Theatre of Action". In 1935 she had been awarded a grant to study at the Moscow Film and Theatre School. She was however unable to accept it as she was denied an exit visa for the USSR. In a review of the "Theatre of Action", published in 1935 in the Manchester Guardian's, their performances were labelled "the nearest thing any British Theatre got to Meyerhold." Howard Goorney, *The Theatre Workshop Story*, (orig. 1981; London: Methuen, 2008).

83 Mordecai Gorelik, *New Theatres for Old*, (orig. 1940; New York: Octagon Books, 1975).

84 "Preliminary Structural Calculations for Individual Trusses". Planning document (not dated), Cedric Price Archive, Canadian Centre for Architecture, Montréal, document folder: DR:1995:0188:165.

85 855 × 375 feet. Reyner Banham, *Megastructures. Urban Futures of the Recent Past*, (London: Thames and Hudson Ltd., 1976).

86 "Complex-Plan (Typical)". Planning document, ink on transparent paper, scale 1:500 (not dated), Cedric Price Archive, Canadian Centre for Architecture, Montréal, document folder: DR:1995:0188:198.

87 Sketch of a longitudinal section through the Fun Palace (not dated), ink, coloured pencil and felt tip on paper Cedric Price Archive, Canadian Centre for Architecture, Montréal, document folder: DR:1995:0188:104.

88 Cedric Price's personal library for example included the original 1900 Paris World Fair exhibition catalogue, which he had bought from an antiquarian bookdealer. "Les Principaux Palais De L'exposition Universelle De Paris 1900" (not dated), Cedric Price Archive, Canadian Centre for Architecture, Montréal, document folder: DRCON 2004:0002:135.

89 Basil Spence. The Sea and Ships Pavilion (Basil Spence Archive, Royal Commission on the Ancient und Historical Monuments of Scotland (RCAHMS), Edinburgh, UK, ca. 1949), photograph of the model. Twenty-five years later Price reused this spatial concept for the Inter-Action Centre (1973–1977), although in this case he adhered very closely to the pavilion's original concept. Cf.: Aerial photograph of the Inter-Action Centre (ca. 1976). Cedric Price Archive, Canadian Centre for Architecture, Montréal, document folder: DR:1995:0252:632:014:001.

90 Frank Newby had met Ludwig Mies van der Rohe in Chicago in 1953, as well as Konrad Wachsman, who was also teaching there at the same time and developed his first universal hall construction as a commission for the US military. Landau, "Newby + Price".

91 Mary Banham notes that Mies van der Rohe's works were an important point of reference for post-war architects in Great Britain. Banham, Authorised interview with the author.

92 Cedric Price, "Structural Systems. Kit of Parts". Sketch, scale not indicated (not dated), Cedric Price Archive, Canadian Centre for Architecture, Montréal, document folder: DR:1995:0188:525-2/5, folder 3.

93 The elements in the structural frame were based on an underlying grid of ca. 1.1 m (= 3 ft 9 in). Cedric Price Architects, "Clamp System. Modular Flexibility Study. 51/78". Scale: ¼ inch = 1 foot (ca. 1 : 200 [the author]; not dated), Cedric Price Archive, Canadian Centre for Architecture, Montréal, document folder: DR:1995:0188:208.

94 Cedric Price, "A Galaxy of Load Bearing Links". Sketch, black ink und coloured pencil, scale not indicated (not dated), Cedric Price Archive, Canadian Centre for Architecture, Montréal, document folder: DR:1995:0188:108.

95 On the life and work of architect Louis Henry Sullivan see: Mario Manieri-Elia, Louis Henry Sullivan, (New York: Princeton Architectural Press, 1996).

96 Price, "A Galaxy of Load Bearing Links".

97 Joan Littlewood, "Joan Littlewood Productions Presents Riverside Pleasure Project". Preliminary design for the Fun Palace Leaflet, typewritten manuscript (ca. 1964), Cedric Price Archive, Canadian Centre for Architecture, Montréal, document folder: DR:1995:0188:525:2/5.

98 Mary Lou Lobsinger had already compared the Fun Palace to a machine. Mary Louise Lobsinger. "Cybernetic Theory and the Architecture of Performance. Cedric Price's Fun Palace", in Anxious Modernisms. Experimentation in Postwar Architectural Culture, Sarah Goldhagen and Rejean Legault, ed. (Cambridge: MIT Press, 2000).

99 Simon Sadler, Archigram. Architecture without Architecture, (Cambridge, MA: MIT Press, 2005).

100 Warren Chalk, Peter Cook, and Dennis Crompton. "Plug in City Study", Archigram Archival Project, Research Centre for Experimental Practice, University of Westminster, http://archigram.westminster.ac.uk/project.php?id=56 (consulted on 6th August 2010).

101 Peter Cook also addressed the conceptual division of architecture into structural elements and spatial elements in his Nottingham Crane Way (shopping viaduct) project, which he had designed in 1962 with David Greene. Sadler, Archigram.

102 Banham, Megastructures.

103 In establishing a distinction between the load-bearing structure and space-forming elements, Cedric Price referenced the concept of "cluster buildings" advocated by Denys Lasdun and Alison and Peter Smithson, which envisaged such a division as an expression of community architecture. On the genesis and content of the "cluster buildings" concept in British architecture: Laurent Stalder. "Cluster Buildings", in Bauten der Boomjahre. Paradoxien der Erhaltung, Uta Hassler and Catherine Dumont d'Ayoy, ed. (Gollion: Infolio Editions, 2009). The architectonic elements of the university extension were composed according to the principle of additive conjoining of infrastructure and usable space and were thus meant to enable growth and change of the building in a fashion akin to the developmental processes found in urban space.

104 As a member of the Groupe d'Étude d'Architecture Mobile (GEAM) Yona Friedman had from 1959–1960 drawn up his design for the "ville spatiale", with a framing structural system developing freely over the old city in Paris. Artist Constant Nieuwenhuys' models of the New Babylon project (1959–1974) showed a megastructure too, also unfolding freely over European cities, and numerous designs for this kind of megastructure had also come into being in Japan both in the context of the Metabolist group, founded in 1960, and in architect Kenzo Tange's circles.

105 Fumihiko Maki, Investigations in Collective Form, (St. Louis: The School of Architecture, Washington University, 1964).

106 "Confidential Fun Palace Project Report".

107 "Possibility of Circuits". Sketch, coloured pencil on transparent paper (not dated), Cedric Price Archive, Canadian Centre for Architecture, Montréal, document folder: DR:1995: 0188:04; Littlewood, "Fun Palace Film. Suggested Model Sequence".

108 The special technical fittings in the rooms included for example: air heating, stage lighting, a loudspeaker system or a movable façade made of a plastic membrane. "Confidential Fun Palace Project Report".

109 Littlewood, "Fun Palace Film. Suggested Model Sequence".

110 "Confidential Fun Palace Project Report".

111 Cedric Price. Axonometry of clamp system (not dated), ink on transparent paper, scale not indicated, Cedric Price Archive, Canadian Centre for Architecture, Montréal, document folder: DR:1995:0188:211.

112 Production figures for motorised vehicles in the United Kingdom increased from 535,000 in 1950 to 1.35 million in 1960. Jeremy Wood, Motor Industry of Britain Centenary Book, (London: Eclat, 1996).

113 In Modernist architecture, for example Le Corbusier's 1927 design for the Citrohan house, which drew on serial production methods, the car served as a model for industrialisation of construction. Joachim Petersen and Friedemann Gschwind. "Die Häuser Der Weissenhofsiedlung. Haus 13", http://www.weissenhof 2002.de/weissenhof.html (consulted on 2nd January 2011).

114 Layout blueprint for an article on the Fun Palace, illustrations and captions (not dated). Cedric Price Archive, Canadian Centre for Architecture, Montréal, document folder: DR:1995: 0188:525:3/5.

115 "Confidential Fun Palace Project Report".

116 Mullin, Authorised interview with the author.

117 Richard Buckminster Fuller, Utopia or Oblivion. The Prospects for Humanity, (New York: Bantam Books, 1969).

118 Richard Buckminster Fuller, Buckminster Fuller. Starting with the Universe, ed. Michael K. Hays, Dana Miller, and Antoine Picon (London: Yale University Press, 2008).

119 Joan Littlewood, "A Laboratory of Fun. Leisure and the Arts in 1984", New Scientist (14th May 1964): 432.

120 Ibid.; Joan Littlewood, "City/Entertainment". Note, typewritten (not dated), Cedric Price Archive, Canadian Centre for Architecture, Montréal, document folder: DR:1995: 0188:525:1/5. Cedric Price had used a similar image in his regional study of the Potteries Thinkbelt to describe the social dynamism of a location with the image of the field and its physical magnetism.

121 Kenneth Browne, "Lea Valley Reclaimed. Proposals for a Linear Park for East London" (July 1964), Cedric Price

Archive, Canadian Centre for Architecture, Montréal, document folder: DR:1995:0188:526:3/5.

122 Joan Littlewood, "Joan Littlewood's Fun Palace Project. Draft Script for Studio Filming" (17th August 1964) Mitras Films Ltd., Cedric Price Archive, Canadian Centre for Architecture, Montréal, document folder: 1995:0188:525:1/5.

123 Sections (not dated), scale 1:500. Cedric Price Archive, Canadian Centre for Architecture, Montréal, document folder: DR:1995:0188:23.

124 Cedric Price, "A Laboratory of Fun. Cedric Price, Architect, Elaborates on the Design of the 'Fun Palace' Envisioned by Joan Littlewood", *New Scientist* (14th May 1964): 433.

125 Littlewood, "Fun Palace Film. Suggested Model Sequence".

126 Banham, "A Home Is Not a House".

127 Reyner Banham, "Horse of Different Colour", *New Society* (November 1967): 637.

128 Sigfried Giedion, *Mechanization Takes Command. A Contribution to Anonymous History*, (New York: Oxford University Press, 1948).

129 William M. Pease, "An Automatic Machine Tool", *Scientific American* 187, No. 3 (1st September 1952): 101.

130 Littlewood, "Joan Littlewood's Fun Palace Project".

131 In the light of his own studies on building services engineering in modern architecture, the design of the Fun Palace as a "responsive environment" reinforced Banham's convictions concerning future uses of technology for architecture. Nigel Whiteley, *Reyner Banham. Historian of the Immediate Future*, (Cambridge MA: MIT Press, 2002); Banham, "A Home Is Not a House".

132 Mathews, "An Architecture for the New Britain".

133 Gordon Pask, "Proposal for a Cybernetic Theatre" (ca. 1963), Cedric Price Archive, Canadian Centre for Architecture, Montréal, document folder: DR:1995:0188:525:3/5; Lobsinger, "Cybernetic Theory and the Architecture of Performance".

134 Gordon Pask. Letter from System Research Ltd. to Cedric Price (8th June 1963). Cedric Price Archive, Canadian Centre for Architecture, Montréal, document folder: DR:1995:0188:525:4/5.

135 Pask, "Fun Palace Project. Cybernetics Committee. Introductory Document".

136 In 1952 Arnold Tustin had defined feedback as the most general principle of systems regulation, applicable not only to electronic machines but also to processes in everyday life and human coexistence: "FEEDBACK It is the fundamental principle that underlines all self-regulating systems, not only machines but also the processes of life and the tides of human affairs." Arnold Tustin, "Feedback", *Scientific American* 187, No. 3 (1st September 1952): 48; *Transformation Des Humanen*, ed. Michael Hagener and Erich Hörl (Frankfurt am Main: Suhrkamp, 2008).

137 Pask, "Fun Palace Project. Cybernetics Committee. Introductory Document".

138 Reyner Banham, "Softer Hardware", *Ark 44* (Summer 1969): 2.

139 Gordon Pask, "The Architectural Relevance of Cybernetics", *Architectural Design* 39 (September 1969): 494.

140 Ibid.

141 Cedric Price, "Systems Investigations" (9th May 1963), Cedric Price Archive, Canadian Centre for Architecture, Montréal, document folder: DR:1995:0188:525:2/5.

142 Richard Surcliffe Engineering Systems Ltd. Offer for "Speedramp" Passenger Conveyors (Horbury Wakefield Yorkshire, 10th January 1964), costs for 10 units ca. 133,000 £. Cedric Price Archive, Canadian Centre for Architecture, Montréal, document folder: DR:1995:0188:525:4/5.

143 "Complex-Plan (Typical)".

144 "Complex-Plan (Typical 1)". Planning document, ink on transparent paper, scale 1:500 (not dated), Cedric Price Archive, Canadian Centre for Architecture, Montréal, document folder: DR:1995:0188:236.

145 Pask, "Fun Palace Project. Cybernetics Committee. Introductory Document".

146 Cedric Price, "Questionnairs". Blank copies and copies filled out anonymously (ca. 1964), Cedric Price Archive, Canadian Centre for Architecture, Montréal, document folder: DR:1995:0188:525:3/5.

147 Gordon Pask and Cedric Price, "In Reply to Your Electronic Enquiries Regarding the F.P. Project" (8th July 1963), Cedric Price Archive, Canadian Centre for Architecture, Montréal, document folder: DR:1995:0188:525:2/5.

148 Pask, "Fun Palace Project. Cybernetics Committee. Introductory Document".

149 Pask, Letter from System Research Ltd. to Cedric Price (8th June 1963).

150 "Control of Total Number of Persons". Memorandum, typewritten (4th June 1965), Cedric Price Archive, Canadian Centre for Architecture, Montréal, document folder: DR:1995: 0188:525:2/5.

151 Price, "Systems Investigations".

152 Pask, Letter from System Research Ltd. to Cedric Price (8th June 1963).

153 Cedric Price, "Fun Palace Project" (29th February 1964), Cedric Price Archive, Canadian Centre for Architecture, Montréal, document folder: DR:1995:0188:525:2/5.

2

1 In 1960 the United States of America topped the league when it came to the reach of television as a mass media, with over 56 million television sets. In comparison: Great Britain ca. 11 million, Japan ca. 6 million, Germany ca. 4.6 million and France ca. 2 million sets. "Statistics on Radio and Television 1950–1960".

2 *The Beatles Anthology*, ed. Brian Roylancen (Munich: Ullstein, 2000).

3 In 1960 the government commissioned Prof. Sir Colin Buchanan to draw up a report on the urban traffic situation. The report was published in 1963 as "Traffic in towns: A study of the long term problems of traffic in urban areas". At that time there were already over 1.5 million vehicles registered in London. The report posited that this would grow to a projected forty million in 1980. Sir Colin Buchanan. "Traffic in Towns. A Study of the Long Term Problems of Traffic in Urban Areas", in *Reports of the Steering Group and Working Group appointed by the Minister of Transport* (Her Majesty's Stationery Office. London: 1963).

4 As part of a report on the planned Lea Valley Regional Park, a slot was scheduled to show the Fun Palace film on 6th August 1964 between 19.30 and 20.30. This was probably as part of Dick Gilling's "Horizon Show", launched in 1964 on the BBC. Cedric Price. Note (15th June 1964), Cedric Price Archive, Canadian Centre for Architecture, Montréal, document folder: DR:1995:0188:525:2/5; Mathews, "An Architecture for the New Britain".

5 Joan Littlewood and Cedric Price, "Being an Account of the Necessity of the Fun Palace as a Temporary 'Valve' in a Late 20th Century Metropolis". Manuscript for *ARK*, the journal of the Royal College of Art (ca. 1963), Cedric Price Archive, Canadian Centre for Architecture, Montréal, document folder: DR:1995: 0188:525:2/5.

6 "The Fun Palace, in its siting relative to the existing city, enables people to use it in passing on to some other destination

[...] thus avoid focal attraction." Cedric Price. Note, typewritten (not dated), Cedric Price Archive, Canadian Centre for Architecture, Montréal, document folder: DR:1995:0188:526:4/5.

7   Constant Nieuwenhuys. Lecture: ICA, London (7th November 1963), Cedric Price Archive, Canadian Centre for Architecture, Montréal, document folder: DR:1995:0188:526:2/5.

8   In the "homo ludens" model, the urge to play is an impetus for human cultural creation and forms the point of departure for all cultural systems, such as politics or science. This concept entered scholarly discourse through Johan Huizinga's eponymous book, Johan Huizinga, *Homo Ludens. A Study of the Play-Element in Culture*, (London, Bosten and Henley: Routledge & Kegan Paul, 1949).

9   Archigram, "Living City", *Living Arts*, No. 2 (June 1963): 112, in: Vittorio Magnago Lampugnani, Katia Frey and Eliana Perotti, ed. *Vom Wiederaufbau nach dem 2. Weltkrieg bis zur zeitgenössischen Stadt*. Vol. 3 (Berlin: Gebrüder Mann Verlag, 2005).

10   Ibid.

11   Price wrote, in respect of the project's relationship to the city's new infrasturcture systems: "Various methods of linking with city communications and activities [...] are employed in order to increase the contribution of the project to a well tuned, highly mechanised city environment." David Price and Joan Littlewood, "Preliminary Report: Fun Palace Project" (1963), Cedric Price Archive, Canadian Centre for Architecture, Montréal, document folder: DR:1995:0188:525:4/5.

12   Graph theory, deployed in the Fun Palace's cybernetic analyses, had been linked to the problem of traffic flows since its development in the 18th century, beginning with Leonhardt Euler's "Seven Bridges of Königsberg" problem. The network's connective qualities were the only relevant factor in determining whether the problem could be solved. Dieter Jungnickel, *Graphen, Netzwerke und Algorithmen*, 3rd edition (Mannheim: BI Wissenschaftsverlag, 1984).

13   The frequency with which connecting routes are selected can be computed with the help of graph theory. In "system dynamics", a language was developed to express system characteristics in the form of flow diagrams rather than in the formula-based language of mathematics.

14   Pask, "Fun Palace Project. Cybernetics Committee. Introductory Document".

15   Cedric Price, "Fun Palace". Layout blueprint for *Fun Palace Leaflet* (ca. 1964) sheet 7, Cedric Price Archive, Canadian Centre for Architecture, Montréal, document folder: DR:1995:0188:525:2/5.

16   Barbara Johnson. Letter to Cedric Price (27th September 1965). Cedric Price Archive, Canadian Centre for Architecture, Montréal, document folder: DR:1995:0188:526:3/5.

17   David Price and Joan Littlewood, "Fun Palace". Original fund-raising folder (ca. 1964), private collection, courtesy of Steven Mullin.

18   Jungnickel, *Graphen, Netzwerke und Algorithmen*.

19   In 1962 Lester Randolf Ford and D. R. Fulkerson published the first book on flow theory available in Great Britain. In 1956 they had developed the first algorithm to determine maximum flow. Implementation methods, such as the "Critical Path Method", were also only developed in 1957, by Remington Rand and DuPont. NASA's "Project Mercury" provided the first demonstration that this new form of project management could handle a highly complex development process.

20   The cyberneticians took on the role of observers engaging in empirical studies of phenomena in an unexplored system, in the sense of a black box. In cybernetics the term "black box" is used to describe a complex system, with an unknown inner structure that makes detailed forecasts of interactions within it impossible. In such systems cybernetics simply analyses incoming and outgoing signals. Psychologist and philosopher of science Karl Popper used the term "black box" in connection with his "Three Worlds Theory".

21   Gordon Pask, *An Approach to Cybernetics*, Science Today Series, (New York: Harper & Brothers, 1961).

22   Price, "Fun Palace".

23   Pask, "Fun Palace Project. Cybernetics Committee. Introductory Document".

24   Stanley Mathews published a list of the people organised in the Fun Palace's Cybernetic Committee in an appendix to his doctoral thesis: Mathews, "An Architecture for the New Britain". A slightly different list appears in the document setting up the committee, drafted by Gordon Pask: Pask, "Fun Palace Project. Cybernetics Committee. Introductory Document".

25   Roy Ascott, "Cybernetics Sub-Committee: Form and Amenities. Minutes of the Meeting Held at Holborn Town Hall" (5th March 1965), Cedric Price Archive, Canadian Centre for Architecture, Montréal, document folder: DR:1995:0188:525:5/5.

26   Price and Littlewood, "Fun Palace".

27   Michael Hughes, "Joan's Fun Palace Nearer Fruition". Newspaper clipping (not dated), Cedric Price Archive, Canadian Centre for Architecture, Montréal, document folder: DR:1995:0188:526:3/5.

28   Joan Littlewood paid particular attention to simple needs like voyeurism and gossip that television could not really satisfy. Littlewood, "Project".

29   Joan Littlewood shot this footage with cameraman Walter Lassaly in London's East End, capturing street life and pub scenes. Littlewood, *Joan's Book*.

30   After the war London City could not return to its previous role as a trade and manufacturing centre. The pre-war furniture industry, located primarily in London's East End, lost fifty-five per cent of its production sites between 1939 and 1955. Jerry White, *London in the Twentieth Century. A City and Its People*, (London: Penguin Books, 2001). In her notes, Joan Littlewood described London's state of decay: "the present riverside slums of docklands with their obsolete wharves, tourist pubs and squalid walks, have fallen into decay [...]" and: "London is a slum [...] with all the squalor and the once rich now patchy patina of slum life." Littlewood, "City/Entertainment".

31   In 1961 the author Ashley Smith addressed changes in the East End: "A pattern that has existed for generations is breaking and what the new pattern will be is unclear even to those who are making their way across the shifting sands." Ashley Smith, *The East Enders. A Social Enquiry into London's East End*, Britain Alive, 2 (London: Secker & Warburg, 1961).

32   In 1964 London County Council was restructured in the course of an administrative reform. It was succeeded by the Greater London Council with different councillors and new administrative districts.

33   White, *London in the Twentieth Century*.

34   380 were built as residential high-rises that drew on pre-war Modernist directives. John R. Gold, *The Practice of Modernism. Modern Architects and Modern Transformation, 1954–1972*, (London: Routledge, 2007).

35   In the light of the growing number of cars, the municipal authorities assigned city-centre plots to investors, using the revenue to fund road construction. Ibid.

36   Buchanan. "Traffic in Towns. A Study of the Long Term Problems of Traffic in Urban Areas".

37   Banham, *Megastructures*.

38   *The Living City Exhibition at the ICA*, ed. Theo Crosby and John Bodley, Living Arts, 3 (London: Institute of Contemporary Arts and Tillotsons, 1964).

39   For Lasdun the typology of the cluster served to establish a new relationship between people and their surroundings by defining a place: "Architecture is about extending and the promotion of human relations." Denys Lasdun, *Architecture of Urban Landscape*, ed. Monica Pidgeon (Audiovisuals, World Microfilms, 1980), record of a lecture. In 1954 Kevin Lynch was the first to define an architectonic design element in the city as a "cluster", which he described as a "unitary social expression in urban form". William J. R. Curtis, *Denys Lasdun*, (London: Phaidon Press, 1994).

40 After graduating from the AA in 1959, Cedric Price worked briefly at Fry, Drew, Drake & Lasdun. In the same year the practice completed the apartment blocks in Greenways Estate, Bethnal Green, as a supplement to Keeling House. Each of the four high-rise blocks was composed internally from individual neighbourhood blocks connected by "vertical streets".

41 David Price, Authorised interview with the author (Faversham, 17th January 2009).

42 Alison and Peter Smithson responded to the problem of transport infrastructure by designing connecting architectonic elements: "It proposes that a community should be built up from a hierarchy of associational elements." Alison Smithson and Peter Smithson, *Urban Structuring*, (London: Studio Vista, 1967).

43 In contrast to the Smithsons' understanding of planning, for Cedric Price the city was not generated by modern architecture and urban planning, but was instead a product of citydwellers' everyday lived culture. On Price's conception of the city, in conjunction with Reyner Banham's essay "City as Scrambled Egg", see Chapter 1, Instruments of Change, in the present book.

44 The Cybernetics Commitee set up four subgroups to address specific aspects of the control system: Form and Amenities, Operational Research, Psychology Experimentation, Cybernetics & Architecture. The Form and Amenities Group, also known as the Ideas Group, included Joan Littlewood and Gordon Pask, cybernetician and artist Roy Ascott and psychology professor John Clark. Ascott, "Cybernetics Sub-Committee: Form and Amenities. Minutes of the Meeting Held at Holborn Town Hall".

45 Littlewood, "Joan Littlewood's Fun Palace Project".

46 Ideas floated included opportunities to test driving or skiing skills on various simulated tracks. B. N. Lewis, "Fun Palace. Counterblast to Boredom", *New Society* (15th April 1965): 8; John Clark, "Memorandum. Ideas for the Fun Palace" (18th November 1965), Cedric Price Archive, Canadian Centre for Architecture, Montréal, document folder: DR:1995:0188:525:3/5. These games were configured for a single player and would adjust their learning goal to each player's skills. To make this possible, a "Teaching Machine" would influence the course of the game. John Clark, "Memorandum. Ideas for the Fun Palace. Serial Numbers 22–28" (9th April 1966), Cedric Price Archive, Canadian Centre for Architecture, Montréal, document folder: DR:1995:0188:525:2/5.

47 In "Tower of Dancing Light" the coloured light fields on a tower were controlled by movements, letting users shape the ambience in the space. Other games, such as "Two Way Panto", required players to interact with other visitors. Various scenarios were envisaged for the game, which could be adjusted by a computer programme in response to players' behaviour. Lewis, "Fun Palace".

48 In installations like "Climb the Tree of Evolution", content less suited to an experience-driven approach was to be explained through films and exhibits. Clark, "Memorandum. Ideas for the Fun Palace".

49 Using mathematical modelling, game theory, which influenced economics and the social sciences from around 1950 on, attempted to forecast statistically the behaviour in conflict situations. The underlying premise is that people pursue their self-interests, taking into account the interests of authors and their supposed negotiation strategies. By way of introduction, see: Gernot Sieg, *Spieltheorie*, 3rd edition (Munich: Oldenbourg Verlag, 2011).

50 Pask, "Fun Palace Project. Cybernetics Committee. Introductory Document".

51 Cedric Price, "Individual Activity Requirement". Diagram of activities and the requisite amenities as a function of room size (ca. 1964), Cedric Price Archive, Canadian Centre for Architecture, Montréal, document folder: DR:1995:0188:209.

52 An attempt to define the term "fun" makes the psychological dimension and educational nature of the Committee's work clear, namely: "'seeking the unfamiliar', and ultimately 'transcending the unfamiliar'." Ascott, "Cybernetics Sub-Committee: Form and Amenities. Minutes of the Meeting Held at Holborn Town Hall".

53 See too William H. Whyte's socio-critical arguments directed at "the ideology of organisation". Whyte refuted the widespread idea that a communication and organisational culture optimised by information technology would inevitably lead to productive behaviour in corporate employees. William H. Whyte, *The Organization Man*, (New York: Simon & Schuster, 1956).

54 Erving Goffman, *The Presentation of Self in Everyday Life*, (New York: Anchor Books, 1959).

55 Gordon Pask, "Fun Palace. Cybernetics Committee" (17th March 1965), Cedric Price Archive, Canadian Centre for Architecture, Montréal, document folder: DR:1995:0188:526:3/5.

56 Pask, "Fun Palace Project. Cybernetics Committee. Introductory Document".

57 Joan Littlewood, "Pensées". Manuscript, typewritten (not dated), Cedric Price Archive, Canadian Centre for Architecture, Montréal, document folder: DR:1995:0188:525:3/5.

58 Joan Littlewood had become acquainted with the influence of the political elites on freedom of opinion as a result of censorship of her plays. She was already fifty when the Committee was set up. Although she did not number among the literary figures dubbed "angry young men", one of the key focuses of her work was a sociocritical engagement with British society and working-class life, as seen in productions such as *The Quare Fellow* (1957) and *A Taste of Honey* (1958) by Shelagh Delaney. See also: Kenneth Tynan, "The Men of Anger", *Holiday* 23 (1958): 93. Reprinted in: Kenneth Tynan, Tynan on Theatre, Pelican Books, A657 (Harmondsworth, Middlesex: Penguin Books, 1964).

59 Joan Littlewood, "Love and Do What You Like". Manuscript (not dated), Cedric Price Archive, Canadian Centre for Architecture, Montréal, document folder: DR:1995:0188:525:3/5.

60 John Barr, "Free Time Britain", *New Society*, No. 133 (April 1965): 5.

61 There was dramatic growth in the market for leisure-related products in Great Britain from the mid-1950s on. For example, sales of sports equipment in Great Britain had increased by forty per cent by mid-1965. Glynn and Booth, *Modern Britain*.

62 Kenneth Frampton had completed his studies at the AA in 1956. The book, recommended to him by his then tutor Thomas S. Stevens, became central to his understanding of American consumer culture as rooted in a new form of division of labour and capitalist production. Stan Allen and Hal Foster, "A Conversation with Kenneth Frampton", *October* 106 (2003): 43.

63 Hannah Arendt, *The Human Condition*, (orig. 1958) 2nd edition (Chicago: University Of Chicago Press, 1998).

64 Historian Johan Huizinga first described the playful, culture-creating human in his concept of the "homo ludens". Huizinga, *Homo Ludens*.

65 As his brother noted, Cedric Price was a Labour Party member. Price, Authorised interview with the author.

66 Peter Dorey, *British Politics since 1945*, (Oxford: Blackwell Publishers, 1995); Des Freedman, *Television Policies of the Labour Party: 1951–2000*, (London: Frank Cass, 2003).

67 Quote from Harold B. Wilson's speech at the 1963 Labour Congress, in Dorey, *British Politics since 1945*.

68 Cedric Price, "Project". Typewriter (18th February 1964), Cedric Price Archive, Canadian Centre for Architecture, Montréal, document folder: DR:1995:0188:525:4/5.

69 Roy Ascott, "Minutes of the Fun Palace Cybernetics Committee" (17th March 1965), Cedric Price Archive, Canadian Centre for Architecture, Montréal, document folder: DR:1995:0188:526:3/5.

70 Roy Ascott, "Meeting No. 2" (Architectural Association, 34. Bedford Square, London, 17th March 1965), Cedric Price Archive, Canadian Centre for Architecture, Montréal, document folder: DR:1995:0188:525:1/5.

71 The wording cites John Clark, who described how myths affect people: "People have been induced to join organisations by setting up a mythical history of the organisation." Ascott, "Minutes of the Fun Palace Cybernetics Committee". The description of the Fun Palace organisation viewed through the prism of a narrative also appears in: Lewis, "Fun Palace".

72 Ascott, "Minutes of the Fun Palace Cybernetics Committee".

73 Banham, "Softer Hardware".

74 Ascott, "Minutes of the Fun Palace Cybernetics Committee".

75 *The Evening Standard*, "Joan Littlewood's 'Dream' Sparks Off a Rumpus Island Residents Protest", 9th September 1963.

76 Charles Greville, *Daily Mail*, "Will This Be a Lot of Fun?", 19th April 1965.

77 It became clear to the Fun Palace design team in autumn 1964 that a site would not be available for the main project in the foreseeable future. Cedric Price had applied for building permission for a plot of land in Mill Meads, but this looked unlikely to suceed in the face of competition from other projects. It was also not clear when the plans for the Lea Valley Regional Park, which included the Fun Palace in its master plan, would be implemented. Political leaders were also put off by the name "Fun Palace", "which evoked for councillors a vision of actors copulating in the bushes." Cf. Mathews, "An Architecture for the New Britain". Quotation: John Ezard and Michael Billington, *The Guardian*, "Joan Littlewood", Obituary, 23rd September 2002 (http://www.guardian.co.uk/news/2002/sep/23/guardianobituaries.arts, accessed on 3rd February 2010).

78 The lack of support led to the Mayor of Hackney, Lou Shermann, withdrawing his assistance to the Fun Palace Project team in their search for a site. Other district authorities followed suit. Joan Littlewood, "Conversation with Lou Sherman". Handwritten record of the conversation (20th December 1965), Cedric Price Archive, Canadian Centre for Architecture, Montréal, document folder: DR:1995:0188:525:5/5. On the initial cost assessment: "Preliminary Cost Indication, Mill Meads West-Ham". Planning document, typewritten (not dated), Cedric Price Archive, Canadian Centre for Architecture, Montréal, document folder: DR:1995:0188:126.

79 By 1974 Joan Littlewood, with Fun Palace Trust participation, had initiated community use schemes on five plots of land in the vicinity of her theatre in Stratford East. In the same year the theatre was listed, after public protests against plans to demolish it. Joan Littlewood and Gerry Raffles, "Uses for Land Awaiting Redevelopment 1967–1975" (15th October 1975), Cedric Price Archive, Canadian Centre for Architecture, Montréal, document folder: DR:1995:0188:525:2/5.

80 Mary Louise Lobsinger, "Das Programm programmieren. Das Inter-Action Centre in London von Cedric Price, 1977", *Werk, Bauen + Wohnen* (December 2007): 38.

81 Hightech as a style had evolved further primarily under the influence of Buckminster Fuller's ideas. Foster cited Buckminster Fuller as an important point of reference in developing his first buildings, e.g.: Reliance Controls Building, Swindon, 1967 or Willis Faber & Dumans Headquarters, Ipswich, 1971–1975.

82 Richard Rogers, Authorised phone interview with the author (2nd November 2006).

83 *Circlorama* was the name of a new projection technique, which immersed the viewers entirely in 360-degree panoramas.

84 On the first evening Cedric Price presented industrial sites slated for demolition, illuminated in white. On the following evening all the areas considered by the authorities to merit preservation were lit in red. Finally, on the third evening, public squares, planned parks and recreational areas were illuminated in green. Cedric Price. "Interview Iv: Cities, Symbols, Lables, Umbrellas", in *Cedric Price*, Hans Ulrich Obrist, ed., The Conversation Series, Vol. 21 (Cologne: Verlag Walter König, 2009).

85 Volker M. Welter, *Biopolis. Patrick Geddes and the City of Life* (Cambridge, MA: The MIT Press, 2002).

86 Ibid.

87 Geddes used the term "the good city", derived from classical antiquity, as an ideal for a possible reconstruction of social community. According to this notion, justice, good city governance and education are the essential foundations of a well-balanced life within a community. Ibid.

88 Hall, *Cities of Tomorrow*.

89 Price's holistic vision of the city as a social and built environment was influenced by his teacher, architect Arthur Korn, who, like many of his other émigré colleagues, brought the concepts of Neues Bauen to London in the 1940s. Korn had moved to London in 1937 and was active in the British section of CIAM and in the Modern Architectural Research Group (MARS), where he became the Urban Planning Secretary. The MARS Group's 1941 plan, largely developed by Arthur Korn, was guided by the developmental principle of the linear city. From 1945 on he taught Urban Planning at the AA School of Architecture in 1945. Taking society and its productive forces as his point of departure, Korn developed a teaching manual for his course, *History Builds the Town*, in which he presented a history-driven and community-oriented urban planning concept. Korn saw the form of the city as arising through the history of transformation processes in society, generated by human beings, in analogy to nature, through their work, new techniques and cultures. Arthur Korn, *History Builds the Town*, (London: Lund Humphries, 1953).

90 In British architectural circles during this period the concept of the "good life" motivated the development of new settlement forms, such as the garden city, which aimed to transpose the values associated with the "good life" into town and country planning. The vision of the regional city was directly linked to re-establishment of communitarian and civil society values. In this vein Geddes' friend Ebenezer Howard envisaged the garden city in 1896 as what he called a "third alternative" to enable workers to enjoy social autonomy and economic independence by combining city and country life. Ebenezer Howard, *To-morrow. A Peaceful Path to Real Reform* (Cambridge: Cambridge University Press, 1898; digital Version, 2010).

91 Since the 1950s the structural transformation of Glasgow, a former hub of heavy industry, had made drastic conversion schemes necessary. On Glasgow's postwar history, see "Official Website of the Stadt of Glasgow", Glasgow City Council, http://www.glasgow.gov.uk/en/AboutGlasgow/History/Industrial+Decline.htm (consulted on 4th October 2010).

92 Price, "Interview Iv".

93 Mathews, "An Architecture for the New Britain".

94 Cedric Price, "Potteries Thinkbelt. A Plan for the Establishment of a Major Advanced Educational Industry in North Staffordshire" (Potteries Thinkbelt, February 1966), Cedric Price Archive, Canadian Centre for Architecture, Montréal, document folder: DR:1995:0216:400:box64.

95 By 1968 only around 60,000 of the 80,000 industrial workers once employed in Stoke-on-Trent's factories were still working there. Steven Birks, "Timeline of Stoke-on-Trent", http://www.thepotteries.org/timeline/index.htm (consulted on 20th September 2010).

96 The deficits Price took as the point of departure in his design were identified in a report commissioned by the British government on "The Potteries" as a region. Department of Economic Affairs. "The West Midlands. A Regional Study" (Her Majesty's Stationery Office. London: 1965); Price, "Potteries Think Belt".

97 Price, "Potteries Thinkbelt".

98 As Price explained in his project report, expanding the state education sector was an inevitable adjustment to the demands of mass society and the state and its institutions were responsible for providing adequate public access to knowledge. Ibid.

99 The report emphasised in particular promotion of technical professions and engineering training, in response to high demand for well-trained skilled workers due to industrial development in the UK. Glynn and Booth, *Modern Britain*.

100 The Robbins Report (1963) recommended that the British government should undertake a huge expansion of the university sector and designate Colleges of Advanced Technology as universities. "Memorandum by the Chief Secretary to the Treasury and Paymaster General", C. (63) 173, Copy No. 62, http://www.filestore.nationalarchives.gov.uk/pdfs/small/cab-129-114-c-173.pdf (consulted on 18th October 2010).

101 For example, the University of York, founded in 1963, was built as a campus, drawing on the role models of Oxford and Cambridge.

102 The six polytechnic universities in the industrial cities of Manchester, Liverpool, Sheffield, Birmingham, Leeds and Bristol were originally described as "red brick universities"; in contrast to Oxford and Cambridge, they have only been founded in the early nineteenth century in response to the demand for technical knowledge in industrial manufacturing.

103 Cedric Price, "Potteries Thinkbelt", New Society (2nd June 1966): 74. Cedric Price Archive, Canadian Centre for Architecture, Montréal, document folder: DR:1995:0216:400.

104 Glynn and Booth, Modern Britain.

105 Price, "Potteries Thinkbelt".

106 "Think". Manuscript, typewritten (not dated), Cedric Price Archive, Canadian Centre for Architecture, Montréal, document folder: DR:1995:0216:400:box64; Price, "Potteries Thinkbelt".

107 Cedric Price and Peter Laslett, "Some Talking Points. New Ways of Teaching". Record of a panel discussion, London (June 1964), Cedric Price Archive, Canadian Centre for Architecture, Montréal, document folder: DR:1995:0216:400.

108 Price, "Madley Transfer Area".

109 Geddes viewed growth of industrial cities as resulting from mechanisation in the world of work. He believed that a city distributed decentrally in the landscape was a prerequisite for comprehensive refashioning of human habitats, both in terms of the built environment and from an economic perspective. Arthur J. Thomson and Patrick Geddes. "A Biological Approach", in Ideals of Science and Faith, James Edward Hand, ed. (London: George Allen, 1904); Welter, Biopolis.

110 On the discussion during that period: "The Architects' Journal", (13th June 1962): 1330; George Grenfell-Baines, The Guardian, "Universities. In Search of a Flexible Unity", 13th June 1965.

111 As Found. Die Entdeckung des Gewöhnlichen, ed. Claude Lichtenstein and Thomas Schregenberger (Baden: Lars Müller Verlag, 2001).

112 Alison Smithson and Peter Smithson, The Charged Void, (New York: Monacelli Press, 2001).

113 Alison Smithson and Peter Smithson, "Cluster City. A New Shape for the Cummunity", Architectural Review (November 1957): 333.

114 Cedric Price Architects, "Housing Types 64/70". Sectional studies (not dated), Cedric Price Archive, Canadian Centre for Architecture, Montréal, document folder: DR:1995:0216:051–069.

115 Geddes summarised this relational system with the term "organism". In the 1880s he transposed the biological principle of mutual dependencies to the social habitat of the city. In this context he included both human behaviour and psychology in his view of the region. Welter, Biopolis.

116 Hall, Cities of Tomorrow.

117 Cedric Price, "Potteries Thinkbelt", Architectural Design 36, No. 10 (1966): 484.

118 Cedric Price Architects, "Existing Landuse 64/12". Planning document (not dated), Cedric Price Archive, Canadian Centre for Architecture, Montréal, document folder: DR:1995:0216:012.

119 Cedric Price Architects, "Housing Types 64/70".

120 Welter, Biopolis.

121 Alison and Peter Smithson had already referred to Patrick Geddes in the 1954 Doorn Manifesto. Volker M. Welter. "Post-War CIAM, Team X, and the Influence of Patrick Geddes' Five Annotations", Department of History of Art und Architecture, The University of Reading, http://www.team10online.org/ (consulted on 22nd September 2010).

122 On Cedric Price's contact with Alison and Peter Smithson: Mathews, "An Architecture for the New Britain".

123 Eric Mumford, The CIAM Discourse on Urbanism. 1928–1960, (Cambridge, MA: MIT Press, 2000).

124 Dirk van den Heuvel. "Valley Sections. A Series of Five Proposals", in Alison Smithson and Peter Smithson. From the House of the Future to the House of Today, Dirk van den Heuvel and Max Risselada, ed. (Rotterdam: 010 Publishers, 2004).

125 For the typology of the small city the Smithsons for example developed a terraced apartment block, with the flats on each floor linked to the adjacent block by gallery access corridors. Mumford, The CIAM Discourse on Urbanism.

126 Angelus Eisinger, Die Stadt der Architekten. Anatomie einer Selbstdemontage, Bauwelt Fundamente, 131 (Gütersloh: Bau-Verlag, 2006).

127 It was exactly this kind of critique that also underpinned Alison und Peter Smithson's Golden Lane Housing competition entry (1952) based on the "Cluster City" concept, in which they suggested the idea of continuous growth of the city in individual units. As Found.

128 "New Town Act. Office of Public Sector Information ", National Archives (not dated), www.opsi.gov.uk/acts/acts1946/pdf/ukpga_19460068_en.pdf (consulted on 20th October 2010). The New Town Act was the result of work by the New Town Committee, which was tasked with developing an appropriate urban reconstruction strategy after the Second World War. The New Town Act, adopted in 1946, paved the way for demolition of parts of the city that had suffered extensive destruction, flanked by construction of new towns in the catchment area of larger cities such as London. The New Town Act also established the requisite legislative framework for founding these new settlements. Hall, Cities of Tomorrow.

129 The main focus here was on development of the London conurbation, where eight New Towns were created. Hall, Cities of Tomorrow.

130 The New Town Committee also recommended renewing transport infrastructure by introducing functional separation of road and rail traffic and pedestrians. "Stepping out to New Cities", The Times (13th January 1966), http://archive.timesonline.co.uk (consulted on 24th October 2010).

131 Thanks to planning work done by Raymond Unwin (1863–1940) and Richard Barry Parker (1867–1947), the garden city concept had become the smallest functional module in regional planning for London's expansion. Hall, Cities of Tomorrow.

132 Cedric Price, "Lecture 1959". Manuscript (1959), Cedric Price Archive, Canadian Centre for Architecture, Montréal, document folder: DR:1995:0235:007:003.

133 In order to improve the quality of the flats, Price took as his yardstick the latest standards, such as those drawn up by the Parker Morris Committee on Public Housing, which entered the statute books in 1967.

134 Price, "Potteries Thinkbelt".

135 Ibid.

136 Cedric Price Architects, "Housing Types Capsule Housing 64/75". Planning document, scale 1:1250, paper print (not dated), Cedric Price Archive, Canadian Centre for Architecture, Montréal, document folder: DR:1995:0216:051–069.

137 Arthur Quarmby, The Plastics Architect, (London: Pall Mall Press, 1974); Der Spiegel, "Arthur Quarmby", 18th July 1966.

138 Cedric Price Architects, "Housing Types Sprawl Housing 64/72". Planning document, scale 1:1250, paper print (not dated), Cedric Price Archive, Canadian Centre for Architecture, Montréal, document folder: DR:1995:0216:051–069.

139 Cedric Price Architects, "Housing Types Battery Housing 64/73". Floor plan and view, scale 1:1250, transparent

paper (not dated), Cedric Price Archive, Canadian Centre for Architecture, Montréal, document folder: DR:1995:0216:051–069.

140 Cedric Price Architects, "Housing Types 64/70".

141 Cedric Price Architects, "Housing Types Battery Housing 64/73".

142 *As Found*.

143 With this typology Cedric Price referenced the low-rise housing block that Alison and Peter Smithson had developed in their 1952 Golden Lane competition entry in London. Cedric Price Architects, "Housing Types Battery Housing 64/73".

144 Cedric Price Architects, "Housing Types Crate Housing 64/74". Axonometric depiction, cross section and view, scale 1:1250, transparent paper (not dated), Cedric Price Archive, Canadian Centre for Architecture, Montréal, document folder: DR:1995:0216:051–069.

145 Le Corbusier, *Creation Is a Patient Search*, (Stuttgart: Praeger, 1960).

146 With his execution of structure and module, he also picked up on one of the central imperatives of Metabolism, realised six years later by Kisho Kurokawa in the Nagakin Capsule Tower in Tokyo. Cedric Price Architects, "Housing Types Crate Housing 64/74".

147 Price, "Potteries Thinkbelt".

148 Cedric Price had a reputation among his friends and colleagues as an expert on England's regional architectural history. Mullin, Authorised interview with the author. His library contained forty works just on the history of traditional building typologies. For a list of the books, see: Eleanor Bron and Samantha Hardingham, *Cedric Price Retriever*, (London: inIVA, 2006).

149 The Smithsons called this the "scale of human association". van den Heuvel, "Valley Sections".

150 Adaptability of the building typologies to a whole host of different social and geographic conditions was one of Price's key design principles to strike a balance between the built environment and the social context: "[…] the consciously planned and purposely built environment that exploits the potential of unevenness of environmental conditioning is likely to become one of the main contributions that architects and planners can make to society." Cedric Price, "Life-Conditioning", *Architectural Design* (October 1966), in *The Square Book* (London: Wiley Academy, 1984. Nachdruck, 2003).

151 Ibid.

152 Cedric Price Architects, "Lifespan & Usage Cycle 64/100". Diagram on transparent paper (not dated), Cedric Price Archive, Canadian Centre for Architecture, Montréal, document folder: DR:1995:0216:372.

153 Cedric Price Architects, "Housing Types Capsule Housing 64/71". Schematic floor plan and view of settlement, scale 1:1250, paper print (not dated), Cedric Price Archive, Canadian Centre for Architecture, Montréal, document folder: DR:1995:0216:051–069; Cedric Price Architects, "Housing Types Crate Housing 64/74".

154 Cedric Price Architects, "Lifespan & Usage Cycle 64/100".

155 Cedric Price Architects, "Housing Types 64/70".

156 Price, "Potteries Thinkbelt".

157 Cedric Price Architects, "Housing Types Sprawl Housing 64/76". Axonometric view and floor plan, scale 1:1250, transparent paper (not dated), Cedric Price Archive, Canadian Centre for Architecture, Montréal, document folder: DR:1995:0216:051–069.

158 Cedric Price Architects, "Lifespan & Usage Cycle 64/100".

159 Adrian Forty, *Words and Buildings. A Vocabulary of Modern Architecture* (London: Thames and Hudson, 2000).

160 Cedric Price, "Link Lecture No.01 Years 1&2". Manuscript for a lecture at the AA School of Architecture for the first and second year (21st March 1963), Cedric Price Archive, Canadian Centre for Architecture, Montréal, document folder: DR:1995:0235:007:003.

161 Cedric Price Architects, "Lifespan & Usage Cycle 64/100".

162 "Think", Manuscript, Typoscript (undated). Cedric Price Archive, Canadian Centre for Architecture, Montréal, Dokumentordner: DR:1995:0216:400:box64.

163 Cedric Price Architects, "P 41". Original drawing for the *Works II* exhibition, version to be copied with glued-on text (not dated), Cedric Price Archive, Canadian Centre for Architecture, Montréal, document folder: DR:2004:1534, folder 2.

164 Welter, *Biopolis*.

165 Lewis Mumford, *The Culture of Cities*, (New Year: Harcourt, Brace & Co, 1938).

166 Ellen Shoshkes, "Jaqueline Tyrwhitt, a Founding Mother of Modern Urban Design", *Planning Perspectives* 21, No. 2 (2006): 179.

167 Bron and Hardingham, *Cedric Price Retriever*; Blake, "Introduction to Arts and Technics".

168 Welter, *Biopolis*.

169 Price's teacher Arthur Korn had previously developed a similar "grassroots democracy" model of the city. Korn, *History Builds the Town*.

170 Mumford updated the 1930s and 1940s concept of "neotechnics" and applied it to the way in which society developed in the electronic age. The starting point for his vision was the decline of the common weal as industrial societies evolved; his harsh critique of this phenomenon also inspired his own counter-model in the form of a vision for the city in the electronic age. Blake, "Introduction to Arts and Technics".

171 Ibid.

172 Mumford's "organic functionalism" drew on concepts devised by Lewis Sullivan and Frank Lloyd Wright that linked modern architecture's so-called machine aesthetic to a formal language rooted in the social and built context of the city, including its history and cultural traditions. Ibid.

173 Price, "Lecture 1959".

174 Cedric Price, "Tales of the City". In *The Square Book* (London: Wiley Academy, 1984, reprint, 2003).

175 Cedric Price, "Transfer Area Madley, 64/65". Axonometric view, scale 1:5000 (not dated), Cedric Price Archive, Canadian Centre for Architecture, Montréal, document folder: DR:1995:0216:279; Cedric Price, "Longsection Madley, 64/62". Cross section, drawing, scale 1:5000 (not dated), Cedric Price Archive, Canadian Centre for Architecture, Montréal, document folder: DR:1995:0216:279; Cedric Price, "Transfer Areas – Aerial Survey, 64/10". Scale 5¾ inch = 1 mile (June 1963), Cedric Price Archive, Canadian Centre for Architecture, Montréal, document folder: DR:1995:0216:205.

176 Price, "Lecture 1959".

177 Price, "Potteries Thinkbelt".

178 "It makes full use of technological resources (like computers) now reserved largely for activities outside of universities. And the rigid requirement about students' age and the length of time they must be at university should be replaced by a more elastic system […]." Cf.: "Think".

179 Price, "Potteries Thinkbelt".

180 Price and Laslett, "Some Talking Points".

181 Price, "Potteries Thinkbelt".

182 On 12th December 1965, MP Tom Driberg introduced Price's ideas into the parliamentary debate on options for further education conducted in the House of Lords. House of Lords. "Official Report Parlamentary Debate" (Her Majesty's Stationery Office. London, 12th December 1965); Mathews, "An Architecture for the New Britain".

183 Mumford elaborated in detail on the idea of the city in the electronic age. Lewis Mumford, *The City in History. Its Origins, Its Transformations, and Its Prospects*, (New York: Harcourt, Brace & World, 1961). Ebenezar Howard had already described the notion of a force field as an expression of a spatial and social unit in the city in his 1898 book *To-morrow*. In his schematic depiction of planning, Howard drew on the metaphor of the magnetic field

to describe the social, political and economic influences of city-dwellers' cultural space in industrial cities. Howard, *To-morrow*.
184   Cedric Price. Layout sketch from a series of eleven sheets for the Fun Palace brochure design (not dated). Cedric Price Archive, Canadian Centre for Architecture, Montréal, document folder: DR:1995:0188:525:001:011.3.
185   On a visit to the medieval city of Viterbo, Le Corbusier talked about an ideal city, as closed and compact as an egg, as a role model for urban reconstruction. Banham's essay appeared in the same year as Price's public statements about a changed attitude towards planning strategies. Reyner Banham, "City as Scrambled Egg", *Cambridge Opinion* 17 (1959): 18.
186   Ibid.
187   Price, "Lecture 1959".
188   Cedric Price, "Magnets". Sketch (not dated), Cedric Price Archive, Canadian Centre for Architecture, Montréal, document folder: DR:2004:0928:001. The sites envisaged for the interventions were in the Greater London Metropolitan Area.

3

1   Littlewood, *Joan's Book*.
2   The Who donated 1,000 pounds to the Fun Palace Trust's initiatives after the concert. Cedric Price, "Camden Town Pilot Project Report" (January 1965), Cedric Price Archive, Canadian Centre for Architecture, Montréal, document folder: DR:1995:0188:525:1/5.
3   The projects were a reaction to the immediate impact of neighbourhood renewal. The theatre was granted conservation status after protests from the neighbourhood over its planned demolition. In 1974 five plots of land were used to run a swimming pool, a garden, sporting facilities and an urban farm. Cf.: Littlewood and Raffles, "Uses for Land Awaiting Redevelopment 1967–1975".
4   "to transform any place if only ephemerally. To place at the disposal of the spectators the technique of learning and the skills which the Workshop team had developed." Shirley Dynevor, "Notes on Steering Comittee Meeting" (Weymouth Street, London, 18th January 1976), Cedric Price Archive, Canadian Centre for Architecture, Montréal, document folder: DR:1995:0188:525:2/5.
5   The Cybernetic Committee used the designs as a kind of test-run for smaller versions of the Fun Palace. Gordon Pask, "Meeting No. 2" (Architectural Assosciation, 34 Bedford Square, London, 17th March 1965), Cedric Price Archive, Canadian Centre for Architecture, Montréal, document folder: DR:1995:0188:525:1/5.
6   Building on this idea, the design team had begun planning three pilot projects in spring 1965, for sites in London, Glasgow and Liverpool. The first, in Camden Town, was a derelict area that had been cleared by London's municipal authorities. Cedric Price, "Fun Palace Project, Further Reference Q5". Sketch with notes (not dated), Cedric Price Archive, Canadian Centre for Architecture, Montréal, document folder: DR:1995:0188:525:2/5; Gordon Pask, "Fun Palace Cybernetic Committee. Minutes of the Meeting Held at the Building Centre, Store Street, London WC1" (27th January 1965), Cedric Price Archive, Canadian Centre for Architecture, Montréal, document folder: DR:1995:0188:525:3/5.

7   Costs for the pilot projects were slashed to 120,000 pounds per site as mechanical and computerised systems were not used. 240,000 pounds were earmarked for running costs. Pask, "Fun Palace Cybernetic Committee".
8   Cedric Price, "Camden Town Pilot Project" (not dated), Cedric Price Archive, Canadian Centre for Architecture, Montréal, document folder: DR:1995:0188:013/014.
9   The cubes' frames were made of steel and wood (dimensions: 7 × 6 × 6 foot). The cubes were screwed together to offer maximum configuration flexibility. Price, "Fun Palace Project"; "Camden Town Project. Typical Details of Junction of 3 Cubes, Full Size, 51/166" (not dated), Cedric Price Archive, Canadian Centre for Architecture, Montréal, document folder: DR:1995:0188:244.
10   Cedric Price decided to keep use stipulations for the cubes very general. Rather than specialised rooms, there were for example panels equipped with a table, chair or bench.
11   In addition to the cubes, inflatable halls were planned to offer space for large events. Taut textile wall-screens could be used to provide privacy and act as acoustic shields.
12   Price, "Camden Town Pilot Project Report".
13   Pask, "Fun Palace Cybernetic Committee".
14   Pask, *An Approach to Cybernetics*. Pask's self-organisation model was derived from biological systems' growth principles. He described cells' adaptation to their environment as a communicative process of self-organisation and underlined cells' "ability to learn" in this paradigm, endeavouring to describe this in a specific language in cybernetics systems. He devised this approach during his research work at the Biological Computer Lab, BCL, under Heinz von Foerster. Erich Hörl. "Das Kybernetische Bild Des Denkens", in *Transformation Des Humanen*, Michael Hagener and Erich Hörl, ed. (Frankfurt am Main: Suhrkamp, 2008).
15   As in the main Fun Palace Project, the pilot projects were to be accessible round the clock. The activity programme here however focused on practical everyday needs, such as shops and restaurants. Courses, musical activities and entertainment rounded off the programme.
16   Cedric Price and Joan Littlewood, "Fun Palace". Script, typewritten (not dated), Cedric Price Archive, Canadian Centre for Architecture, Montréal, document folder: DR:1995:0188:525:4/5. Individual members of the Cybernetics Committee were tasked with drawing up plans for the project's growth. For example, Richard J. Goldacre, a medical practitioner at the Royal Cancer Hospital in London, drafted a study explaining how the project could draw inspiration from cellular growth processes. Goldacre envisaged that dialogue between the building and its users could offer scope for adaptation. He dubbed this conception "the opposite of evolution." Richard J. Goldacre, "Biological Models, the Fun Palace. Part 2, Evolution and Growth" (21st April 1965), Cedric Price Archive, Canadian Centre for Architecture, Montréal, document folder: DR:1995:0188:525:2/5–5/5.
17   Price returned repeatedly to this science-tinged language in many of his projects, for example comparing architecture's impact on the cityscape to the functioning of catalysts and enzymes: "The chief innovation […] is that the fixed amenities (cinemas, restaurants, novel arrangements) act as catalysts or enzyme systems in an analogous biological system […]". Pask, "Fun Palace Cybernetic Committee".
18   The project developed by Le Corbusier for the Venice Hospital (1964) had a similar structure. Cf.: Hashim Sarkis, *Le Corbusier's Venice Hospital and the Mat Building Revival*, (Munich: Prestel, 2002).
19   Both approaches were rooted in the principle of an adaptable layout and a cellular structure. However the building by Candilis, Josic & Woods had a less radical notion of organic growth. On the work of Candilis, Josic & Woods: Arnulf Lüchinger, *Strukturalismus in Architektur und Städtebau*, vol. 14, Dokumente der Modernen Architektur, (Stuttgart: Karl Krämer Verlag, 1980).
20   Every bifurcation within the flow diagram represented a developmental step in the project's timeline. Connections

between the bifurcations indicated the activities needed to implement a particular step. This overview made it possible to consider various trajectories, starting from a range of different developmental stages.

21 Aldo van Eyck coined the term in the architectural magazine *Forum* in 1959. Arnulf Lüchinger. "Structuralism Reloaded. Notizen zum Strukturalismus", http://www.arch-edition.nl/structuralism.html (consulted on 1st November 2009).

22 In parallel, Price also worked on smaller projects, such as conversion of the Oxford Corner House and redevelopment planning for the Birmingham and Midland Institute.

23 During the 1960s it had been assumed that working time per week would have dropped from 47 to 32 hours a week by 2000. However, by 1968 working hours had only actually dropped to 44.7 hours for male employees. Sabine Haustein, *Vom Mangel zum Massenkonsum. Deutschland, Frankreich und Großbritannien im Vergleich 1945–1970*, (Frankfurt am Main: Campus Verlag, 2007).

24 On Great Britain's economic development under Harold B. Wilsons' Labour government (1964–1970): Susan Howson. "Money and Monetary Policy in Britain, 1945–1990", in *The Economic History of Britain since 1700*, Roderick Floud and Deirdre McCloskey, ed. (Cambridge: Cambridge University Press, 1994). On the development of waged labour: Stephen Broadberry. "Employment and Unemployment", in *The Economic History of Britain since 1700*, Roderick Floud and Deirdre McCloskey, ed. (Cambridge: Cambridge University Press, 1994).

25 Reyner Banham, "A Clip-on Architecture", *Design Quarterly* (1965): 11.

26 The conference in Folkestone was organised by the BASA (British Architecture Student Association) in conjunction with the Archigram Group, and pitched as a meeting for young architects. Renowned architects travelled to the conference in various international delegations; they included Reyner Banham, Arthur Quarmby, Yona Friedman, Claude Parent and Paul Virillio, Hans Hollein as well as students from the Hochschule für Gestaltung, Ulm and the École des Beaux Arts, Paris.

27 Cedric Price, "Statement of Intention and Aim" (IDEA Folkestone Conference, 1966), Cedric Price Archive, Canadian Centre for Architecture, Montréal, document folder: DR:2004: 1433 3/3.

28 At the conference Metzger presented a dramatic staging of his idea of "Auto Destructive Art" by claiming that he had a bomb in a suitcase next to the speaker's lectern that he could ignite at any moment. Mullin, Authorised interview with the author; Eleanor Bron, ibid. (8th December. Cf. also: Sadler, *Archigram*.

29 Price and Metzger, twelve years his senior, were old friends. Both were involved in CND (Campaign for Nuclear Disarmament) and active in the anti-apartheid movement until the late 1970s. They had met in the early 1960s when Gustav Metzger was staging his early Happenings in London. Bron, Authorised interview with the author.

30 In his first Happening in 1959, Metzger publicly dissolved a television set's packaging in acid. Gustav Metzger. Cardboards selected and arraged by G. Metzger at 14 Monmouth Street, W.C. 2 near Cambridge Circus (1959). Cedric Price Archive, Canadian Centre for Architecture, Montréal, document folder: DR:1995:0188:525:2/5 No. 3.

31 Reyner Banham drew on Sant'Elias' architectural designs in conceiving a new stance in Modernist architecture. He saw them as generating a new aesthetic of "mechanical sensibility". Banham, *Theory and Design in the First Machine Age*.

32 Cedric Price, "International Dialogue of Experimental Architecture" (Introductory Lecture at the Folkestone Conference, 10th June 1966), Cedric Price Archive, Canadian Centre for Architecture, Montréal, document folder: DRCON:2004:0002:033, DR:2004:1434.

33 Cedric Price, "CP ART:12/1962, Urban Planning". Typewritten (not dated), Cedric Price Archive, Canadian Centre for Architecture, Montréal, document folder: DR:1995:0235:007:003.

34 The fundamental incompatibility of the various approaches became apparent for example in the cynical question from one participant in the discussion, who asked how the aesthetic of Archigram's collages could solve Third World hunger. Cedric Price, "Discussion Panel, Gustav Metzger and Cedric Price" (IDEA Folkestone Conference, 12th June 1966), Cedric Price Archive, Canadian Centre for Architecture, Montréal, document folder: DR:2004:1434.

35 Franz-Josef Brüggemeier, *Geschichte Großbritanniens im 20. Jahrhundert*, (Munich: C.H. Beck Verlag, 2010).

36 In this project Ron Herron designed cities as mechanically operated machines for living that could move wherever the labour of their inhabitants was needed. Sadler, *Archigram*. On the discussion at the IDEA Conference: Price, "Discussion Panel, Gustav Metzger and Cedric Price".

37 Sadler, *Archigram*.

38 Cedric Price. Letter to Colin Ward with a copy of the National School Plan (29th November 1965). Cedric Price Archive, Canadian Centre for Architecture, Montréal, document folder: DR:1995:0188:525:5/5.

39 Reflections on educational policy had already influenced both the Fun Palace Project and the Potteries Thinkbelt project. Price understood the latter as introducing a new method for urban architectural and social revitalisation through self-organisation. Price, "International Dialogue of Experimental Architecture".

40 "Polyark" (not dated), Cedric Price Archive, Canadian Centre for Architecture, Montréal, document folder: DR:2004:0002:131; Peter Murray, "Ad/ Poly Arch/ Bus: Letter No 1". Press release (not dated), Cedric Price Archive, Canadian Centre for Architecture, Montréal, document folder: DR:2004:0002:131; Peter Murray, "Cosmorama", *Architectural Design* (April 1973). Cedric Price Archive, Canadian Centre for Architecture, Montréal, document folder: DR:2004:0002:131.

41 "Provisional Programme Dates". Photocopy (not dated), Cedric Price Archive, Canadian Centre for Architecture, Montréal, document folder: DR:2004:0002:131.

42 In summer 1972 the Inter-Action Group travelled to the Olympic Games in Munich with their double-decker bus.

43 The group's action exuded the hippy flair of the "San Francisco Summer of Love" and symbolised a seamless blend of creative freedom of expression, social projects and architectural experimentation. Price was familiar with the group from their *Astro Daze* performance in Houston, Texas, which coincided with his period as a guest lecturer at the Rice University's School of Architecture in 1969, at the same time as ANTFARM. Constance Lewallen and Steve Seid, *Ant Farm: 1968–1978*, (Berkeley: University of California Press, 2004).

44 "Polyark".

45 Hall, *Cities of Tomorrow*.

46 Steven Mullin recalls Joan Littlewood bringing photos of settlements such as Glen Farba in Hertfordshire and Jaywick Sands in Essex along to Price's office. They studied the simple wooden constructions of cabins and allotments, later replaced by houses. Mullin, Authorised interview with the author. A note in Colin Ward's 1984 book suggests that Cedric Price also visited Jaywick Sands. Colin Ward and Dennis Hardy, *Arcadia for All*, (London, New York: Mansell, 1984). Also: Bron and Hardingham, *Cedric Price Retriever*.

47 The issue of land ownership was for example linked to the question of planning that would give everyone an opportunity for free self-development. Ward and Hardy, *Arcadia for All*.

48 Paul Barker. "Thinking the Unthinkable", in *Non-Plan. Essays on Freedom, Participation and Change in Modern Architecture and Urbanism*, Jonathan Hughes and Simon Sadler, ed. (London: Architectural Press, 2000). The younger generation of architects, including Cedric Price and John C. F. Turner, was more interested in adapting planning processes inhabitants' needs than in studying urban typologies. Since the 1970s self-help had grown

much more popular in residential construction due to the emphasis on systemic interaction, activity and agency. Richard Harris, "A Double Irony: The Originality and Influence of John F. C. Turner", *Habitat International* 27, No. 2 (2003): 245.

49 Planning fell within the remit of state institutions in Great Britain, with planning hierarchies and large-scale settlement plans that the authors described as "hang-overs from the days of collectivism in left wing thought".

50 Cedric Price, "Approaching an Architecture of Approximation", *Architectural Design* 42, No. 10 (1972): 645.

51 Reyner Banham et al., "Non-Plan. An Experiment in Freedom", *New Society*, No. 338 (20th March 1969): 435.

52 "[...] It was the revelation that a different kind of city was developing there. [...] based on the freedom that the automobile gave. [...] it was creating a tremendously exciting new urban form which in a way was totally unconventional, even crazy". Peter Geoffrey Hall, Authorised interview with the author (London, 29th August 2006).

53 Reyner Banham, "The Art of Doing Your Thing" BBC Radio Lecture, *The Listener* 80 (12th September 1968). Cf. also: Whiteley, *Reyner Banham*.

54 Charles Moore. "You Have to Pay for the Public Life" (1965), in *You Have to Pay for the Public Life. Selected Essays from Charles W. Moore*, Kevin Keim, ed. (Cambridge, MA: MIT Press, 2001).

55 Banham et al., "Non-Plan".

56 Herbert J. Gans, *Urban Villagers. Group and Class in the Life of Italian-Americans*, (New York, NY: Free Press of Glencoe, 1962).

57 "Non-Plan" was also an indirect response to *The Neophiliacs*, a recently published work by Christopher Booker that portrayed the yearning for societal reform and technical transformation in Great Britain as the naïve dream of a romantically inclined movement that tragically celebrated the eternally new. Christopher Booker, *The Neophiliacs. A Study of the Revolution in English Life in the Fifties and Sixties* (London: Collinsi, 1969); Barker, "Thinking the Unthinkable".

58 Banham et al., "Non-Plan".

59 To shed light on instruments for this kind of Functionalist vision of planning, the "Non-Plan" authors discussed to what extent state planning should be deployed as a counterweight to the dynamic of the free market. They cited left-wing liberal economist John Kenneth Galbraith (1908–2006), who had propounded the idea of "social balance" in *The Affluent Society* (1958) and *The New Industrial State* (1967), asserting that planning decisions should be guided by both individual and societal interests. John Kenneth Galbraith, *The Affluent Society*, (New York: Houghton Mifflin, 1958); John Kenneth Galbraith, *The New Industrial State*, (Princeton, NJ: Princeton University Press, 1967).

60 Peter Hall described the reaction to the manifesto's publication as akin to watching a "set of crazy people talking to themselves". Hall, Authorised interview with the author.

61 The first supermarket in England with a central customer car park was opened just one year after the "Non-Plan" manifesto was published. Ibid.

62 E.g.: Martino Stierli, *Las Vegas im Rückspiegel. Zum Stadtbegriff von Robert Venturi und Denise Scott Brown*, (Zürich: gta Verlag, 2011).

63 Denise Scott-Brown, Robert Venturi, and Steven Izenour, *Learning from Las Vegas*, (Cambridge, MA: The MIT Press, 1972); Denise Scott-Brown, "Learning from Pop", *Casabella* 359-360 (December 1971): 62, in *Architecture Theory since 1968*, hrsg. Michael K. Hays (Cambridge, MA: MIT Press, 2000).

64 Kevin A. Lynch, *The Image of the City*, (Cambridge, MA: MIT Press, 1960).

65 Price, "Life-Conditioning".

66 Ben Franks. "New Right/New Left. An Alternative Experiment in Freedom", in *Non-Plan. Essays on Freedom, Participation and Change in Modern Architecture and Urbanism*, Jonathan Hughes and Simon Sadler, ed. (London: Architectural Press, 2000).

67 Bruno Latour and Albena Yaneva. "Give Me a Gun and I Will Make All Buildings Move. An Ant's Approach to Architecture", in *Explorations in Architecture. Teaching, Design, Research*, Reto Geiser, ed. (Basel: Birkhäuser, 2008).

68 Reyner Banham, *Los Angeles. The Architecture of Four Ecologies*, (orig. 1971; Berkeley CA: California Press, 2009).

69 As Mary Banham noted on her husband's friendship with Cedric Price, the latter challenged Banham "to testify in public on L.A." Banham, Authorised interview with the author. Cf. also: Bron and Hardingham, *Cedric Price Retriever*. Both viewed the architect's new role as that of an enabler. Cf.: Whiteley, *Reyner Banham*.

70 Lawrence Alloway, "The Long Front of Culture", *Cambridge Opinion* 17 (1959): 298, cited according to Whiteley, *Reyner Banham*.

71 Banham, "The Art of Doing Your Thing".

72 Cf. also Cedric Price. "Cedric Price Im Interview Mit Hans Ulrich Obrist", in *Re:Cp*, Hans Ulrich Obrist, ed. (Basel, Boston, Berlin: Birkhäuser Verlag, 2003).

73 In particular, the motivation for each individual's rational action was identified not solely in maximising economic gain, but in fulfilling hedonistic goals like fun, enjoyment and contentedness.

74 Jane Jacobs, *The Death and Life of Great American Cities*, (Harmondsworth: Penguin Books, 1961). Cf. also: Anthony Vidler. "Foreword to the 2000 Edition", in ed. Reyner Banham, *Los Angeles. The Architecture of Four Ecologies* (Berkeley CA: California Press, 2000).

75 Cedric Price had already incorporated the Los Angeles model into his Potteries Thinkbelt design from an urban planning perspective, in reconfiguring the region socially and architecturally into a field of exchanges, in the broadest sense of the term.

76 Participatory observation was a practice that had already been used by the members of the Independent Group, including Nigel Henderson; he had moved to Bethnal Green in 1945 with his wife, social anthropologist, Julia Stephens, to study the local population's quotidian culture as part of the research project "Discover your Neighbour". Ben Highmore, "Hopscotch Modernism. On Everyday Life and the Blurring of Art and Social Science" Special issue: "Modernism and the Everyday", *Modernist Cultures*, No. 2 (2006): 70; *As Found*.

77 Banham's concept of ecology thus extended beyond the established view of "social ecology" in the social sciences, as formulated for example by George Herbert Mead (1863–1931) or Robert E. Park (1864–1944); it only applied an ecological perspective to the power structures and relationships manifested in urban areas. Egon Becker, *Soziale Ökologie. Grundzüge einer Wissenschaft von den gesellschaftlichen Naturverhältnissen*, (Frankfurt am Main: Campus Verlag, 2006).

78 As early as the mid-1960s, Reyner Banham viewed the car as an object that conveyed a sense of a new lifestyle and at the same time generated a new relationship of drivers to space. In this context Banham saw architecture as part of ecology. Banham, *Los Angeles*.

79 Vidler, "Foreword to the 2000 Edition".

80 Banham's interpretation of the term "ecology" symbolises a system-based, Functionalist perspective, as elucidated in the 1960s for example by sociologist Talcott Parsons in his theory of structural functionalism. His work on a systemic concept of functions within society addressed the debate on social order in modern democracy and was grounded in values such as integration and social balance. Cf.: Uta Gebhardt, *Talcott Parsons, an Intellectual Biography*, (Cambridge, New York: Cambridge University Press, 2002).

81 Vidler, "Foreword to the 2000 Edition".

82 Price, "International Dialogue of Experimental Architecture".

83 "Declaration of the UN Conference on the Human Environment", UNO (1972), http://fletcher.tufts.edu/multi/texts/STOCKHOLM-DECL.txt (consulted on 10th January 2011). UN General Assembly Resolution 2398, 1968.

84 Ulrich Grober, *Die Entdeckung der Nachhaltigkeit. Kulturgeschichte eines Begriffs*, (Munich: Verlag Antje Kunstmann, 2010).

85 "Three Die as Tower Block Collapses", Report from 16th May 1968, BBC News Archive, http://news.bbc.co.uk/onthisday/hi/dates/stories/may/16/newsid_2514000/2514277.stm (consulted on 8th December 2009).

86 Both quotations from: "Architecture on TV or It Won't Be Always Be This Easy", *Architectural Design* (September 1971): 572.

87 Giancarlo De Carlo, "The Housing Problem in Italy", *Freedom* 9/12 (1948): 2.

88 Hugo Scornik, "Hugo Scornik Continues the Saga of His Travel in Africa and Arrival in the Canary Islands" Reader's Letter, *Architectural Design* (August 1972): 513.

89 Gordon Pask, "The Architectural Relevance of Cybernetics", ibid. 39 (September 1969): 494.

90 From 1971 on Price was involved with activities organised by the Inter-Action Group as the architect of the Inter-Action Centre, designing and constructing what was dubbed Europe's first community arts centre: the project, set in London's Kentish Town, was completed in 1979. The building was intended to form the design frame for the group's various activities, uniting them literally under one roof. Price opted here for prefabricated components and mobile spaces such as containers and a log cabin that could be combined flexibly within a roof grid. In the Inter-Action Centre Price created a cultural centre that combined ideas from the Fun Palace Projects with the notion of open design. However, he did encounter practical problems in implementing his ideas, principally due to the still undefined process of participation in planning. E.g.: Lobsinger, "Das Programm programmieren".

91 Cedric Price, "E15. EA.74". Notes and sketches (16th February 1974), Cedric Price Archive, Canadian Centre for Architecture, Montréal, document folder: DR:1995:0188:525:2/5. "EA.74" is an abbreviation for "Easter Fair 1974".

92 Ibid.

93 In contrast, Reyner Banham and Lawrence Alloway described the decentralised organisation of cities like Los Angeles as "modern arrangements of knowledge in non-hierarchic forms." In contrast to an elitist culture of the monument based on the principle of design heightening, Los Angeles symbolised a democratic model of the city, organised "from the bottom up". Banham identified the petrol station as the monument of this new typology of urban culture. Alloway, "The Long Front of Culture". In addition, Lawrence Alloway countered the pyramid city with its "top-down" planning strategy in his concept of the city as a field, which he defined as a continuum of parallels in an inclusive counter-concept.

94 Charles Moore had identified the monument in places such as Disneyland. Although the political dimension of public space was excluded from Disneyland, it had all the characteristics of a collective locus – and thus of a monument. Moore, "You Have to Pay for the Public Life". Price ignored other approaches to interpreting the monument, for example Aldo Rossi's *L'architettura della città*.

95 In the Generator project Cedric Price deliberately opposed the idea of an artificially staged environment and described Walt Disney's World Resort in Orlando as a "warning […] what one must not do". Cedric Price. Letter to Howard Gillman (6th September 1977). Cedric Price Archive, Canadian Centre for Architecture, Montréal, document folder: DR:1995:0280:651:5/5.

96 Cf. e.g. the pseudo-historical replica of American "Main Street" in Disneyland.

97 Steve Bruce and Steven Yearley. "Max Weber", in *The Sage Dictionary of Sociology* (London: Sage Publications, 2006).

98 Price's proposal to set up a Ferris wheel on London's South Bank in 1984 was a logical consequence of further development of this idea of an appropriate form of representation in architecture through individual appropriation. "Possibilities. 159/53". Planning document, scale not indicated (not dated), Cedric Price Archive, Canadian Centre for Architecture, Montréal, document folder: DRCON:2004:051. With a view to making his idea of the monument in mass culture clear, Price had postcards printed for the South Bank study, bearing the question, beneath sketches of e.g. church towers, "Why do we always have to look up?" Price, Authorised interview with the author. For Cedric Price, action and personal appropriation were key aspects of design that allowed people to create their own form of expression. Price, "Man-Made Style".

99 In 1964 Alistair McAlpine became London District Director of the family firm Sir Robert McAlpine & Sons, one of the leading British construction companies. Cedric Price described the baron, who was eight years younger than he, as his tutor, with whom he regularly honed his opinion on topical political issues. They shared an acute interest in politics and art. Alistair McAlpine referred to these meetings as "mental gymnastics". Robert Alistair McAlpine, *Once a Jolly Bagman*, (London: Weidenfeld & Nicolson, 1997).

100 Six months before the start of the project, the recently founded construction workers union UCATT (Union of Construction Allied Trades and Technicians) had initiated the first national construction workers strike. In summer 1972 UCATT members began a thirteen-week strike with a view to abolishing day work ("the lump"), which had been common practice until this time. The strike was followed by two convictions for lock-outs, which the general public interpreted as state overreaction due to the draconian prison sentences imposed. One of the employers of those sentenced was Sir Robert McAlpine & Sons. "The Shrewsbury Trial". Photocopy, typewritten (not dated), Cedric Price Archive, Canadian Centre for Architecture, Montréal, document folder: DR:1995:0263:032:2/8. However, Alistair McAlpine stated that the project was not triggered directly by the strike. Cedric Price, "Draft Terms of Agreement". Typewritten (28th March 1974), Cedric Price Archive, Canadian Centre for Architecture, Montréal, document folder: DR:1995:0263:032:1/8.

101 Cedric Price, "Confidential Meeting CP Al. McAl". Handwritten memorandum (28th August 1973), Cedric Price Archive, Canadian Centre for Architecture, Montréal, document folder: DR:1995:0263:032:1/8.

102 Cedric Price Architects, "McAppy Angel Court Story". Office copy (June 1975), Cedric Price Archive, Canadian Centre for Architecture, Montréal, document folder: DR:1995:0263:032:4/8.

103 Cedric Price, "Work Programme". Memorandum, typewritten (27th February 1973), Cedric Price Archive, Canadian Centre for Architecture, Montréal, document folder: DR:1995:0263:032:2/8.

104 Price, "Confidential Meeting CP Al. McAl".

105 Cedric Price's paternal uncle had been an active member of the labour movement and was one of the founding members of the Industrial Artists' Union and of a local branch of the Labour Party in the Midlands. Bron, Authorised interview with the author.

106 In Socialist Liberalism, social and cultural emancipation as well as the formation of the bourgeoisie through property were central arguments for freedom defined in positive terms, which was to be established through a new form of the social state. Cf.: Theo Schiller. "Liberalismus", in *Kleines Lexikon Der Politik*, Dieter Nohlen and Florian Grotz, ed., 2nd edition (Munich: C. H. Beck Verlag, 2007). Cedric Price clearly set himself apart from the influential British Establishment through his political stance and advocated that society should open up and become more democratic, albeit without calling the social market economy into question. Contemporary social science theories of the post-war era were also based on this social-liberal attitude.

107 Neo-liberal theories highlighted the absolute freedom of the individual and trusted in the free play of capitalist market forces as the most efficient and certain route to positive development of society. From 1979 this line of argument also underpinned Margaret Thatcher's economic policy; Alistair McAlpine was Treasury Minister for some time in her Cabinet.

108 Cedric Price, "Meeting on 40 Bernard Street, London WC1". Minutes, typewritten (8th March 1973), Cedric Price Archive, Canadian Centre for Architecture, Montréal, document folder: DR:1995:0263:032:1/8.

109 Cedric Price Architects, "McAppy Angel Court Story".

110 "Stage, Content, Form". Handwritten manuscript (not dated), Cedric Price Archive, Canadian Centre for Architecture, Montréal, document folder: DR:1995:0263:001:0012.

111 In March 1973 Cedric Price began, in an initial project phase, to document working conditions on a selection of ca. twenty building sites in London and the surrounding area. This included many large building sites, for example for Shakespeare Tower on the Barbican Estate and for Intercontinental Hotel in central London. Cedric Price Architects, "List of Mcalpine Sites Visited" (McAppy, January 1974), Cedric Price Archive, Canadian Centre for Architecture, Montréal, document folder: DR:1995:0263: 032:4/8.

112 During the three years of work on the project, there was some fluctuation in the team. Will Alsop, who was involved in the Inter-Action Centre during the same period, also worked on the McAppy project. Observations were noted in records of site visits, and there are around fifteen of these in the project archives. E.g: David Price, "Site Visit and Discussion London Bridge". Memorandum (21st August 1973), Cedric Price Archive, Canadian Centre for Architecture, Montréal, document folder: DR:1995:0263:032:1/8.

113 E.g.: "Site Visit: New Covent Garden". Memorandum (7th March 1973), Cedric Price Archive, Canadian Centre for Architecture, Montréal, document folder: DR:1995:0263:032:2/8; "Site Visit: London Bridge". Memorandum (16th March 1973), Cedric Price Archive, Canadian Centre for Architecture, Montréal, document folder: DR:1995:0263:032:2/8.

114 Cedric Price Architects, "McAppy Angel Court Story".

115 Cedric Price, "Operative Structure of McAppy. Meeting Cedric Price/John Racker". Memorandum, typewritten (9th August 1973), Cedric Price Archive, Canadian Centre for Architecture, Montréal, document folder: DR:1995:0263:032:1/2.

116 Cedric Price argued in the context of the PEP programme's introduction that the usual wooden site sheds could not be moved as construction progressed, which caused problems in the construction sequence. The option of stacking mobile construction containers could in contrast help overcome the lack of work space. Cedric Price Architects, "PEP Reference" (January 1974), Cedric Price Archive, Canadian Centre for Architecture, Montréal, document folder: DR:1995:0263:032:4/8.

117 Cedric Price Architects, "Angel Court Site Planning Phases and Accomodation" (January 1974), Cedric Price Archive, Canadian Centre for Architecture, Montréal, document folder: DR:1995:0263:032:4/8.

118 The team tested two container systems, from Rollalong and Terrapin. They examined e.g. costs, practicability and possible fittings. Cf. for example the sketches: "Rollalong PP 5.0, Angel Court. Drawing 38/Ac/046c,29". Scale 1:100 (30th June 1974), Cedric Price Archive, Canadian Centre for Architecture, Montréal, document folder: DR:1995:0263:032:2/8.ss. And: "Terrapin Application Angel Court. Drawing 2b/Ac/020". Scale 1:100 (7th April 1974), Cedric Price Archive, Canadian Centre for Architecture, Montréal, document folder: DR:1995:0263:032:2/8.ss

119 There was no statutory requirement for firms to ensure the workplace was safe or provide suitable work gear and food for building-site workers, nor was this standard practice in the building industry. Price, Authorised interview with the author.

120 Cedric Price, "Meeting: Small Contractors Manager". Typewritten (16th August 1973), Cedric Price Archive, Canadian Centre for Architecture, Montréal, document folder: DR:1995:0263:032:2/8.

121 Cedric Price, "More Operational Originality, Less Three Dimensional Ingenuity, More Social Structures", The Architects' Journal (December 1977), in The Square Book (London: Wiley Academy, 1984; Nachdruck, 2003).

122 The nomenclature he chose reflected the distinction between social interaction and interactions between humans and their environment.

123 In addition to a building site in Bankside, London, the firm had also selected a building site close to Angel Court as a test platform. This was chosen for a pilot study as the work was not so far advanced there. Price, "Draft Terms of Agreement"; "Stage 1–3" (not dated), Cedric Price Archive, Canadian Centre for Architecture, Montréal, document folder: DR:1995:0263:001–012; Price, Authorised interview with the author.

124 Constant adaptation of the building site facilities were intended to optimise the cost-benefit relationship as the number of workers on site varied between 42 in April 1974 and over 300 in 1976. Cedric Price Architects, "Angel Court Site Planning Phases and Accomodation".

125 E.g.: David Price, "Rollalong PP 15.05 Angel Court 10 Units Phase Ii… Control". Sketch on photocopy, photocopy (30th June 1974), Cedric Price Archive, Canadian Centre for Architecture, Montréal, document folder: DR:1995:0263:032:2/8; Cedric Price Architects, "McAppy Angel Court Story".

126 He indicated the type of communication, the reason, location and time involved. Cedric Price Architects, "PEP Reference. Chief Engineer George Bruce". Photocopy with handwritten notes, drawing 2 (January 1974), Cedric Price Archive, Canadian Centre for Architecture, Montréal, document folder: DR:1995:0263:032:4/8. He also drew on contemporary specialised literature on safety in the workplace and job satisfaction, for example: The Manual of Accident Prevention in Construction, 6th edition (Washington: The Associated General Constructors of America Inc., 1971); John Fraser. "Tripartite Steering Group on Job Satisfaction. Making Work More Satisfying" (Her Majesty's Stationery Office. London: 1975).

127 Cedric Price Architects, "PEP Reference. Personal Communications Face to Face. Control Office Arrangement" (January 1974), Cedric Price Archive, Canadian Centre for Architecture, Montréal, document folder: DR:1995:0263:032:4/8.

128 Cedric Price Architects, "Rollalong MCA Control. Phase Ii & Iii. Angel Court Internal Arrangement". Photocopy, drawing 2C/AC/026, scale 1:100 (not dated), Cedric Price Archive, Canadian Centre for Architecture, Montréal, document folder: DR:1995:0263:032:2/8.

129 The term "radio phone" is more or less synonymous with "walkie-talkie." Cedric Price Architects, "PEP Reference. Site Communications First Aid Box Locations" (January 1974), Cedric Price Archive, Canadian Centre for Architecture, Montréal, document folder: DR:1995:0263:032:4/8; Cedric Price Architects, "PEP Reference. Communications Requirements" (January 1974), Cedric Price Archive, Canadian Centre for Architecture, Montréal, document folder: DR:1995:0263:032:4/8.

130 Pask, "The Architectural Relevance of Cybernetics".

131 Research on the company's accident statistics revealed that seventy-six percent of all accidents on building sites occurred on the ground; falling construction materials ranked as the second main cause of accidents. Cedric Price Architects, "McAppy Angel Court Story".

132 E.g.: Cedric Price Architects, "First Floor Kitchen / Canteen". Photos of the canteen after completion, drawing: 38/AC/057, scale 1:100 (June 1975), Cedric Price Archive, Canadian Centre for Architecture, Montréal, document folder: DR:1995:0263:032:4/8; "Catering Options for McAppy Sites". Memorandum (24th June 1974), Cedric Price Archive, Canadian Centre for Architecture, Montréal, document folder: DR:1995: 0263:032:4/8.ss

133 Cedric Price Architects, "McAppy Angel Court Story".

134 Ibid.

135 Cedric Price Architects, "Locker/Drying Facilities in Rollalong Units at Angel Court". Black and white pho-

tograph (June 1975), Cedric Price Archive, Canadian Centre for Architecture, Montréal, document folder: DR:1995:0263:032:4/8.ss

136 230,000 Sikhs lived in Great Britain after the 1947 division of territory in Punjab, previously a region of northern India, between Pakistan and India. Cf.: Martin Sökefeld. "Diaspora der Sikh", Vorlesung am Institut für Ethnologie der Ludwigs Maximilian Universität München, (26th November 2008), http://ebookbrowse.com/07sikh-diaspora-pdf-d60087924 (consulted on 12th February 2011).

137 "Stage, Content, Form".

138 Cedric Price Architects, "PEP Reference. Policy Formulation and Application, Health and Safety" (January 1974), Cedric Price Archive, Canadian Centre for Architecture, Montréal, document folder: DR:1995:0263:032:4/8.

139 Price presented his methodology in the context of a lecture at the 1966 "Planning for Diversity and Choice" conference at MIT.

140 Cf.: Banham, *Los Angeles*.

141 Cedric Price, "Ced's Lecture. lid/55". Note cards for lecture, handwritten (17th August 1970), Cedric Price Archive, Canadian Centre for Architecture, Montréal, document folder: DR:2004:1433:3/4.

142 Cedric Price Architects, "PEP Reference. Test and Monitoring Procedure" (January 1974), Cedric Price Archive, Canadian Centre for Architecture, Montréal, document folder: DR:1995:0263:032:4/8; Cedric Price Architects, "PEP Reference. Office Layouts" (January 1974), Cedric Price Archive, Canadian Centre for Architecture, Montréal, document folder: DR:1995:0263:032:4/8.

143 Cedric Price, "Job Description". Memorandum, typewritten (16th April 1975), Cedric Price Archive, Canadian Centre for Architecture, Montréal, document folder: DR:1995:0263:032:3/8.

144 Cedric Price Architects, "McAppy Action Summary" (1975), Cedric Price Archive, Canadian Centre for Architecture, Montréal, document folder: DR:1995:0263:032:2/8–4/8; David Price, "Draft Management-Handbook" (January 1975), Cedric Price Archive, Canadian Centre for Architecture, Montréal, document folder: DR:1995:0263:032:2/8.

145 Cedric Price Architects, "McAppy Angel Court Story".

146 Certain aspects of these reflections were already incorporated into a wide-reaching discussion in the 1950s and 1960s on a democratic principle to strike a balance between different forces in society. Cf. for example Karl Popper's theory of a third way in society. Karl Raimund Popper, *Unended Quest*, (orig. 1974; London: Routledge, 1992). Drawing on this, in 1976 Anthony Giddens developed a third- way approach to sociology. Anthony Giddens, *The Third Way*, (Cambridge: Polity Press, 1998).

147 Jeffrey C. Alexander. "The Modern Reconstruction of Classical Thought. Talcott Parsons", in *Theoretical Logic in Sociology*, John Rex, ed. (London: Routledge Kegan, 1984).

148 In 1951 initial studies by the Tavistock Institute in London had revealed that automated processes in coal mining could not entirely control productivity increases if workers were also involved in the production process alongside the machines. Instead it became apparent that the group's social organisation and the behaviour of individual workers influenced productivity as much as the technical aspects of the mining process. Eric Trist and Ken Banforth, "Some Social and Psychological Consequences of the Long Wall Method of Coal Getting", *Human Relations*, No. 4 (1951): 3.

149 Tom Burns, "Micropolitics. Mechanisms of Institutional Change", *Administrative Science Quarterly* 6, No. 3 (December 1961): 257.

150 Ibid.

151 Price had been familiar with these ideas for some time, particularly thanks to his cooperation with Gordon Pask and his contacts with the co-founder of operations research, Stafford Beer, who was also periodically involved in the Fun Palace Project.

152 In the McAppy project Cedric Price based his analyses of work on the latest reports from the working group on job satisfaction, a copy of which he received in 1975. The foreword to the committee report demonstrated a new awareness of the need to transform the definition of work: "Until fairly recent times it has been accepted, without much questioning, that the scope of many jobs is bound to be determined by the demands of technology, processes and systems. Employees have been given little opportunity to become involved in the planning and organisation of work. [...] There is now however a growing realisation throughout all sectors of industry and commerce that jobs restricted in this way are the source of problems." Fraser. "Tripartite Steering Group on Job Satisfaction. Making Work More Satisfying"

153 Aldo Rossi, *L'architettura Della Città*, 1st edition (Padua: Citta Studi, 1966).

4

1 Gilman Paper Company. Official press release (13th December 1977), Cedric Price Archive, Canadian Centre for Architecture, Montréal, document folder: DR:1995:0280:651:2/5. Price met Gilman through a curator at the Museum of Modern Art, Pierre Apraxine. The latter provided support during the initial project phase and acted as an intermediary between Howard Gilman and Cedric Price in subsequent stages of the project. C.f.: Terence Riley and Paola Antonelli. "Pierre Apraxine Interview by Paola Antonelli", in *The Changing of the Avant-Garde. Visionary Architectural Drawings from the Howard Gilman Collection* (New York: The Museum of Modern Art, 2002). Over and above this professional contact, a friendship soon developed between them, making it possible to agree to a feasibility study for a "fine arts building" after an initial meeting in autumn 1976. Cedric Price, "Letter of Appointment" (November 1976), Cedric Price Archive, Canadian Centre for Architecture, Montréal, document folder: DR:1995:0280: 651:5/5.

2 The centre also offered them living and study quarters. Cedric Price, "What Offered" (not dated), Cedric Price Archive, Canadian Centre for Architecture, Montréal, document folder: DR:1995:0280:651:1/5.

3 Gilman was already actively involved in fine arts sponsorship and wanted to expand his focus with a long-term commitment to the performing arts, such as dance, opera and theatre through this new project. Ibid.; Riley and Antonelli, "Interview Von Paola Antonelli Mit Pierre Apraxine"; Cedric Price Architects, "Minimal Initial Brief as Noted by P.A.". Memorandum (12th December 1976), Cedric Price Archive, Canadian Centre for Architecture, Montréal, document folder: DR:1995:0280:651:5/5. P.A. is probably an abbreviation for Pierre Apraxine. The programme sketches for the project mention a planned Artist-in-Residence programme, to enable famous artists to develop work at White Oak.

4 Cedric Price. Letter to Douglas Smith, quantity surveyor (28th July 1977). Cedric Price Archive, Canadian Centre for Architecture, Montréal, document folder: DR:1995:0280: 651:5/5.

5 Cedric Price, "Polariser Notes. Who Are You?" (24th February 1978), Cedric Price Archive, Canadian Centre for Architecture, Montréal, document folder: DR:1995:0280:651:5/5.

6 Pierre Apraxine described Howard Gilman as a man who loved grand ideas, as a philanthropist and conser-

vationist. Riley and Antonelli, "Pierre Apraxine Interview by Paola Antonelli".

7   The working documents Price sent to Gilman included a file on the McAppy project along with the two questionnaires ("mutual work assessment" and "work improvement scheme") that he had developed for the McAppy project: Cedric Price, "Scope of the McAppy Programme" (21st December 1976), Cedric Price Archive, Canadian Centre for Architecture, Montréal, document folder: DR:1995:0280:651:3/5.

8   Price, "Generator".

9   Cedric Price Architects, "Grid Layout Menu 24". Planning document, scale 1:250 (not dated), Cedric Price Archive, Canadian Centre for Architecture, Montréal, document folder: DR:1995:0280:467.

10   Cedric Price Architects, "Minimal Initial Brief as Noted by P.A."; Gonçalo Furtado, "Generator and Beyond. Encounters of Cedric Price and John Frazer" (Doctoral thesis, University College of London, 2004).

11   Cedric Price Architects, "Initial Layout of Bases". Planning document, layout number 132/126, scale 1:250 (not dated), Cedric Price Archive, Canadian Centre for Architecture, Montréal, document folder: DR:1995:0280:037:449.

12   Cedric Price Architects, "Key to Dwngs 132/175–176". Scale 1:250, Indian ink on transparent paper (not dated), Cedric Price Archive, Canadian Centre for Architecture, Montréal, document folder: DR:1995:0280:651:1/5. During development of the design the foundation grid was scaled and measured out by Frank Newby and F J Samuely and Partners. F J Samuely und Partners, "Generator. Bases Layout". Scale 1:250 (not dated), Cedric Price Archive, Canadian Centre for Architecture, Montréal, document folder: DR:1995:0280:651:1/5.

13   Cedric Price Architects, "Modular Activity Spaces". Layout number 132/24, scale 1:250, transparent paper (not dated), Cedric Price Archive, Canadian Centre for Architecture, Montréal, document folder: DR:1995:0280:254.

14   Cedric Price Architects, "Grid Layout + Menu 24 + Gl Walk G". Planning document, layout number 132/167, scale 1:250 (not dated), Cedric Price Archive, Canadian Centre for Architecture, Montréal, document folder: DR:1995:0280:462.

15   "Structures, enclosures, plant equipment and services that together, with the 'existing' environment, generate a unique series of conditions to encourage and precipitate creative activity – both individual & collective." Cedric Price, "General Design Notes". Memorandum (10th February 1977), Cedric Price Archive, Canadian Centre for Architecture, Montréal, document folder: DR:1995:0280:651:5/5.

16   Price's considerations on this point ranged from development of processes for planning and decision-making right through to operation and upkeep of the ensemble.

17   As a result the northern grid area was rotated by ten degrees. F J Samuely und Partners, "Bases Layout".

18   Cedric Price Architects, "Modular Activity Spaces".

19   Price, "Generator".

20   Price took a very literal approach in engaging with the menu analogy. He derived an initial proposal for the Generator's spatial design from the traditional British breakfast, arranging its various "structural components" like egg, beans and sausage on a plate. This referenced his concept of a useable style of architecture, devised to allow users to tap into the leeway the design offered for individual appropriation of the space.

21   For example he titled one of the first design sketches for the Generator "The Menu & Table Setting". Cedric Price Architects, "The Menu & Table Setting". Layout number 132/11, drawing on copy, orange pencil and ball pen on photocopy, scale 1:500 (not dated), Cedric Price Archive, Canadian Centre for Architecture, Montréal, document folder: DR:1995:0280:409.

22   Cedric Price, "Rough Analysis of Combined Menus". Memorandum, handwritten on transparent paper, A4 (1st March 1978), Cedric Price Archive, Canadian Centre for Architecture, Montréal, document folder: DR:1995:0280:651:5/5.

23   Cedric Price Architects, "Menu 15 View a–D". Layout number 132/169, scale 1:500 (not dated), Cedric Price Archive, Canadian Centre for Architecture, Montréal, document folder: DR:1995:0280:651:4/5. Price's design method essentially corresponded to the "rational model", developed by Allen Newell and Herbert A. Simon in the late 1960s. Their pioneering work on artificial intelligence and cognitive research demonstrated that computer programmes are capable of actions for which human beings use intelligence. The principle essentially corresponds to generative design as practiced today.

24   Cedric Price Architects, "Modular Activity Spaces".

25   Cedric Price Architects, "Grid Layout + Menu 24". Layout number 132/153, scale 1:250, copy (not dated), Cedric Price Archive, Canadian Centre for Architecture, Montréal, document folder: DR:1995:0280:467; Cedric Price Architects, "The Menu & Table Setting".

26   Cedric Price Architects, "The Menu & Table Setting".

27   Cedric Price, "Menu, Table Setting & the Meal". Layout number sk46, drawing with black and red felt pens on photocopy of registry entry, scale 1:1056/1:88', A4 (not dated), Cedric Price Archive, Canadian Centre for Architecture, Montréal, document folder: DR:1995:0280:651:5/5.

28   Price, "Rough Analysis of Combined Menus"; Cedric Price Architects, "Group a Envelopmess". Layout number 132/098, scale 1:250 (not dated), Cedric Price Archive, Canadian Centre for Architecture, Montréal, document folder: DR:1995:0280:420.

29   Cedric Price Architects, "Key to Dwngs 132/175 –176".

30   A series of 1:250 plans for "Menu 24" still exist. C.f.: Cedric Price Architects, "Menu 24 – the Circle". Planning document, scale 1:250 (not dated), Cedric Price Archive, Canadian Centre for Architecture, Montréal, document folder: DR:1995:0280:462; Cedric Price Architects, "Menu 24 – Inbetween Spaces". Planning document, scale 1:250 (not dated), Cedric Price Archive, Canadian Centre for Architecture, Montréal, document folder: DR:1995:0280:465; Cedric Price Architects, "Menu 24 – Junctions". Planning document, scale 1:250 (not dated), Cedric Price Archive, Canadian Centre for Architecture, Montréal, document folder: DR:1995:0280:466; Cedric Price Architects, "Menu 24 – Uses". Planning document, scale 1:250 (not dated), Cedric Price Archive, Canadian Centre for Architecture, Montréal, document folder: DR:1995:0280:467. Price did more in-depth work on the detailing of walkways and platforms, drainage ditches, curbs and planted areas.

31   "Menu 25, Detail of S/W Zone Ii". Sketch, scale 1:250 (not dated), Cedric Price Archive, Canadian Centre for Architecture, Montréal, document folder: DR:1995:0280:651:2/5.

32   "The Notion of a (Friendly) Barrier". Sketch, scale not indicated (not dated), Cedric Price Archive, Canadian Centre for Architecture, Montréal, document folder: DR:1995:0280:110.

33   At a later stage in the planning Price produced a comparative sketch in which he placed the dimensions of the Generator's urban planning situation over Manhattan's urban grid to compare their proportions. Another sketch shows a similar comparison with a section of central London. Cedric Price Architects, "Where It's At". Planning document, layout number 132/027, scale not indicated (not dated), Cedric Price Archive, Canadian Centre for Architecture, Montréal, document folder: DR:1995:0280: 409–411.

34   Price, "Never Feel Empty, Never Feel Full".

35   A number of plans and sketches point to this type of study. C.f. inter alia: Cedric Price Architects, "Triple Cube. Transverse Sections with Sight Lines", layout number 132/137, scale 1"=2ft (not dated), Cedric Price Archive, Canadian Centre for Architecture, Montréal, document folder: DR:1995:0280:464–474; Airbrush perspective (not dated). Cedric Price Archive, Canadian Centre for Architecture, Montréal, document folder: DR:1995:0280:594; Cedric Price Architects, "Cube Grid Perspective", planning document,

layout number 132/060, scale not indicated (not dated), Cedric Price Archive, Canadian Centre for Architecture, Montréal, document folder: DR:1995:0280:508.

36   Cedric Price Architects, "Generator", sketch, coloured pencil on A4, scale not indicated (not dated), Cedric Price Archive, Canadian Centre for Architecture, Montréal, document folder: DR:1995:0280:651:5/5.

37   Price planned to have a model of the cube produced in England in order to run trials in a clay quarry in Thurrock to explore how various changes impacted on the ambience created.

38   Cedric Price conducted several studies on the communicative dimension, which was such a vital design component for him, even going so far as to carry out a 1:1 test in 1979 during a visit to the plantation. In order to investigate how the cube related to the outdoor space, he reproduced the outlines of a few cubes with wooden panels and covered the cubes' sides with sheets of paper at various different heights to check the vistas revealed by the varying degrees of opening. "The Site Is Tested", photocopy of a colour photograph (not dated), Cedric Price Archive, Canadian Centre for Architecture, Montréal, document folder: DR:1995:0280:651:5/5.

39   Cedric Price and A. Meadowcold, "Notes on Generator Drawings No.132/161, 132/162" (15th June 1979), Cedric Price Archive, Canadian Centre for Architecture, Montréal, document folder: DR:1995:0280:651:5/5.

40   Barry Fox, "A Building That Moves in the Night", *New Scientist* (19th March 1981): 743.

41   The crane that was to assist with placement of the cubes needed a certain amount of room to manoeuvre. Having studied the outdoor areas in "Menu 23" Cedric Price therefore concluded that these areas had to be at least three times the size of the adjacent cubes. He noted a further rule on the margins of a sketch that simulated the crane's trajectory during construction of the ensemble: "There shall be no cube more than two cube squares from a crane route." This rule also served as the basis for the practical requirements for the finishing incorporated into the cubes. Cedric Price, "Minimum Crane Route", layout number sk87, scale 1:250 (not dated), Cedric Price Archive, Canadian Centre for Architecture, Montréal, document folder: DR:1995:0280:651:2/5.

42   Cedric Price, "Assembly. Stage 1–8", layout number sk69–sk76, scale 1:100 (not dated), Cedric Price Archive, Canadian Centre for Architecture, Montréal, document folder: DR:1995:0280:651:2/5.

43   In 1978 the detailing for the subsequent tender was completed. Surveying work on the site began in October 1978 and at the end of that year Frank Newby carried out the scaling for the cubes.

44   Cedric Price, "General Design Notes". Memorandum (10th February 1977), Cedric Price Archive, Canadian Centre for Architecture, Montréal, document folder: DR:1995:0280:651:5/5.

45   Cedric Price Architects, "Friendly Barriers", layout number 132/57, scale not indicated (not dated), Cedric Price Archive, Canadian Centre for Architecture, Montréal, document folder: DR:1995:0280:272. In addition to the external surfaces of the cubes, a diagonal dividing wall could be introduced into the cube so that a bathroom could be installed. Cedric Price Architects, "Key to Dwngs 132/175–176"; Photo of the cube study, black and white print (not dated). Cedric Price Archive, Canadian Centre for Architecture, Montréal, document folder: DR:2004:1264:013.

46   Cedric Price Architects, "Triple Cube with Sight Lines Iii + Ii Upright", layout number 132/136, scale 1"=2ft (not dated), Cedric Price Archive, Canadian Centre for Architecture, Montréal, document folder: DR:1995:0280:438; Cedric Price Architects, "Triple Cube. Transverse Sections with Sight Lines".

47   Sandy Brown Associates, "Generator Acoustics Report No. 2" (29th September 1978), Cedric Price Archive, Canadian Centre for Architecture, Montréal, document folder: DR:1995:0280:651:1/5.

48   Cedric Price Architects, "Multi-Use Fixings", series of axonometric depictions: sk80–sk83, A4, copies (not dated), Cedric Price Archive, Canadian Centre for Architecture, Montréal, document folder: DR:1995:0280:651:1/5; Cedric Price, "Multi-Use Fixings", drawing sk84, scale 1:100 (not dated), Cedric Price Archive, Canadian Centre for Architecture, Montréal, document folder: DR:1995:0280:651:2/5.

49   Cedric Price, "Group Growth", drawing sk31 (not dated), Cedric Price Archive, Canadian Centre for Architecture, Montréal, document folder: DR:1995:0280:651:2/5.

50   Price, "Cedric Price Im Interview Mit Hans Ulrich Obrist".

51   Ibid.

52   "Network", planning document 132/29, scale not indicated (not dated), Cedric Price Archive, Canadian Centre for Architecture, Montréal, document folder: DR:1995:0280:411.

53   In the primary and secondary sources on the subject, both the British spelling ("Polariser") and the American spelling ("Polarizer") are used. This text primarily uses the British spelling, with the exception of direct quotations.

54   Cedric Price, "Polariser Potential. Draft" (4th August 1977), Cedric Price Archive, Canadian Centre for Architecture, Montréal, document folder: DR:1995:0280:651:3/5.

55   "Factor" in this connection means, roughly, a representative/broker. Although the position and job description for the "Factor" are not defined in as much detail as for the Polariser, a comprehensive description of the remit can nonetheless be compiled from various sources. On the Factor's role in maintenance and reconfiguration of the Generator c.f.: Cedric Price and Barbara Johnson, "Polariser's Predictions on Behavioral Patterns of Generator Users" (15th March 1978), Cedric Price Archive, Canadian Centre for Architecture, Montréal, document folder: DR:1995:0280:651:5/5. For a further definition of his tasks, which Cedric Price described as "One of the key components of any operation that contributes to a result" c.f.: Cedric Price, "Further Respectably Zany Definitions", memorandum (5th March 1977), Cedric Price Archive, Canadian Centre for Architecture, Montréal, document folder: DR:1995:0280:651:5/5. C.f. in addition the address list of contact persons for the Generator project, which includes an entry for the "Factor" with the name "Wally" (short for Wallace) Prince and his phone number.

56   "Polariser Notes" (28th February 1978), Cedric Price Archive, Canadian Centre for Architecture, Montréal, document folder: DR:1995:0280:651:1/5.

57   Price, "Polariser Potential".

58   "Network".

59   Cedric Price, "Draft Brief for Polariser (P.)" (6th March 1978), Cedric Price Archive, Canadian Centre for Architecture, Montréal, document folder: DR:1995:0280:651:5/5.

60   Price, "Polariser Potential".

61   Cedric Price, "Draft Brief to Polariser" (6th March 1978), Cedric Price Archive, Canadian Centre for Architecture, Montréal, document folder: DR:1995:0280:651:3/5.

62   Cedric Price, "Generator Florida US", memorandum (25th March 1980), Cedric Price Archive, Canadian Centre for Architecture, Montréal, document folder: DR:1995:0280:651:3/5.

63   Cedric Price. memorandum (12th December 1976), Cedric Price Archive, Canadian Centre for Architecture, Montréal, document folder: DR:1995:0280:651:3/5.

64   Cedric Price Architects, "Polariser Draft Work Definition No. 02", Confidential memorandum (11th November 1977), Cedric Price Archive, Canadian Centre for Architecture, Montréal, document folder: DR:1995:0280:651:5/5; Price, "Polariser Potential".

65   Both the Gestalt psychology approach and the concept of group psychology that Cedric Price referred to in the Generator project had been developed by social psychologist Kurt Lewin (1890–1947) as "dynamic" theories that examined how users' perceptions of their surroundings influenced their behaviour.

66 What was known as "shape-shifting" appeared for example in the "cube experiment", in which the perspective view "flipped" if viewed at length from a three-dimensional projection to a two-dimensional representation. "Generator", sketch (not dated), Cedric Price Archive, Canadian Centre for Architecture, Montréal, document folder: DR:1995:0280:651:1/5.

67 Oksana Bulgakowa. "Von Der 'Komödie Des Auges' Zum Verhaltensdrama. Eisensteins 'Glasshausprojekt'", in Wahrnehmung und Geschichte. Markierungen zur Aisthesis Materialis, Bernhard J. Dotzler and Ernst Müller, ed. (Berlin: Akademie Verlag, 1995).

68 With a view to ensuring that the space offered as much leeway for interpretation as possible, Cedric Price laid out the Generator grid to allow for multiple readings, in a manner akin to Gestalt psychology experiments on perception. He achieved this for example by turning the grid through ten degrees. The movement of visitors on the street was filtered through a varying experience of space depending on the viewer's position: "The resultant visual ambiguity is sufficient to suggest from the roadside crowding of structures viewed in one direction with a corresponding exfoliation in the other. Thus both FRIENDLY BARRIERS are created for those arriving and a GENEROUS FAREWELL given to those departing." "Generator. Above You the Grid" (not dated), Cedric Price Archive, Canadian Centre for Architecture, Montréal, document folder: DR:1995:0280:651:5/5.

69 Since the 1940s Kurt Lewin had been developing a model of psychological ecology in field theory in which human behaviour was viewed as mutually dependent on the surroundings. Analogously to electromagnetic field physics, Kurt Lewin sketched out a rational explanatory model for the way in which people behaved in groups and also used mathematical instruments to compute dynamic field strengths as a possible forecasting option. His position was bolstered by systems-theory approaches to self-organisation theory and the theory of non-dynamic linear systems. Kurt Lewin, Field Theory in Social Science, (New York: Harper Brothers, 1951). In psychological field theory, the constellations of all current experiences, memories and expectations of the psychological field of the structured life space formed the group through dynamic forces of social interaction, and led the individual to take on certain social roles. Kurt Lewin's theories were based on a host of experimental behavioural studies, in which the influence factors could be described with the help of mathematical topology.

70 Cedric Price probably became acquainted with this particular interpretation of dynamic spatial perception through works on architectural theory written by his friend Reyner Banham. Banham, Authorised interview with the author. In Theory and Design in the First Machine Age Banham had dismantled the polarities between rational and anti-rational trends in the "Modern Movement" and advocated an extended view of modernity. In his discussion on Le Corbusier's Villa Savoye, he identified spatial perception triggered specifically by human psychology, which he referred to as "material-immaterial illusionism", growing out of the tension between the user's movements and the spatial elements he or she perceived. Whiteley, Reyner Banham.

71 Price envisioned that the spatial and social environment would foster free development, creativity and diversity as fundamental human attributes. In addition, the Polariser was given the task of building up "differences in potential" in the psychological field of the Generator to unleash unknown human energies and forces.

72 No written commissioning of John Frazer is extant. Nick Bailey, who worked for Cedric Price at the time, simply contacted Frazer. Furtado, "Generator and Beyond".

73 The arrangement of the Generator cubes on the ensemble's grid was to be simulated on the Tektonix computers there. Ibid.

74 John Frazer, "Intelligent Modelling System", copy of a publication about the Generator project, A4 (not dated), Cedric Price Archive, Canadian Centre for Architecture, Montréal, document folder: DR:1995:0280:651:5/5. John Frazer received the grant with support from Price. Cedric Price, "Letter of Recomendation for John Frazer's Interactive Computer Aided Design Programme Based on the Concept Seeding Technique", letter to N. L. Wiliams (8th December 1980), Cedric Price Archive, Canadian Centre for Architecture, Montréal, document folder: DR:1995:0280:651:5/5. The grant was for 6,000 pounds. Student Paul Coats from Liverpool University also received funding support.

75 Nick Baily and Cedric Price, "Generator Notes for John Frazer", memorandum (1st August 1979), Cedric Price Archive, Canadian Centre for Architecture, Montréal, document folder: DR:1995:0280:651:5/5.

76 In 1979 John Frazer, together with his wife Julia Frazer, set up the firm Autographics, which was involved in developing CAD. The computer programme for Generator was also developed further through this firm. There were links between Autographics and Cedric Price until the 1990s. The two parties became entangled in a conflict over payment for models that had already been produced, including disputes over correct commissioning, cost computation and invoicing. John Frazer continued work on the project with his firm independently. John Frazer. Letter to Cedric Price (6th June 1989). Cedric Price Archive, Canadian Centre for Architecture, Montréal, document folder: DR:1995:0235:651:5/5; John Frazer. Letter to Cedric Price (11th July 1989). Cedric Price Archive, Canadian Centre for Architecture, Montréal, document folder: DR:1995:0280:651:5/5.

77 Fox, "A Building That Moves in the Night".

78 For a detailed account of the use of computers in the Generator project and John Frazer's role c.f.: Furtado, "Generator and Beyond".

79 This form of mathematical modelling, used in physics, biology, economics and the social sciences, as well as later in computer sciences, to simulate dynamic processes or conduct combinatorial computational processes, was developed in 1940 by two researchers on the Los Alamos project, Stanislaw Ulam and John von Neumann. "Game of Life" was developed by mathematician John Horton Conway in 1969 at Cambridge University. In his book Rechnender Raum (translated into English as Calculating Space), Konrad Zuse had already established a connection between the theory of cellular automata and simulation of natural development processes. However, in the "exact" natural sciences, explanatory models based on this kind of simulation were viewed critically, as they were not based on scientific laws. The cellular automata model is also used in ecological studies to make statistical statements about the development of complex systems. The issue at stake is often habitat stability and the prerequisites to produce what is dubbed an ecological balance. Heinz Zemanek. "Konrad Zuse Und Die Systemarchitektur", in Geschichte der Informatik, Hans Dieter Hellige, ed. (Berlin: Springer Verlag, 2004).

80 In Gestalt psychology the field of experience and action is a term used to describe reality as perceived and experienced by human beings. This also determines experiences and behaviour.

81 "Thinking for Fun. Cedric Price's Generator Project in Florida", Building Design, No. 492 (18th April 1980): 8.

82 Socio-economic theories of action and the use of mathematical models were discussed in the context of the socio-political debates during the student uprisings, and in critical theory. Having originally been used by institutions such as the American RAND Cooperation to design military deterrence strategies during the Cold War, game theory seemed to entail reducing human behaviour to simple utilitarian relationships in which the human individual was simply a plaything of totalitarian power structures. Reinhold Martin, Utopia's Ghost. Architecture and Postmodernism, Again, (Minneapolis: University of Minnesota Press, 2010).

83 American sociologist James Coleman developed this relationship in his action model. Heike Diefenbach. "Die Theorie Der Rationalen Wahl", in Soziologische Paradigmen nach Talcott Parsons, Ditmar Brock, et al., ed. (Wiesbaden: VS Verlag für Sozialwissenschaften, 2009).

84 Thomas C. Schelling, *Micromotives and Macrobehaviour*, (New York: W.W. Norton & Company, 1978).

85 Hall, *Cities of Tomorrow*.

86 Charles Jencks, *The Language of Post-Modern Architecture*, (orig. 1977) 2nd edition (New York: Rizzoli, 1988).

87 Against the backdrop of the 1965 riots in Los Angeles, Reyner Banham questioned the influence of modern architecture in improving living conditions. Banham, *Los Angeles*.

88 Beginning with the Fun Palace Project, where a cybernetic system was to transpose user preferences into machine commands, and continuing with the information system for the Potteries Thinkbelt project, Price once again elaborated this idea in 1965 in a "Pop-Up Parliament" project sketch. In his piece on remodelling the historic parliamentary building, he advocated introducing a computer system that would provide parliamentarians with open access to all the information needed for parliamentary work, making the communication and information exchange into the foundation of democratic parliamentary culture. Price viewed this new communicative culture as an important contribution to greater openness in parliamentary work, which needed to focus more on content and rise above the individual interests of parties and politicians. Cedric Price devised the project as a commentary on Martin Buchanan's plan for Whitehall. Cedric Price, "Pop-up Parliament", manuscript (1965), Cedric Price Archive, Canadian Centre for Architecture, Montréal, document folder: DR:1995:0235:007:003; Cedric Price, "Pop-up Parliament", *New Society*, No. 148 (29th July 1965): 7.

89 In concrete terms, the software was intended to assist with design designs and to correlate users' wishes and the imperatives of the surroundings. Fox, "A Building That Moves in the Night".

90 Furtado, "Generator and Beyond". The Commodore PET was launched in 1977 with 4 KB memory, later increased to 8 KB.

91 Cedric Price mentioned only two rules in his design. He evolved these on the basis of the ensemble's functional conditions. In addition, in the Polariser's job description, Price incorporated self-organisation processes such as "self-selection and user booking". Price, "Draft Brief to Polariser". Cedric Price had already become acquainted with an automated booking system during his visit to the 1969 Montréal Expo. Along with Price's office calendars, the archive files also contain the entrance tickets, hotel information and 360-degree panoramic view from the 1969 "Man and his World" Expo in Montréal.

92 Frazer, Letter to Cedric Price (11th July 1989).

93 Cedric Price, "Generator Florida US. Computer Programmes", memorandum (25th March 1980), Cedric Price Archive, Canadian Centre for Architecture, Montréal, document folder: DR:1995:0280:651:3/5.

94 Frazer, Letter to Cedric Price (11th July 1989).

95 Ibid.

96 "Thinking for Fun".

97 John Frazer's contacts with Gordon Pask dated back to his student days at the AA School of Architecture, where Pask taught. During development of the Fun Palace, Pask elaborated the idea of a self-organising system that would adjust autonomously to changed conditions in its surroundings on the basis of organic principles of growth and adaptation. For Pask cybernetics was to a large extent about influences from psychological and social systems, so that machines, with the help of cybernetics, also had to be adapted to human perceptions, sensibilities and behaviours. The devices Pask devised in his firm, such as the Self Adaptive Keyboard Instructor, SAKI, or the automated learning environment, EUCRATES, were inspired by the design idea that specific cybernetic shaping of interactions could influence human creativity and capacity to learn. Gordon Pask, "Comments on the Cybernetics of Ethical, Psychological and Sociological Systems", *Progress in Biocybernetics* 3 (1966): 158. His partner Robin McKinnon-Wood identified the Musicolour machine as one indication of the success of Pask's efforts: it was no longer perceived by those nearby as a machine but as part of the natural environment: "[…] one bends the machine to adapt to the person in such way that he doesn't notice. It worked fine." Robin McKinnon-Wood, "Early Machinations", *Systems Research and Behavioral Science* 10, No. 3 (1993): 129; Gordon Pask. "Musicolour", in *The Scientist Speculates. An Anthology of Partly-Baked Ideas*, I. J. Good, ed. (New York: Basic Books, 1962).

98 Howard Gilman. Letter to Cedric Price (29th October 1979). Cedric Price Archive, Canadian Centre for Architecture, Montréal, document folder: DR:1995:0280:651:5/5.

99 Nathaniel Coleman, *Utopias and Architecture*, (New York: Routledge, 2005).

100 This approach was very similar to Lewis Mumford's idea of "neotechnic communities". To reinvigorate his vision Mumford drew in his writings on the technological developments of the second Industrial Revolution. In his view these new technological achievements could give rise to new organisational forms for social communities and strike a new balance between the rural culture of the pre-industrial era and the urban culture of the industrial age. However, this egalitarian vision of community ran against the grain of the actual implementation of the technological revolution, which he saw as being in the hands of planning elites and specialists such as technicians, artists and intellectuals. Blake, "Introduction to Arts and Technics"; Lewis Mumford, *Interpretations and Forecasts. 1922–1972 Studies in Literature, History, Biography, Technics, and Contemporary Society*, (New York, London: Hartcourt, Brace, Jovanovich, 1973); Lewis Mumford, *The Urban Prospects. Essays*, (New York, London: Hartcourt, Brace, Jovanovich, 1968).

101 By deliberately choosing short lifecycles for individual elements, Price envisioned that it would be possible to ensure openness in the long-term social organisation of the space, and thus to shape it in a pluralistic spirit.

102 In addition, legal disputes concerning issues within the family over management of the Gilman Paper Company also contributed to suspension of the project, as funding for the scheme was no longer secured. In one of Howard Gilman's last letters to Price, written three years after the first temporary halt to the project, Gilman explicitly blamed the legal dispute with his brother and the latter's wife for the postponement of the project. Howard Gilman. Letter to Cedric Price (24th November 1982). Cedric Price Archive, Canadian Centre for Architecture, Montréal, document folder: DR:1995:0280:651:5/5.

103 Riley and Antonelli, "Pierre Apraxine Interview by Paola Antonelli".

104 Ibid.

Epilogue

1 The project exhibition was held from 18th April to 8th June 1997 in the Architecture Foundation, London. "Magnets", Invitation Card (not dated), Cedric Price Archive, Canadian Centre for Architecture, Montréal: unfiled Box CP#5 (archive state: August 2009).

2 Price described the function of the Magnets in the following terms: "Magnets are installed on existing metropolitan sites at present UNDERUSED or MISUSED. […] Their SITING enriches the intensity of the city grain the STRUCTURES act as both INSERTS and TRANSPLANTS providing socially beneficial movement routes." Cedric Price. Report (1st July 1996), Cedric Price Archive, Canadian Centre for Architecture, Montréal, document folder: unfiled Box CP#11, Subfolder 1 (archive state: August 2009).

3 Cedric Price, "Parc De La Villette", planning documents (not dated), Cedric Price Archive, Canadian Centre for Architecture, Montréal: filed Box "Projet #156 de l'ajout 2004", 1051 folder DE01303 (archive state: August 2009); Cedric Price.

"Ducklands", in *Opera*, Samantha Hardingham, ed. (London: Wiley Academy, 2003); "IFCCA Prize for the Design of Cities" (New York, Montréal: Canadian Centre of Architecture, 5th–20th October 1999).

4   Cedric Price, "Presentation Draft" (15th March 1996), Cedric Price Archive, Canadian Centre for Architecture, Montréal: unfiled Box CP#11, (archive state: August 2009).

5   Price, "Generator".

6   The term "postmodern" was first used by Jean-François Lyotard in *La condition postmoderne.* He also coined the phrase "the end of grand narratives" that shaped the modern era. According to Lyotard the three grand meta-narratives of modernity are the Enlightenment, Idealism and Historicism. Jean-François Lyotard, *The Postmodern Condition. A Report on Knowledge*, (Manchester University Press, 1984), orig.: *La condition postmoderne. Rapport sur le savoir* (Paris: Èditions Minuit, 1979).

References

Interviews

Banham, Mary. Authorised interview with the author (London, 14th February 2007).

Bron, Eleanor. Authorised interview with the author (London, 8th December 2006).

Hall, Peter Geoffrey. Authorised interview with the author (London, 29th August 2006).

Mullin, Steven. Authorised interview with the author (London, 24th June 2006).

Price, David. Authorised interview with the author (Faversham, 17th January 2009).

Rogers, Richard. Authorised phone interview with the author (2nd November 2006).

Periodicals

Allen, Stan, and Hal Foster. "A Conversation with Kenneth Frampton", *October* 106 (2003): 43.

Alloway, Lawrence. "The Long Front of Culture", *Cambridge Opinion* 17 (1959): 298.

Archigram. "Living City", *Living Arts*, No. 2 (June 1963): 112.

Banham, Reyner. "The Art of Doing Your Thing" BBC Radio Lecture, *The Listener* 80 (12th September 1968).

——————. "City as Scrambled Egg", *Cambridge Opinion* 17 (1959): 18.

——————. "A Clip-on Architecture", *Design Quaterly* (1965): 11.

——————. "A Home Is Not a House", *Art in America* (April 1965): 73.

——————. "Horse of Different Colour", *New Society* (November 1967): 637.

——————. "Softer Hardware", *Ark 44* (Summer 1969): 2.

——————. "Towards a Pop Architecture", *Architectural Review* (July 1962): 43.

——————. "Zoo À La Mode", *New Statesman* (12th March 1965).

Banham, Reyner, Paul Barker, Peter Geoffrey Hall, and Cedric Price. "Non-Plan. An Experiment in Freedom", *New Society*, No. 338 (20th March 1969): 435.

Barr, John. "Free Time Britain", *New Society*, No. 133 (April 1965): 5.

Burns, Tom. "Micropolitics. Mechanisms of Institutional Change", *Administrative Science Quarterly* 6, No. 3 (December 1961): 257.

Colomina, Beatriz. "Friends of the Future. A Conversation with Peter Smithson", *The Independent Group* 94 (October 2000): 3.

De Carlo, Giancarlo. "The Housing Problem in Italy", *Freedom* 9/12 (1948): 2.

Ezard, John, and Michael Billington, *The Guardian*, "Joan Littlewood", Obituary, 23rd September 2002.

Fox, Barry. "A Building That Moves in the Night", *New Scientist* (19th March 1981): 743.

Gough, Maria. "In the Laboratory of Constructivism. Karl loganson's Cold Structures", *October* 84 (1998): 90.

Grenfell-Baines, George, *The Guardian*, "Universities. In Search for a Flexible Unity", 13th June 1965.

Greville, Charles, *Daily Mail*, "Will This Be a Lot of Fun?", 19th April 1965.

Harris, Richard. "A Double Irony: The Originality and Influence of John F. C. Turner", *Habitat International* 27, No. 2 (2003): 245.

Highmore, Ben. "Hopscotch Modernism. On Everyday Life and the Blurring of Art and Social Science" Special issue: "Modernism and the Everyday", *Modernist Cultures*, No. 2 (2006): 70.

Lewis, B. N. "Fun Palace. Counterblast to Boredom", *New Society* (15th April 1965): 8.

Littlewood, Joan. "A Laboratory of Fun. Leisure and the Arts in 1984", *New Scientist* (14th May 1964): 432.

Lobsinger, Mary Louise. "Das Programm programmieren. Das Inter-Action Centre in London von Cedric Price, 1977", *Werk, Bauen + Wohnen* (December 2007): 38.

McKinnon-Wood, Robin. "Early Machinations", *Systems Research and Behavioral Science* 10, No. 3 (1993): 129.

Moffat, Isabelle. "A Horror of Abstract Thought. Postwar Britain and Hamilton's 1951 'Growth and Form' Exhibition", *The Independent Group* 94 (October 2000): 89.

Murray, Peter. "Cosmorama", *Architectural Design* (April 1973).

Pask, Gordon. "The Architectural Relevance of Cybernetics", *Architectural Design* 39 (September 1969): 494.

——————. "Comments on the Cybernetics of Ethical, Psychological and Sociological Systems", *Progress in Biocybernetics* 3 (1966): 158.

Pease, William M. "An Automatic Machine Tool", *Scientific American* 187, No. 3 (1st September 1952): 101.

Price, Cedric. "Approaching an Architecture of Approximation", *Architectural Design* 42, No. 10 (1972): 645.

——————. "Buckminster Fuller, 1895–1983" Obituary, *Architectural Design*, No. 4 (1983).

——————. "Chat. Extracts from the Tape", *Architectural Design* 41 (April 1971): 231.

——————. "Conversion at Oldham, Lancashire", *Architectural Review*, No. 714 (June 1956).

——————. "Home, Sweet Home", *Time & Tide* (20th January 1961).

——————. "A Laboratory of Fun. Cedric Price, Architect, Elaborates on the Design of the 'Fun Palace' Envisioned by Joan Littlewood", *New Scientist* (14th May 1964): 433.

——————. "Life-Conditioning", *Architectural Design* (October 1966).

——————. "More Operational Originality, Less Three Dimensional Ingenuity, More Social Structures", *The Architects' Journal* (December 1977).

——————. "Pop-up Parliament", *New Society*, No. 148 (29th July 1965): 7.

——————. "Potteries Thinkbelt", *Architectural Design* 36, No. 10 (1966): 484.

——————. "Potteries Thinkbelt", *New Society* (2nd June 1966): 74.

——————. "Towards a 24-Hour Economic Living Toy", *Interior Design* (September 1967).

——————. "What's the Use of Piccadilly?", *Time & Tide* (2nd March 1961).

Scornik, Hugo. "Hugo Scornik Continues the Saga of His Travel in Africa and Arrival in the Canary Islands" Reader's Letter, *Architectural Design* (August 1972): 513.

Scott-Brown, Denise. "Learning from Pop", *Casabella* 359-360 (December 1971): 62.

Shoshkes, Ellen. "Jaqueline Tyrwhitt, a Founding Mother of Modern Urban Design", *Planning Perspectives* 21, No. 2 (2006): 179.

Smithson, Alison, and Peter Smithson. "Cluster City. A New Shape for the Cummunity", *Architectural Review* (November 1957): 333.

Trist, Eric, and Ken Banforth. "Some Social and Psychological Consequences of the Long Wall Method of Coal Getting", *Human Relations*, No. 4 (1951): 3.

Tustin, Arnold. "Feedback", *Scientific American* 187, No. 3 (1st September 1952): 48.

Tynan, Kenneth. "The Men of Anger", *Holiday* 23 (1958): 93.

Books

Arendt, Hannah. *The Human Condition*. (orig. 1958) 2nd edition (Chicago: University Of Chicago Press, 1998).

Banham, Reyner. Design by Choice. (London: Academy Editions, 1981).

—————. *.Los Angeles. The Architecture of Four Ecologies*. (orig. 1971; Berkeley CA: California Press, 2009).

—————. *.Megastructures. Urban Futures of the Recent Past*. (London: Thames and Hudson Ltd., 1976).

—————. *.Theory and Design in the First Machine Age*. (London: Architectural Press, 1960).

Becker, Egon. *Soziale Ökologie. Grundzüge einer Wissenschaft von den gesellschaftlichen Naturverhältnissen*. (Frankfurt am Main: Campus Verlag, 2006).

Booker, Christopher. *The Neophiliacs. A Study of the Revolution in English Life in the Fifties and Sixties*. (London: Collinsi, 1969).

Braun, Edward. *Meyerhold. A Revolution in Theatre*. University of Iowa Press, 1995).

Brock, Ditmar, Rainer Junger, Heike Diefenbach, Rainer Keller, and Dirk Villany, ed. *Soziologische Paradigmen nach Talcott Parsons*. (Wiesbaden: VS Verlag für Sozialwissenschaften, 2009).

Bron, Eleanor, and Samantha Hardingham. *Cedric Price Retriever*. (London: inIVA, 2006).

Brüggemeier, Franz-Josef. *Geschichte Großbritanniens im 20. Jahrhundert*. (Munich: C.H. Beck Verlag, 2010).

Coleman, Nathaniel. *Utopias and Architecture*. (New York: Routledge, 2005).

Conrads, Ulrich, ed. *Programs and Manifestoes on 20th-Century Architecture*. (Cambridge, MA: MIT Press, 1970).

Crosby, Theo, and John Bodley, ed. *The Living City Exhibition at the ICA*. Livings Arts, 3. (London: Institute of Contemporary Arts and Tillotsons, 1964).

Curtis, William J. R. *Denys Lasdun*. (London: Phaidon Press, 1994).

Dorey, Peter. *British Politics since 1945*. (Oxford: Blackwell Publishers, 1995).

Dotzler, Bernhard J., and Ernst Müller, ed. *Wahrnehmung und Geschichte. Markierungen zur Aisthesis Materialis*. (Berlin: Akademie Verlag, 1995).

Eisinger, Angelus. *Die Stadt der Architekten. Anatomie einer Selbstdemontage*. Bauwelt Fundamente, 131. (Gütersloh: Bau-Verlag, 2006).

Floud, Roderick, and Deirdre McCloskey, ed. *The Economic History of Britain since 1700*. (Cambridge: Cambridge University Press, 1994).

Forty, Adrian. *Words and Buildings. A Vocabulary of Modern Architecture*. (London: Thames and Hudson, 2000).

Freedman, Des. *Television Policies of the Labour Party: 1951–2000*. (London: Frank Cass, 2003).

Fuller, Richard Buckminster. *Utopia or Oblivion. The Prospects for Humanity*. (New York: Bantam Books, 1969).

Furtado, Gonçalo. "Generator and Beyond. Encounters of Cedric Price and John Frazer." Doctoral thesis, University College of London, 2004.

Galbraith, John Kenneth. *The Affluent Society*. (New York: Houghton Mifflin, 1958).

—————. *.The New Industrial State*. (Princeton, NJ: Princeton University Press, 1967).

Gans, Herbert J. *Urban Villagers. Group and Class in the Life of Italian-Americans*. (New York, NY: Free Press of Glencoe, 1962).

Gebhardt, Uta. *Talcott Parsons, an Intellectual Biography*. (Cambridge, New York: Cambridge University Press, 2002).

Geiser, Reto, ed. *Explorations in Architecture. Teaching, Design, Research*. (Basel: Birkhäuser, 2008).

Giddens, Anthony. *The Third Way*. (Cambridge: Polity Press, 1998).

Giedion, Sigfried. *Mechanization Takes Command. A Contribution to Anonymous History*. (New York: Oxford University Press, 1948).

Glynn, Sean, and Alan Booth. *Modern Britain. An Economic and Social History*. (New York: Routledge, 1996).

Goffman, Erving. *The Presentation of Self in Everyday Life*. (New York: Anchor Books, 1959).

Gold, John R. . *The Practice of Modernism. Modern Architects and Modern Transformation, 1954–1972*. (London: Routledge, 2007).

Goldhagen, Sarah, and Rejean Legault, ed. *Anxious Modernisms. Experimentation in Postwar Architectural Culture*. (Cambridge: MIT Press, 2000).

Good, I. J., ed. *The Scientist Speculates. An Anthology of Partly-Baked Ideas*. (New York: Basic Books, 1962).

Goorney, Howard. *The Theatre Workshop Story*. (orig. 1981; London: Methuen, 2008).

Gorelik, Mordecai. *New Theatres for Old*. (orig. 1940; New York: Octagon Books, 1975).

Grober, Ulrich. *Die Entdeckung der Nachhaltigkeit. Kulturgeschichte eines Begriffs*. (Munich: Verlag Antje Kunstmann, 2010),

Hagener, Michael, and Erich Hörl, ed. *Transformation Des Humanen*. (Frankfurt am Main: Suhrkamp, 2008).

Hall, Peter Geoffrey. *Cities of Tomorrow. An Intellectual History of Urban Planning in the Twentieth Century*. 6th edition (London: Blackwell Publishers, 2001).

Hand, James Edward, ed. *Ideals of Science and Faith*. (London: George Allen, 1904).

Hardingham, Samantha, ed. *Opera*. (London: Wiley Academy, 2003).

Hassler, Uta, and Catherine Dumont d'Ayoy, ed. *Bauten der Boomjahre. Paradoxien der Erhaltung*. (Gollion: Infolio Editions, 2009).

Haustein, Sabine. *Vom Mangel zum Massenkonsum. Deutschland, Frankreich und Großbritannien im Vergleich 1945–1970*. (Frankfurt am Main: Campus Verlag, 2007).

Hays, Michael K., *Architecture Theory since 1968*. (Cambridge, Mass.: MIT Press, 1998).

Hays, Michael K., Dana Miller and Antoine Picon, ed. *Buckminster Fuller. Starting with the Universe*. (London: Yale University Press, 2008).

Hellige, Hans Dieter, ed. *Geschichte der Informatik*. (Berlin: Springer Verlag, 2004).

Howard, Ebenezer. *To-morrow. A Peaceful Path to Real Reform* (Cambridge: Cambridge University Press, 1898; digital Version, 2010),

Hughes, Jonathan, and Simon Sadler, ed. *Non-Plan. Essays on Freedom, Participation and Change in Modern Architecture and Urbanism*. (London: Architectural Press, 2000).

Huizinga, Johan. *Homo Ludens. A Study of the Play-Element in Culture*. (London, Bosten and Henley: Routledge & Kegan Paul, 1949).

Jacobs, Jane. *The Death and Life of Great American Cities*. (Harmondsworth: Penguin Books, 1961).

Jencks, Charles. *The Language of Post-Modern Architecture*. (orig. 1977) 2nd edition (New York: Rizzoli, 1988).

Jungnickel, Dieter. *Graphen, Netzwerke und Algorithmen*. 3rd edition (Mannheim: BI Wissenschaftsverlag, 1984).

Keim, Kevin, ed. *You Have to Pay for the Public Life. Selected Essays from Charles W. Moore*. (Cambridge, MA: MIT Press, 2001).

Korn, Arthur. *History Builds the Town*. (London: Lund Humphries, 1953).

Krause, Joachim, and Claude Lichtenstein, ed. *Your Private Sky*. (Baden: Lars Müller Verlag, 1999).

Lampugnani, Vittorio Magnago, Katia Frey, and Eliana Perotti, ed. *Vom Wiederaufbau nach dem 2. Weltkrieg bis zur* zeitgenössischen Stadt. Vol. 3 (Berlin: Gebrüder Mann Verlag, 2005).

Landau, Royston. "Newby + Price", AA files In *Enigneers and Architects Series*, 27 (1994).

Le Corbusier. *Creation Is a Patient Search*. (Stuttgart: Praeger, 1960).

Leach, Robert. *Theatre Workshop. Joan Littlewood and the Making of Modern British Theatre*. (Exeter: University of Exeter Press, 2006).

Lewallen, Constance, and Steve Seid. *Ant Farm: 1968–1978*. (Berkeley: University of California Press, 2004).

Lewin, Kurt. *Field Theory in Social Science*. (New York: Harper Brothers, 1951).

Lichtenstein, Claude, and Thomas Schregenberger, ed. *As Found. Die Entdeckung des Gewöhnlichen*. (Baden: Lars Müller Verlag, 2001).

Littlewood, Joan. *Joan's Book. Joan Littlewood's Peculiar History as She Tells It*. (London: Methuen, 2003).

Lüchinger, Arnulf. *Strukturalismus in Architektur und Städtebau. Dokumente der Modernen Architektur*. Vol. 14 (Stuttgart: Karl Krämer Verlag, 1980).

Lynch, Kevin A. *The Image of the City*. (Cambridge, MA: MIT Press, 1960).

Lyotard, Jean-François. *The Postmodern Condition. A Report on Knowledge*. Manchester University Press, 1984), orig.: *La condition postmoderne. Rapport sur le savoir* (Paris: Èditions Minuit, 1979).

Maki, Fumihiko. *Investigations in Collective Form*. (St. Louis: The School of Architecture, Washington University, 1964).

Manieri-Elia, Mario. *Louis Henry Sullivan*. (New York: Princeton Architectural Press, 1996).

Martin, Reinhold. *Utopia's Ghost. Architecture and Postmodernism, Again*. (Minneapolis: University of Minnesota Press, 2010).

Massey, Anne. *The Independent Group. Modernism and Mass Culture in Britain 1945–1959*. (Manchester: Manchester University Press, 1995).

Mathews, J. Stanley. "An Architecture for the New Britain. The Social Vision of Cedric Price's Fun Palace and Potteries Thinkbelt." Doctoral thesis Columbia University, New York, 2003.

——————— .*From Agit Prop to Free Space. The Architecture of Cedric Price* (London: Black Dog Publishing, 2006).

McAlpine, Robert Alistair. *Once a Jolly Bagman*. (London: Weidenfeld & Nicolson, 1997).

Mumford, Eric. *The CIAM Discourse on Urbanism. 1928–1960*. (Cambridge, MA: MIT Press, 2000).

Mumford, Lewis. *Art and Technics*. 2nd edition (New York: Columbia University Press, 2000).

——————— .*The City in History. Its Origins, Its Transformations, and Its Prospects*. (New York: Harcourt, Brace & World, 1961).

——————— .*The Culture of Cities*. (New Year: Harcourt, Brace & Co, 1938).

——————— .*Interpretations and Forecasts. 1922–1972 Studies in Literature, History, Biography, Technics, and Contemporary Society*. (New York, London: Hartcourt, Brace, Jovanovich, 1973).

——————— .*The Urban Prospects. Essays*. (New York, London: Hartcourt, Brace, Jovanovich, 1968).

Obrist, Hans Ulrich. *Cedric Price*. The Conversation Series, 21. (Cologne: Verlag Walter König, 2009).

Obrist, Hans Ulrich, ed. *Re:Cp*. (Basel, Boston, Berlin: Birkhäuser Verlag, 2003).

Pask, Gordon. *An Approach to Cybernetics*. Science Today Series. (New York: Harper & Brothers, 1961).

Popper, Karl Raimund. *Unended Quest*. (orig. 1974; London: Routledge, 1992).

Price, Cedric. *The Square Book*. (London: Wiley Academy, 1984; reprinted 2003).

Price, Cedric, Frank Newby, Robert H. Suan und F J Samuely and Partners. *Air Structures. A Survey*. (London: Department of the Environment/HMSO, 1971).

Quarmby, Arthur. *The Plastics Architect*. (London: Pall Mall Press, 1974).

Rex, John, ed. *Theoretical Logic in Sociology*. (London: Routledge Kegan, 1984).

Rossi, Aldo. *L'architettura Della Città*. 1st edition (Padua: Citta Studi, 1966).

Sadler, Simon. *Archigram. Architecture without Architecture*. (Cambridge, MA: MIT Press, 2005).

Sarkis, Hashim. *Le Corbusier's Venice Hospital and the Mat Building Revival*. (Munich: Prestel, 2002).

Schelling, Thomas C. *Micromotives and Macrobehaviour*. (New York: W.W. Norton & Company, 1978).

Scott-Brown, Denise, Robert Venturi, and Steven Izenour. *Learning from Las Vegas*. (Cambridge, MA: The MIT Press, 1972).

Sieg, Gernot. *Spieltheorie*. 3rd edition (Munich: Oldenbourg Verlag, 2011).

Smith, Ashley. *The East Enders. A Social Enquiry into London's East End*. Britain Alive, 2. (London: Secker & Warburg, 1961).

Smithson, Alison, and Peter Smithson. *The Charged Void*. (New York: Monacelli Press, 2001).

——————— .*Urban Structuring*. (London: Studio Vista, 1967).

Stierli, Martino. *Las Vegas im Rückspiegel. Zum Stadtbegriff von Robert Venturi und Denise Scott Brown*. (Zürich: gta Verlag, 2011).

Tynan, Kenneth. *Tynan on Theatre*. Pelican Books, A657. (Harmondsworth, Middlesex: Penguin Books, 1964).

van den Heuvel, Dirk, and Max Risselada, ed. *Alison Smithson and Peter Smithson. From the House of the Future to the House of Today*. (Rotterdam: 010 Publishers, 2004).

Wachsmann, Konrad. *Wendepunkt im Bauen*. (Wiesbaden: Krausskopf Verlag, 1959).

Ward, Colin, and Dennis Hardy. *Arcadia for All*. (London, New York: Mansell, 1984).

Welter, Volker M. *Biopolis. Patrick Geddes and the City of Life*. (Cambridge, MA: The MIT Press, 2002).

White, Jerry. *London in the Twentieth Century. A City and Its People*. (London: Penguin Books, 2001).

Whiteley, Nigel. *Reyner Banham. Historian of the Immediate Future*. (Cambridge MA: MIT Press, 2002).

Whyte, William H. *The Organization Man*. (New York: Simon & Schuster, 1956).

Image credits

Preface

1   Ian Finch, "Fun Palace Architect", *The Guardian*, 4th July 1964.

1

1   Cedric Price, "PRICE", series 2/4, photomontage for the Sheffield University Festival, ca. 1966. Cedric Price Archive, Canadian Centre for Architecture, Montréal, DR:2004_0036_002_D1.

2   Cedric Price, "PRICE", series 3/4, photomontage for the Sheffield University Festival, ca. 1966. Cedric Price Archive, Canadian Centre for Architecture, Montréal, DR:2004_0036_002_D2.

3   Richard Buckminster Fuller, Dymaxion House and Tensegrity structure, New Scientist, 8th February 1962, 312.

4   Cedric Price, Auditorium for the American Museum in Britain, Claverton near Bath, ca. 1963. Cedric Price Archive, Canadian Centre for Architecture, Montréal, DR:1995_0207_001_008.

5   Cedric Price, "New Aviary: London Zoo", London, photograph of model, ca. 1963. Cedric Price Archive, Canadian Centre for Architecture, Montréal, DR:1995_0207_001_006.

6   Cedric Price, New Aviary: London Zoo, axonometric projection, ca. 1963. Cedric Price Archive, Canadian Centre for Architecture, Montréal, DR:1995_0185_270.

7   Cedric Price, New Aviary: London Zoo, exterior view, 2008, photograph by the author.

8   Cedric Price, New Aviary: London Zoo, roof structure, 2008, photograph by the author.

9   Cedric Price, "Lea River Site", Fun Palace: Perspective for Lea Valley, ca. 1964. Cedric Price Archive, Canadian Centre for Architecture, Montréal, DR:1995_0188_522.

10   Joan Littlewood and Cedric Price, Fun Palace Leaflet: Cover, ca. 1964. Private collection, curtosy of Steven Mullin.

11   Joan Littlewood and Cedric Price, Fun Palace Leaflet: Interior pages, ca. 1964. Private collection, curtosy of Steven Mullin.

12   Cedric Price, Fun Palace Project, interior sketches, 29th February 1964. Cedric Price Archive, Canadian Centre for Architecture, Montréal, DR:1995_0188_525_003_019.

13   Cedric Price, Fun Palace, "Complex: Typical short section", ca. 1964, scale 1:500. Cedric Price Archive, Canadian Centre for Architecture, Montréal, DR:1995_0188_197.

14   Cedric Price, Fun Palace, "Complex: Plan typical", ca. 1964, scale 1:500. Cedric Price Archive, Canadian Centre for Architecture, Montréal, DR:1995_0188_198.

15   Cedric Price, "a galaxy of load bearing links", structural elements of the Fun Palace, ca. 1964. Cedric Price Archive, Canadian Centre for Architecture, Montréal, DR:1995_0188_106.

16   Cedric Price, untitled, sketch of Fun Palace with technical equipment and skin in pink and orange. ca. 1964, Cedric Price Archive, Canadian Centre for Architecture, Montréal, DR:1995_0188_109.

17   Cedric Price, "Star gazing", punch card, ca. 1964. Cedric Price Archive, Canadian Centre for Architecture, Montréal, DR:1995_0188_525_004_001.

18   Cedric Price, Fun Palace, questionnaire, ca. 1964. Cedric Price Archive, Canadian Centre for Architecture, Montréal, DR:1995_0188_525_003_005.

19   Gordon Pask, Diagram 5, from: "Proposal for a Cybernetic Theatre", ca. 1963. Cedric Price Archive, Canadian Centre for Architecture, Montréal, DR:1995_0188_525_001_009_014.

20   Cedric Price, "Servicing for Mass Activities", table, ca. 1964. Cedric Price Archive, Canadian Centre for Architecture, Montréal, DR:1995_0188_188.

21   Cedric Price, "Individual Activity Requirments", table, ca. 1964. Cedric Price Archive, Canadian Centre for Architecture, Montréal, DR:1995_0188_209.

22   Joan Littlewood and Cedric Price, Fun Palace Leaflet: Interior pages, ca. 1964. Private collection, curtosy of Steven Mullin.

2

1   Cedric Price, sketch with ballpen on yellow paper, ca. 1964. Cedric Price Archive, Canadian Centre for Architecture, Montréal, DR:1995:0188:525:002:002:020.

2   Cedric Price, *Fun Palace*, layout draft for: Fun Palace Leaflet, sheet 3, ca. 1964. Cedric Price Archive, Canadian Centre for Architecture, Montréal, DR:1995:0188:525:001:011:003.

3   Cedric Price, *Fun Palace*, layout draft for: Fun Palace Leaflet, sheet 7, ca. 1964. Cedric Price Archive, Canadian Centre for Architecture, Montréal, DR:1995:0188:525:001:011:007.

4   Cedric Price, *Fun Palace*, layout draft for: Fun Palace Leaflet, sheet 18, ca. 1964, Cedric Price Archive, Canadian Centre for Architecture, Montréal, DR:1995:0188:525:001:011:007!1.

5   Cedric Price, *Fun Palace*, layout draft for: Fun Palace Leaflet, sheet 5, ca. 1964. Cedric Price Archive, Canadian Centre for Architecture, Montréal, DR:1995:0188:525:001:011:005.

6   Cedric Price, Perspective drawing on paper, nocturnal view of the Fun Palace in Mill Meads, pencil, undated. Cedric Price Archive, Canadian Centre for Architecture, Montréal, DR:1995:0188:012.

7   Cedric Price, Potteries Thinkbelt, "Master Diagram: All elements and key", ca. 1964. Cedric Price Archive, Canadian Centre for Architecture, Montréal, DR:1995: 0216:012.

8   Cedric Price, Potteries Thinkbelt, "Aerial Photograph", aerial view with clear foil and red, blue and black felt pen, ca. 1964. Cedric Price Archive, Canadian Centre for Architecture, Montréal, DR:1995: 0216:012.

9   Cedric Price, Potteries Thinkbelt, "sidings, tracks and stations existing suggested usage", ca. 1965. Cedric Price Archive, Canadian Centre for Architecture, Montréal, DR:1995:0216:032.

10   Cedric Price, Potteries Thinkbelt, "Transfer Areas: Aerial Survey", scale 5 ¾" = 1 mile, ca. 1963. Cedric Price Archive, Canadian Centre for Architecture, Montréal, DR:1995:0216:205.

11 Cedric Price, Potteries Thinkbelt, "Transfer Areas: Madley Axonometric View", scale 1:1250, ca. 1965. Cedric Price Archive, Canadian Centre for Architecture, Montréal, DR:1995: 0216:279.
12 Cedric Price, Potteries Thinkbelt, "Housing types adaptation to site condition", ca. 1965. Cedric Price Archive, Canadian Centre for Architecture, Montréal, DR:1995:0216:076.
13 Cedric Price, Potteries Thinkbelt, "Housing site 7, housing site 17", photo montages, ca. 1965. Cedric Price Archive, Canadian Centre for Architecture, Montréal, DR:1995:0216:014.
14 Cedric Price, "Housing types: sprawl housing", scale 1:1250, ca. 1964. Cedric Price Archive, Canadian Centre for Architecture, Montréal, DR:1995:0216:078.
15 Cedric Price, "Housing types: battery housing", scale 1:1250, ca. 1964. Cedric Price Archive, Canadian Centre for Architecture, Montréal, DR:1995:0216:082.
16 Cedric Price, "Life span & Use cycle chart", diagram, ca. 1965. Cedric Price Archive, Canadian Centre for Architecture, Montréal, DR:1995:0216:372.
17 Cedric Price, "The City as An Egg", illustration, Cedric Price Propositions I, undated. Cedric Price Archive, Canadian Centre for Architecture, Montréal, DR:2004:1520.1.
18 Cedric Price, "The City as An Egg", illustration, Cedric Price Propositions II, undated. Cedric Price Archive, Canadian Centre for Architecture, Montréal, DR:2004:1520.2.

3

1 Author unknown, without title, Inter-Action Centre, use diagram, undated. Cedric Price Archive, Canadian Centre for Architecture, Montréal, DR:1995:0252:621.
2 Cedric Price, Camden Town Pilot Project, site plan, without scale, ca. 1965. Cedric Price Archive, Canadian Centre for Architecture, Montréal, DR:1995:0188:135.
3 Cedric Price, Camden Town Pilot Project, axonometric projection, ca. 1965. Cedric Price Archive, Canadian Centre for Architecture, Montréal, DR:1995:0188:128.
4 Cedric Price, "Basis units + control systems: F.P. Pilot Project", without scale, ca. 1965. Cedric Price Archive, Canadian Centre for Architecture, Montréal, DR:1995: 0188:256.
5 Cedric Price, Camden Town Project, "Network Analysis", ca. 1965. Cedric Price Archive, Canadian Centre for Architecture, Montréal, DR:1995:0188:246.
6 Cedric Price, "Atom", collage on photographic negative, undated. Cedric Price Archive, Canadian Centre for Architecture, Montréal, DR:2004:0036:001.
7 Author unknown, "Polyark Lectures No. 1", poster, ca. 1970. Cedric Price Archive, Canadian Centre for Architecture, Montréal, DR:2004:1448:002:001.
8 Reyner Banham, Paul Barker, Peter Geoffrey Hall und Cedric Price, Cover von: "Non-Plan: An Experiment in Freedom", *New Society*, Nr. 338 (20th March 1969): 435.
9 Cedric Price, "Volumetric Zoning: Fun Palace Project", Easter Fair, sketch, 16th February 1974. Cedric Price Archive, Canadian Centre for Architecture, Montréal, DR:1995:0188:525: 001:018.1.
10 Cedric Price, "X26: Fun Palace Project", Easter Fair, sketch, 16th February 1974. Cedric Price Archive, Canadian Centre for Architecture, Montréal, DR:1995:0188:525:001:018.2.

11 Cedric Price, "Possibilities G: Fun Palace Project", South Bank, collage, ca. 1983. Cedric Price Archive, Canadian Centre for Architecture, Montréal, DR:2004:1131:001.
12 Cedric Price, "McAlpine Present", organisational diagram, 1974. Cedric Price Archive, Canadian Centre for Architecture, Montréal, DR:1995:0263:032:005:005.
13 Cedric Price, "McAlpine Future", 1974, organisational diagram, 1974. Cedric Price Archive, Canadian Centre for Architecture, Montréal, DR:1995:0263:032:005:003.
14 Cedric Price, "Safety and Health", organisational diagram, 1974. Cedric Price Archive, Canadian Centre for Architecture, Montréal, DR:1995:0263:032:005:001.
15 Cedric Price, "Work Information", organisational diagram, 1974. Cedric Price Archive, Canadian Centre for Architecture, Montréal, document folder: DR:1995:0263:032:005:002.
16 Cedric Price, "Spider/Frog", organisational diagram, 1974. Cedric Price Archive, Canadian Centre for Architecture, Montréal, DR:1995:0263:032:005:004.
17 Cedric Price, "Programme Pep Now", organisational diagram, 1974. Cedric Price Archive, Canadian Centre for Architecture, Montréal, DR:1995:0263:032:005:006.
18 Cedric Price, McAppy, "The Angel Court Story: An Extract", ca. 1978, project presentation, part 1, ca. 1978. Cedric Price Archive, Canadian Centre for Architecture, Montréal, DR:1995:0263: 028.
19 Cedric Price, McAppy, "The Angel Court Story: An Extract", project presentation, part 2, ca. 1978. Cedric Price Archive, Canadian Centre for Architecture, Montréal, DR:1995:0263 :029.
20 Cedric Price, McAppy, "Angel Court", documentation of building site equipment, ca. 1975. Cedric Price Archive, Canadian Centre for Architecture, Montréal, DR:1995:0263:032:004 :001.
21 Cedric Price Architects, "Locker/Drying Facilities", photography, from: "McAppy Angel Court Story", June 1975. Cedric Price Archive, Canadian Centre for Architecture, Montréal, DR:1995:0263:032:004:002.
22 Cedric Price Architects, "Terrapin: Drying/Changing", photography, ibid.
23 Cedric Price Architects, "Portable Enclosures Programme: Example 'First Aid'", photography, ibid.
24 Cedric Price Architects, "First Aid", photography, ibid.

4

1 Cedric Price, Generator, "The cube as a hood", sketch, ca. 1977. Cedric Price Archive, Canadian Centre for Architecture, Montréal, DR:1995:0280:110:003.
2 Cedric Price, Generator, "Activity compatibility, sk021 CP", diagram, May 1977. Cedric Price Archive, Canadian Centre for Architecture, Montréal, DR:1995:0280:651:004:009.
3 Cedric Price, Generator, "Activity compatibility, sk021 M", diagram, May 1977. Cedric Price Archive, Canadian Centre for Architecture, Montréal, DR:1995:0280:651:004:007.
4 Cedric Price, Generator, "Activity compatibility, sk021 CP May 77", diagram, May 1977. Cedric Price Archive, Canadian Centre for Architecture, Montréal, DR:1995:0280:651:004: 008.

5 Cedric Price Architects, "Menu 15", schematic plan, undated. Cedric Price Archive, Canadian Centre for Architecture, Montréal, DR:1995:0280:406.

6 Cedric Price Architects, photograph of model mounted on cardboard, undated. Cedric Price Archive, Canadian Centre for Architecture, Montréal, DR:1995:0280:640.

7 Author unknown, Generator model, "132 P129", Polaroid photograph, 6th February 1978. Cedric Price Archive, Canadian Centre for Architecture, Montréal, DR:2004:1264:001.

8 Author unknown, Generator model, "132 P131", Polaroid photograph, 6th February 1978. Cedric Price Archive, Canadian Centre for Architecture, Montréal, DR:2004:1264:007.

9 Cedric Price, "Menu & Table Settings & The Meal", sketch, undated. Cedric Price Archive, Canadian Centre for Architecture, Montréal, DR:1995:0280:193.

10 Cedric Price, "Menu 22", 4th October 1978, sketch, 4th October 1978. Cedric Price Archive, Canadian Centre for Architecture, Montréal, DR:1995:0280:651:001:013.

11 Cedric Price Architects, "Modular Activity Spaces", plan, undated. Cedric Price Archive, Canadian Centre for Architecture, Montréal, DR:1995:0280:254.

12 Cedric Price Architects, "Initial Layout of Bases", plan, undated. Cedric Price Archive, Canadian Centre for Architecture, Montréal, DR:1995:0280:441.

13 Cedric Price Architects, "Grid Layout + Menu 23 + External Spaces II", plan, 1979. Cedric Price Archive, Canadian Centre for Architecture, Montréal, DR:1995:0280:464.

14 Author unknown, airbrush perspective, undated. Cedric Price Archive, Canadian Centre for Architecture, Montréal, DR:1995:0280:644.

15 Author unknown, 1:1 Test, Polaroid photograph, undated. Cedric Price Archive, Canadian Centre for Architecture, Montréal, DR:2004:1265:005.

16 Author unknown, 1:1 Test, Polaroid photograph, undated. Cedric Price Archive, Canadian Centre for Architecture, Montréal, DR:2004:1265:006.

17 Author unknown, 1:1 Test, Polaroid photograph, undated. Cedric Price Archive, Canadian Centre for Architecture, Montréal, DR:2004:1265:007.

18 Author unknown, 1:1 Test, Polaroid photograph, undated. Cedric Price Archive, Canadian Centre for Architecture, Montréal, DR:2004:1265:008.

19 Author unknown, 1:1 Test, Polaroid photograph, undated. Cedric Price Archive, Canadian Centre for Architecture, Montréal, DR:2004:1265:004.

20 Author unknown, 1:1 Test, Polaroid photograph, undated. Cedric Price Archive, Canadian Centre for Architecture, Montréal, DR:2004:1265:003.

21 Cedric Price Architects, Generator cube, photocopy, ca. 1979. Cedric Price Archive, Canadian Centre for Architecture, Montréal, DR:2004:1264:013.

22 Cedric Price Architects, Generator cube model, photograph, ca. 1979. Cedric Price Archive, Canadian Centre for Architecture, Montréal, DR:1995:0280:651:005:003.

23 Cedric Price Architects, "Multi-Use-Fixings: 7–8", axonometric drawing, undated. Cedric Price Archive, Canadian Centre for Architecture, Montréal, DR:1995:0280:651:001:014.

24 Cedric Price Architects, "Multi-Use-Fixings: 9–10", axonometric drawing, undated. Cedric Price Archive, Canadian Centre for Architecture, Montréal, DR:1995:0280:651:001:010.

25 Cedric Price Architects, „Network", planning diagram, undated. Cedric Price Archive, Canadian Centre for Architecture, Montréal, DR:1995:0280:259.

26 Author unknown, Generator Computer, photograph, undated. Cedric Price Archive, Canadian Centre for Architecture, Montréal, DR:1995:0280:108.

27 Cedric Price Architects, "The Symbol – any size – only one shape", Polaroid photographs on paper, undated. Cedric Price Archive, Canadian Centre for Architecture, Montréal, DR:1995:0280:651:005:002.

Epilogue

1 Author unknown, "Magnet 220", collage, ca. 1997. Cedric Price Archive, Canadian Centre for Architecture, Montréal, DR:2004:0766:001.

2 Author unknown, "Magnet 220: 1–10", collage, ca. 1997. Cedric Price Archive, Canadian Centre for Architecture, Montréal, DR:2004:0772:001.

3 Author unknown, "Magnet K., 22", sketch, September 1995. Canadian Centre for Architecture, Montréal, DR:2004:0928:001.

4 Author unknown, "Magnet K. Ass.", sketch, 8th September 1995. Canadian Centre for Architecture, Montréal, DR:2006:0018:008.

5 Author unknown, "Your Play Space Needs You", Talacre Action Group NWS and Inter Action, poster, ca. 1971. Cedric Price Archive, Canadian Centre for Architecture, Montréal, DR:1995:0252:632:014:002.

6 Author unknown, West Kentish Town Neighbourhood Festival, Inter-Action Community Calender, 1977. Cedric Price Archive, Canadian Centre for Architecture, Montréal, DR:1995:0252:632:015:001:007.

7 Cedric Price Architects, photograph of the Inter-Action Centre, Camden Town, London, ca. 1976. Cedric Price Archive, Canadian Centre for Architecture, Montréal, DR:1995:0252:632:014:001.

9 Cedric Price, "PRICE", series 4/4, ca. 1966, collage for the Sheffield University Festival. Cedric Price Archive, Canadian Centre for Architecture, Montréal, DR:2004:0036:003:D1.